ALSO BY ROSABETH MOSS KANTER

The Challenge of Organizational Change: How Companies Experience It and Leaders Guide It (coauthored), 1992

When Giants Learn to Dance: Mastering the Challenges of Strategy, Management, and Careers in the 1990s, 1989

Creating the Future (coauthored), 1988

The Change Masters: Innovation and Entrepreneurship in the American Corporation, 1983

A Tale of "O": On Being Different in an Organization, 1980

Life in Organizations: Workplaces as People Experience Them (coedited), 1979

Men and Women of the Corporation, 1977

Work and Family in the United States, 1977

Another Voice (coedited), 1975

Communes: Creating and Managing the Collective Life (edited), 1973

Commitment and Community, 1972

SIMON & SCHUSTER

NEW YORK LONDON TORONTO SYDNEY

TOKYO SINGAPORE

ROSABETH MOSS KANTER

WORLD CLASS

THRIVING LOCALLY IN THE GLOBAL ECONOMY

SIMON & SCHUSTER
Rockefeller Center
1230 Avenue of the Americas
New York, NY 10020

Designed by Karolina Harris

Manufactured in the United States of America

10 9 8 7 6 5 4 3 2 1

Library of Congress Cataloging-in-Publication Data
Kanter, Rosabeth Moss.
World class : thriving locally in the global economy / Rosabeth Moss Kanter.
p. cm.
Includes bibliographical references and index.
1. Small business—United States—Management. 2. Competition, International. 3. Community development—United States. I. Title.
HD62.7.K367 1995
338.973—dc20 95-11210
CIP

ISBN 0-684-81129-4

To Barry and Matthew, loving husband and son, always and forever

To Myra, Wendy, and Willa

CONTENTS

Preface 11

PART ONE
TOWARD A NEW CENTURY

1. The Rise of the World Class 17

PART TWO
COSMOPOLITANS: THE POWER OF NETWORKS

2. Winning in Global Markets 39
3. The New Business Cosmopolitans 60
4. "Best Partner": Transforming Supply Chains to Global Webs 90

PART THREE
LOCALS: THE DANGERS OF DISCONNECTION

5. Wallets and Ballot Boxes 119
6. Workplaces, Careers, and Employability Security 145
7. Business Leadership in the Community 174

PART FOUR
MAKING THE GLOBAL ECONOMY WORK LOCALLY

8. Thinkers: The Brains of Boston 201
9. Makers: Foreign Manufacturing in South Carolina 242
10. Traders: International Connections Through Miami 283

PART FIVE
BECOMING WORLD CLASS: HOW TO CREATE COLLABORATIVE ADVANTAGE

11. World Class Businesses: Leadership across Boundaries 327
12. World Class Regions: Strengthening the Infrastructure for Collaboration 353

Acknowledgments 381
Appendix Research as Civic Action: A Note on Sources, Methods, and Collaborations 385
Notes to Chapters 390
Index 403

PREFACE

Globalization is surely one of the most powerful and pervasive influences on nations, businesses, workplaces, communities, and lives at the end of the twentieth century.

Information technology, communication, travel, and trade that link the world are revolutionary in their impact. Global economic forces—and desires—are causing regimes to topple, enemies to bury the political hatchet in a common quest for foreign investment, large corporations to rethink their strategies and structures, governments to scale back and privatize services, consumers to see the whole planet as their shopping mall, and communities to compete with cities worldwide for prominence as international centers that attract the best companies and jobs.

For many years I have helped carry a message of change to leaders of businesses and governments worldwide that need to reinvent their organizations to meet the challenges of these dramatic economic shifts. In North America and other parts of the industrialized world, corporate giants and smaller competitors are well on their way to espousing, if not yet fully implementing, a new organizational model. They are becoming more focused, fast moving, flexible, and friendly to external partners; as they free themselves from the shackles of rigid bureaucracies, a few of them may even be starting to have fun—to use my fifth "f" for success.

But increasingly, the daily skirmishes of globalization are being played out not at international summit conferences or in conglomerate boardrooms, but in local Town Halls and small-business conference rooms. A new wave of social concerns and a growing desire for community spirit have come in the wake of economic change. Once preoccupied primarily with economic issues, the public is more and more concerned about social issues. Once focused primarily on the competitiveness of large-business corporations, leaders are more and more concerned about the strength of communities and the competitiveness of cities, states, and regions. At the same time, rising numbers of small and midsize businesses are joining the giants in their desire for a higher share of international growth markets. And every business or profession, even those that still believe they are purely domestic, is affected by global trends.

Is there a basic conflict between social and community interests that are largely domestic or even local, and business competitiveness issues that are often international in scope? Many people think so. I do not agree. In this book, I show how to manage global challenges to the advantage of both businesses and communities.

The sum of many technological and geopolitical developments, globalization brings both opportunities and anxieties. As with any significant change, people want to know two things: "What's in it for us?" and "Are we prepared to handle it?"

Good answers to those questions overcome resistance and help people master change. So I set out to provide answers to the questions lying just below the surface of current economic, political, and managerial challenges:

- How does globalization change the requirements for business and individual success, in small as well as large companies, in domestic as well as international pursuits? What kinds of companies are best prepared to take advantage of opportunities in the global economy? What kinds of leadership skills must be cultivated?
- As companies reinvent themselves and pursue international markets, how do changes in business affect people as managers, workers, consumers, voters, and community residents?

- What is the meaning of "community" in a global economy? Do communities matter, and to whom? Can the spirit of community be restored and people reengaged in meaningful civic action to ensure a strong economy and high quality of life?
- How can cities and regions attract and hold the best companies and the best jobs? How can they harness global forces for local advantage? How can they be masters, not victims, of change?

I wrote *World Class* for all who aspire to excellence. This book is for those involved in making businesses work—executives, managers, entrepreneurs, professionals, employees and associates, consultants, investors, advisers and directors—and those involved in making communities work—elected officials, national and regional policy makers, civic association members, community activists, social sector innovators, philanthropists, and leaders helping cities create strategic plans and economic visions. Indeed, this book is about how business leadership and community leadership can work together.

Since the mid-1980s new companies and industries have risen to prominence, unexpected places have emerged as international centers, and long-established companies have taken dramatically different form and direction—or died. Accordingly, the cases and examples in this book are fresh, even surprising, success stories. Of course, many of these business and community stars have been rising for a long time—like the proverbial musician who practiced for years to become an "overnight sensation." The people, companies, and places I feature as examples of how the future is being created are relatively new to the public spotlight.

Change did not wait for me to finish the book. A week after I met with the head of a software company for a final fact check, for example, his company announced a major merger, and I retrieved the manuscript to make note of this. But it is a good thing that people, companies, and communities are continuing to change. Leaders in some of the places I describe are already acting on recommendations contained in this book, solving some of their problems. Some businesses have already found new partners and are working with them effectively. Specific details are always subject to change as a company shifts strategy, a community gets its act together, or today's hero stumbles and becomes tomorrow's fallen star; it is a fact of life that no success endures for very long without both discipline and flexibility, both persistence and change.

What I try to convey here are not just intriguing stories about successes and struggles, but underlying themes that combine to create enduring lessons, a kind of road map for the future. I hope these lessons can help us all make our way productively into the twenty-first century.

PART ONE

TOWARD A NEW CENTURY

The Rise of the World Class

A friend who lives year-round on Martha's Vineyard recounts the questions his five-year-old son asked him while walking on the beach one day:

"We live on an island, right?"

Right, my friend replied.

"We're surrounded by water, right?"

Right again.

Pause.

"Are we connected to the world?"

The answer to that question is, of course, yes. We are all connected to the world in many and various ways. But economic ties are surely among the strongest—and the most complex. Today, the world economy is in a period of rapid and dramatic change, and the question of just how we will connect to this new world is the single most important issue of our lifetime. Even people who think that international trade means patronizing the Chinese restaurant down the street or that foreign relations are in-laws living in another country, even those who build their lives around neighborhood and family, must make that determination, because their businesses, their jobs, and the quality of community life are at stake.

On every continent and in every city of the world, large or small, companies that need customers, people who need jobs, and communities that need quality of life are asking how they fit in the new global economy. And government leaders, who are responsible for the political order that follows the already global economic order, are often failing to provide answers. Observing the problem in obtaining cooperation among nations on world environmental standards at the 1992 summit in Rio de Janeiro, Brazil, an analyst commented: "America, Europe, and Japan are groping for a redefinition of roles in the post–cold war era. Actually, Japan hasn't had a role and requires one. Europe is uncertain of its new role, because it hasn't yet defined itself. America continues to possess the wherewithal for solving yesterday's problems but lacks the resources and, many diplomats would say, the rigor and the coherence for dealing with the problems of today and tomorrow."[1]

As the world's last superpower, is the United States stuck in the past or creating the future?

THE LAST SUPERPOWER'S MIDLIFE CRISIS

Americans are living in a time of contradictions, a time of role reversals, a time in which old expectations are violated so frequently that new expectations cannot form. Many of these contradictions center around connections to the world.

Americans enjoyed a rare period of cultural and economic dominance after World War II, a period during which the United States set the standards for the world. Americans called its baseball championship the World Series. English became the language of air traffic control and international business. American dollars were strong and welcomed everywhere. American products became the first global products—Gillette razors, Coca-Cola, Disney characters—often succeeding by selling images of American culture, like Marlboro's cowboy or Levi's blue jeans. The United States exported political models along with its technology and pop culture. U.S. multinational companies—IBM, Citicorp, Caterpillar—taught American management principles to managers throughout the world, spreading a universal culture of commerce. American colleges and universities, the most extensive and best (overall) higher education system in the world, educated the elite of many countries.

Americans assumed that everyone liked them and that everyone wanted to be like them. America's place as the standard setter was clear. But by the 1990s America's place in the world had changed. A recent *New Yorker* cartoon pictured a man, apparently an American executive, saying his nightly prayers: "I pray that we continue to deserve to consume a disproportionate share of the world's resources." Now some are questioning whether the United States will continue to consume the same skewed share or deserve to.

The American economy has recovered from a period of stagnation, but few believe that security—let alone unchallenged superiority—has returned. Other countries do not automatically follow American leadership on international matters; European allies pursued their own course on Bosnia, and China refused to cave in to U.S. human rights requirements for retaining its most favored nation status. The most dynamic growth markets lie in other regions, regions that are unfamiliar territory to many American businesses. Some American companies face still formidable foreign competition. America's reputation for quality products has had to be reearned. America's secondary schools are not the world's best, while its outstanding colleges and universities are enrolling an increasing percentage of foreign students. America's universalistic culture—from core curricula on college campuses to the English language in use commercially worldwide—is being challenged even on American shores by bilingual and multicultural movements.

Yet the United States is still the world's most productive economy and most desirable market. As proof of that, increasing numbers of American businesses are owned by foreign companies, and foreign investment plays an ever larger role in the life of American communities. American popular music dominates the world, but five out of the top six record companies in the world featuring American music are owned by foreign corporations. Economically, the role of Americans has changed. Once primarily actors, they are now also being acted upon; once always initiators, they are now also recipients.

As I listen to Americans starting to come to terms with a changed place in the world, I can't help thinking of an image derived from male-female relationships. In her book *The Second Sex*, Simone de Beauvoir wrote about what it means to be the "other" in a relationship in which one kind of person—the man—is always dominant.[2] The dominant party assumes, almost unconsciously, that his way of thinking and being holds for everyone; he takes it all for granted. The "other," however, must become very attuned to the dominant person in order to sense his needs and wishes and accommodate them (or manipulate them). The "other" suppresses her own sense of self in order to learn to read the dominant person.

Americans—particularly American-born white male business executives—are no longer the dominant parties whom everyone else must accommodate. In increasing numbers, they are taking on the role of the "other"—the ones who must learn how to accommodate (or manipulate) foreign bosses or read the signals sent by foreign partners whose collaboration is necessary to tap export markets or develop new ventures. This creates anxiety and confusion.

Consider these contradictions, reversals, and confusions of images:

• *Who's on top?* Recent weaknesses in the Japanese economy caused smiles of smug superiority on the faces of some American managers. Perhaps there is no longer any reason to learn management lessons from Japanese companies if there is so much trouble in Japan and the American economy is doing so much better? Then a listing of the top-quality automobiles is released by J. D. Powers in 1993, and Japanese models win ten of the top twelve places.

• *Does foreign ownership hurt local economies?* Cleveland, Ohio, is often cited for its revival of local leadership and community spirit that has resulted in tourist attractions such as a national rock and roll museum, conversion of industrial wastelands into entertainment centers, and a new stadium. During this same period, ownership of major Cleveland companies moved outside of Cleveland and even outside of the United States; Nestlé bought Stouffer's and BP (British Petroleum) bought Sohio. A Cleveland company featured at a U.S. Labor Department conference on exemplary workplaces was a joint venture with a Japanese company. Local leadership grew after foreign ownership increased.

• *Saved by the French?* The city of Worcester, Massachusetts, fought hard to keep its largest employer, Norton Company, under local control in a takeover battle with the British BTR. One benefit of local control cited often by management was the preservation of local jobs. Ultimately Norton was rescued by a French "white knight," St. Gobain, which folded it into its international family and fired a range of Norton managers. "They were right to fire us," one said later. "The French outclassed us."

• *Where is the Third World?* The scene is central Jakarta, 1993. I am sitting with two British executives in the offices of a Japanese company on the seventeenth floor of a modern high-rise. Outside the window the scene could be downtown Los Angeles—the glistening glass-and-steel ARCO tower across the street, the Citibank tower nearby, the luxurious Grand Hyatt Hotel with elaborate fountains. Then my Indonesian client shows me pictures of the golf course community the company is building on the outskirts of Jakarta, a Southern California–style suburban enclave designed by Americans. Meanwhile, parts of Los Angeles look like Jakarta after World War II: bombed out, burned out, and torn with racial tensions.

The United States in its youth was characterized by isolationism and limitless opportunities. All things were possible. America attracted people and enterprises that turned their backs on their places of origin. Now the country faces middle age. Other places with younger and more modern economies and populations—for example, the big and little Asian "tigers" who have come to industrial maturity in recent years—are catching up and occasionally surpassing the United States, which has aging plants and equipment and an aging work force. And older industrial economies are showing surprising signs of rejuvenation —consider Britain's northeastern corner, recently named the most attractive site for manufacturing in the world by the prestigious World Economic Forum.

The American economy in midlife faces limits to growth and is no longer self-sufficient. In many dimensions and by many measures, America is still number one and is likely to remain so. American values of enterprise and achievement are envied elsewhere. But there is an importance difference between being number one and *alone* or being number one among a set of peers that also have assets and attractions. The gap is closing between the leaders and the also-rans. And in a global economy, it is hard for traditional centers to monopolize power, even if they remain dominant. For example, Boston's Route 128 and

California's Silicon Valley are still preeminent high-tech centers, but they are now joined by Silicon Gulch, Mountain, Forest, Prairie, and Desert in the United States, Silicon Bog in Ireland, Silicon Glen in Scotland, and Silicon Jungles in India and Singapore.

Furthermore, what makes America strong is not just a singular entity called a nation, but a series of strong companies and strong communities, popularly dubbed "citistates"[3]—some of which make their own foreign policy. The National League of Cities has argued that the image of a single "national" economy is incomplete and inaccurate; America instead is a "common market" of local economic regions, a league position paper said.[4] It has been suggested that there are not three nations in North America (the United States, Canada, and Mexico) but nine regions, some of them crossing borders, that have distinctive economic and political interests.[5] A civic activist group in Seattle, for example, has created a vision of "Cascadia"—a Pacific Northwest economy that includes Washington, Oregon, British Columbia, and Alberta. In Europe, an "Alsace 2000" vision in France links that region's future with Germany and Switzerland. Regions, not nations, are increasingly identified as operative economies that spill over political jurisdictions.[6]

No wonder the last superpower is having a midlife identity crisis. A passage is under way from one life stage to another. The American century—and the European half millennium—is coming to an end. The world century is beginning. And for American business and communities to prosper in a global economy, the standards to meet and the groups to join are the "world class."

WHO IS "WORLD CLASS"?

"World class" is a play on words suggesting both the need to meet the highest standards anywhere in order to compete and the growth of a social class defined by its ability to command resources and operate beyond borders and across wide territories.

If the class divide of the industrial economy was between capital and labor or managers and workers, the class divide of the emerging information economy could well be between cosmopolitans and locals.

Cosmopolitans are card-carrying members of the world class—often literally card carrying, with passports or air tickets serving to admit them. They lead companies that are linked to global chains. Comfortable in many places and able to understand and bridge the differences among them, cosmopolitans possess portable skills and a broad outlook. But it is not travel that defines cosmopolitans—some widely traveled people remain hopelessly parochial—it is mind-set.

Cosmopolitans are rich in three intangible assets, three C's that translate into preeminence and power in a global economy: *concepts*—the best and latest knowledge and ideas; *competence*—the ability to operate at the highest standards of any place anywhere; and *connections*—the best relationships, which provide access to the resources of other people and organizations around the world. Indeed, it is because cosmopolitans bring the best and latest concepts, the highest levels of competence, and excellent connections that they gain influence over locals.

Cosmopolitans carry these three C's with them to all the places in which they operate. As they do so, they create and become part of a more universal culture that transcends the particularities of place—and, in the eyes of some locals, threatens the distinctive identity of groups and communities. And cosmopolitans argue for a "qualitocracy"—that the highest quality matters more than place of origin—because then cosmopolitans who tap into the best in the world automatically win out over those who are more restricted.

At one extreme of the cosmopolitan class is a small global elite of business leaders creating powerful, border-spanning networks. These cosmopolitans have unlimited opportunities because of their ability to tap resources or gain access to knowledge anywhere in the world. Their community and even national affiliations are weak, although they may feel sentimental attachments to places of their youth or current residence, and they may ally themselves with local politicians—a source of their power.

Locals, by contrast, are defined primarily by particular places. Some are rooted in their communities but remain open to global thinking and opportunities. Others are simply stuck. The isolates at the extreme end of the local class are those whose skills are not particularly unique or desirable, whose connections are limited to a small circle in the neighborhood, and whose opportunities are confined to their own communities. In contrast with the limitless horizons for cosmopolitans, isolates face increasing limits to opportunity. They lack control over resources and knowledge, which can move rapidly in and out of their communities. Because they are dependent on decisions made by cosmopolitans about where to invest and where to locate, they can easily become nativists, resisting and resenting globalism.

Cosmopolitans often have strong feelings of membership in particular communities. They are not antilocal, they are supralocal, connected with communities but transcending them. But their linkages to wider networks give them opportunities and options that local isolates lack. Consequently cosmopolitans often value choices over loyalties—even in terms of which relationships deserve their loyalty. Local nativists value loyalties over choices, preferring to preserve distinctions and protect their own group. Cosmopolitans characteristically try to break through barriers and overcome limits; nativists characteristically try to preserve and even erect new barriers, most often through political means.

These differences create one of the great tensions and paradoxes of our time. While economies are globalizing, politics in many parts of the world are localizing. Large countries and large companies are burying the political hatchet in order to reach foreign customers or attract foreign investment—one impetus for peace in the Middle East—while smaller, more isolated entities are engaged in a kind of tribal warfare, trying to achieve or restore local sovereignty.[7] Many of the tragic trouble spots of the world are places insufficiently linked to the global economy, where internecine warfare or jurisdictional disputes are at the root of bitter battles over the distribution of crumbs rather than collaborative efforts to enlarge the pie.

Global economic interests and local political interests potentially clash in a wide variety of domains. Even organized crime is crossing borders to work in dishonest global harmony, while lawful society is "haggling over legal jurisdiction and perpetuating a multitude of police agencies carefully keeping secrets from each other," according to one study.[8] Globalizing economic interests are often uncontrolled by territory-oriented political bodies. When Banco Latino International became the first bankruptcy of an international bank in the United States in 1994 because of a run on the Miami bank after its Venezuelan parent was seized for corruption, neither the Federal Reserve in the United States nor Venezuelan banking authorities seemed clear about who had jurisdiction and who could have prevented the crisis.

Business is increasingly global, but "all politics is local," in the late Speaker of the House Tip O'Neill's oft quoted remark. Businesses generally want the freedom to pursue resources or markets anywhere. But as business mobility increases, the fate of local populations becomes tied to distant forces they do not control. In reaction, politicians court local votes by capitalizing on the discontent and insecurity of their constituents and promising to protect local businesses and provide job security by placing restrictions on entry or exit from the area. In the United States, political battles arise between cosmopolitan internationalists and nativists. Nativists act as self-styled economic patriots—buy-domestic protectionists who mistrust foreign investment and want to close borders, as did the anti-NAFTA forces mobilized by populist millionaire and erstwhile presidential candidate Ross Perot.

Cosmopolitans, therefore, must play a high-order political game. Businesses, even as they globalize, must know how to be responsive to the needs of the communities in which they operate. Communities, for their part, must determine how to best connect cosmopolitans and locals, how to create opportunities and an atmosphere that will both attract and hold footloose companies. In the middle are vast numbers of businesses and people whose prospects have already been reshaped by globalization, although they do not yet know how pervasively—businesses and people whose future prosperity depends upon their knowledge of what it takes to become "world class."

THE END OF AUTOMATIC PREEMINENCE AND GUARANTEED JOB SECURITY

American companies, like their counterparts across the Atlantic, will continue to do well in the global economy, and America will remain one of the world's most desirable markets, ensuring reasonable prosperity for its citizens. But excellence is no longer to be taken for granted nor future success guaranteed by past performance. Success will come from the ability to meet world standards and join world networks.

The newest technologies are inherently border crossing, such as computers and electronic communications, and the strong American companies that develop and use them are rapidly creating alliances and networks with numerous companies in many parts of the world. As for job creation, small businesses and service companies have been responsible for a lion's share. It is claimed by advocates that women-owned businesses alone employ more people in America than the Fortune 500. But now even small companies must learn how to gain power from their relationships with larger companies and with international networks.

Capitalism, which was once assumed to be exemplified by American individualism, finds some of its most successful recent practitioners flourishing under other value systems. In 1904, the German scholar Max Weber attributed America's growth to values such as hard work and sacrifice for the future, as described in his classic book, *The Protestant Ethic and the Spirit of Capitalism.* Almost a century later such a book could also be titled *The Confucian-Buddhist Ethic and the Spirit of Capitalism.* Asceticism, diligence, and thrift were associated in recent decades with rapidly growing Asian nations. Singapore, South Korea, and Hong Kong enjoyed the world's highest mean economic growth between the 1970s and 1990s; Taiwan and Japan were not far behind. The entrepreneurial success of the overseas Chinese—a group that dominates the economies of many other emerging Southeast Asian nations—is impressive. Furthermore, such cultures are characterized by communitarian values that foster greater business-government cooperation than in the United States. Singapore and Hong Kong are often referenced by American cities crafting strategic plans. Seattle civic leaders visited Japan in search of models for city management.

Entrepreneurship is an American strength that can serve as a counterweight to corporatism in terms of images of success. James Fallows has urged America to build on this strength, to become "more like us" rather than emulating Asia.[9] In the last fifteen years feisty smaller companies have become heroes of "Jack and the Beanstalk" tales of their climb to the top by outwitting the giants—such as MCI taking on AT&T in long-distance telephone services. But the small business sector, too, reflects the trend toward globalism, as many smaller and midsize enterprises are seeking export markets, especially in expanding economies in Asia and Latin America.

Some small businesses will still occupy local niches and serve local needs. But increasingly, new companies in emerging industries are "born global"—competing on a world stage even for local business. Software, telecommunications, and health care technologies are already global industries with universal world standards, and companies in those fields are sought by communities everywhere as sources of future jobs. Professional groups with relevant expertise easily cross borders, whether they are medical researchers or engineers. And for industries requiring interconnectivity, such as software and telecommunications, start-up companies must think about world standards and large partners even before they sell a single product into a foreign market.

At the same time, older industrial countries and regions envy the vitality of the American small-business sector and its job creation potential and are rushing to catch up. Scottish Enterprises, for example, a quasi-governmental agency, has targeted entrepreneurship as a key part of its development plan for Scotland, borrowing ideas from Massachusetts and Silicon Valley.

Foreign direct investment has also become a more important influence on American soil, almost as important as it already is in other countries. Over about a decade, foreigners have paid $316 billion to acquire U.S. companies, in addition to the many international firms that have started new operations in the United States. Nearly five million Americans work in foreign-owned companies or their U.S. affiliates.[10] This means that foreign competition exists next door to American companies, on their home territory. The presence of Japanese auto industry transplants has been particularly controversial—to American companies, not to the Japanese. Toyota cheerfully advertises all the states in the United States contributing to its cars under the banner "We buy the best parts in the world, no matter which state they're from." While some companies and communities turn their backs on foreign investment, others, such as Spartanburg, South Carolina, or Newcastle, England, woo it and use it to raise local standards and serve global markets.

Both a global perspective and the small-business renaissance make it clear how rigid and parochial the traditional large industrial corporation had become, whether American giants or European "national champions." Now, even large American companies have started to emulate the innovation and team spirit of smaller ones as well as to look beyond their boundaries for ideas about how to be competitive. The process of change, seeded in the 1980s and accelerated in the 1990s, is loosening structures and breaching boundaries. Such changes, coupled with unprecedented downsizing in large companies, dramatically alters the career context for corporate men and women. Managers and professionals in traditional corporations once focused inwardly, on the job, on their own career games, on good soldiering. They led a circumscribed existence, anchored by the safety of their company and backed by the might of the U.S. economy. Thoughts of the competition rarely intruded upon daily life. International divisions were separated from U.S. operations by a wide gulf. They were referred to as "overseas" operations, although some shared the continent and hemisphere. International operations were headed by U.S. expatriates, many of whom worried that service in remote locations was a career-limiting move. Overseas operations were a source of raw materials and markets for excess production, not a source of expertise.

Today, people up and down the line spend every day under the shadow of macroforces that can dramatically alter their fortunes. The message has been driven home: People's ultimate career fates may be determined less by their own performance ratings than by decisions in the boardroom—and not only the boardroom of their own company, but the boardrooms of their key suppliers, major customers, institutional investors, or aggressive foreign competitors. They must listen to the voices of many stakeholders and learn from many parts of the world.

Companies are opening their boundaries, and people are enlarging their perspectives, not because they are farsighted, but because they must. The competitive pressures of the global economy are forcing them to manage issues well outside their own walls. This, in turn, is dramatically changing the nature of work, the structure of power and success, and the nature of everyday life—in the choices people make as workers, consumers, and citizens.

The competitive business battles of the future will be fought not among nations (the United States versus Japan versus Europe), although there will be contests between government-backed consortia in fields such as aerospace and some countries will contain a higher proportion of members of the world class. The competitive battles will be among global networks whose participants span many countries or regions. Depending on the industry, the range of locations and the sizes of the companies represented in the networks will vary; companies do not have to be giants to flourish in the new global networks.

The route to success for people, companies, and localities is to become links in these global chains and to ensure that local activities meet world standards of excellence. Thus, cities and states—local and regional economies—will flourish to the extent that they provide linkage to global activities and networks. They must become world centers of distinctive world class skills. They must join the world class.

FROM COMPANIES TO COMMUNITIES

The development of a world commercial class came into sharp focus for me when I started a journey in 1990 to explore emerging business alliances and partnerships around the world. Eventually my Harvard Business School research group and I examined the alliance and partnership activity of over thirty-seven companies involved in over fifteen countries, including the United States, Canada, Mexico, Brazil, the United Kingdom, the Netherlands, France, Germany, Switzerland, Sweden, Turkey, Indonesia, Hong Kong, China, and Japan. I saw that these companies were often surpassing their peers by linking forces in international networks. But I also saw that their actions were controversial in their own countries and headquarters cities and that they were irretrievably altering life back home. COMCO, for example, an entrepreneurial Swiss holding company, was buying out small German and Austrian industrial cleaning and transportation companies, steering them away from local priorities to network priorities.

Each time I returned to my own home near Boston, I wondered which international networks had altered local company priorities in Massachusetts while I was away. American cities have been struggling to remain viable in the midst of fiscal crises, racial tensions, aging infrastructure, reports of deteriorating public schools, and a decline of "social capital"—the informal connections among people that build trust and a foundation for civic engagement.[11] As a contributor to economic development efforts in my own area and elsewhere, I wondered why any company has to be in any particular place once it joined the world class—and how the local work force, the middle class, already reeling from reengineering and recession, could deal with its loss of job security. I wondered how the rise of the world class changes the meaning of community—a source of identity and well-being that is largely place rooted.

While global networks pass overhead like satellite transmissions, most people continue to operate firmly on the ground. How can global forces be corralled for the benefit of communities, rather than causing their destruction?

My focus flipped from the global to the local side when I embarked on a research and consulting tour of eight American cities and hundreds of businesses in them. My project on local challenges in the global economy included extensive work in five places that face the global economy in different ways—Seattle, Miami, Cleveland, Boston, and the neighboring South Carolina cities of Greenville and Spartanburg. The project was designed to stimulate civic dialogue and action as well as produce information in collaboration with leading civic associations.

Over 2,650 business heads in those five places returned questionnaires; almost one hundred companies were profiled in depth after extensive interviews; hundreds of community leaders and public officials were interviewed; and hundreds more participated in civic forums to decide how to act on the results. In addition, the voices of about 300 ordinary people—middle managers and professionals, direct production and service workers—were included via more than 40 two- to three-hour focus group discussions in four cities. Briefer interviews were also conducted in Marysville, Ohio, home base for Honda; and in Asian communities in San Francisco and Los Angeles. (The appendix describes my choice of places and the methods I used.)

By approaching these cities and regions through the lens of business, I was able to view local economies not as abstractions or aggregate statistics, but from inside the organizations that struggle every day to make and sell goods or services.[12] I was able to sound out business and civic leaders about their strategies to improve their economy and quality of life in light of global changes. And I identified three archetypal ways that the global economy can work locally, built around the golden triumvirate of world class resources: concepts, competence, and connections. Cities specialize in using those assets to link their local population to the global economy. Thus they develop preeminence in one of three generic ways: as *thinkers*, *makers*, or *traders*.

Thinkers specialize in concepts. They are magnets for brainpower, which in turn is channeled into knowledge industries. Their competitive edge comes from continuous innovation. They set world standards and export both knowledge and knowledge-based products that enjoy temporary monopolies because of their innovation and command premium prices. Thinkers count on their cleverness and technological creativity to win a niche in world markets; as their original concepts pass into common use, they must think up new ones. The Boston area provides a good example. Boston's preeminence in thinking enables new industries to spring up as others mature or decline—a shift from hardware to software, for example, or from health care to health technologies. Other places with strength as thinkers include the San Francisco Bay Area (also a trader) and regional centers such as Seattle.

Makers specialize in executional competence. They are characterized by skills that must meet high process-quality standards and an infrastructure that supports high-value, cost-effective production. Makers attract world manufacturing because of their competence, and they are thus magnets for foreign investment. Spartanburg and Greenville, South Carolina, which together have the highest per capita diversified foreign investment in the United States, are good examples of makers. Cleveland, an industrial comeback city, is also a good example of a maker, along with others in the midwestern manufacturing belt. Makers differ from thinkers in which world class skills predominate. Greenville-Spartanburg's blue-collar work force is considered world class by business leaders; its professional work force is not particularly distinctive. In Boston, the reverse is true.

Traders specialize in connections. They sit at a crossroads of cultures, helping move goods and services from one country to another, managing the intersections. Miami, with its Latin American connections and, increasingly, global connections, as well as an airport that handles more international cargo than any other U.S. airport and more international passengers than any but New York's JFK, is a quintessential trader. Indeed, Miami is often identified as an international city rather than an American city; companies such as AT&T choose Miami for Latin American headquarters because it is a panhemispheric place and no one Latin American country can represent a whole continent. Miami bridges Anglo and Latin cultures, just as the great trading cities Singapore and Hong Kong link Anglo and Chinese cultures.

What distinguishes the world class from the merely good is the ability to be a global center of thinking, making, or trading. World class regions demonstrate excellence in at least one of these three domains. After all, great companies can start anywhere—usually where the entrepreneur is already living. Both Boston's home region and Miami's home region have spawned new office supply superstore concepts. There is nothing inherently Boston linked in Staples, which started in Massachusetts, nor Miami linked in Office Depot, which started in south Florida; indeed, the Staples start-up was financed in part by Latin American investors more commonly associated with Miami. But neither city derives its strength from being the headquarters of an office supply superstore chain. Boston's unique advantages are in software, health care, and telecommunications; Miami's is in international trade. It would be easier for Staples to leave Boston than for an advanced technology firm; easier for Office Depot to leave south Florida than for a Latin American exporter. For a place to be world class, it must feature a concentration of skills that are hard to uncouple from local assets—for example, colleges and universities in Boston, Latin American experts in Miami.

Of course, the three C's and local assets are not enough to make an area world class without attention to basic strengths, because cosmopolitan companies even in industries benefiting from local assets can move part or all of their operations more easily today. For an area to remain viable as other areas around the world compete to attract and retain businesses, minimum standards must be maintained. Every area must contain a range of support institutions, provide a modern infrastructure such as transportation and telecommunication facilities, engage in a variety of activities that provide employment and amenities, and ensure a positive business climate. Every area needs to identify and refurbish deteriorating or underutilized assets—parklands, ports, or public schools.

Here, too, world class resources and skills can be applied—the three C's on a community level: new concepts through investment in innovation; increased competence through investment in education; and strengthened connections through an investment in collaboration. Boston cannot monopolize thinking any more than Miami can monopolize trading. To support world class businesses, communities must also seek to become world class.

Thus, communities need both *magnets* and *glue*. They must have magnets that attract a flow of external resources—new people or new companies—to renew and expand skills, broaden horizons, and hold up a comparative mirror against world standards. The flow might involve customers, outside investors, foreign companies, students, business travelers, or even immigrants. Communities also need social glue —a means for social cohesion, a way to bring people together to define the common good, create joint plans, and identify strategies that benefit a wide range of organizations and people in the community. In addition to the physical infrastructure that supports daily life and work —roads, subways, sewers, electricity, communications systems—communities need a social infrastructure, an infrastructure for collaboration to solve problems and create the future.

Excellence, in short, is the best protection against global competition. Communities must be connected to the world through world class skills.

THE MOOD OF A NATION

Some people feel excited about international opportunities as ways to grow their businesses or careers, but others are frightened or demoralized by changes in their communities and their lives. That's why an economic recovery does not translate immediately into optimism. During times of change, job displacement and career insecurity are rampant, and some nativists retreat into protectionism in the futile hope that the doors can be closed and globalism will go away. New forms of security are urgently required. What seem to some like hostile forces, such as foreign ownership of American companies, must be converted into sources of benefits for locals. Community spirit must be restored, unifying people across groups and sectors in a common quest for excellence that will link their region to the rest of the world.

Many Americans no longer believe that Washington can fix things. Although they mistrust government at all levels, they have slightly more faith in state and local attempts to revitalize regional economies, as my five-city survey shows. They believe that things are out of control nationally but possible to deal with regionally, especially if businesses commit to specific local projects. Some people think there is more hope of solving social problems through business than through government. If this is true, then community institutions that depend on business support—civic associations, not-for-profit social and cultural organizations—also require reinvention.[13]

The companies that will make their cities world class are not just the global giants, but numerous small and medium-size enterprises. After corporate giants have been fine-tuned, reengineered, downsized, streamlined, or dressed up for sale, communities are left with the fact that most of their jobs and businesses are in smaller organizations. Small and medium-size enterprises—manufacturers, professional firms, trading companies, service providers, software developers—must become cosmopolitans. It is essential to help those companies become world ready, to innovate, educate, and collaborate so they can join the world class through their direct exports or memberships in international networks.

That's why many entrepreneurial companies join larger ones as the heroes of this book. For example, Hans Balmer's Symtech in Spartanburg is an equipment distributor that also sets up its customers' factories. Maria Elena Ibanez's International High-Tech Marketing in Miami is a company that has sold computers to Africa and Japanese consumer electronics bought in the United States back into the Japanese market. Tech Ridge is a thirty-person manufacturer of photo-identification cameras with technology so desirable that much larger Polaroid took it as a partner to Mexico. Cohen & Wilks International is a small British apparel supplier whose joint venture with a giant Japanese trading company gives it a desk in 189 offices worldwide.

Just consider Boston's two most globalized companies. One is Gillette, giant manufacturer of razors and other consumer products, with over 70 percent of its sales and employees outside of the United States. The other is the Bamboo Fencer, a four-person craft shop near a brewery in a neighborhood close to the inner city. Its bamboo comes from a company in Panama that it partly owns or from surplus imported from China by Orvis, which uses bamboo for the fishing rods it makes in New England. The Bamboo Fencer's employees are from Nepal, Laos, Puerto Rico, and Texas. It sells its fences nearly anywhere but Boston, and it expects future growth from a new venture with an Italian designer to make Japanese-style fences for the German market.

Both companies are led by cosmopolitans. In its own way, each is connected to the world. And while leaders of both have deep local roots in their home communities, they are also members of the world class.

In this book, I examine the many ways in which the global economy is transforming businesses, workplaces, politics, communities, and everyday lives. I offer numerous lessons from successful companies and communities that can help many others make the transition to world class excellence. These lessons are addressed to those who want to understand and master the changing conditions under which they work and live as a new century gets ready to be born.

I want to help leaders and average citizens understand economic and political changes occurring globally that affect them locally. I want to encourage them not to be afraid of globalization, but to learn to embrace its possibilities. I want to rally them to become active in their communities, wherever they are, to ensure that economic prosperity extends throughout local areas and that the local population can join the world class.

PART TWO

COSMOPOLITANS: THE POWER OF NETWORKS

The world is becoming a global shopping mall in which ideas and products are available everywhere at the same time. This puts the power of choice in the hands of customers, changing the terms of competition forever. To succeed, companies need abundant stocks of three global assets—concepts, competence, and connections—which derive from investments in innovation, education, and collaboration.

To stock the global shopping mall, international giants are increasingly developing world concepts, coordinating every aspect of their operations on a cross-border basis and empowering cosmopolitan leaders who can operate across boundaries and borders. These new business cosmopolitans push further convergence as they carry ideas from one place to another. The upper end of the cosmopolitan class forms a global elite active in cross-border networks.

No business, however locally focused, is immune from these changes, because they rattle the supply chain. Smaller businesses feel the impact of globalization through the demands of their customers, who want the world's best quality, extra services, and closer partnerships with fewer suppliers. So companies need global mind-sets whether or not they seek global markets. As they expand their horizons they must also widen their networks, for alliances and partnerships can make them seem bigger than they are and offer their customers global reach.

Winning in Global Markets

Whenever you fly on an airplane, you are experiencing the world's most globalized environment—even if you never leave your own country.

Consider the components of the airline industry: a world fleet of aircraft whose numbers and exact locations are almost always known. Manufactured by a handful of giants such as Boeing, Lockheed, or Airbus. Financed by one of the few world leasing groups such as Guinness Peat Aviation in Ireland. Virtually identical interiors, regardless of the carrier's name on the exterior. World safety standards and a world air traffic control system using English as the common language. A work force with universal training determined by the technology of the plane that can deploy its knowledge over many employers of many nationalities. International agreements covering everything from route structures to baggage liabilities. Reservations and ticketing by computer, making it possible to go nearly anywhere on nearly any combination of carriers on a single ticket.

Air travel also stirs chauvinistic political sentiments, reflecting another aspect of globalization: the anxiety it arouses. National pride, concerns about sovereignty, and local economic interests encourage countries to subsidize flagship airlines or set rules that favor their own carriers.

What the automobile did to promote suburbanization, the jet airplane did to promote globalization. It makes places more similar as they become more accessible. From 1960 to 1988 the real cost of international travel dropped nearly 60 percent. In the United States alone during the same period, the number of foreigners entering on business rose by 2,800 percent.[1] In early 1995, the World Travel and Tourism Council, a global coalition of CEOs of seventy leading travel-related companies—from aircraft manufacturers to hotels—claimed that this industry cluster, including products for travel and services purchased by travelers, would produce 10.5 percent of 1995's total U.S. GDP.

The airport duty-free shopping area was the first global shopping center. Featuring brand-name items known around the world as well as a few local products, it is almost a prototype for today's enclosed shopping mall. Indeed, the British Airport Authority has developed Pittsburgh Airport into a shopping area so attractive that local nontravelers come to spend the day.

Is the world becoming a global shopping mall? For more affluent economic groups a similar array of choices is becoming available. Take teenage boys as a world consumer segment. My teenage son, Matthew, has gone on outings with peers in Rome, São Paulo, Manila, and Jakarta to experience local culture. In each city he visited a local shopping mall, where the boys—all wearing Levi's—played video games and ate a McDonald's hamburger.

Whether or not the world is becoming a global shopping mall, many believe that it *should* be. Some Americans fervently proclaim their desire to put quality first in their purchases and products from anywhere available without restriction, arguing against "Buy American" marketing campaigns as though the "right to shop" is one of the freedoms guaranteed by the Constitution. Political shifts toward democracy and free market systems throughout the world can be understood as choice-led revolutions in a search for the best of competing goods and services. A Hungarian economic minister's wife impressed a group of American leaders at a dinner I attended by giving a better explanation than her husband for the fall of communism in Eastern Europe. While he invoked oil prices, trade relations, and monetary policy, she said simply, "My friends and I wanted to go shopping." Transformations in Eastern Europe seem to have been fueled by people's desire to buy rather than their desire to vote, by dreams of purchasing rather than dreams of participating.

Actual cross-border shopping is common only in certain border towns, such as Bellingham, Washington, just north of Seattle, whose biggest industry is retailing, serving Canadian shoppers. Or at world crossroads, such as Miami. The big shopping centers of Miami report that between 35 and 45 percent of purchases are made by foreign visitors who come with empty bags and leave with full ones, according to Miami airport officials. Dadeland Shopping Center across from a large hotel earns almost half its revenues from Latin American visitors who come to see their doctor, visit their kids in American schools, and buy consumer goods. In California, Japanese tourists can be found buying Japanese electronic devices because they are cheaper in the United States. Business travelers also shop across borders, such as the Scottish executive I met in Glasgow who lives down the road from the distillery making his favorite Scotch whiskey but buys it in airport duty-free shops.

The global shopping mall is becoming a reality because people everywhere want to purchase the world's best without leaving home. They are demanding that producers for the home market meet higher standards, using their knowledge of what's available elsewhere and their theoretical access to it to push for more choices.

THE FOUR PROCESSES OF GLOBALIZATION

Globalization is a process of change stemming from a combination of increasing cross-border activity and information technology enabling virtually instantaneous communication worldwide. And it promises to give everyone everywhere access to the world's best.

Four broad processes are associated with globalization: mobility, simultaneity, bypass, and pluralism. Together they help put more choices in the hands of individual consumers and organizational customers, which, in turn, generates a "globalization cascade"—mutually reinforcing feedback loops that strengthen and accelerate globalizing forces. Two phenomena occur simultaneously: the regulated are getting deregulated (which loosens political control), while the unorganized are getting organized (which increases industry coordination).

■ PROCESS #1: MOBILITY—CAPITAL, PEOPLE, IDEAS

Key business ingredients such as capital, labor, and ideas are increasingly mobile. Not only do investors have the world to choose from, but information technology makes it possible to complete transactions from anywhere without even necessarily passing through central banks or leaving a formal trace.[2] When Banco Latino was seized by the Venezuelan government in January 1994, top executives fled the country and allegedly altered certain accounts from offshore by modem. The 1995 collapse of Barings plc, a venerable 233-year-old British investment bank, was attributed to the electronic movement of capital; a twenty-eight-year-old Englishman working for Barings in Singapore traded in leveraged Japanese securities, losing hundreds of millions of dollars suddenly, apparently without the firm's knowledge, shaking the world's financial markets.

Capital mobility has been oft noted, especially in contrast with the greater rootedness of labor. But migrant professionals and managers are now joining migrant workers in an international labor force. When Boston teaching hospitals had a shortage of nurses, they recruited from Ireland and the Philippines; and international medical centers in Switzerland and Scotland are trying to lure Boston physicians. There is a world labor market for engineers whose technical skills are easily transferred. Software expertise has extended to Singapore and India; Bangalore, India, has more routine computer-programming companies than Boston. In 1994 Digital Equipment paid $45,000 in fines and back wages for violating immigration laws by undercompensating twenty-four foreign computer programmers brought from India (and paid Indian wages) under a program allowing U.S. companies to use foreign workers temporarily for hard-to-fill jobs—in Massachusetts, supposedly one of the world's great sources of software talent.[3]

Companies in my five-city project reported they recruit locally for unskilled workers, nationally for higher-skill levels, and internationally at the highest levels. Because scientific expertise is fungible, Boston's biotechnology companies are noteworthy for an international mix in key positions. By 1986 a high proportion of the world's scientific brainpower came from developing countries. In absolute numbers, the United States, Soviet Union, and Japan produced the largest number of total college graduates, but Brazil, China, and the Philippines were next, ahead of Germany, France, the United Kingdom, and Canada.[4]

Furthering the international flow of knowledge workers, a highly disproportionate number of the world's Ph.D.'s are produced by American universities, which attract college graduates from other countries. In 1992 U.S. universities granted noncitizens about 59 percent of the doctorates in engineering, 33 percent in life sciences, 42 percent in business, and 44 percent in physical sciences.[5] Scientists and engineers from countries such as Korea, China, or Taiwan who stay to work in the United States often return home at some point, cross-fertilizing ideas. And those retired from the work force take capital as well as ideas with them when they move across borders, whether Latin Americans in Miami, Japanese in Hawaii, Americans in Mexico, or Swedes and British in Spain and Portugal.

Ideas also move quickly around the world through more extensive global media. CNN, available in 140 countries, was viewed by about 123 million households in 1994, up from 1.6 million individuals in 1980. *The Wall Street Journal*, with a U.S. circulation of 1.8 million, has increased the circulation of its European edition from 20,000 in 1983 to 59,201 in 1994 and its Asian edition from 13,700 in 1978 to 45,957 in 1994. In August 1994 it started an Americas edition with a circulation of 977,000, inserted into most major Spanish-language newspapers in Latin America. The *International Herald Tribune* has increased its printing plants along with world circulation—from one in Paris in 1974 to eleven, including facilities in Singapore, Hong Kong, Tokyo, and the United States. And on-line computer services and databases make it possible to find specialized knowledge from any media source quickly.

High-speed information transfer makes place irrelevant. In 1983 AMR, American Airlines' parent, moved its data entry for tickets from Tulsa, Oklahoma, to Bridgetown, Barbados. Saztec, an information services company started in Australia by a former IBM employee from New Zealand, uses its Philippines office to enter data for American hospitals, British credit bureaus, European patent offices, and the switching networks of the Mountain Bell and Pacific Bell telephone systems. The Malmö, Sweden, fire department reaches its database of street routes by contacting a General Electric computer in Cleveland, Ohio.[6]

■ PROCESS #2: SIMULTANEITY—EVERYWHERE AT ONCE

The process of globalization means that goods and services are increasingly available in many places at the same time. The time lag between the introduction of a product or service in one place and its adoption other places is declining precipitously, especially with respect to new technologies. The slow rollout from local test to home country launch to adjacent country availability is less and less common. One consumer goods company that licenses products based on films told me that it had taken thirty years for one of its concepts to move from North America to Europe and finally to Asia; now it plans new product promotions that travel the world from the moment a film is released.

In consumer electronics, once wide gaps have disappeared. For black-and-white televisions, there was a twelve-year gap between full market penetration in the United States and equal penetration in Europe and Japan. For color TVs, the gap was five or six years for Japan, slightly more for Europe. For VCRs, Europe and Japan were three or four years ahead of the United States. For CDs, penetration everywhere evened out within a year.[7] But video products were still country specific, using different formats. Contrast the fax machine, both a symptom and a cause of globalization. Fax machines using a common standard emerged almost everywhere by 1988, about two years after affordable fax machines became widely available. Global simultaneity is essential for products requiring interconnectivity.

The market basket of food and packaged goods available to consumers in supermarkets in many countries is more and more similar, despite differences in brand names, even in the developing countries, and new items are traveling across countries faster.[8] Industrial products serving the needs of large international manufacturers are even more likely to be the same products everywhere.

The newer the technology or application, the more likely it is to be designed with the whole world in mind. And products based on fresh technologies *can* be designed with the whole world in mind, since there is no established infrastructure with which they must contend: for example, country differences in average kitchen space, which means that home appliances must vary in size and features by country, or country differences in the number of bakeries, which affect the market for American products such as frozen dough—more neighborhood bakeries, fewer home bakers. New technologies can create their own infrastructure, the same everywhere. But even in older categories such as appliances or autos, producers are trying to develop world products or regional products that cross markets—such as Ford's Contour, a world car, or a single Eurostandard paper towel instead of highly variable lengths, widths, and textures.

■ PROCESS #3: BYPASS—MULTIPLE CHOICES

Globalization is also aided by cross-border competition supported by easier international travel, deregulation, and privatization of government monopolies, all of which increase alternatives. Innovators can use alternative channels and new technology to go around established players rather than competing with them head-to-head.

"Bypass" first referred to the rise of private switching networks that went around American regional telephone operating companies' wires. Now wireless networks such as cellular and satellite systems bypass land-wire systems altogether. Companies establish their own networks more easily. By 1994 the number of leased international telephone lines for private communication networks more than doubled from 17,000 in 1988. Texas Instruments' fifty worldwide facilities can beam messages to each other via eight leased satellite channels.[9]

Bypass implies numerous alternative routes to reach and serve customers. As these routes multiply and customers are able to choose among them, dominating particular channels is no longer a long-term advantage. For example, the rise of world overnight package delivery services bypasses government postal services. So does the fax machine. Some electronic funds transfers bypass central banks. In transactions never appearing on balance of trade reports, Texas Instruments "imports" software used to design semiconductors via satellite from its Bangalore, India, software facility.[10] Japanese subscribers to mail-order catalogs find an increasing number of brochures mailed from Hong Kong; Japanese companies save 20–30 percent on postage costs by sending bulk mail outside for remailing back to Japan, bypassing Japan's expensive postal service monopoly.[11]

Consider the literal multiplication of television channels: from the original 3 national broadcast networks in the United States to over 62 national and 9 regional cable networks—and still more programming originating from 1,100 local cable systems. Or the development of alternatives for buying computers: from dealing directly with a company's in-house sales force to computer stores to direct mail, when Dell Computer bypassed even the stores by selling computers by catalog. Retail trade in general is also evolving channels, from small neighborhood shops to large department stores to discounters to warehouse clubs to catalogs to home shopping.

Entrepreneurs change the nature of industries through bypass, finding or creating new routes outside of established channels. Ruth Owades founded Calyx & Corolla to sell fresh flowers by catalog, thereby going around Florists Telegraph Delivery, the network that permitted local florists to fulfill orders for one another around the United States. Calyx & Corolla is an attractive alternative built around an alternative network, a partnership between Owades's company, a score of leading growers, and Federal Express (itself a classic example of bypass), which guarantees overnight delivery of flowers picked to order.

The wealthy have always had ways to bypass inadequate or inconvenient public systems, such as private schools, private transportation (their own planes), or discreet private banks in other countries. When regulations are loosened or affluence grows, some private systems become more widely accessible. An air charter service on Martha's Vineyard and Nantucket became a scheduled short-hop airline; some private schools are becoming "charter schools," receiving Massachusetts education funds to experiment with alternatives on behalf of the public.

Newer channels are not run by old-style government-backed monopolies. They are more universal, less place specific; they can be tapped into from anywhere. And many of them coexist.

■ PROCESS #4: PLURALISM—"THE CENTER CANNOT HOLD"

The fourth process associated with globalization is the relative decline of monopolistic "centers" once activities concentrated in few places disperse to multiple centers of expertise and influence.

"The center cannot hold," predicted Irish poet William Butler Yeats. Throughout the world, centers are being decentralized. While Hollywood is still the film capital, there are now important studios for MGM, Disney, and Universal in Orlando, Florida, and Miami is taking film business from Orlando. Detroit, once the most powerful determinant of automotive standards in the world, housing the three American giants that had emerged after industry consolidation following World War II, had to learn to share power with Japan. The U.S. portion of world car production dropped from 18.4 percent in 1982 to 15.3 percent in 1992, bouncing back to 16.9 percent in 1993; within the United States, Michigan now shares the distinction of housing North American headquarters for auto companies with Tennessee, Ohio, and

South Carolina. New York City as a world financial capital has been joined by Tokyo and London, and Boston is a leader in new financial services such as mutual funds. High-tech research and innovation has spread from Northern California and Boston's Route 128 to many other U.S. and world locations. And the share of U.S. patents issued to foreigners increased from 38 percent in 1980 to 47 percent in 1990, although U.S. companies are on the comeback trail, with the foreign share decreasing to 45 percent in 1993.

Traditional centers often still thrive as directors of the action and its main beneficiaries, even while activities disperse elsewhere. But their automatic dominance or power to shape events declines when expertise and influence spread. As President Clinton discovered, the role of "Superpower" is difficult to sustain when other nations have become strong in their own right, pursue independent paths, and recognize that they have alternatives. European allies felt no compulsion to follow America's lead on Bosnia. China could refuse to bend to U.S. pressure on human rights because Japan and Europe are alternative sources of foreign investment and technology.

Within countries, giants that enjoyed favored and protected status as "national champions," especially government-owned enterprises, are being privatized, broken up, or opened to competition. In the United States, AT&T, broken up in 1983, is joined as a telecommunications giant not only by new rivals in long-distance service, but by its seven former children, which are now powerful industry forces in their own right. AT&T is still strong, with excellent performance and a bright future. But it is no longer virtually alone.

"The center cannot hold" with respect to corporate headquarters, too. Pluralism is reflected in the breakup and dispersion of corporate headquarters functions and the creation of centers of excellence in many parts of the world. In 1990 IBM broke up Armonk's monopoly by transferring 120 executives and the headquarters of its $10 billion communications business from suburban New York to Europe. Hewlett-Packard, whose strong performance made it the world's third largest computer company by 1993, has its corporate headquarters in Palo Alto, California, but its world center for medical equipment in Boston; for personal computer business in Grenoble, France; for fiber-optic research in Germany; for computer-aided engineering software development in Australia; and for laser printers in Singapore. Asea Brown Boveri, a $25 billion company that competes effectively with

General Electric and is often heralded as the model for the new "federated" organization, has a small headquarters with one hundred people in Zurich and runs the rest of its worldwide business and staff functions from wherever key executives are located, reporting results in U.S. dollars and using English as its official language. CEO Percy Barnevik calls his office at headquarters the place "where my mail arrives before the important letters are faxed to wherever I happen to be."[12]

Products increasingly reflect linkages among many organizations in many parts of the world. Take Jhane Barnes, a New York menswear designer. The collection one season was designed in New York; wool from Australian sheep was woven into suit fabric in a Japanese textile factory using a spinning technique invented in Italy; cotton from Brazil and Peru and special fabrics from Finland were found for shirts; buttons and linings were made in Italy; the final items were tailored in Hong Kong and Italy; and the advertising campaign was directed from New York.[13] Similarly, Mazda's MX-5 Miata was designed in California, financed from Tokyo and New York, created in prototype in Worthing, England, and assembled in Michigan and Mexico using advanced electronic components invented in New Jersey and fabricated in Japan. To catalog part of the Helsinki Library, the information service company Saztec microfilmed the card catalog in Helsinki, then did partial data entry in Manila, computer formatting in Sydney, Australia, database searching for full entries in Toronto, conversion to the Finnish catalog system in Dayton, Ohio, and final checking in London.[14]

THINK LIKE THE CUSTOMER: THE GLOBAL BUSINESS LOGIC

Among many now discredited ideas of the industrial economy is the theory that power comes from control over the means of production. In the global information economy, power comes from influence over consumption. As mobility and alternatives give customers more choices, power shifts from those producing goods and services to those buying them.

Pick an industry. Computers? Manufacturers once told customers what to buy and charged a premium for it. Now hardware is a commodity, and the hot growth area is software, an industry in which customers tell producers what to make. Pharmaceuticals? Drug companies were once darlings of the American stock market for surefire profits, with "detail men" telling physicians what to prescribe and hospital pharmacies carrying out the orders. Now hospital chains, hospital purchasing cooperatives, and health maintenance organizations tell the drug industry what prices they are willing to pay and how they want products delivered. Retailing? Food manufacturers in North America once told grocery stores when they needed to reorder the brands their advertising made consumers crave. Now supermarkets equipped with scanners have real-time information about consumer preferences and tell manufacturers when to produce and ship.

Customer power derives from industry consolidation and networking, which join smaller players to create big clout. It stems from increased competition and channel proliferation, which give customers the power of choice. It is based on easily accessible information, which increases customer knowledge and sophistication. World standard setters and databases give customers information to compare suppliers across regions and countries. ISO 9000, a European process assurance standard from the International Organization for Standardization, is a de facto world minimum standard, sometimes called an international visa for quality. America's Baldrige Award criteria for business excellence are used in many countries.

As globalization of markets increases customers' choices, those who supply them must move from thinking like producers to thinking like customers. "Producer" logic differs from "customer" logic in fundamental ways.

• *Producers think they are making products. Customers think they are buying services.* From a customer's standpoint, a product is nothing more than a tangible means for getting a service performed. In addition to the primary use, customers want more services delivered along with particular goods.

In a customer-centered world, industries are defined by patterns of consumption or similiarities of use, not by patterns of production. Visionary companies are reaching across industry lines to create future technology: C&C (computers and communication) for NEC of Japan; IM&M (information movement and management) for AT&T. Competing in the computer systems integration business are hardware manufacturers (like IBM), software developers (such as Oracle), and spinoffs of accounting firms (Andersen Consulting).

• *Producers want to maximize return on the resources they own. Customers care about whether resources are applied for their benefit, not who owns them.* By most financial measures, producers are successful when they can extend the value of their investment in tools, capabilities, facilities, people, or products they already possess. They want to sell more of what they already have the capacity to make. But customers do not necessarily care about the ownership of particular resources; they want the best resources pulled together from any source that will meet their needs.

If company A's widget works better in combination with company B's gasket, why should customers be forced to take only what company A offers? If company A wants to keep its widget customers, it might be compelled to stop pushing its own gaskets and form an alliance with company B to offer customers a joint system. This shift of logic leads companies toward greater flexibility: less ownership of fixed capacity, including its own captive parts and service suppliers, and more partnering with other companies to meet the needs of particular customers.

• *Producers worry about visible mistakes. Customers are lost because of invisible mistakes.* Producers want smooth, error-free processes. Customers want to have their problems solved and dreams fulfilled.

Some companies worship at the quality altar, hoping that zero defects will guarantee business salvation. But during the past decade, quality programs have been criticized for being too narrowly producer oriented, focusing merely on reducing the costs of visible mistakes. Farsighted managers now worry more about invisible mistakes—failing to take risks, failing to innovate to create new value for customers.

In a sense, every business today, not just those in the garment trade, is a "fashion" business. To compete effectively, companies must innovate continually and in ever shorter cycles. Keeping customers as well as attracting new ones requires constantly offering new and better products, with design innovations based on new technologies. To be truly customer oriented, managers must be concerned about what they do not yet see. Where there is a customer wish but no way yet to fulfill it, there is an opportunity for innovation. Fulfill it yourself, or someone else will. Surrounding every business are both invisible opportunities —customers' hopes and dreams—and invisible enemies—new companies outside the country or outside the industry possessing capabilities better able to fulfill those hopes.

• *Producers think their technologies create products. Customers think their needs create products.* Producers believe they are market oriented when they ask customers their opinions of products that already exist. Customers think companies are market oriented when they themselves set priorities for design.

Companies sometimes find it hard to take customer needs seriously even when they try. In a leading computer company trying to move from pushing specific products to offering total system solutions, a senior executive said, "If customers don't like our solutions, they must have the wrong problems." In contrast, successful technology companies increasingly let customer needs and desires guide product design, turning customer questions into immediate improvements and agendas for the next innovation.

Some companies try to get everyone involved in customer-centered innovation. Because Ocean Spray asked its employees to be idea scouts, inviting them to regular product development forums, the company scored several important wins with customers. It was the first juice producer in the United States to use innovative packaging technology—the paper bottle—from Tetrapak of Sweden.

• *Producers organize for internal managerial convenience. Customers want their convenience to come first.* In producer logic, managerial considerations are paramount: organizing functions, describing jobs, or controlling systems. What makes a company manageable, however, might detract from serving the customer. For example, from a producer standpoint, uniformity and standardization are easiest to manage. But customers want variety and customization. When a company serving world markets from London closes its switchboards at five o'clock Greenwich mean time, international customers cannot ask questions or make appointments during their own workday. Whose needs are being met, the customers' or the company's? After all, if every product is really a service, then every contact or communication with customers is also the product.

Thinking like the customer requires companies to develop an abundant stock of the three primary assets for global success: *concepts*—the guiding premises behind the company's work, including leading-edge ideas, designs, or formulations for products or services that create value for their customers; *competence*—the ability to execute to the highest-quality standards, to run routine production effectively, as ideas are translated into applications for customers; and *connections*—close relationships with partners that can augment resources, join in creating still more value for customers, or simply open doors and widen horizons. Possession of these three C's make companies and people world class. They are the basis for business excellence.[15]

Unlike tangible assets tied to particular places—facilities, equipment, product inventory—these intangible resources are portable and fluid. They decline in value rapidly if not replenished constantly. Therefore world class companies are more *entrepreneurial*, continuously seeking even better concepts, investing in customer-driven innovation. They are more *learning oriented*, searching for ideas and experience through informal inquisitiveness as well as formal education, holding their staffs to a high performance standard, and investing in their people's knowledge and skills. And they are more *collaborative*, valuing relationships and willing to work closely with other companies as their partners in achieving a common objective.

PROGRAMMING SUCCESS THROUGH CONCEPTS, COMPETENCE, AND CONNECTIONS: THE POWERSOFT CASE

Information technology is one of the prime movers of the global economy, helping to create the global shopping mall. And computer software is one of the fastest-growing occupations for the future. Software is also one of those boundary-blurring categories: classified with service industries yet manufacturing packaged products. It is no surprise, then, that a Boston-area software company illustrates how companies respond to the new global logic by embedding the three C's in their business practice.

Powersoft's roots are in a computer programming service bureau started in the 1970s by Mitchell Kertzman, a Brandeis University dropout and radio disc jockey. But its blossoming is more recent, stemming from the decoupling of software from hardware that created explosive growth in the American software industry. Kertzman transformed his service bureau in the 1980s into a producer of manufacturing automation software. It received its first $150,000 state venture capital investment in 1983 when sales were still under $1 million.

Kertzman soon saw that mainframe computers would be bypassed and that networking tools were the wave of the future. In 1987 Powersoft researched the requirements of its manufacturing customers and saw that they shared the same need Powersoft had: for tools for developing and managing software. Kertzman found David Litwack, former head of R&D for Cullinet, a large mainframe software company in the area, who had a business plan to try to develop the software. Both had grown up in the same part of Boston. Powersoft funded the development of Litwack's tools and then rebuilt its own product using them. Litwack is now Powersoft's president, Kertzman chairman and CEO. Kertzman also chairs the Massachusetts Software Council.

Powersoft has grown rapidly since the 1990 launch of its PowerBuilder client/server software tools that allow programmers to link independent computers. In 1993 Powersoft introduced PowerViewer and PowerMaker; issued its first public stock offering; and earned $8 million on sales of $51 million, up from $3.5 million on $20 million in sales in 1992. In 1994 Powersoft outgrew its facility in Burlington, Massachusetts, one of the "edge cities" near Boston housing high-technology firms, moving into a former Digital Equipment building a few stops away on Route 128. This move was fraught with symbolism: a small software innovator replacing a downsizing hardware giant. Then, in November 1994, Powersoft announced its intention to merge with Sybase, forming the world's seventh-largest software company and one of the largest in the client/server field.

CONCEPTS: SETTING WORLD STANDARDS

Powersoft's goal is innovation on a world scale derived from the understanding of customer needs. Ever shorter lead times in the software industry mean that only the best survive; Powersoft's competitive edge comes from setting world standards for its category. "Technology is a global business," Kertzman said. "We must get critical mass around the world faster and faster to become a standard. Competitive leads last a very short time. The minute you poke your head out in the leadership position, everybody is after you."

Having a significant amount of international business is thus a necessity even to sell products at home. Leadership in software must be world leadership, and corporate customers using Powersoft tools must be supported wherever they are. Powersoft sold overseas as soon as PowerBuilder was ready. Four years later Powersoft had distribution joint ventures in forty-four countries and had just released the Kanji edition of PowerBuilder in Japan. Early in 1994 Powersoft acquired Watcom International Corporation of Waterloo, Ontario, Canada. Powersoft's European headquarters is in Berkshire, England. In 1992 it opened a customer service and support center in London, then in June 1994 acquired some of its European distributorships, established service and support centers in Paris and Brussels, and planned Pacific Rim offices.

But success today, gone tomorrow. In an industry characterized by cutthroat competition and a blinding speed of change, the company needs constant innovation. "This is war, make no mistake about it," a Powersoft executive observed. Formidable competitors include Gupta, Oracle, Sybase, Knowledgware, Microsoft, and "the competition du jour"—emerging companies going after Powersoft's niches. American companies dominate software now, but Kertzman watches the rest of the world; Japan has targeted the software industry.

Powersoft has to be entrepreneurial, innovating constantly. Its leaders wanted to be the first to bring manufacturing systems to a new platform. Kertzman still seeks the "next bench"—something new that will be needed in the future. "Every time we do a new release," he said, "we must redefine the category."

Innovation comes from listening to customers and empowering associates to act on what they hear. A senior manager reported: "Our developers are dedicated to developing a product which is exactly what our customers want. The customer service organization is one of the things that differentiates us from our main competition and makes us head and shoulders above the rest: how we leverage technology to make things easier for our customer and get them the information they need to be successful." Customer relations specialists listen to customer questions, make spot changes for those customers, and then incorporate the ideas into long-term technical plans. At "Q review" sessions they tear apart customers' questions and give the findings to management and product designers as the basis for further innovation.

Powersoft tools are customer friendly. PowerBuilder, for example, is easily understood by traditional mainframe MIS programmers. They do not have to learn a new language; Powersoft software is graphical and intuitive. The benefit for customers is that they can use their existing programmers, who were generally hired to manage a system, not create a new one. "The artists coming out of graduate schools who can create new systems are very good, very smart, but they cost a lot of money and they take a lot of time to get things done," Kertzman says. "Our tools let mainstream banks and corporations get productivity out of the programmers they have."

COMPETENCE: INVESTING IN LEARNING

Rapid technological change poses a challenge: how to ensure that new knowledge constantly enters the organization and that people have skills for both today's and tomorrow's work. Without new knowledge, the company falls behind. Without encouragement for the current work force to learn, employees become obsolete with each new technological wave.

A low attrition rate at Powersoft is attributed to hiring "only the best" through a rigorous process including interviews by at least six people and family visits to the company. One professional previously with a computer hardware company claimed that Powersoft's strength as a place to work is its "interesting, motivated, highly intelligent people. Hopefully I'm interesting, intelligent, and highly motivated myself!" Human resource vice president Traci Weaver urges managers not to hire out of desperation when rapid growth makes them hungry for people, but to maintain standards for excellence. Powersoft's training commitments include about three weeks a year of technical training for everyone and extra courses for managers; additional learning is encouraged by a full tuition reimbursement program. "Training is part of the culture," Weaver said. So is cosmopolitanism. Powersoft hires engineers of diverse national origins, the older ones with international experience; participants in my focus groups say they have their pick of the world's best places but chose the Boston area and Powersoft.

Coleman Sisson, vice president of customer services, sees a direct connection between Powersoft's culture of caring for people and its ability to satisfy customers. "A lot of companies say that customer satisfaction is their number one goal. Of course it is. Can you imagine 'customer dissatisfaction' being the number one goal? That's obvious. But I think if you want to achieve satisfaction, you should focus on satisfying your employees. Because if you do that, they are the ones who are going to talk to the customers anyway. I'm not. Not five thousand customers a day." Employees report that Sisson responds to comments and criticisms about Powersoft products on the Internet, giving people his direct call-in number.

Similarly, Kertzman and other top executives are lauded by workers for their friendliness, accessibility, and interest in their ideas, which encourages initiative. "If you have an idea and they like it," one associate said, "they'll suggest that you write it up so you get credit." Rewarding enterprising employees with the chance to move their ideas into action, and get recognized for this, is characteristic of high-innovation, learning-oriented companies.

Powersoft gives people abundant information and the tools to succeed at their jobs. Education is a daily process, as folders of competitive intelligence are passed around the company. An engineer praised the support he gets. "Our computers are top of the line, the fastest available," he said. "If we need CD-ROM drives, we get CD-ROM drives; it's never a question. If you need it, you get it. Whenever we're exploring problems, if it involves a third-party software package, we just go get it. You don't have the excuse of not having the tool to get the job done."

Powersoft people have to become multiskilled experts who understand all their customers' needs, supporting customers that use other multiple-application software. High-innovation companies are known for giving people broad jobs that cut across territories. "It is not sufficient to be able to service just your own product; you must be able to help customers with all of their interfacing products," a systems engineer said. "When customers call our support line and the problem involves another piece of software or includes hardware, we don't say it's not our problem. We help them solve it."

CONNECTIONS: CASUAL COLLABORATIONS TO THE LOTUS KEIRETSU

With under eight hundred people, Powersoft is far from a giant, but its reach is vast. Powersoft's partnership network mushrooms to include tens of thousands of people working in its interest; for example, thirteen thousand developers received PowerBuilder training in 1993 and serve as extended family. In an industry characterized by dense ties, Powersoft's emphasis on relationships stands out; it has a department to manage relationships, guided by an executive for alliances.

Multiple advantages come from a major relationship with Lotus Development, one of the world's major software companies, a short drive away in Cambridge. Powersoft has enough Lotus connections for Kertzman to dub Powersoft part of the "Lotus keiretsu," in a comparison with Japanese business networks. A former Lotus marketing head serves on Powersoft's board, and Powersoft shares manufacturing space with Lotus.

Having consolidated manufacturing just outside of Boston, closing a facility in Puerto Rico, Lotus had some downtime in the local facility. A new Powersoft employee formerly with Lotus told operations director Peter Barker about this. Coincidentally, Powersoft was not happy with the company it used to duplicate, package, and ship its software. Barker made a call to Lotus mostly as a courtesy but discovered a significant opportunity. Lotus liked the idea of converting manufacturing to a profit center earning revenues from outside; the Powersoft deal would also help ensure that the facility could produce steadily.

Now Powersoft gets cost savings, access to innovation, and a set of relationships that lead to still other opportunities. Combining Lotus and Powersoft raw material purchasing provides savings to both companies. Powersoft reduces other costs by piggybacking on Lotus relationships. Lotus is the second-largest regional user of Federal Express shipping after L. L. Bean, and Powersoft gets the benefits of Lotus's high-volume discount with Federal Express. Powersoft uses Lotus packaging advances, because it is easier for Lotus to manufacture more of its own boxes than to change setups for Powersoft. The industry standard is cardboard packaging that costs from $11 to $13 per software box. Lotus developed a different kind of packaging out of corrugated paper, more functional and only $.85 a box. Powersoft saves over $10 a package because of the Lotus connection.

Barker calls the relationship synergistic: each company teaches the other. For example, Powersoft is developing the PowerBuilder Library for Lotus Notes, extending the reach of Lotus databases into mainstream corporate and commercial application development. But the Lotus product development agreement is only one example among hundreds. External collaboration is rampant at Powersoft. Powersoft's products are more appealing when they can interact with others' products, and Powersoft's reach is greater when it can tap into many distribution and support networks. As users want more services and applications, it becomes less likely that any one company can provide all of them.

For *development*, Powersoft has two hundred CODE partnerships ("client/server open development environment") with complementary companies to integrate its tools with other programs. The biggest names in computing—IBM, Digital, Novell, Hewlett-Packard, Microsoft, Oracle, and Knowledgware—are partners as well as competitors; Sybase is a development partner, competitor, and Powersoft's new corporate parent. Other CODE partners range from Texas Instruments to a former Burlington neighbor, Bachman.

Relationships are both cooperative and wary. "Microsoft in Utah and Sybase and Oracle in California helped make us famous" as tools vendors, according to Bill Critch, director of alliances and business development. "We were small and neutral, the Switzerland of our field. But as we get larger we're a competitive threat."

For *marketing*, Powersoft has partnerships with almost one hundred resellers, companies affectionately known as "power channels"—consultants, systems integrators, and project developers in the client server industry, which together account for 55 percent of its North American sales. Marketing partners include large systems integrators such as the Big Six accounting firms, the consulting organizations of IBM, Digital, EDS, and Perot Systems, and independent software vendors such as Dun & Bradstreet, which has six hundred developers working on PowerBuilder applications. AT&T includes PowerBuilder with other tools to its customers. Thirty of sixty customer training partners also sell Powersoft products.

Some relationships have multiple dimensions, such as Powersoft's international technology and marketing alliance with Attachmate, a leader in networking software and a neighbor of Microsoft in the Seattle area with 1994 revenues of $391 million. Attachmate launched a cooperatively developed product, EXTRA! Tools for PowerBuilder, which enables corporate developers using mainframes to integrate data quickly and easily into applications created with PowerBuilder, opening a large new market for Powersoft tools.

These relationships are delicate balancing acts. To work with so many competing companies, Powersoft has to help each feel it is gaining an edge against other competitors by investing in Powersoft programs. To avoid conflicts between resellers and Powersoft's own sales force, Powersoft representatives are considered territory managers, compensated in terms of total sales even if resellers close the deal. And particular relationships wax and wane in importance as technology changes. But Powersoft's connections are one of its major assets; the company could not succeed without them.

INNOVATORS FOR THE GLOBAL SHOPPING MALL

The processes of globalization come to life in companies of the future like Powersoft: mobile people and ideas, technologies for simultaneous use worldwide, new information channels that bypass stand-alone mainframes and offer tools for new computer links to form, and a flexible network of pluralistic partnerships instead of a single powerful hierarchy.

Companies fit to win in global markets share an emphasis on innovation, learning, and collaboration. They

- *organize around customer logic:* rapidly feed customer needs and desires into new product and service concepts and transform the overall concept of the business when technologies and markets shift;
- *set high goals:* try to be the world standard setter in the niches they pursue and seek to "redefine the category" with each new offering;
- *select people who are broad, creative thinkers:* define their jobs broadly rather than narrowly, encourage them to become multiskilled at working across territories, and give them the best tools for those jobs;
- *encourage enterprise:* empower people to seek new product and service concepts, let them act on their ideas, and provide abundant recognition for initiative;
- *support constant learning:* circulate information widely, track competitors and innovators throughout the world, measure themselves against world quality standards, and offer continual training to keep everyone's knowledge current;
- *collaborate with partners:* combine the best of their own and their partners' expertise for customized customer applications.

Their cultures combine apparent opposites: tough standards with caring for people, an emphasis on proprietary innovations with an ability to share with partners. And their principal assets are the three C's: concepts, competence, and connections, which they continually nurture and replenish.

Companies like these are creating the global shopping mall of the future. And in the process of globalization, they become world class: focused outward rather than inward, steeped in the latest knowledge, and comfortable operating across the boundaries of function, industry, company, community, or country.

The New Business Cosmopolitans

The process of globalization easily becomes a self-fulfilling prophecy, both a cause and effect of change. Globalization requires businesses to become more cosmopolitan, and the cosmopolitans who rise to leadership in these companies promote further globalization.

Cosmopolitans are, by definition, members of the world class. They carry concepts from place to place and integrate activities spread throughout the world. They act as global Johnny Appleseeds, planting seedlings wherever they go, which grow into similar orchards throughout the world. Cosmopolitans bring alternatives from one place to another. They are familiar with many places and aware of distinctively local characteristics but see beyond the interests of any one place because they are linked to a wider world and can move between and among places.

Cosmopolitans have a career and financial stake in finding commonalities or creating a more universal way that transcends the particulars of places, which gives them power and control. Some locals, in contrast, benefit from maintaining differences, arguing for the distinctiveness of their own particular way—which gives them jobs as experts, interpreters, gatekeepers, and local managers. Business cosmopolitans have an economic interest in making places more similar—not by reducing choices to a single one-size-fits-all, but by increasing the range and variety available everywhere. This is a subtle but important distinction. Similarity of places emerges in the global economy not because of homogenization, but because the same diversity coexists everywhere. There is more variety everywhere and a similar variety everywhere, with differences only in emphasis.

As cosmopolitans spread universal ideas and juggle the requirements of diverse places, they manage resistance to change from locals who see their power eroding. Cosmopolitans face decentralizing pulls in their own organizations, such as reasons why an idea from one place won't work in another, resentment of world concepts because they restrict local identity and options, and legitimate concerns about how well concepts from other places fit local needs. The job of cosmopolitans is to bridge such differences and resolve them so that companies can operate efficiently on a global basis. Cosmopolitanism is a mindset that finds commonalities across places. And globalization in one aspect of business inevitably leads to globalization in others.

THE PUSH FOR COSMOPOLITANISM: THE GILLETTE CASE

The first place to look for cosmopolitans is inside large international consumer goods companies such as Gillette, a company that is both responding to the global shopping mall and creating it.

Founded in Boston in 1901 by King Gillette, the Gillette Company was already selling in eight countries by the start of World War I thirteen years later, joining only a handful of American international companies such as Singer, Hershey, Kodak, and Standard Oil. Today more than 70 percent of Gillette's $6 billion in sales and 75 percent of its thirty-one thousand employees are outside the United States. The company's impressive financial performance is a result of its global growth strategy; profits grew 13 percent a year from 1989 to 1994.

Gillette is the world leader in the manufacture and marketing of blades and razors, reaching over two hundred countries and territories. Gillette also holds a major position in North America in toiletries and is the world's top seller of writing instruments, with Parker Pen and Waterman of France recent acquisitions. Braun, a German acquisition, is the number one marketer of electric shavers in Germany and is among the leaders in Europe, North America, and Japan, as well as a strong competitor in other small-appliance segments. Oral-B, another recent acquisition, is a leading seller of toothbrushes in the United States and other markets. Gillette has fifty-eight facilities in twenty-eight countries.

Over the last ten years Gillette has evolved from a classic multinational to a self-described global company with world class products that are sold in nearly every country. "For us," CEO Alfred Zeien said, "nothing is a core category unless it's global, and we can have clear leadership."

FROM STONE AGE TO WORLD CLASS

In the 1980s Gillette discovered the new consumer who knows about the world's latest and best and wants it now. Prior to 1987 the company operated by what Zeien called the "Stone Age theory" of marketing, which dictated a slow spread of concepts from the home market to the hinterlands. "Just as mankind progressed in stages from the Stone Age to the Bronze Age to the Iron Age," he told me, "we thought we had the right product for a market based on the stage of social development of the country. In the 1950s we made carbon blades. We moved to stainless steel in North America in the 1960s, but carbon was still okay in Latin America because we thought people there would have to go through the carbon period. With this theory, we could write the Papua New Guinea marketing plan for the year 2040, when American products from the 1980s would finally arrive there."

That theory broke down with experiences in the mid-1980s, such as the one in 1984 with a fifty-fifty joint venture in China. The venture was in competition with a government company, so output was restricted to 9 percent of the market, but Gillette was able to develop a sales force in China. "After a few years we found that our sales force was selling in dollar value more in imported Gillette products than the products made in China," Zeien recalled. "This meant that enough people in China knew about advanced shaving systems and didn't want old-style local blades."

A changing world would kill Gillette's business under the Stone Age theory, he said, because "the consumer in other parts of the world wouldn't accept what was sold in the United States fifteen years ago. World communications had fundamentally changed the theory. If you go to Jakarta, people read the same kind of news, watch the same kind of TV. There was no reason that X percent of the population there was not ready for an Atra razor." Now Gillette is moving its latest technology to China—cartridges with lubricating strips for its 70 percent joint venture with the largest government-owned manufacturer; it has about a 60 percent market share. In India the push now is Atra, a new shaving system. And in a reversal of past practice, if product launches cannot be perfectly simultaneous, the home market is not always the first to get the newest product; SensorExcel was made in the United States but appeared first in Europe.

New retail trade behavior is another force for global products and simultaneous rollout. Standing between Gillette and its more sophisticated world consumers are ever more powerful retail chains. In the 1970s Gillette first launched its TracII razors and blades regionally in the United States, then nationally. But large retailers, starting to consolidate nationally and seeking economies of scale, rejected that approach. To sell to major trade customers such as discounters Target, Kmart, or Wal-Mart in the United States or Safeway supermarkets and Boots pharmacies in the United Kingdom, Gillette now must launch products simultaneously in all of its large customers' markets.

INNOVATION AND GLOBALIZATION

For Gillette to dominate its central razor-and-blade category and avoid a slide into producing a commodity at the hands of demanding trade customers—who can make or break products while squeezing a producer's profit margins—requires substantial innovation. The magnitude of investment necessary for a leap forward in both product and process technology is a further reason why new products are increasingly global products. Economics dictates international markets for products that require investment too heavy for a single market to carry.

"The name of this business is products," Zeien said. "We are not magicians of marketing; we are only as good as our products." In 1987 the Sensor razor concept had the potential to make a significant difference among consumers and trade customers. Sensor was an innovative product idea linked to a series of significant technologies neither Gillette nor its competitors had available, such as high-speed precision laser welding. The new technologies Gillette pursued for the Sensor required for payback a market much bigger than the U.S. home base. At about 3 percent of sales, Gillette's research spending was unusually high for the industry. The Sensor project required about a quarter billion dollars in technical resources and equipment alone.

Gillette needed to marshal global resources to develop, produce, and launch Sensor across many markets starting in January 1990. Sensor was the first product of great magnitude Gillette rolled out globally, although the company had tried it previously with lesser products. The time lag between launch in North America, Western Europe, Japan, and most major countries elsewhere was just a matter of months. Exceptions such as Brazil and Turkey, where the product was held back a little longer because of special circumstances, followed quickly.

A simultaneous world launch is possible only if the company can treat the world as one, planning advertising, marketing, and packaging on a global basis. Gillette consolidated global advertising at headquarters, working with fewer global agencies that could design world campaigns for translation and adaptation to local markets. For new products such as Sensor or Gillette Series toiletries, a world strategic marketing plan is done in Boston. A commercial such as the "Best a Man Can Get" is the same across the North Atlantic, with the local language dubbed in.

REORGANIZING FOR GLOBALIZATION

Global structure follows global strategies. Gillette restructured to strengthen its global focus after the successful conclusion to a takeover battle in 1987–1988, adopting a "transnational" organization for its core products similar to that of other global giants. North American and European shaving and personal care activities were grouped into one seamless transatlantic body. The North Atlantic group integrates all functions in North America and Europe, putting most of the developed countries under one head. Gillette International focuses on the developing countries.

Manufacturing, R&D, and engineering for razors, blades, and toiletries were combined on a North Atlantic basis. R&D had formerly reported up through a chief technical officer, manufacturing and marketing were under a division marketing president, and technical operations reported to a corporate senior vice president, coming together in the chairman's office. Gillette's new world products needed "concurrent risk taking" in which all functions worked together, mutually agreeing to invest and "all finishing in the same bobsled," as an executive put it. The functions can thereby balance costs that differ with project stage. And factory operations report no longer to a country manager, but to a group operations manager in Boston.

In deference to the growing power of retail customers, country managers now concentrate on local trade marketing. Gillette has increasingly put more of its best people in trade relations positions, mounting teams to work with key customers in the United States and Europe on strategies for production planning, warehousing, distribution, or pricing across product categories. Key account managers are connected through a sophisticated computer network system.

WORLD STANDARDIZATION

When a global structure is adopted, global systems and procedures soon follow. In internal functions such as personnel or finance, Gillette's systems are also consistent across the world. Human resource policies are standardized globally to facilitate personnel transfers. For example, the duties of a senior programmer at grade level fourteen are the same in Germany and the United States, although exact compensation is determined by local market rates. A single system of job evaluation supports exchange of people. Financial records are kept identically so that an assistant controller in one unit can become a controller in a new unit elsewhere. Gillette managers acknowledge country differences but still prefer to treat the world as one. "Language and social things are different," an executive said. "We try to get people to speak the local language. But we also require operating committees in small countries to speak English."

To staff its professional and managerial ranks, Gillette taps a world labor market, competing across the United States and the world for marketing talent, for example, with Procter & Gamble, Johnson & Johnson, or Colgate-Palmolive. Furthermore, a cosmopolitan perspective is required to make global integration work everywhere. Thus, world transfers are common at management levels, in R&D, and at the highest levels in the factories, although the absolute number serving outside their home country at any one time is about four hundred out of about eight thousand professionals. Of that four hundred, fewer than fifty are from the United States, but as former human resource chief William McMorrow observed, "Of the top twenty officers, under 20 percent have *not* served abroad." CEO Zeien, a first-generation American, spent nine years abroad, mostly in Germany.

A sampling of key people in Boston underscores the importance of world transfers. The South Boston factory facility manager came there after a similar post in Britain. The new head of Oral-B was a Dane who worked for Braun in Finland, Germany, and then headed Braun's U.S. operations. His boss, the new diversified products group chief, was French; he had started with Gillette in France, left to teach at a business school in Lyons, returned to Gillette in France, then ran Oral-B in California and Braun in Germany. Tours of duty through Boston are one element reinforcing a common Gillette world culture. People from international facilities are in and out of corporate offices frequently. Divisions convene people worldwide for regular conferences. The North Atlantic group holds operations meetings on both sides of the ocean.

Gillette aspires to abide by the same principles everywhere. With respect to environmental issues such as air pollution, Gillette's policy is that there is the same standard in Boston as in Bhiwadi, India (a place Zeien invoked often because he visits frequently). "After all," he said, "it's the same world, the same air." However, execution of those standards might not occur at the same time, he added, because "the wherewithal to accomplish it is different—local government, local contractors, infrastructure support."

Creating a world company in which people move easily across places makes it inevitable that ideas and standards also converge across places. "Much of what we do is because we couldn't live with our employees otherwise," Zeien said. "Our culture would reject anything else. We can't have people come to Boston from international operations and learn that we treat them differently."

WORLD MODELS

Gillette's role models are the companies it considers the best in the world. Urged on by strategic planning chief Paul Fruitt, Gillette compares itself to companies such as Johnson & Johnson for management style; Coca-Cola, Rubbermaid, L'Oréal, and Sony for new-product, high-performance orientation; and 3M and Hewlett-Packard for innovation.

"We never lose sight of competition," said Edward De Graan, head of manufacturing and technical operations. "We study Bic and Warner-Lambert's Schick to make sure our products perform better for the consumer." Benchmarking occurs item by item. For plastic components, De Graan might look at other companies that produce billions of parts the way Gillette does for Sensor, comparing performance against Kodak cameras or toy companies. Gillette seeks best practices worldwide in cycle time, material handling, statistical controls, and measurement techniques.

As technical talent becomes more portable and useful ideas pop up anywhere, Gillette's sources of ideas are increasingly international. The home base Boston area has MIT, but it is also only a plane ride away from other sources of technology, including Europe. Massachusetts is no longer Gillette's primary research site; R&D is dispersed over ten centers, including the U.K. lab that did the initial research work for Sensor and constructed its prototypes. "We know we have to compete on a world stage," De Graan said. "We have to be in front using the most sophisticated technology. . . . Maybe it helps to be surrounded by high technology in Boston, but we are moving around the world, bumping into technology. There's a world cross-fertilization of ideas. There's an explosion of technology all around us. We can't put our arms around it only in Massachusetts or the U.S. Technology is exploding worldwide, and it's easily available."

WORLD SOURCING

It's an easy step from finding good ideas anywhere to finding good suppliers anywhere. About sixty-two cents out of every dollar of product cost is spent with suppliers, who play a key role. "We look around the world for what's best," De Graan said.

World class suppliers develop custom tools and machinery, such as the innovative equipment for SensorExcel that performs a two-color molding process joining two dissimilar materials in a single setup. Klockner Ferromatik, the press maker in Germany, ships this sophisticated technology around the world, including into a Chinese industrial zone near Hong Kong.

Gillette's South Boston razor-and-blade factory works with an array of certified vendors whose products can be shipped without incoming inspection. Because the company does not see the infrastructure to support industry as leading edge in Massachusetts, it searches the world for production components. Nypro, a plastic molder in western Massachusetts, is among a handful of suppliers not because it is local, but because it is world class, serving as Gillette's partner for its Sensor for Women line. For the most part, machinery comes from German manufacturers, steel from Hitachi Metals and British Steel, mold makers from California and Europe, die makers from Pennsylvania and the Midwest. In the factory, I spotted American flag stickers adorning a German machine and wondered what message local workers were trying to send about the presence of so many foreign suppliers.

WORLD PRODUCTION

Gillette's manufacturing operations are standardized worldwide so that production can move from place to place rapidly. Worldwide standards with the same specifications and tolerances everywhere permit maximum geographic flexibility. "We have about sixty factories making several hundred different products in more than a thousand versions in about two hundred markets," said Zeien, an architect of global production. "For every finished product, we are also moving parts around. Every day we are trying to figure out where to make product A to go to market B—based on exchange rates, who has capacity, or anything else that offers cost advantages. If there's a shortage in production runs in Istanbul, tomorrow we can supply from elsewhere."

Computers and faxes significantly increase the feasibility and efficiency of global scheduling. Daily production reports from each location reach the Boston headquarters forty-eighth-floor control point quickly, replacing the previous system of time-consuming phone calls and labor-intensive manual recording of data transmitted through armies of clerks before reaching decision makers. To Zeien, having teleconferencing equipment in the room next to his office means that "now it doesn't matter if the manager is five hundred or five thousand miles away. Major communication, such as updates on the status of a program, used to be face-to-face. A manager couldn't just send in a report or communicate on the telephone; he came to Boston with a carousel of slides, had dinner. Now communication is so simple here." Boston staff can telecommute from their households to world operations.

Manufacturing has been consolidated into fewer plants worldwide. The company "never ceases evaluating our manufacturing capacity," according to William McMorrow, especially as it enters new markets with local production in countries like China and India. But total productivity is more important than wage rates, so Gillette operates some of its most important factories in some of the world's most expensive places.

With 1.45 million square feet, Gillette's South Boston plant is almost twice the size of the next largest U.S. facility and alone over a quarter the size of aggregate manufacturing space for razors and blades and toiletries outside the United States. Three thousand people work there, two-thirds of them in manufacturing, the rest in research and sales. South Boston is the leading world manufacturing center for razors and blades; Berlin, known for highly skilled workers, is the only comparable one in size and sophistication and the only other plant making Sensor. Plants in Brazil, Mexico, and Great Britain also make razors and blades.

Technology requirements affect human resource requirements. To match Berlin's highly productive, highly skilled work force, the Boston Sensor workers have to be upgraded. Sally Harrison, production head for Sensor, recalled the evening meetings in the cafeteria every Thursday with all operating managers during the start-up crunch for Sensor in Boston. One big problem department managers faced initially was worker computer and numeric literacy. Longtime Gillette employees and new hires alike took training programs for the sophisticated, computerized work systems and measurement techniques that would come with Sensor technology. People were comfortable with an entirely visible operation; now the operator's job is one where the product and process are machine controlled and not visible—for instance, 13 laser welds in a millisecond for a single part and 150 parts per minute. "When it's going that fast you can't control it visibly," Harrison explained. "You need instrumentation. You need to look at quality measures like sigma limits. This is not an easy concept if you don't understand averages." So Gillette stepped back to teach computer language and math classes in the plant. "People, especially longtime employees, resent being told to change—'You never told me that when you hired me. I was not hired to be a computer operator.' " Nonetheless, a relentless pursuit of productivity within the plant involves constant training and puts workers on teams suggesting improvements.

Throughout South Boston, production workers have become more aware of their place in worldwide manufacturing. Production workers for SensorExcel in 1993, for example, knew that their product was not to be sold in the United States yet, that it was for Europe first. Press clippings from around the world adorn employee bulletin boards, such as stories about Gillette's activities in India. Berlin and Boston exchange improvement ideas and performance information. Long walls in the factory are covered with graphs about every aspect of production in both places; Sally compares notes weekly with Rudy, her Sensor counterpart in Germany.

LEADERSHIP FROM ANYWHERE

Gillette corporate headquarters is small, unpretentious, and largely invisible to the public—"much less important than the factory and facility in South Boston," an executive said. Far from the opulent symbol of corporate power many companies erected in the past decades, Gillette's headquarters occupies a dozen almost anonymous floors in the Prudential Tower high-rise. The number of people at headquarters continues to shrink, from one thousand down to six hundred, as activities are shifted to other locations, nearby and around the globe.

As Gillette becomes more globally integrated, locations away from headquarters serve as the lead for projects or planning on behalf of the world. Divisional headquarters for Oral-B, for example, is in California, its lead manufacturing facility in Iowa. Braun, headquartered in Germany, runs plants in Germany, Spain, Ireland, and Mexico. A corporate unit coordinates information technology, but dispersed manufacturing staff might lead projects for new software developments.

Increasingly, "headquarters" is portable, replacing staff pilgrimages to the center with executive visits to the field. Key managers come to Boston quarterly, but Zeien travels outside the United States monthly, because, he said, "it's different when managers come here with their Kodak carousels than when you see them on their home ground, see them around a table with their key people. And it affects commitments. It's easy to agree in Boston, but it means more when they make a commitment in front of their people."

Gillette contributes to its Boston headquarters community through high-wage manufacturing jobs, charitable donations, and participation by some executives in high-profile civic causes. But that's just a form of dues paying. Gillette's supply base is worldwide, it can easily shift production anywhere, its local markets are trivial, recent acquisitions are international, and none of its top ten U.S. retail customers are in Boston.

THE GLOBALIZATION CASCADE

Gillette executives liken their new global system to operating across "five hundred states," the same way companies operate across fifty states in America. They acknowledge that Kansas City and Kuala Lumpur are different just as New York and New Orleans are, but these differences can be taken into account by local sales offices, without challenging the company's global strategy.

This model of the fully globalized company has been realized only by a handful of giants. Some integrate all operations on a world or regional basis, like Ford, whose new North Atlantic unit resembles Gillette's. Some organize production on a world basis while maintaining strong country product strategy and marketing systems, like Nestlé. Still others, like Disney Consumer Products, maintain strong country organizations but look for synergies across markets. And hybrids call themselves "globally local," like Asea Brown Boveri (ABB), which considers itself a federation of 1,200 national companies with global coordination. Organization structures differ—and so do the terms for them, from "multidomestic" to "international" to "transnational."[1] Yet regardless of form of formal organization, the increasingly cosmopolitan outlook of large companies sets the tone for international competition.

Businesses are becoming more coordinated across borders, not necessarily more centralized. They transfer ideas across places, even if they do not move facilities or people. And once companies reach for world class concepts, the logic of world coordination in other areas follows. World coordination then pushes the development of world standards. To the extent that larger companies seek the means to transfer resources, ideas, and people smoothly and quickly across borders—from communication infrastructure and air transportation to a more universally educated population—smaller companies also gain access to mechanisms that help them form networks. To succeed involves being well connected, not necessarily big. This helps explain why the argument still rages about whether globalization favors large multinationals or small-niche competitors. The answer: Neither or both.

To some analysts, the large globalized company is associated with market dominance so great that it transcends the efforts of the nation-state to control economic life. One group proposes that giant global companies have already lost their national identities and have replaced governmental power. They argue that a few hundred giant "imperial corporations" control the flow of money, goods, and information across the world: Sony, Bertelsmann, Philips, Time-Warner, Matsushita, and Disney dominating a "global cultural bazaar" for information and entertainment; Philip Morris, RJR Nabisco, Nestlé, Sara Lee, and Heinz dominating a "global shopping mall" for consumer products; Citibank leading in a "global financial network."[2]

It might be farfetched to say that international corporations replace governments, but certainly their ability to operate effectively in more than one place gives them immense bargaining power in negotiations with governments. When Asea of Sweden merged with Brown Boveri and moved to Zurich in 1987, its power grew. "Fifteen years ago, Asea was a Swedish electrical company with 95 percent of its engineers in Sweden," CEO Percy Barnevik observed. "We could complain about high taxes, about how the high cost of living made it difficult to recruit Germans or Americans to come to Sweden. But what could Asea do about it? Not much. Today I can tell the Swedish authorities that they must create a more competitive environment for R&D or our research there will decline."[3]

Still other observers, noting fragmentation in the European Community and the success of smaller, entrepreneurial high-technology firms operating through networks of partners, see just the opposite.[4] Indeed, it is not hard to find examples of competent local, or regional, niche players outcompeting global giants even in industries once considered prime targets for global consolidation. The success of niche competitors such as Southwest Airlines, for example, challenges common wisdom that only a few large international airlines will survive. Deep knowledge of a local or regional market and a cost structure appropriate to it offer advantages against giants.

This controversy itself reflects the paradoxical nature of the global economy: the coexistence of globalizing consumption and localized distribution—with cosmopolitan leaders helping them to live together.

Globalism leads in information and communication, and that, in turn, supports convergence of tastes. Protected markets dominated by national champions are disappearing. Nearly every industry is being opened up to some form of competition from outside the traditional territory, even if it is only "theoretical" competition from knowledge of the existence of better products in other markets—realized by travelers who cross borders to shop. Within any country of the world, there is a growing pool of more sophisticated customers with access to the best the world has to offer. They no longer have to choose the local product or service as the only alternative. Among many problems for Euro Disney, for example, was the fact that European tourists could almost as easily, and sometimes more cheaply, go to sunnier Disney World in Orlando, Florida.

Localism prevails in politics and distribution—the differences in infrastructure and logistics to get goods and services to customers. Even when people accept, and sometimes even prefer, foreign products (why else would McDonald's be one of the best-known American brands worldwide?), they support local sovereignty. The French go wild for American movies but support legislation banning English from billboards.

Local jurisdictions set the rules. Local distribution channels require specific, differentiated relationships within a country. When Japanese management guru Kenichi Ohmae exhorts companies to undergo "insiderization" in order to be globally effective, he is referring to relationship building with local officials, distributors, and opinion leaders.[5] Large international companies are not immune to local and national politics. The Renault-Volvo alliance fell apart not on economic grounds, but on political ones: Volvo's Swedish stockholders' concerns about continuing French government involvement in Renault. This is why there will always be a need for people with deep local connections who are trusted by the locals. In fact, global companies need them more than others, to permit local acceptance of their world products.

Even highly local activities, however, are becoming more cosmopolitan. As large international companies globalize, they create a "globalization cascade" effect. Integration across markets in one industry pushes integration across markets in adjacent industries, which, in turn, reinforces and extends integration in the first. Global consolidation in one industry pushes that industry's suppliers and customers to develop international bases and meet world standards in all of their local sites. Each then has a stake in reinforcing the others' cosmopolitan thrust. Together they encourage governments to loosen local restraints, develop policies compatible with the rest of the world, and facilitate cross-border activity. And they develop cosmopolitan leaders who carry concepts from one place to another, pressuring local units to reduce their differences and join the world class.

The next place to look for cosmopolitans, then, is in the professionals who help international companies spread their concepts throughout the world. Whether they are taste reflectors, tastemakers, or taste manipulators, advertising agencies have followed clients like Gillette in accelerating globalization by increasingly treating people everywhere the same way.

COMMUNICATING WORLD MESSAGES: INSIDE AN ADVERTISING ALLIANCE

Changes begun in the 1980s have accelerated in the 1990s to increase international linkages in what was once a locally focused industry. The network formed by Chicago-based Foote Cone Belding (FCB) and Paris-based Publicis in 1988 is a response to the globalization cascade and a force for further change.[6]

The globalization cascade in advertising works through a set of mutually reinforcing feedback loops. Global media create consumer demand for the world's best products. Consumer products companies increase the number of multicountry products. One effect is to increase competition, as companies once centered in particular markets invade others. Increased competition increases the need for aggressive marketing, which increases advertising expenditures. To gain efficiencies in advertising as they implement global strategies, companies consolidate advertising through fewer agencies that can serve them across markets. To keep the business of the biggest spenders, advertising agencies then seek global scale through mergers or alliances. Once agencies become large and international, they profit from internal global efficiencies. They give priority to international clients. They tout multicultural approaches and maintain faith in global commonalities even in the face of local resistance. They create champions of world concepts. And they push their clients to develop still more world concepts.

MULTICOUNTRY AND WORLD PRODUCTS

Growth of global media encourages the development of world products and messages. Print media such as *Reader's Digest*, with 11,990,000 copies in circulation outside the United States in 1994, are one force. Television is even more important. CNN is available in over 140 countries. Rupert Murdoch operates a film studio (Twentieth Century–Fox), the United States's fourth-largest TV network (Fox), a satellite TV channel (Skychannel) covering Continental Europe, and a number of Australian TV stations.

Associated with the growth of international media outlets is a growing interest in consolidating product lines and selling those products into more markets. A decade ago there were still relatively few "world products" with the same content sold the same way everywhere—McDonald's burgers, Kodak film, Hyatt hotels, Timex watches, and Gillette razors. But companies increasingly want products that easily cross borders. Some marketing experts declare the death of the purely domestic business as countries invade each other's shelf space.

MORE COMPETITION, MORE MARKETING, MORE ADVERTISING

Heightened cross-border competition in the 1980s encouraged more aggressive marketing. More imported consumer goods were penetrating North American and European markets, and product variations were proliferating dramatically—sixty-six thousand new products and brands introduced in the United States alone between 1985 and 1990.[7] Retailers' private-label products were threatening manufacturers' brands in some markets. And, of course, the growth in scope and number of free-market economies around the world through deregulation, privatization, and opening of trade relations created more arenas for selling consumer products.

In 1970 worldwide advertising expenditure was just over $33 billion. By 1988 expenditure had grown to $200 billion, with the United States accounting for $109.8 billion, Western Europe for $42 billion, and the Asia/Pacific region (predominantly Japan) for $29 billion. In 1993 advertisers around the world spent an estimated $312.3 billion dollars promoting their products through the major media, according to Brian Jacobs, international media director for Leo Burnett. Advertising as a percentage of private consumption expenditure was highest in the United States at over 3 percent, next in the United Kingdom, and lowest in Germany, Italy, and France, among major markets.

The advertising industry was slower to develop in West Germany because of government restrictions on television advertising, which was limited to twenty minutes per day, to be aired before eight P.M. and not on Sundays. Germany's decentralized economic structure (four commercial hubs—Düsseldorf, Hamburg, Frankfurt, and Munich—instead of one large business center like London or Paris) meant that domestic agencies tended to be small, without international capabilities. But the German situation, too, changed in 1989, with the reunification of Germany, anticipation of European union, and eased regulations.

CLIENTS CONSOLIDATE ADVERTISING

With multicountry products, consumer goods companies can stretch their resources by mounting multicountry campaigns. Beginning in the 1980s, they sought international agencies that could handle their business in every market.

From the time large brand-name consumer goods manufacturers moved into international markets in the early 1900s, advertising agencies followed them. Coca-Cola drove McCann-Erickson's global expansion, Ford was behind J. Walter Thompson's increased international involvement, and Philip Morris used Leo Burnett to disseminate the Marlboro cowboy worldwide.

FCB grew to thirty-seven offices in eighteen countries by the 1970s. However, its clients were expanding internationally at an even faster rate. "When we presented to new clients, we would talk about our international capabilities, and wherever we had holes, we could see them wince," recalled former chairman Norman Brown.

In the 1980s international consumer goods companies like Gillette dramatically reduced the number of agencies employed to handle worldwide accounts. By 1987, when Gillette focused on fully global strategies, three-fifths of the world's top forty advertisers had consolidated their accounts in fewer agencies, and over 130 multinational companies had handed their accounts to single agencies. This tendency was strongest in Europe, in which six of the seven largest advertisers consolidated on a worldwide basis: Unilever, Nestlé, Grand Metropolitan, Volkswagen, Philips, and Renault. In the United States, which accounted for twenty-six of the top forty advertisers, seventeen had consolidated advertising internationally: Philip Morris, Procter & Gamble, General Motors, Ford, RJR Nabisco, PepsiCo, McDonald's, Kellogg, Eastman Kodak, Anheuser-Busch, Mars, Coca-Cola, General Mills, Colgate-Palmolive, Sara Lee, H. J. Heinz, and Campbell Soup. The financial impact was huge; Procter & Gamble's total advertising budget for 1990, for instance, was $2.4 billion.

AGENCY MERGERS AND ALLIANCES

In response to increasing demand for agencies with global presences, and in an environment demanding economies of scale and standardized quality, large advertising groups began to merge, buy out smaller, "boutique" shops, or form alliances with competitors overseas.

Although there had been some notable mergers in the 1960s and 1970s, the current frenzy began with London's Saatchi & Saatchi's merger with the New York agency Compton in 1982. Days later giant agencies Doyle Dane Bernbach, Needham Harper, and BBDO merged into a $5 billion agency, Omnicon. During 1985 and 1986 alone there were thirty-four major mergers. Although large international groups had significant management problems and occasional financial disappointments—Saatchi & Saatchi stumbled after its acquisition binge made it the world's largest agency—agencies rushed to snap up potential partners before their competitors did. As agencies merged, they retained competing clients' accounts by spinning off independently managed separate units ("streams") under a different name.

Foote, Cone & Belding's Brown foresaw in the mid-1980s that a few major global agencies would eventually dominate the market and that FCB needed to double in size and strength if it hoped to be one of them. According to FCB analyses, by 1987 international advertising agencies commanded 24.3 percent of the market, up from 14 percent in 1977; FCB estimated that by 1997 international agencies would have 35 percent world market share. FCB wanted to gain greater global scale.

Client desire to work with fewer agencies that could handle more markets had spread to regional players, accelerating the merger trend. In 1988 German household goods producer Henkel asked Düsseldorf agency BMZ to work on a well-known hair care product on condition that it coordinated the account throughout Europe. As there was no time to establish its own agencies in other countries, BMZ's only recourse was to join forces with FCB, which already had a European network.

Meanwhile, Nestlé had just announced that it was planning to reduce its ninety-plus advertising agencies to five preferred groups to service Nestlé worldwide. If FCB did not increase its global scale quickly, it risked being dropped from Nestlé accounts. Publicis, working for Nestlé out of Paris, heard the same news and faced the same problem. When a Spanish FCB executive, whom Publicis had once tried to hire, introduced Brown to Publicis head Maurice Lévy in 1988, the two agencies saw in each other an immediate solution to the problem of gaining global reach. Within months they designed a global alliance that would link their agencies without a full merger.

Publicis was the top-ranked agency in France with a useful network in Europe but virtually nonexistent elsewhere; founder Marcel Bleustein-Blanchet had long preached that advertising was fundamentally a national business predicated on national cultures. FCB, on the other hand, was strong in the Americas and had an Asian capability but lacked a significant European presence. Together they would have the reach and critical mass necessary to be among Nestlé's chosen five, but apart they would not. Publicis and FCB both worked for S. C. Johnson and Colgate-Palmolive in addition to Nestlé and had few competing clients. Brown felt an immediate rapport with Lévy, whom he saw as bright, energetic, and ambitious. A 1988 FCB memo called it "love at first sight."

Together FCB and Publicis have grown to a network of 173 agencies in forty-three countries with more than US$6 billion in worldwide billings. The partners constitute the second-largest agency in Europe, the second-largest in North America, and the eighth-largest in the world. In Europe they have 105 offices and two networks, one headed by Publicis in Paris and a second "stream" led by BMZ in Germany. The network provides global strategy and strength; local offices determine the fit with local culture based on client strategy.

GLOBAL COMMONALITIES: CULTURAL FAITH AND ECONOMIC INTEREST

International advertising agencies profit from global efficiencies. For example, advertising in global media can be handled at a single point, thus economizing on production costs and providing the client with volume discounts. Once organized to work globally, agencies have a stake in finding more things that can be done globally. The cascade continues.

Agencies encourage clients to see the value of brand consistency in all markets. That is both reasonable in light of the speed with which information crosses borders and a benefit to larger international groups. Easy-to-globalize products include those with simple, pragmatic applications, such as toilet tissue and insecticide. Where local tastes (rather than price or effectiveness) might drive a product's acceptance or rejection (as in foods or perfumes), an agency seeks an underlying principle or motivation inducing the consumer to buy.

FCB research encourages a strong belief that fundamental consumer motivations are similar from country to country even for culturally laden products such as cosmetics. FCB and Publicis leaders understand that communication can and will vary locally—"You don't automatically run one commercial around the world for everybody," one said—but they seek commonalities, permitting campaigns appealing to numerous audiences across markets. They might use a model whose features could be appreciated in any market; Isabella Rossellini appears in L'Oréal's Lancôme advertisements because she "translates well." Publicis invented "single concept campaigns" for Renault across countries, with minor details varying by market. For example, if the concept in France was that a Renault model was "beautiful to look at," the British campaign would be deterred from focusing its advertising on some other feature of the model, such as excellent engineering. Products do not have to lose their identification with particular countries to be sold globally; the network builds on country images to sell cheese from France and dairy products from Ireland.

Thus, FCB and Publicis give priority to international clients with future global development potential over accounts that are important only to a local agency. In Spain, for example, to keep FCB's S. C. Johnson and Zenith Data Systems accounts, Publicis gave up American Cyanamid and Alcatel. By 1992, four years into the alliance, FCB-Publicis handled thirty-seven world brands.

MELDING CULTURES

"One articulates multicultural melding from a comfortable CEO position in Paris or Chicago," Brown said as he assessed how well the alliance worked. "Then the rubber meets the road," stirring up predictable cultural tensions.

• *Country differences:* The organization of Publicis in 1988 mirrored the configuration of its French homeland, whereas FCB had a freewheeling American style. In France, politics, culture, and business tend to be highly centralized, with the seats of power and influence residing almost completely in the capital city; Publicis had its own singular source of power in Marcel Bleustein-Blanchet, known as *le patron.* The general problem-solving style taught at French management universities is more abstract than the style promoted at empirically minded American universities. Moreover, Europe is a more fragmented market than the United States, with language differences even within countries, such as Flemish and French in Belgium or four languages and cultural groups in Switzerland. Americans learn to brush aside differences; Europeans notice them everywhere.

• *Country rivalries:* Publicis had to prove it did not sell out to Americans—a hot button in France and a consideration for French government-owned clients such as Renault. FCB had to reassure its American multinational clients (and American expatriates in Europe hoping to return home on career rotation) that it was not abandoning its European operations to the French. Across another divide, BMZ's German managing director, Klaus-Jürgen Müller, recalled his concerns after his well-liked American acquirer "married" a French agency: "France is a very important country in Europe with a rich culture. But there are other important countries whose people don't like the the way the French think they're the greatest, especially Germans, who can be very tough and ambitious. While there is partnership between the two, there is also competition."

• *Local interests:* When the FCB and Publicis alliance formed, some local agencies were consolidated or eliminated while others enjoyed a sudden increase in revenues from servicing growing, worldwide accounts initiated elsewhere, such as Intel, L'Oréal, and Nestlé. But even those with opportunities from global connections experienced a loss of power. They were forced to work with unknown overseas counterparts, often also reluctant to cooperate.

Global organizations use formal mechanisms to build relationships that reduce tensions, from FCB and Publicis's world operating committee to worldwide seminars and conferences for managing and creative directors in local agencies. The most potent mechanism is explicit assignment of people to the role of global integrator. This puts power in the hands of the network's most cosmopolitan members, which further promotes globalization.

GLOBAL INTEGRATORS CHAMPION WORLD CONCEPTS

For advertising agencies, worldwide account directors (known as WWADs) are global integrators on behalf of client interests. The complexities as well as the opportunities of globalization are embedded in the role. WWADs are quintessential cosmopolitans: multilingual, well traveled, at ease in many places. Referring to themselves as "HQ watchdogs," "troubleshooters," "cross-fertilizers," "unquestionable experts," "peacemakers between local client and local agency," "consultants," and "the cement of center and periphery," they work across several boundaries:

- between FCB and Publicis offices within the alliance, each with a different heritage and reporting relationships;
- between offices located in different countries, each with local pride and country culture;
- between the network and clients, who have varying and changing cross-border strategies;
- between levels and units of client organizations;
- between client units and local network agencies.

In practice they promote the global over the local. For example, local offices have an investment in using their own ads, out of creative pride, pressure from a client's local representative, or, with the advent of a recession in the advertising industry, job security. Sometimes cultural inappropriateness or a regulatory infringement (country requirements for proof of claims) is cited as the reason for wishing to modify an ad or create a whole new campaign. WWADs intervene when a local office objects to an international campaign. WWADs try to convince the local parties of the ad's excellence, fit with the overall international strategy for the brand, or economies. WWADs marshal research evidence from another major market to support their arguments.

Integrators like the WWADs are strong advocates of globalization, even when client organization and strategy vary: from global centralization in the case of L'Oréal to Colgate-Palmolive's evolution away from decentralization to Nestlé's strong decentralization. Although each WWAD operates differently, each extends globalism.

L'Oréal: Beauty products manufacturer L'Oréal is highly centralized; local offices have little control over advertising in their countries. The company's product philosophy stresses technical innovation rather than culturally variable beauty standards; a single creative idea is executed the same way in every country for five world brands: Lancôme,

Plénitude, Garnier, Salon, and Armani. Publicis in France, lead agency for most L'Oréal products, handles creative work while local agencies translate copy into the local language, modify claims to fit local regulations or seasons, and choose local media. WWAD Claude Pradere's job is to guide a world message from his Paris office.

Colgate-Palmolive: In the early 1980s historically decentralized Colgate, maker of personal care products, made strides toward global integration by establishing worldwide product strategy groups at New York headquarters and consolidating advertising with three worldwide agencies in 1983. Many of Colgate's successful products had been local brands with country-specific positioning, packaging, and names. Colgate's most successful businesses in countries such as France, Mexico, Australia, Colombia, and the Philippines had operated autonomously, linked only by financial reporting requirements.

Colgate wanted a substantial increase in multicountry campaigns, such as a successful Ajax commercial aired in five European countries. When Ned Wiley started as Colgate's WWAD in April 1992, he and Colgate's new advertising manager set as the top priority "to create more great ads that could travel the world." Wiley's structure mirrors Colgate's organization: local agency teams, regional coordination teams, and Wiley's global coordination team responsible for strategy and integration. By drawing on world resources to solve local problems, Wiley spreads expertise across countries, using a special fund dedicated to cross-fertilization. He sent the creative director from the Philippines, Palmolive soap's most successful market, to South Africa for a week to help the local FCB office develop a campaign for the launch of five different "flavors" of Palmolive. His group found commonalities for a campaign for dishwashing detergent in France (where the brand name stood for skin care) and the United States (where cleaning efficacy was important).

Nestlé: Food producer Nestlé maintains high degrees of country autonomy even as it uses world product formulas and manufacturing. Local managers have full discretion over marketing, even though corporate units are responsible for Nestlé strategic brands, such as Chambourcy, and there is no central sourcing of creative material. At one point, forty different commercials for Nescafé were in use around the world because of an assumption that language differences required this variety.

Salomon Salto knows Nestlé well, having handled the account for Publicis for ten years before being appointed WWAD for Publicis-FCB in 1989. He avoids words like "guideline" and "framework" for fear of offending country subsidiaries. But he develops ten-year global marketing strategies using universal core concepts, which gently steers local thinking in a common direction.

Salto draws on cosmopolitan skills to make his case: "My job is more diplomacy and negotiation than power," he said. "In Latin America I speak Spanish; in English-speaking countries I speak English. My associate speaks German and uses it in Switzerland, Austria, and Germany. In some countries I speak French. I just returned from Asia where I spoke English." Because of thirteen years' experience with Nestlé, he has credibility on Nestlé matters and, therefore, little trouble commanding respect. He also studies the market before he visits. "I do my homework and it shows," he said.

Salto, Wiley, Pradere, and other global champions feel immediate rapport with one another as fellow cosmopolitans. Salto refers to FCB's Asian and Latin American regional directors, whom he met for the first time when he toured their areas, as friends. When the alliance convened WWADs for the first time in June 1992 in Paris, strangers enjoyed instant camaraderie. FCB's Terry Peigh, WWAD for Kimberly-Clark, said he could not tell who at the meeting was from Publicis and who was from FCB. A counterpart from Publicis observed: "I met FCB account directors from the United States and had the feeling that I had been working with those guys for years. Everything was natural, smooth—really easy."

Cosmopolitans share a mind-set, a worldview—literally. And they are adept at finding each other, even in localized industries, to begin to globalize minds as well as methods.

GREAT CONNECTIONS: THE FORMATION OF GLOBAL ELITES

Cosmopolitans spread world concepts and reinforce a global culture of management through their leadership of international companies like Gillette or their work as global integrators for clients and customers, like the worldwide account directors at FCB and Publicis. They also know how to extend their reach through network building, through cultivation of connections in many parts of the world that provide business advantages.

Members of the world class are not only cosmopolitan in outlook, they are also highly interconnected with each other. They may start with loose social ties within industry sectors and regions, but then, as their companies link their fates more tightly through alliances, joint ventures, cross shareholding, or exchange of people, cosmopolitans become more tightly connected to their counterparts around the world. The interactions that occur through these networks create a need for common vocabularies, tools, and systems, and they encourage transfer or sharing of capabilities. Convergence of organizational competence—the development of a world culture of management—then permits world class companies to operate anywhere, taking advantage of differences among localities (such as in natural resources or wages) without sacrificing quality.

Networks form around both industry and ethnic cosmopolitans. Pierre Everaert, for example, is an industry cosmopolitan with extensive ties across many countries and an instinct for collaboration. A Belgium-born American citizen experienced in consumer goods companies in Europe and the United States, Everaert was the first nonfamily head of Ahold, a Dutch supermarket company that owns American chains in the Boston-Cleveland-Atlanta triangle—Bi-Lo (headquartered in Greenville, South Carolina), First National, Tops, Giant, and Red Food Stores. Before he moved from Ahold to Philips, Everaert transformed informal industry acquaintances into formal allies, helping create networks that share resources and know-how among independent companies from many countries.

One of Everaert's network visions, the European Retail Alliance (ERA), links the chief executives and, increasingly, top management, of three companies in a quest for mutual learning: Ahold; Groupe Casino, a French supermarket giant; and Argyll, owner of the British Safeway stores purchased from Kohlberg Kravis Roberts of the United States.[8] ERA members mount joint projects around logistics and systems, sharing resources and ideas. They take advantage of one another's strengths for product and concept innovation and tap new international suppliers already tested by another ERA company, resulting in new offerings that enhance the companies' reputations as taste leaders in their home markets. Associated Marketing Services, an alliance of the ERA partners with another eight companies from another eight countries, works with manufacturers to create efficiencies that can be shared with retailers—for example, an agreement to develop a Eurostandard paper towel by Scott Paper in Philadelphia (at that time Everaert was on the Scott board of directors).

As the ERA partners share information and capabilities, each adopts another's products or merchandising style, and global commonalities grow. Argyll drew from Casino's strengths in wine and delicatessen design; now French delicatessens operate in British Safeway supermarkets. Casino used Safeway suppliers to introduce Scottish smoked salmon to French consumers.

Industry networks nudge companies to subordinate local differences to international commonalities; ERA companies developed a common international accounting standard to help them compare information item by item, although the Dutch and the French are still not convinced that English cash registers are more user friendly. But although people at lower ranks do not let go of localism easily, the cosmopolitans at the top will continue to look outward, across countries, for ideas and opportunities.

For ethnic cosmopolitans, international commonalities already exist in a shared ethnic culture that transcends particular places.[9] The most powerful examples of ethnic cosmopolitans are the overseas Chinese in the Pacific Rim, heading business groups that extend from Southeast Asia to the United States. Among these ethnic cosmopolitans, one of the most successful practitioners of networking is Mochtar Riady, founder and chairman of Lippo Group, a financial services conglomerate with dual headquarters in Indonesia and Hong Kong and an important American base in California. I first met him in 1991 before his photo graced stories in *Time* or *Fortune* about the new Asian tigers. Now Riady has moved beyond his ethnic base to create a web of significant international political and business connections in America, Europe, Japan, and China that help Lippo Group tap new markets while bringing American ideas and products to Southeast Asia.[10]

Riady is a master of the network universe who is equally well connected with the president of the United States and the premier of China. Over a thirty-five-year period Riady (born Lie Wen Chen in Indonesia to Chinese immigrant parents) created a financial empire out of nothing but his personal drive, ethnic ties (Chinese moneylenders gave him his start in banking), and skills as a collaborator who knows that the first principle of networking is to make friends, not deals —to take advantage of every connection for the future doors it might open. One story illustrates how those with cosmopolitan instincts move from a local base to international prominence through relationships. In 1976 this then obscure Indonesian banker made a bold bid for Bert Lance's 30 percent share of National Bank of Georgia. Lance, President Carter's director of the Office of Management and Budget, was selling his share through Arkansas investment banker Jackson Stephens. The bank board was impressed by Riady's proposal to internationalize this American regional bank.

Although pressure from Indonesia caused Riady to withdraw his bid, he built on the connections. In 1977 Riady and Stephens developed a fifty-fifty joint venture in Hong Kong, which was one of Lippo Group's eventual platforms for expansion in Hong Kong and now China. The Stephens connection also led to Riady's ownership of Worthen Bank in Arkansas (later divested), where he sent his son James for training and developed a warm relationship with young Governor Bill Clinton. Today James is one of the World Economic Forum's two hundred Global Leaders for Tomorrow, and John Huang, the former head of Lippo Group's American business activities, is now principal deputy assistant secretary of the U.S. Department of Commerce.

In addition to providing connections with opportunities, networks are important sources of new concepts and competence. And Lippo Group, like the European Retail Alliance or FCB and Publicis, uses its relationships to spread a common culture of management across places, increasing the cosmopolitan outlook of managers and facilitating the development of global business concepts. Riady sought seasoned executives with experience in American multinational companies, especially Citibank, which provided Lippo Group's first nonfamily managing director and cosmopolitan leaders like José ("call me Joe") Hanna, a Brazilian who speaks six languages and had worked for Citibank on four continents. Lippo uses venture partners as teachers—such as IBM, Mitsubishi, and, among its most recent, Kmart and J.C. Penney; hires foreign expatriates to mentor local managers; uses its California banks to train Asian bankers; communicates in English; and convenes its managers from across the Pacific Rim for "synergy conferences" to reinforce a common culture that transcends country affiliations.

NETWORK POWER AS A BUSINESS ADVANTAGE

The new cosmopolitans can come from anywhere, as long as they have the desire and ability to seek concepts, competence, and connections from outside their home territory. Small local networks, like Riady's first ventures in Indonesian banking with other overseas Chinese business heads where shared ethnicity provided the basis for trust, can create resources for entry into wider global networks. Networks are strengthened when members develop joint projects and bet on each other's future, as FCB and Publicis or the ERA partners did in exchanging ownership shares, but the network is more than the specific deal. Networks are options on future opportunities, as Riady found with Stephens or with his major current partner in banking in Hong Kong and China, China Resources, the Chinese government's principal international investment group.

Ongoing broadening of network ties creates still more opportunities; relationships for one purpose in one place, if successful, can open new opportunities or bring prestige in other places with other partners. Thus, the value of any part of a network, any particular venture, cannot be calculated solely on the basis of the direct economic value located in that part; it needs to be viewed in terms of increased benefits to other parts of the network. Lippo Group's California banks bring value far beyond the earnings (or more likely, losses) of four small branch banks in San Francisco, Los Angeles, Orange County, and San Jose; they anchor one end of trade financing for the rest of the Pacific Rim, solidify Chinese-American ties, train Asians in U.S. banking, and reinforce American political connections.

The result of the networks that cosmopolitans create is a "global elite" at the pinnacle of the world class. This global elite consists of top executives who are well acquainted with one another, are fluent in each other's corporate languages, and often stand on an equal footing with heads of governments that court them as sources of new investment regardless of their passport (or multiple passports). On a 1992 trip to the mountain resort of Davos, Switzerland, for the annual meeting of the World Economic Forum, a premier networking opportunity for leaders of companies and countries, I heard political leaders ranging from Nelson Mandela to new heads of state from the Soviet bloc's now independent CIS sound a common theme: "Invest here, and we'll bury the political hatchet." So much for ideologies. In the rush for foreign investment, nationalism seems an internal luxury. At Davos, when with the cosmopolitans, think cosmopolitan.

Cosmopolitans have the vision, skills, and resources to form networks that extend beyond the home base. Such cosmopolitans lead international companies and networks bcause they are *integrators* who can see beyond obvious differences among countries and cultures; *diplomats* who can resolve conflicts among local ways and influence locals to accept world standards or commonalities; and *cross-fertilizers* who can bring the best from one place to another. Creating formal roles for integrators, diplomats, and cross-fertilizers is one way the new business networks organize for success.

Networks produce a self-reinforcing cycle of advantage that help the rich get richer. Extensive cross-border networks permit world class companies to offer their customers wide access to goods and services that transcend territories. These networks, in turn, create still more opportunities, both at home and abroad, because they enlarge the pool of the three C's available to cosmopolitans. Access to state-of-the-art concepts, global competence, and powerful connections then solidify membership in the world class. Here's how the cycle works:

• *Strong partners offer each other access to the best and latest concepts*: products and processes that can be brought to the home market for local advantage or used to enter new ones.

• *Network membership forces learning, whether or not that is an explicit intent*. Gradual convergence of competence is a necessary outgrowth of forging a link between companies. Absorbing partners' know-how puts cosmopolitans on an equal footing almost any place in the world and augments the skills they can use locally—to gain advantage over local competitors or defend the home territory against foreign companies.

• *Powerful connections open doors to still more introductions to powerful people*. This puts cosmopolitans on the inside track in other places and makes them the preferred local partner(s) for foreign interests that come to the home base.

Cosmopolitans reproduce themselves. Cosmopolitans create conditions that require additional cosmopolitan leaders with boundary-crossing skills. And the actions of cosmopolitans to move concepts around the world reinforce the power of customers, wherever they are, to demand the world's best.

"Best Partner": Transforming Supply Chains to Global Webs

Customer power brings global markets home—even for local companies doing business only in the area. To survive, local businesses must become more cosmopolitan.

Cosmopolitanism is a matter of mind-set as much as markets. Businesses must enlarge the geographic scope of their sources of ideas, standards, processes, raw materials, parts, and people in order to find and serve increasingly cosmopolitan customers. They must be linked to networks that help them look beyond their home region or nation for resources to add value at home.

Although most economic transactions occur within national borders and relatively few companies are involved in exports—only about 10 percent of the U.S. GDP is trade related, according to economist Paul Krugman—the global economy casts a shadow on all business relationships. It puts the power of choice in the hands of more demanding customers who are no longer forced to settle for what's locally available. They bring global criteria to bear on decisions about where to buy goods and services they need for local operations, gradually erasing the line between domestic and international competition.

Being best in the neighborhood isn't good enough anymore. Companies must look good against the best in the world just to survive in the neighborhood. Inward-focused organizations must become outward focused, and isolated ones must become network linked. Small and local businesses must join the world class.

"Small" and "local" are not identical, although they are correlated. The more international of the 2,655 companies in my five-city survey tend to be much larger in revenues and employment, as well as faster growing, more innovative, and more likely to be involved in networks and alliances.[1] But some large companies are still quite local in inputs, outputs, and outlooks: for example, banks, hospitals, and utilities—the traditional downtown organizations that formed the leadership base of many American cities throughout most of the century. And some small companies are highly cosmopolitan: newer businesses in knowledge-intensive high-technology industries or local affiliates of large international networks.

The most familiar arguments for why companies must become more cosmopolitan revolve around the value of exports for market growth, economies of scope, and learning. Exports to fast-growing markets, such as those in Asia or Latin America, create or preserve jobs at home when domestic markets are stagnant. Furthermore, economies of geographic scope enable companies to be more innovative, spreading the costs of new technology or product development over markets of much greater size than a single country, even one as large as the United States. This rationale, which was behind Gillette's formation of a single North Atlantic division, works for small as well as for large companies. Merlin Metalworks, a small manufacturer, can afford to make high-quality, premium-priced titanium bicycles for a relatively small market niche because of its international distribution; over a third of the sales of this young company come from outside the United States. Growing numbers of midsize American health care product companies seek product approval overseas before or concurrently with the U.S. approval process because of the value for global competitiveness of early focus on markets large in aggregate size that can be developed quickly.[2]

Companies also gain intangible benefits from international marketing, such as access to concepts and competence required for foreign trade that prove useful in the home market. An international presence exposes companies to innovations developed elsewhere. And exporting requires additional competence. For example, customers at home are sometimes more forgiving because problems can be resolved quickly through easy access to company headquarters; for more distant customers, it might be more important to anticipate problems to ensure that they do not arise in the first place, thereby raising operational quality standards.

A second set of reasons to become more cosmopolitan affects a larger number of local companies, many of which may never export anything. The growing presence of international companies in their home territories confronts smaller local businesses with competitors and customers who bring different standards and have access to different, and often greater, resources. For example, Morrie Olson of Olson's Food Stores in Seattle, a fifteen-store regional operation, competes with national and foreign-owned chains that have deep pockets for real estate, advanced information technology, and direct supply relationships bypassing food wholesalers. Allen Funk of Funk's Wallpapers in Spartanburg, another retailer, has changed his product mix to reflect the tastes of European expatriates staffing international companies in South Carolina. Parts suppliers to Honda's American plant in Marysville, Ohio, must match the competence of Honda's Japanese supply base.

The third and most important force for cosmopolitanism affects still more businesses: the growth of customer power. Global consolidation and the cascade effects that stem from it are changing the ways companies deal with their suppliers. The implications ripple through the supply chain to reach all suppliers, from equipment makers and parts producers to bankers and law firms. Customers want access to the best in the world, but they do not want to have to go far to get it, and they want it at attractive prices with extra services. They want fewer suppliers who do more for them. And large customers have the power to demand that suppliers themselves become cosmopolitans. "Indirect exporters" (domestic suppliers to companies who include their components in products for export) must become as world savvy as their international company customers.

In short, a shift from localism to cosmopolitanism is often customer driven. As customers consolidate and move around the world, their suppliers have to be able to move quickly with them—or ahead of them. Dynatech, a $500 million maker of video voice data systems and other telecommunications equipment, has built facilities and ties outside of America in order to keep its American telecom customers as they seek foreign markets. And to serve ever-larger global customers, Dynatech must integrate the capabilities of forty-two largely independent local units, driving cosmopolitanism throughout the organization. It must balance entrepreneurship through local "ownership" with the ability to tap the power of the whole.

To succeed in a global economy, companies must be "world-ready" whether or not they are world-active. This is why emerging companies in industries of the future are born global. They develop a cosmopolitan mind-set from the start, even before they sell a single product into international markets. They are capable of serving the most demanding customers with the best concepts because they stress global competence and connections.

Successful growth companies like Powersoft, described in chapter 2, develop concepts that not only meet world standards, but redefine them. They devise product strategies from the beginning with global elements in mind—market needs, supply sources, international standards, quality processes, technology developments. And they find international partners to extend their reach. Genzyme, for example, a biotechnology leader, has alliances with European, Japanese, and American companies; satisfies both U.S. and European regulatory standards; and obtains specialized materials internationally, such as serum from New Zealand, enzyme from Thailand, and tissue from France. Medical research, its managers said, has no borders. Tiny health technology start-ups still in an incubator in Miami agree; one newborn, VideoMed, provides physician consultations to developing countries by satellite.

Similarly, Harvard Design and Mapping (HDM), a computer-mapping company founded in 1988 by Katja Kim, a young woman émigrée from Korea to the United States, had a representative and joint venture in Japan and development groups in Russia and Canada within four years of its formation. Although small—under $5 million in sales—the company is recognized as an international player because it opened a niche. Like Genzyme, HDM has a multinational, multilingual staff. As a subcontractor to large engineering firms and computer companies, HDM must meet world technology standards.

PURCHASING PRESSURE AND THE EROSION OF LOCAL ADVANTAGES

Local suppliers, like it or not, are competing in national and international markets for local business, under conditions that do not favor them. As cosmopolitanism grows in large companies, local-area operations of companies headquartered elsewhere make fewer purchasing decisions, and local relationships decline in importance—except when local suppliers are world class.

Hewlett-Packard, the widely admired global computer and instruments manufacturer whose products are world leaders, was known for many years as a model of decentralization and local control. Traditionally, considerable decision-making autonomy resided in units such as its medical equipment division, based in Andover, Massachusetts, on the northern outskirts of Boston, a market leader with 1993 revenues of $1.14 billion. Today H-P operates like other global companies. Worldwide purchasing is coordinated by a headquarters team in California. There are fewer decisions left to make in Andover and little opportunity for the community-conscious Andover executives to pump more money into the local economy by buying locally. "Making decisions about worldwide sourcing as a resident of the North Shore shakes the conscience a little," said general manager Ben Holmes, with twenty years in Andover under his belt. "But we have to compete globally to succeed."

A Hewlett-Packard corporate group oversees procurement and funds training in it worldwide. Major purchases of electronic components are coordinated at Palo Alto corporate headquarters, which negotiates long-term agreements with suppliers. True to H-P tradition, there is an element of decentralization left. Divisions offer feedback on their best suppliers, the corporate group negotiates price, then divisions choose their suppliers from an approved list. Even for those less significant items for which purchasing is still decentralized, there is much worldwide coordination and global information exchange, putting pressure on local decision makers to accept world products.

For the medical products group in Andover, fifty key suppliers account for 80–90 percent of its purchasing dollars. The division seeks the best quality worldwide, formally measuring supplier performance on "TQRDCE" (technology, quality, responsiveness, delivery, cost, and environmental standards). If local or regional firms are world class, they can compete. Massachusetts and New England are favored for plastics because of high-quality manufacturers in the region, such as Nypro, which supplies Gillette; indeed, the Greater Boston unit of H-P can influence sites in Germany and Oregon to buy plastics from New England. But at the same time, Andover must look to the world for most of its supplies.

Hewlett-Packard's Holmes is not the only one to have his conscience shaken. In every city, major institutions with deep community connections are moving quietly from traditional local suppliers to distant sources that offer performance advantages and worldwide service. An executive of a bank with strong local commitments, marketing itself as a local institution, lowered his voice to a whisper in my interview when he revealed that the bank was getting ready to outsource its software services to India, which is now a world center for programming. That bank could be one of many. It could be Chase Manhattan Bank in New York, which struck a deal with Tata Unisys Ltd. in Bombay (a joint venture of India's Tata with America's Unisys) to coordinate programming design in Hong Kong and the United States and oversee it in India. "You consider all the available resources," said Gene Friedman, vice president of applied technology. Labor costs are 50 percent less expensive in India than in the United States, but what Friedman claimed was equally important is that Chase can get leading-edge business applications and world class quality at that price.[3]

The likelihood that companies operating a unit in a particular place will find their suppliers primarily in that place continues to decline—a long-term process of change enlarged and accelerated by globalization. Consolidation of manufacturing in fewer sites to achieve economies of scale, and higher productivity within that smaller number of sites, make it less likely that companies in any single city will find most of what they need locally. And local offices or distributors for global companies make it easier to shop the world from home.

In the Boston area, for example, the biggest purchasers across industries spend their largest dollars for high-ticket goods and services outside the region:

- A big biotech company buys its raw materials from Iowa, France, and Thailand and its laboratory supplies and equipment from an American multinational outside the region.

- A telephone operating company buys $1 billion a year in switching equipment from Canadian, Japanese, and American manufacturers, only one of which has a facility in the area.
- A large insurance company gets $80 million a year in information systems support from a national systems firm that flies in consultants to augment its small local office.
- A computer manufacturer spends only 10 percent of its $500 million of purchasing dollars in Massachusetts; its mechanical components and electronics come from the West Coast, its semiconductors and peripherals from the Far East, and its printers from Italy.

Even those companies that are highly locally focused in their markets and orientation are global shoppers in their purchasing; a local newspaper's biggest purchase is $70 million a year of newsprint, obtained entirely outside the local area, a quarter of it from across the border in Canada.

In contrast, in all five places in my survey, larger companies use local businesses primarily for labor-intensive, low value-added services. Services such as cleaning, maintenance, security, and local transportation are increasingly outsourced by big companies and obtained from local suppliers. In short, the things left to local decision makers for local purchase are less valuable commodities: services and office supplies. An electronic device manufacturer, for example, buys half of its nonproduction materials and services locally but only 10–15 percent of its production materials. A defense contractor buys computer chips centrally for all its national facilities from U.S. multinationals in the Midwest and California and other components from Singapore and Hong Kong, then uses local suppliers on a decentralized basis at each of its facilities for lower-value work such as cabinetry.

Professional services such as legal work and accounting tend to be purchased locally, and most companies use local banks for routine services such as payrolls and checking accounts. But local preferences are disappearing even for professional and financial services. A Boston-area telecommunications equipment manufacturer splits its legal work geographically among four firms because of their specialties, not their location: one each in Washington for labor relations, New York for patent issues, California for litigation, and Boston for technology knowledge. A Miami company moved its major commercial banking relationship from south Florida to South Carolina because of turmoil related to the takeover of a bank in its region.

Even temporary employment agencies, whose use is generally a local decision, are not immune to these trends. Although the ten thousand estimated temporary help offices in the United States are predominantly local companies, temp services are increasingly purchased from multinational chains. ADIA personnel services, for example, was founded in Lausanne, Switzerland, in 1957, expanded throughout Europe, and entered the United States in 1972, moving its world headquarters to Menlo Park, California, in 1993. It has about 1,500 offices worldwide, 600 of them in the United States. Such service chains offer sophisticated staff training, computer networks and databases, and international contracts for international companies.

Proximity has not disappeared as one of the criteria for suppliers; but it has been joined by so many other criteria that it no longer confers an automatic advantage. There are opportunities for local suppliers to win new business from cost-conscious companies if the local companies meet world standards. For example, a defense contractor reports a slight preference for local suppliers due to recent cost controls that limit travel budgets. Sometimes there are national preferences, although not necessarily local ones. Wal-Mart, the innovative discount retail giant that pioneered in supplier partnerships, created its "Bring It Home to the USA" program in 1985 to encourage American manufacturing of items Wal-Mart was importing.

But just because large customers want their suppliers to be nearby—the way Honda does in keeping only three hours' worth of inventory in its Marysville, Ohio, plant—does not mean that they settle for what's already in the neighborhood. Increasingly they entice global suppliers to locate facilities close to theirs. Roger Milliken, chairman of textile giant Milliken & Co. and a pioneer in the quality movement, brought new industry to Spartanburg and neighboring South Carolina counties by encouraging European textile equipment manufacturers to establish American operations there.

BEST-IN-WORLD: THE NEW RESPONSIBILITIES OF SUPPLIERS

Companies want things J-I-T (just-in-time), but they also want them B-I-W (best-in-world). They want things right now right here, but they also want that same service everywhere. Cosmopolitan customers seek greater cosmopolitanism in their suppliers. They expect suppliers to

- meet the highest world standards;
- provide extra, "value-added" services, to increase convenience for the customer or benefits for the end user;
- serve them wherever they are located;
- draw on the best resources from any part of the world;
- become a partner expert in the customer's business, contributing to combined supplier-customer teams and knowledgeable about end users, whether domestic or international.

Throughout the supply chain, closer collaboration is replacing arm's-length transactions. Supplier-customer transactions are evolving toward fewer but closer relationships in which suppliers perform more services for customers but must also meet higher standards. Customers and suppliers alike report increasing "partnering." In my five-area survey, over a third of all companies indicate they have established closer relationships with major suppliers and intend to do more of this in the future. On the supplier side, over half say they are deepening their relationships with major customers. And these trends are even stronger for companies with greater international activity. Even giant corporations once preferring self-sufficiency and unilateral control are increasing their partnering activity.

Closer relationships mean fewer relationships, each one carrying a heavier load. Ocean Spray, a billion-dollar producer of fruit juices, has reduced its supply base from 900 to 170 suppliers. About 90 percent of its purchases come from thirty core suppliers, none of them located in Ocean Spray's home state of Massachusetts. Ocean Spray demands more of suppliers and manages supplier relationships as a seamless part of the company. The company wants just-in-time delivery with fewer inspections, which means greater investment with fewer suppliers. It evaluates suppliers through prequalifying plant audits and reviews of their financial and management history, then sends a multifunctional Ocean Spray team from purchasing, process engineering, and manufacturing for site visits to suppliers. Ocean Spray gives awards for suppliers; it encourages competition by holding contests centered on innovation—for example, to develop material for new plastic containers. To manage the new supplier relationships, purchasing managers must have quality experience and international expertise. Instead of talking price first, they now discuss specifications and quality first.

Companies in both manufacturing and services expect those fewer preferred suppliers to do more things and to do them everywhere the company operates. A large insurance company I'll call "Lifeco" still uses 1,600 vendors nationally, but 30 suppliers account for 60–70 percent of dollars spent. Price has fallen to a distant third among criteria for suppliers. The company has developed four highly significant relationships, none of them with local companies, although in one case a local sales office is the liaison. The single most important criterion for these significant relationships is the ability to supply Lifeco on a national basis. Second is the ability to work in a partnership arrangement to improve operations. For example, a furniture supplier has helped Lifeco find considerable savings through better spacing of facilities; a business forms supplier has helped it reengineer its forms processing, showing how to print more forms by computer, thereby saving storage costs. Furthermore, Lifeco no longer wants to store supplies, it wants vendors to do it.

As powerful customers demand value-added services, suppliers regain some power only if they redefine their roles to become indispensable to their customers—for example, through continual innovation or partnering to upgrade or perform essential functions. Excellent quality is no longer a competitive advantage for suppliers. Without it, suppliers are out of the game. Even with it, suppliers must be ready to perform a wide range of services for customers. As an American computer executive argued, "The quality of the supplier is now assumed; all companies we deal with have excellent quality. Now suppliers need more than quality for us to talk to them."

A new division of labor between suppliers and customers is reinventing industries. In Spartanburg, for example, Symtech Systems and Technology no longer simply sells equipment to its manufacturing customers. It designs and oversees their manufacturing processes as they use the equipment. In Aberdeen, Scotland, oil company customers such as BP (British Petroleum) and Conoco work with suppliers such as engineering firm Brown & Root to rethink the supply chain. They want suppliers to move from simply constructing rigs and platforms to maintaining and even operating them. Up to a dozen subcontractors work with BP in teams to design and manage complete projects formerly carved into discrete activities.

Extra services include those that involve shifting activities from customers to suppliers. Customers might expect their suppliers to warehouse a customer's inventory, finance it by withholding billing until well after goods are received, ship on demand, customize design, inspect for quality, ticket goods for retail sale, and serve on joint teams to solve problems or develop innovations. Suppliers and customers must speak the same language, know the same technology, use the same business systems, and understand the needs of end users. Thus, small suppliers must be at least as knowledgeable and sophisticated as their large company customers—sometimes more so. Meeting international quality certification standards is only an admissions ticket, not a winning strategy.

To meet the B-I-W requirements of customers requires collaborative strategies: partnerships between suppliers and customers and membership in networks that give small and midsize companies access to the world's best resources. Thus, companies that know how to be "best partners" to their customers, allies, and their own suppliers will remain on the list when suppliers are pruned and industry responsibilities redistributed.

"BEST PARTNER" IN ACTION: HOW A SMALL PLAYER WINS GLOBAL WARS

As an illustration of the value of networks and relationships that extend in many directions, consider the following case of a company in the apparel industry that is reinventing the supply chain in North America and Europe. Cohen & Wilks International (CWI) shows how all the new forms of partnering work together as a global survival strategy. CWI gets many benefits as a "best partner," uses the benefits from one relationship to build another, and manages far-flung relationships effectively. The CWI story also sheds light on the partnering activity of global trading companies and major retail customers.[4] In this case, the supply chain is truly a global web of blurred boundary relationships.

CWI's managing director, Bryan Spink, and marketing director, Derek Doyle, took the train from Leeds to meet me for lunch at the Royal Automobile Club in London in March 1992 at the request of its largest customer, BhS (originally British Home Stores), whose American chief executive was engineering a dramatic turnaround. I expected two typical "locals" from a small company in the heartland. I found instead a pair of world-savvy cosmopolitans.

Once family owned and run, CWI is now a joint venture with a giant partner. Once manufacturing primarily locally, it now guides production through a network of foreign factories. Once supplying a large number of arm's-length retail customers, it now has a small number of deep, dedicated customer relationships.

CWI, formerly Britain's largest manufacturer of raincoats, faltered when British garment manufacturing declined in the 1960s because of competition from Asia. But CWI joined the global thrust instead of fighting it. In 1966 Spink traveled to Japan and was introduced to Mitsui & Co., which had relationships with numerous textile factories, including Toray Industries, the world's largest synthetic-fiber company. Cohen & Wilks supplemented its product offering with goods purchased through Mitsui and manufactured in Japan. A few years later Cohen & Wilks International was reinvented by Spink and Doyle to become a joint venture with Mitsui as 50 percent co-owner.

CWI supplies apparel primarily for the British market but plans to increase business in continental Europe. A small CWI staff of one hundred orchestrates a network of ten stitching factories spanning six countries in east Asia and the Middle East, overseeing the manufacture of about two million garments annually, while drawing on the resources of 189 Mitsui offices worldwide and earning a steady profit on sales in the range £15–£20 million.

THE SMALL PLAYER'S BIG PARTNER: MITSUI AND GLOBAL ACCESS

Mitsui & Co. is the trading arm and core of one of Japan's oldest, most distinguished business groups *(zaibatsu)*, tracing its history back nearly three hundred years. Sales in 1992 exceeded ¥16.5 trillion (then $145 billion) and assets ¥8 trillion. In 1993 Mitsui operated 189 offices worldwide, each office equipped with an administrative and financial staff. One of the world's largest trading companies, Mitsui subsidiaries are active in steel, machinery, chemical products, foodstuffs, and petroleum; textile trade accounts for 13 percent of the company's business. Most Mitsui offices employ textile managers who can offer on-site support to CWI. In Japan, about 255 people are dedicated to textiles in Tokyo, Osaka, and Nagoya; outside of Japan, about 75.

Mitsui's role with CWI was initially largely administrative and financial, with occasional introductions, such as enhancing CWI's image by connecting it with an important design firm with which Mitsui had worked in Japan. Keiichi Kotake, a Mitsui computer specialist, moved to Leeds in 1992 to learn the business and help CWI, such as opening letters of credit for overseas business directly from CWI rather than from Mitsui London. As Mitsui moves to integrate its diverse independent companies, to gain strength in unity as other international companies are doing, joint ventures outside of Japan, once considered exile, are now career development opportunities for younger staff like Kotake.

Giant Mitsui needs small companies like CWI to supply local know-how for Mitsui's global strategy. "In the past," Kotake said, "Mitsui was more like just a shareholder, giving money but not mouth. Cohen & Wilks is the entire front of the operation. We need the existing local human relationships, know-how. English people speak to English people; everywhere we go we are still Japanese. But we are getting more involved, as we have done elsewhere, especially in textiles in the downstream of the market, with wholesalers and retailers. I go everywhere with Cohen & Wilks. My job is to grasp completely what is going on in this company. We are looking to enlarge our know-how. We can't do it if we just put money in and don't learn from others' experience. In the textile field Japanese people have always looked at the Japanese market only, never for export. Foreign countries were seen for their supply value only. Now Cohen & Wilks will help us penetrate Europe."

CWI needs Mitsui even more. When CWI staff travel, the local Mitsui office provides support on a fee basis. When CWI seeks new sources of supply, Mitsui's textile experts conduct a worldwide search, providing in-depth background information about local conditions, introductions to relevant government officials, and information about the local factory owner. For example, Mitsui Dubai's 1988 introduction of CWI to the United Arab Emirates led to CWI's switching nearly all its trouser manufacturing operations there.

Mitsui's relationships with local officials give CWI advance warning of trends and changes, such as shifts in quotas, currency rates, or laws that might affect the business. Mitsui also works with CWI on capital needs for new factories, which Mitsui views as an investment in the future of CWI. "Our joint ventures are not about money but about human relationships," Kotake said. "We feel a sense of *giri*—obligation—toward Cohen & Wilks and want to see them do well for relationship reasons."

ENSURING COMPETENCE IN PRODUCTION

Between 1988 and 1993 CWI reduced its foreign supply partners from about twenty-five to ten, insisting on their exclusive services to CWI quality standards in return for volume guarantees. This requires skill at developing and maintaining the competence of far-flung factories not wholly owned by CWI.

Historically, Korea had been an excellent source for fabrics and manufacturing. The work force was well educated, skillful at garment construction, and, for a long time, inexpensive. In the mid- to late 1980s, however, the cost of labor in Korea skyrocketed. Many Korean manufacturers purchased sites in Southeast Asia and offered to service existing customers through these new factories. CWI entered Indonesia in 1989, in the wake of financial deregulation, continuing its relationships with Korean companies such as Samsung. Gradually CWI trained local Indonesian workers in non-Korean companies.

To ensure meeting customers' needs for high quality and fast delivery, CWI transferred casual jackets head Jim Alton and his wife, also a CWI employee, to Jakarta in 1993. Before joining CWI in 1968, Alton had been a technician checking production quality in Korea and Eastern Europe. Alton, like other CWI managers, is a seasoned traveler who can adjust negotiating styles and expectations to local culture and innovate or compromise according to a country's garment quota and capacity for efficiency. He can also manage long distance. While based in Indonesia, Alton still heads his sales division for jackets in Leeds, eight thousand miles away.

In Indonesia as elsewhere, Mitsui helps CWI to analyze potential factories and factory owners to decide whether to invest in a relationship with CWI. "If you just turn up with a suitcase and say I'm Joe Bloggs," Alton observed, "they would probably ignore you. The fact that we're a Mitsui joint venture means that people know the kind of backing we've got." On the CWI end, CWI checks out suppliers by sending people to work in the factory for several weeks and observe supervisors and workers outside of the workplace.

CWI's Indonesian base is the textile desk in the local Mitsui office in a central Jakarta high-rise—literally a set of tables and desks forming a large block in the middle of a large room, a Japanese-style open office. Several Mitsui staff support CWI exclusively, reporting to the Japanese textile manager; a group of technicians work directly for Alton. To support CWI, Mitsui increased its Indonesian quality control staff by three people; this function was less important in Korea's more sophisticated manufacturing environment.

CWI might provide suppliers with equipment such as sewing machines, pressers, or hanging rails for garments. Smaller suppliers get occasional financial help. CWI's biggest investment is time to train local workers to the mind-set for quality clothing for a foreign market. Factory managers are invited to Britain to see their goods in the stores, often videotaping their store visits to show workers. Looking back through the supply chain to ensure quality, CWI requires factories to procure fabrics or accessories from sources CWI and Mitsui have approved.

Indonesian factories are often criticized in the West for low wages, poor working conditions, and environmental pollution. Because CWI brings buyers from its British retail customers to Southeast Asia to tour the places manufacturing the garments they buy, the company seeks the most modern, environmentally correct, highest-wage facilities that fit British and American sensibilities.

THE CUSTOMER CHALLENGE: BHS'S STRATEGIC SOURCING

CWI's five largest customers constitute about 80 percent of sales, of which casual jackets account for 57 percent. Until 1983 CWI had supplied about six hundred small accounts and employed a sales force of ten people. But as industry consolidation brought a smaller number of much larger retailers, CWI focused on private label production of a few items in depth for large customers, becoming its customers' manufacturing arm.

CWI began supplying clothing to BhS, a large apparel retail chain, in 1977. In the mid-1980s Sir Terence Conran directed BhS into high-priced fashion clothing, with disastrous results; Conran's American retail ventures also failed. David Dworkin, American former president of Neiman-Marcus, became CEO of BhS in 1989 to revitalize the company.

Changing the way BhS worked with suppliers meant reducing their numbers. "We cannot have meaningful relationships with over 650 suppliers. Far from being meaningful, that number is almost promiscuous," a buyer explained. Spink and Doyle met Dworkin for the first time in 1991 at a meeting for BhS's largest suppliers. Four hundred suppliers had already been connected to a new electronic data interchange system, getting the equipment at a special price BhS negotiated with IBM. Now Dworkin told the suppliers he wanted BhS to develop a partnership with an even smaller group of suppliers.

Prospects for CWI to be among that group looked good. Dworkin and his new BhS team liked CWI's established record, secure financial backing (through its relationship with Mitsui), and sufficient depth of management to work effectively with a larger company. They also liked CWI's international connections, as BhS wanted to increase its use of imported goods, which accounted for 35 percent of sales but were bought inefficiently in small quantities from over 125 suppliers. In some categories, such as women's separates, almost all BhS merchandise was made locally in Britain. But in leisure menswear, CWI's specialty, 80 percent of the stock was imported from the Far East, especially in the high-volume jeans category. Much lower costs of goods sourced from Asia, around 20–25 percent below British figures, offset longer shipping time.

To expand its business with BhS, CWI had to outperform large, well-connected competitors on the ground in the Far East, such as Swire & McLaine, a buying agent in Hong Kong attached to the powerful Swire Group and a sophisticated regional trade facilitator whose largest customer is Wal-Mart. Swire Group had begun out of British shipping interests in Shanghai in the early nineteenth century, eventually growing to become one of the largest companies in Hong Kong, involved in aviation (Cathay Pacific Airways), industrial and consumer products, insurance, and property. When I visited Swire & McLaine's Hong Kong headquarters in a crowded industrial district in Kowloon during the period in which BhS was defining its global supply strategy, I counted more computers than garment racks, which highlighted the importance of electronic linkages for a Hong Kong company operating throughout Southeast Asia on behalf of American and British customers.

I saw in Swire the kind of sophisticated Asian enterprise (most staff have MBAs) with which American companies would be increasingly competing, and I wondered how small suppliers such as CWI could win the competition. It turned out to be a matter of value. By partnering closely with BhS and performing additional services that saved BhS the costs of internal departments, CWI could beat a larger, well-endowed insider. But, of course, CWI had also invested years in becoming close to an insider in Korea and Indonesia, had Jim Alton in

Jakarta, and was willing to link its operations closely to that of BhS back home.

VALUE-MANAGED RELATIONSHIPS: HOW THE "BEST PARTNER" WINS

By the end of 1992 BhS had decided not to pursue the Swire & McLaine connection. BhS deepened the relationship with CWI, giving more of its business to the little player from Leeds. The win for CWI stemmed from BhS's focus on "value-managed relationships" with selected suppliers. Suppliers offering value-added services that allow BhS to focus on retail marketing win a larger share of BhS business. CWI could be a B-I-W partner to BhS because of its ability to share the three C's.

- *World class concepts:* CWI provides BhS with product innovation. CWI in-house designers visit stores weekly and consult well-known outside designers to be able to help BhS assemble upcoming clothing lines. BhS buyers and CWI designers attend fashion shows together and visit stores in Europe, Asia, and North America in search of the best ideas. CWI develops new technology in support of BhS, such as a software program improving the reorder system.

- *World class competence:* After products are designed, CWI offers not only high-quality production through its close oversight of Asian factories, but also a range of value-added services:

- design and stitching expertise useful at the design stage;
- preproduction prototype creation, offering a wide range of samples and remakes through Korean experts;
- discounts from bulk orders with single factories;
- quality control before garments leave the factory;
- full shipping and importing services, including management of apparel quota under trade agreements;
- warehousing and inventory carrying costs (CWI pays up front, BhS pays when the goods are delivered);
- item processing: pressing, bagging, tagging, and bar coding;
- quality guarantees: for example, CWI takes back faulty garments even after they have been displayed in shops;
- access to international financing and expertise through Mitsui.

The monetary value of such extra services—quantified for BhS by an independent consultant—means that there are no discernible cost advantages on basic garments if BhS were to buy them directly at lower cost, bypassing CWI by going directly to factories or through an agent such as Swire & McLaine. BhS would use up savings from the lower garment cost on the costs of an infrastructure for handling various stages of the supply process. CWI performs such services for BhS with greater quality and reliability.

• *World class connections:* CWI's competitive advantage stems from collaborative advantage—maximizing its ties with Mitsui, contract factories, and BhS. For BhS, CWI has invested in strong and seamless links to every BhS function.

Counterparts meet counterparts throughout each organization. Spink and Doyle discuss strategic issues regularly with top managers at BhS: how to expand BhS's market share, global structuring of buying, or incentive schemes such as a retrospective discount Spink proposed to give BhS if its purchases in a given year exceeded projections. CWI's sales and division directors work with product division controllers at BhS. BhS's distribution arm has daily contact with CWI's sales/stock controller and warehouse manager to coordinate delivery schedules. CWI's quality engineers talk frequently with BhS's quality directors in London. CWI people join other BhS key suppliers on joint improvement teams to make BhS's computer linkup more user-friendly or help BhS outsource trucking.

For CWI, close ties with BhS provides more stability in sales, which encourages CWI to make BhS-specific investments. For example, CWI hired an additional quality manager in 1992 to reassure BhS about its concern for quality. Cooperative relationships among CWI designers and store buyers and merchandisers encourage CWI employees to stay abreast of developments in fashion and in the marketplace, to learn at least as much about BhS consumers as BhS does. CWI staff often make tactical recommendations—how to fill a product gap or the introduction of a new type of fabric, such as a chino cotton for a successful trouser line. "There is more input from us, it is more welcomed, and they are more ready to receive it," Spink said. "We have a genuine trading partnership."

Being enmeshed in a global web of blurred-boundary relationships —whether Powersoft's numerous alliances or CWI's partnerships—

brings business advantages for cosmopolitan companies that know how to nurture and build on every tie to the benefit of customers. But each set of threads in the global web also contains risks and vulnerabilities. Pull one thread, and perhaps the whole web unravels. Powersoft, for example, collaborates with competitors; one shift of technology and its partners could become predators. CWI would be endangered if BhS—or for that matter, Mitsui—shifted strategy and no longer needed the small player from Leeds. Alliances are notoriously fragile.[5] That is why some companies prefer independence. But independence can easily slide into isolation. Contrast the situation of more independent companies with that of CWI.

KGR is one such independent. An apparel manufacturer founded in 1976 in Lawrence, Massachusetts, just north of Boston, where the textile industry started in the nineteenth century, KGR has enjoyed an average annual growth rate of 20 percent for the past ten years, while most of the American garment manufacturing industry declined. The company makes private label apparel for U.S. retailers such as Talbots, Nordstrom, Dillard's, Dayton Hudson, and L. L. Bean. It competes effectively with Southeast Asia because it offers world class competence, fast turnaround time, and value-added services. It delivers fashionable clothing of high quality with a "passion," owner-CEO Chet Sidell said, for restocking its customers' shelves in three weeks.

But new technology in the industry and cheaper labor costs overseas have opened up competition all over the world. KGR often finds itself competing with China and Central America. This has caused the company to begin to source overseas, although the majority of KGR's product is still manufactured in New England in factories employing immigrant labor from Puerto Rico, the Dominican Republic, Turkey, Cambodia, Vietnam, and China. Many of these immigrants come to the United States with apparel skills.

Others in KGR's neighborhood reported that skills have moved out. Two decades ago, all of the sewing contractors for another apparel company were local; now only 15 percent are. Industry expertise resides abroad; the company hired an Italian woman from Milan as its pattern development specialist. Like KGR, this company is adaptable and innovative. But as small independent companies and novices in international trade, will they have the means to respond to more intense competition and more demanding customers?

Look who's coming to America to compete with the independents:

the competitors a company like CWI faces in Asia. In January 1994 the apparel industry in Miami was joined by a newcomer from Taiwan. Febena Fashion Co. Ltd. opened its headquarters for the Americas in south Florida. The Beacon Council, Dade County's economic development organization, announced this proudly with the hope that more companies from Taiwan would follow. So far Febena supplies different segments from KGR's—such as Target, the Gap, Kids "Я" Us. But Asian companies have a history of moving up the scale, and Febena's global network is close to KGR's home.

Family-owned Febena is part of a large network with yarn-spinning and fabric mills in Taiwan, two hundred factories in Korea, and twenty to thirty Taiwanese-owned factories in Central America and the Caribbean, the latter now managed out of the Miami office. Febena moved to Honduras along with other Taiwanese and Korean companies to cut labor costs. The Miami office handles sales, purchasing of goods and services for the Honduras plant, and coordination of production process. Febena might eventually move mills to south Florida; meanwhile it is using an increasing quantity of U.S. fabrics, often from South Florida, which it has cut in Florida and assembled in Honduras. Febena is expanding its label printing operations in Florida and will manufacture boxes there.

Globalism eventually brings the competition home. Isolated companies find it harder to succeed. Networks become a necessity.

THE GROWING NECESSITY OF NETWORKS

Business networks are not new, but their proliferation and visibility have increased their power. Smaller companies recognize the benefits —and necessity—of collaboration in order to be world-ready for their customers. And the corporate giants are dancing with partners.

Strategic alliances are especially prominent at business frontiers where there are new opportunities but also great uncertainties: for example, at the crossroads of computers and communication as well as the crossroads of Southeast Asia, China, and other emerging markets. Alliances are a way to join forces to address the opportunities yet hedge bets to counter the risks and uncertainties. They are a way for global players to gain local know-how through local partners. Networks presage the shape of future competition: not country against country, and not just company against company, but groups of companies joined in a network competing with other multicompany groups.[6]

In telecommunications alone, groups are forming so frequently that it is hard to keep up with the composition of emerging networks. Take the announcements during just one week in September 1994: Bell Atlantic allied with Nynex, U.S. West, and AirTouch for wireless long-distance services, while Bell Atlantic's spurned suitor, the cable company TCI, joined with Sprint, Comcast, Teleport, and Cox Communications for a similar purpose. Both groups formed to compete with the AT&T/McCaw Cellular team. At the same time, Bell Atlantic formed a joint venture to produce video programming with Nynex, Pacific Telesis, and Creative Artists Agency, a talent firm, in order to face off against a group consisting of Ameritech, BellSouth, Southwestern Bell (now SBC Communications), and Walt Disney Company.

The new networks are often loose and fluid. Their membership overlaps with that of other networks, and allies cooperate for only some purposes. When Powersoft's Kertzman called his company part of the "Lotus *keiretsu*" because it shares some facilities, concepts, and people with Lotus, he was referring to a looser kind of network than the formal marriage between Powersoft and Sybase.

Loose or tight, networks are critical for young technology companies and novices in emerging markets. One study shows that collaborators make more money; technology-intensive new ventures engaging in a variety of cooperative arrangements for product development enjoy higher sales growth.[7]

Companies derive considerable benefit within their local markets from industrywide and geographically diverse partnerships. These networks can then help propel smaller companies into global markets or gain collective strength to recapture a portion of the purchasing dollars giant companies now spend outside the region.[8] To gain the advantages of larger companies' reach over many locations, smaller companies have to form cross-company networks, such as the joint marketing groups organized by Latin American airlines in Miami. Indeed, Miami's local landscape is being transformed by networks. Fifteen years ago most hotels in Miami Beach were independent; a large percentage of them are now franchised, which helps them stay in business by augmenting their marketing reach. Since Ramada Resort Deauville became part of a chain in August 1992, convention and tour business has increased dramatically, sales are up by 40 percent, and access to

Ramada's Rocket 2001 reservation system produces daily information about potential customers, giving the Miami unit the chance to make adjustments such as discounting blocks of rooms. The hotel's general manager recalled that Miami Beach hoteliers were among the last in the United States to affiliate with chains; before the turning point in 1978, when the Fontainebleau became a Hilton, the only franchise had been a Sheraton.[9]

Network membership is a core element of the business concept for some small and midsize companies. For example, an employee benefits consulting firm's head office manages a network of independent local service providers wherever its large national clients have facilities. A specialty construction craft shop works through a network of builders and other groups in skilled trades and crafts to bid together on large contracts. For others, alliances and networks expand markets and distribution. Membership in an international law network provides referrals to a Cleveland law firm and a network of experts to service its clients elsewhere. In Seattle, a group of nine small software companies have formed a cooperative; this maintains each company's independence but offers collective clout.

A&A/Carey Limousine, a small car service operating in Greater Boston, is a good example of how network advantages build greater cosmopolitanism for a local service operation. Carey's international network has more locations around the world than any other limousine service, far ahead of the number two company. The cosmopolitan mind-set of Carey's staff comes through its international network ties and also the work itself; Carey gets a high share of rides for foreign visitors to Boston who have booked cars through an international reservations line. Attendance at the network's international meetings encourages A&A/Carey to raise standards: development of its own automated reservations/dispatch system and extensive driver training. No-tech Carey employees echo high-tech Powersoft associates in their international knowledge.

NETWORK LOCALLY, GROW GLOBALLY

Companies on the rise benefit most from local networks. For emerging companies, industry clusters provide opportunities for informal exchange of people and ideas as well as more formal alliances. As companies get larger and extend well beyond a local area, they no longer depend on purely local contacts within their industry, but they may collaborate locally for other purposes. Collaboration provides an opportunity for smaller companies to share scarce resources and derive mutual benefits, but smaller companies in nongrowth industries are less likely to have ways to make relevant connections.

Over half of the 2,655 companies in my five-city survey engage in widespread informal local networking; over a quarter occasionally collaborate locally on marketing or special promotions and management education, over 15 percent on research or worker skills training. Local business collaboration is associated with collaboration elsewhere. Companies engaging in more local collaboration of both kinds are likely to be larger, to be involved in alliances or joint ventures elsewhere in the United States, to be much more oriented toward community service, to be more positive about the business climate, and to be less protectionist. In short, they have a pattern of open boundaries and connectedness. And companies that have not been active report that they plan to seek greater involvement. Local joint activities and local networking are slightly more likely to be found in growth industries in new technology areas with international aspirations and somewhat less likely to be found in older, capital-intensive manufacturing companies serving primarily national markets.

The power of networks is confirmed by studies throughout the world. In Britain, entrepreneurs succeeding at product innovation are involved in more professional organizations and have the highest percentage of strangers in their personal networks. In the successful companies, managers other than the founder also have many contacts, and they travel more.[10] In two Italian industrial districts, network ties among 103 small and midsize firms ensure learning as well as reduced costs through flexible specialization. Competitiveness is network embedded, a matter of connections across companies. For innovation, an entrepreneur must create, manage, and recombine sets of relationships with external suppliers. The ability to glue together external expertise and capabilities in original and unique ways is a key factor for innovation. Entrepreneurs act as "orchestrators of interfirm linkages."[11]

When small, single-location companies meet the criteria for B-I-W partnerships—continual innovation, world-quality standards, value-added services, and the ability to work collaboratively, thereby enhancing their stock of concepts, competence, and connections—they can find new national and international market opportunities through their larger partners.

RIDING COATTAILS TO THE WORLD: TECH RIDGE AND POLAROID

Tech Ridge's success shows how a small supplier flourishes at home by being world-ready and is then invited to join the world class. Tech Ridge's large partner, Polaroid, has helped grow the company's local manufacturing through international contracts.

Started in 1957 as a machine shop in South Chelmsford, on the outskirts of Boston, Tech Ridge specializes in manufacturing identification cameras and components, earning steady profits on sales of close to $10 million a year. In 1962 founder Leonard Comeau designed a camera useful for instant photo ID cards for colleges, hospitals, sports clubs, driver's licenses, and the like. His purchase of Polaroid film and camera backs began an important relationship with Polaroid, headquartered nearby in Cambridge. "They call us Polaroid Chelmsford," said his son and vice president, Stephen Comeau. The partnership with Polaroid has been maintained because Tech Ridge

- creates world class concepts—"At the moment I think we are setting world standards for ID cameras," Stephen Comeau said. Even its competitors buy die cuts from TR;
- meets world standards—quality training with the help of a Polaroid quality expert, ISO 9000 certification;
- provides extra service with flexibility—low overhead, fast decisions, willingness to go into weekend shifts if necessary, good relationships with the customer representatives who are treated "like part of the family";
- is reliable and fast, with turnaround for repairs in twenty-four hours compared to weeks for competitors—"We never once missed a delivery date. Not once";
- collaborates with its own suppliers—Screw Machine House makes handles for Tech Ridge equipment, cheaper, better, faster, allowing TR to focus on its core technology;
- innovates in production technology.

Being physically close to Polaroid is a bonus. At one point a Polaroid executive came to Tech Ridge with a map on which he drew a circle, saying, "I want a company inside this circle I can drive my car to, talk

English to"—a daily relationship, which he contrasted with "eighty-two trips to Germany to get a little plastic piece right."

Tech Ridge's world class concepts and competence are valuable to its much larger partner. In 1987 TR pioneered in designing an electronic camera to replace a mechanical product, a move that landed its biggest distributor. TR's next-generation camera competed effectively with a large competitor's high-priced camera; TR can sell its offering for under half because of its low overhead. Now TR and Polaroid are exploring electronic imaging, which could replace instant film. Because of TR's superior ID camera technology and Polaroid's focus on film, Polaroid is weighing whether to outsource more manufacturing to TR. "Big companies are finding that small companies like us can do things cheaper, better, faster. We don't have the layers of management a decision has to go through," Comeau said.

TR's relationship with Polaroid is complex, like many alliances and partnerships in the global economy. TR is simultaneously a supplier, a customer (for film), and a competitor in the camera business. But because this long relationship has worked well ("Relationships are my most favorite thing; they are what I like to do," the younger Comeau said), Polaroid included TR on a large contract in Mexico to produce ID cameras to make government-issued voter ID cards for Mexico's 1994 voter registration drive. IBM had recommended Polaroid after the Mexican government sought a less expensive alternative to computer imaging; TR supplied cameras while Polaroid supplied film. This venture constituted one of the biggest orders in history for both companies —50 million sheets of film sold by Polaroid and 11,600 cameras by Tech Ridge in nine months (in contrast with TR's usual volume of 3,500 per year).

Because of its success in Mexico, Kodak asked Tech Ridge to join on a similar proposal in the Dominican Republic. Tech Ridge went to Polaroid for clearance. Because Polaroid stood to sell 4 million sheets of film to Kodak under the proposal, Tech Ridge got the go-ahead and went to the Dominican Republic with Kodak.

World class companies are learning oriented as well as entrepreneurial and collaborative. Tech Ridge used its experience in Mexico, under Polaroid's guidance, to learn about international markets and to further innovate, preparing for a shift in technology. TR is now working on a rechargeable battery-powered camera with improved circuits, an innovation for the U.S. market that would also help Tech Ridge compete internationally, especially in developing countries where electricity is unreliable and erratic. The Comeaus saw this firsthand when they spent several weeks watching TR equipment being used in Mexico and the Dominican Republic. "In the Dominican Republic, they would plug in a camera, hear a sizzle, and it would short out. We had to bring in our own power source," Stephen Comeau recalled.

This Third World–friendly innovation will also add value to U.S. products and give Tech Ridge an edge. For example, a large bank wanted a battery-operated ID camera, which TR could not yet supply, so the bank bought an Italian model for which TR supplied some parts. Now the bank is having trouble with the Italian camera because the batteries have to be replaced often and create a disposal problem. They eagerly await TR's new product.

"We would never have been able to access the international market without the steadfast support of Polaroid," Comeau said. "They guided us every step of the way. Someone virtually lived with us." Tech Ridge has another venture now pending in Mexico. Eyeing opportunities in Guatemala, Peru, Puerto Rico, and Argentina, it expects to enter Europe with Polaroid and Kodak.

For world-ready companies, local supply partnerships can open doors to export markets. And when their partners offer them training for world class competence and international connections, their entrepreneurial and learning-oriented skills enable them to take advantage of new opportunities.

OPEN MINDS, OPEN MARKETS, OPEN BOUNDARIES

Cosmopolitan companies operate in ways that transcend the boundaries of particular places, even when their market scope is local or regional. They are desirable partners for their customers, suppliers, and network allies because they

- measure themselves against B-I-W (best-in-world) standards;
- understand the needs of partners and follow them into new places;
- invest in innovation to create new concepts, which means that they continue to have something unique and valuable to offer;
- learn from their experience, absorbing new knowledge quickly;

- develop the competence to perform many services effectively to high process-quality standards;
- operate as a member of their partners' organizations, connecting their capabilities across many functions.

Cosmopolitan companies and their leaders are joiners, in every sense of the word. They are members of networks that form the global web. They also serve as links among organizations and links among places. By being open to the new possibilities that the global economy brings, they help create them.

PART THREE

LOCALS: THE DANGERS OF DISCONNECTION

Although large international businesses can seemingly locate anywhere, most people live and work in particular places, as members of groups to which they feel loyal and attached.

From a local vantage point, globalization brings concerns as well as opportunities. It puts new political, individual, and social issues on the agenda. World products from international companies compete with those made nearby. Foreign investors run U.S. facilities. Workplaces change and then change again, to respond to new competition. Career planning becomes murky. The composition and priorities of a community's business leaders shift in response to new pressures or a new location for their corporate headquarters.

As consumers, citizens, workers, managers, entrepreneurs, or community activists, people operate in a new context. Some see only disadvantages, losses that concern them so deeply that they erupt into nativism and fuel class warfare between locals and cosmopolitans. But other people and organizations are already creating new forms of economic security and new kinds of civic engagement that respond to global realities and build advantages for locals: exemplary workplaces rich in the three C's, for example, or cosmopolitan companies contributing community service.

The real problem for locals is not globalization, it is isolation. The challenge is to forge linkages to each other, to cosmopolitans, and to global networks.

Wallets and Ballot Boxes

"I agree with open markets," a computer company manager said. "But on a gut level, when I hear the issue my stomach turns. I believe we need to be more global. But I still have some parochialism and respond emotionally to having our economic community controlled by foreigners."

The global economy comes home through international products, foreign investment, and trade. Cosmopolitanism is a two-way street. While domestic companies are internationalizing, foreign companies are "domesticating"—that is, enlarging their presence on American soil and in American markets. But nonlocal ownership of assets makes many Americans uneasy. Attitudes tend to be mixed at best. An American CEO described his reactions to his firm's takeover by a British company: "Initially there were apprehensions about being bought by foreigners. Foreigners to us are anyone outside the local community."

Even people who support open markets, whose own jobs are secure in companies benefiting from global ties, and who are generally positive about the growth potential of the global economy ponder local consequences and draw lines in the sand. A production worker at Kohler, world leader in plumbing fixtures, said, "As far as the Japanese buying companies, that doesn't bother me. I just don't approve of the Japanese buying up land."

When American companies fumble in foreign markets, it is sometimes because their products are strange and different—jarring. Perhaps they don't fit local use patterns, like the left-hand-drive American cars exported to right-hand-drive Japan, or the flat dinner plates exported to Southeast Asian countries, where the people eat rice from bowls. But backlash against the global economy in American communities is not because "foreign" is equated with "strange." Just the opposite. The foreign has become familiar, too familiar; foreign companies are seen as too successful at selling Americans what they want. Few remember the days when products from Asia came with garbled English instructions or mysterious extra parts. People don't say that foreign products should be feared because "we want things *our* way," or "those foreigners don't understand us." The fears, instead, are that foreign companies understand Americans all too well. They succeed all too brilliantly at supplying exactly what Americans need. That's why many fear they will win economic wars.

In whatever part of the world they arise, tensions between cosmopolitans and locals tend to center around threats to control and identity. Such concerns surfaced repeatedly when my research team asked about experiences with and attitudes toward foreign products, foreign investment, and foreign trade in 40 two-to-three-hour focus group discussions with almost three hundred people in a range of occupations in over thirty companies in four cities.

• *Loss of control:* As control over major institutions passes out of local hands, politicians try to get it back, using jurisdictional weapons ranging from outright bans on outsiders to hurdles that favor local producers. Separatist movements to increase local sovereignty—whether the Québécois in Canada or the brief attempt of the African-American neighborhood of Roxbury to secede from the city of Boston—seek additional power to set territorial rules. Locals fear invasion—that cosmopolitans can swamp them with superior resources gathered from all the places cosmopolitans operate. But they not only dread the power of cosmopolitans, they fear their mobility; they are often as much concerned about local companies that globalize as about global companies that enter locally. If invasion is one fear, flight is another. Cosmopolitans can easily pull up stakes. What they bring in jobs, resources, or prestige, they can easily remove.

Many worry about losing control over the country's destiny. An American manager reported feeling "sick" that the country is "gradually being sold off to foreigners" and that, in his view, technology is leaking out of the country, eroding the United States' competitive edge. "I get pissed because people are importing software where they [foreigners] have taken our ideas and reprogrammed them in a minor way and ship them back," he said. Some people are suspicious that foreign companies that move capital into a community will all too easily move it out again, and locals will have no power to stop it.

Others see local ownership as essential to preserve local communities. Foreign-owned businesses, they fear, won't understand the local environment or support the community, repatriating corporate profits to the parent company instead of spending them in the United States. Employees in other companies worry that if foreigners take over, they will lose career opportunities that come from being close to headquarters.

Even those in favor of globalization sometimes see it as an inevitable fact of economic life to which they must adjust, not as the best of all possible worlds in which gains from trade will make them prosperous. Those with "no opinion" say that leaders don't know what open markets will bring and are just speculating.

• *Blows to pride:* Cosmopolitans can also threaten locals' identity and self-esteem, by dilution and by comparison. Cosmopolitan people and companies bring not only different standards, which threatens the "purity" of local culture, they also invoke comparisons. And cosmopolitans are hard to write off or ignore because of their proven success elsewhere.

Some Americans are uncomfortable with the reversal of roles implied by foreign company successes. A Kohler employee, who often notices the origins of goods and finds many foreign products better than U.S. ones, lamented: "The foreigners got us beat, I'm sorry to say." A co-worker is offended that some foreigners are better educated than Americans. After midlevel managers at a software company spent a few minutes listing the U.S. products they considered the best in the world, one of them remarked: "It's a sad commentary that we have to struggle to come up with ten things." Another executive searches for evidence that American supremacy in his industry is unassailable, falling back on sweeping stereotypes: "Americans are more creative. Otherwise the Japanese would already have taken over the software industry or the Indians would have the application development industry."

A foreign company's acquisition of an American company is often viewed as a sign of failure. Another Kohler employee remarked: "I'm not concerned if they're starting a new business, but if they're buying a business, I'm concerned, because that makes me think what happened to the business they're buying. Where did we fail?" Reported a manager at a gun maker flourishing in a happy relationship with its British acquirer: "We would rather have been bought by a U.S. company. There is an element of national pride, especially in our industry. We are very patriotic. There is no one in the company who would say we are a British firm. We all wear and buy 'Made in USA' products."

The desire to favor one's own runs high and deep in America among both workers and management. On my five-areas survey, a large percentage of 2,655 business leaders endorse local preference, many agreeing that businesses should put local loyalties above economic self-interest. Some 72 percent want state and local governments to give preference to local companies in their purchases. Roughly 50 percent want banks to be required to give some loan preferences to local businesses even if the deals are riskier. And 36 percent feel that local loyalties should transcend financial interests, agreeing that "to ensure a strong local economy, businesses should purchase local products of comparable quality to support local suppliers even if the price is higher." At one company production workers want to vote for candidates who will promote products made only in their city.

Yet some people who care about their community reject that kind of economic isolationism and are decidedly more positive about globalization. Those whose work identification and company affiliation provide linkages to the global economy—those in world-ready companies—are more likely to hold the internationalistic attitudes associated with cosmopolitans. They see similarities across boundaries. They value choices. They reject isolationism because they see that communities and nations are interdependent.

Whereas internationalists value choices over loyalties, isolationists value loyalties over choices. And they may even become "nativists" who want to preserve their present identity and take back control.

NATIVISTS

"Nativists" are concerned primarily about globalism's downside. They are usually isolated from the global economy, without means to deal with their economic discomforts and distress. Self-styled "economic patriots," they close ranks, mistrust foreigners, and buy domestic. Among this group are

1. *smaller, domestic, service companies.* In a 1991 survey of twelve thousand managers in twenty-four countries, more "economic patriots" are found at the helm of smaller service companies that operate within one country. Those most in favor of free trade and open markets work for larger, older manufacturing companies—the type of company most likely to benefit from trade.[1]
2. *local "protectionists"—smaller, locally dependent companies.* On my five-areas surveys, heads of companies whose markets, competitors, supply sources, employment, and product or process ideas are based almost entirely in their immediate local area are more protectionist. They are more likely to be smaller companies that desire government and business preferences for local suppliers, do not support free trade or government solicitation of foreign investment. Their protectionist views are associated with economic vulnerability and isolation. Their companies are more likely to be struggling financially and caught in price wars because they somewhat more often compete on the basis of low costs rather than superior quality. They are less likely to be involved in local networks and much less likely to be engaged in community service.
3. *dislocated employees in distressed communities.* In my focus groups, those with work experiences in companies that have downsized, been disrupted by international competition, or isolated from the benefits of global networks are more likely to espouse nativist views.

Nativists can be found everywhere: from manufacturing belts most hurt by global industry restructuring to ethnic communities in Miami, where some black workers feel that immigrants—first Cubans, then Nicaraguans—take their jobs. Those with nativist views say they want to "buy American" to a radical extent. They want to curtail foreign ownership of American companies. They want trade policies to protect

American jobs first and do not care about opening foreign markets. Such backlash against globalization cuts across occupations.

"Class warfare" between internationalists and nativists often concerns the politics of purchasing; the theater of war is the shopping mall, and the choice of automobile is a test of the new class solidarity. Not too long ago cars were sold as symbols of "manhood." Now they are sold as tests of patriotism.

FORMS OF "ECONOMIC PATRIOTISM"

The association between economic distress and nativism is an old one in the United States. Historians have noted opposition to other than English immigration as soon as it began: "Zealous Protestants were concerned about the purity of manners and doubted the loyalty of Roman Catholics. There was discrimination against foreign-born Catholics before the Civil War and against Chinese immigrants in northern California in the 1870s."[2] Nativism flared up whenever there was competition for scarce resources; and organized labor was often hostile to immigration. "Labor disputes of [the mid-nineteenth century] redefined national loyalty as commitment to equality—i.e., equal access of all classes of indigenous Americans to American prosperity."[3] In 1930 economic depression and national sentiment against other countries' protectionist policies, especially Great Britain's Buy British movement, generated Buy American momentum in Congress to pass the Smoot-Hawley Tariff Act. One senator declared that the U.S. Treasury was "not the world's community chest."[4]

The 1980s brought a new wave of debates. Foreign direct investment in the United States increased nearly 3,000 percent between 1970 and 1990, according to Commerce Department figures.[5] In 1988, for the first time since World War I, foreign direct investment in the United States, totaling $329 million, exceeded the $327 million that American companies invested abroad.

Economic difficulties—such as an extended recession beginning in 1990, plant closings, and the need for extensive retraining for displaced workers—led to a search for explanations. Some people found it easier to blame other countries' tricks than poor American management, attributing America's ills to an influx of imported products and foreign acquisitions of domestic companies. Imports and foreign takeovers were blamed for causing a negative balance of trade, repatriation of profit, and higher U.S. unemployment. Because the trade deficit was largely a product of trade with Pacific Rim countries (the United States enjoyed a trade surplus with the European Community), most of the concern centered around the success of Japanese companies in America. Headline-grabbing Japanese takeovers of U.S. companies, such as Sony's purchase of CBS Records for $2 billion and Columbia Pictures for $3.4 billion, helped put the spotlight and heat on Japan.[6]

Japanese success in the auto industry was especially controversial. Even as Japanese companies responded to backlash against imports by moving production to the U.S. heartland, as Honda did in Marysville, Ohio, criticism continued. Some decried the large incentive packages offered by states vying for Japanese auto transplants and later for German carmakers like such BMW, which chose Spartanburg, South Carolina. Union supporters argued that Japanese auto factories in the United States cost more jobs by displacing small American suppliers than they saved by employing American workers in assembly plants.[7]

One response was legislative protection. The Exon-Florio Amendment to the Omnibus Trade and Competitiveness Act of 1988 gave the president power to block foreign investment on the basis of national security; one title, the Buy American Act, put domestic content rules into government procurement. The United States is not the only country to respond to global change with Buy Domestic programs. Virtually every government in the world today has official policies encouraging or mandating government purchases from domestic companies and allowing discrimination against foreign suppliers.[8]

Domestic content laws extend to consumer products. The American Automobile Labeling Act of 1992 requires domestic content labels on car windows in showrooms as of October 1994. Although over half of the Japanese cars sold in America are U.S. assembled, labor unions and the Big Three automakers claim Japanese carmakers get their parts mostly from Japan. The act does not include assembly plant labor in domestic content, such as Honda's large numbers of American workers in American factories; nor does it distinguish between U.S. and Canadian parts.[9]

LANGUAGE POLITICS

A second weapon is to seek cultural and linguistic purity. The Québecois separatists in Canada have made language rights the centerpiece of a secession movement; in the United States, language politics have centered around immigrants. In 1983, a Michigan ophthalmologist, John Tanton, formed US English, an antibilingualism group with former California senator S. I. Hayakawa as honorary chair and former Reagan aide Linda Chavez as executive director. The group argued that despite cultural diversity, Americans must share a language as well as civic virtues. In 1986 an official English referendum passed in California; by 1988 thirteen states had enacted laws declaring English to be the state's official language.[10]

Florida English, US English's state affiliate, had tried unsuccessfully since 1983 to get the legislature to pass a law declaring English the state's official language. It worked loosely with Citizens of Dade County United to Protect English, which in 1980 had mobilized the voters to pass a county ordinance that prohibited "the expenditure of any county funds for the purpose of utilizing any language other than English or any culture other than that of the United States." In a poll taken just a few months before the 1988 election, with an English-only amendment on the ballot, half the likely voters agreed, "We are losing control of our state to foreigners." The amendment was approved by 84 percent of the voters in 1988.

While American states were trying to protect English, movements in other countries were attempting to ban it. English might be the universal language of air traffic controllers, but it is far from locally accepted. In 1993 the city of Jakarta, Indonesia, issued a decree that all English-language billboards must switch to the local language, Bahasa Indonesia. In the spring of 1994 the French parliament prepared to pass a bill with huge popular support banning foreign words from television, billboards, public signs and announcements, work contracts, and advertising and requiring simultaneous translation into French for all scientific conferences held in France. To guard against the use of English terms ("Franglais"), the "High Committee for the Defense and Expansion of the French Language," formed by Premier Pompidou in 1966, creates a yearly list of French equivalents to replace Anglicisms —changing "data processing" to "informatique" or "le blackout" to "occultation."[11]

BUY DOMESTIC CAMPAIGNS

Some groups emerged to protest and protect not by keeping foreign products out, but by encouraging consumers to buy American products, sometimes taking positive steps to raise their quality. In the spring of 1984, for example, the Crafted with Pride in USA Council was organized to strengthen the competitive positions of the American textile, apparel, and home furnishings industries. With Roger Milliken, chairman of Milliken & Co., headquartered in Spartanburg, as its first chair, it attracted over three hundred members by mid-1986. Convinced by poll data that it had a solid basis for a national campaign, the CWP Council mounted a three-year, $40 million ad blitz in 1985. The number of consumers reporting they had refused to buy a product because it was foreign made rose from 21 percent in 1985 to 39 percent in 1989.[12]

Wal-Mart began a "Bring It Home to the USA" program for suppliers in 1985, when imports were over a third of its sales. To encourage manufacturers to produce goods in the United States, founder Sam Walton issued a mandate: "Find products that American manufacturers have stopped producing because they couldn't compete with foreign imports." Buyers targeted import items and gave lists to state industrial development agencies to find manufacturers for conversion to Wal-Mart's program.[13] Walton wrote three thousand domestic suppliers, asking them to commit to improving facilities, machinery, and employee productivity; some 1,800 suppliers agreed. Southwest Missouri University conducted evaluations to help suppliers qualify for Wal-Mart business.

Between 1991 and 1992, Buy American promotions mushroomed. In 1992 Monsanto offered employees $1,000 toward the purchase of a new car assembled in North America. Ads linked car buying with patriotism; an Anchorage dealer showed scenes of the Japanese attack on Pearl Harbor.[14]

Buy American campaigns appeal emotionally to the desire to help American workers.[15] A sign reading "This lot reserved for American vehicles only" adorns a parking lot of the International Brotherhood of Electrical Workers Local 1505 on the corner of Main and Liberty Streets in Waltham, Massachusetts, a Boston suburb with many high-tech companies where Local 1505 members work. Arthur Osborn, local president, said the sign symbolizes members' support for the American system and solidarity with American workers displaced by foreign products and expansion. When a neighboring church asked to use the lot, the local gave permission with the proviso that church members driving foreign cars park elsewhere.

Buy American campaigns also arouse skepticism. Experts say too many groups are competing, doubt these groups can raise money, and believe consumers want the best products regardless of origin. Although polls show that people would buy domestic goods if the origin issue is brought to their attention, patriotism alone has limited appeal.[16] And considerable controversy surrounds Made in the USA labels, especially ambiguous domestic content requirements. Wal-Mart grants apparel suppliers an "American made" label even though they might cut goods in the United States but sew or assemble them in Mexico or the Caribbean.

But for the people rattled by the global economy in my focus groups, "buying American" is seen as the only direct action they can take. "Jobs are disappearing. Other than buy American, I'm not sure what I can do about it," a high-tech manager said. Thus they use their wallets to protest and protect.

MILITANT NATIVISTS: DISTRESS IN "MILLVILLE"

On a bleak wintry night, I sat around a kitchen table in "Millville," pseudonym for a small city near Boston, with seven people who felt they were victims of the global economy. Their names and circumstances are disguised, but all of them wanted their views in my book in the hope, they said, that others will listen.

These hardworking people, most of them college educated, held a range of white-collar and blue-collar jobs, from engineering managers to union activists. Two lost jobs in downsizings; one now held two part-time jobs, the other scraped by on freelance assignments. They were also locally focused. The boundaries of their community were Millville and its environs. They did not read Boston newspapers and thought of it as just another big city, even though Millville is technically a part of the Boston statistical area. They couldn't imagine leaving Millville; family was nearby. Touched personally by displacement in an area that has lost tens of thousands of manufacturing jobs, they wanted to fight back with nativist weapons: protectionism, favoritism toward their own, and closing the doors to foreigners.

They did not agree on every issue, and the value of free trade was occasionally invoked. But as that night wore on and the cake and doughnuts disappeared, their comments fed on one another's, raising the rancor against foreigners and showing how easily vague discontent might become a political force.

These Millville residents felt they had lots to be angry about and thought they knew whom to blame. They were anti-Japanese because the Japanese "buy up America," "displace American management," "don't integrate with our culture," "believe in the supremacy of their way of life." They were anti-Hispanic because they "live together in clumps," "insist on bilingual everything," and "pay cash"—which arouses suspicions of drug money. They were anti-immigrant out of anger over welfare payments to minority groups who, they said, had made the city unsafe.

Moreover, they were concerned that they didn't know about the hidden foreign presence in their community—for example, that a Japanese company owned a favorite retail chain, Talbots. Several called Wang Laboratories "disguised foreign ownership" because the founder (now deceased) was born in China, even though he was an American citizen ("But for how long?" one person asked suspiciously). The group opposed NAFTA despite arguments from their congressman about benefits to companies, and thus jobs, in their area; for instance, the nearby Hewlett-Packard division exported $225 million of goods to Mexico and expected a post-NAFTA 15–20 percent increase.

Charlotte—a pseudonym, like the other names—was the ringleader of movements against globalism. In her mid-fifties, she worked for a large manufacturing company, where she had held both management and nonmanagement jobs; she was now an active union leader. She and her husband worked split shifts, his the early shift beginning at 6:00 A.M., hers from 3:30 P.M. through the evening after working mornings at the beauty parlor she owned. Her children were grown, but she still had a thirteen-year-old niece living with her whom she had raised since infancy, and she took care of grandchildren to save her daughter child care fees. Charlotte's work ethic was amazing; she juggled her job, the union, her business, and child care. But she was very angry that hard work, even award-winning excellent work, didn't protect workers. "Everybody's killing themselves," she said of her company, "and for what? They bring us out for dinner, we get an award, and a week later, a thousand people are out the door."

Charlotte mistrusted workplace changes. "Management puts out all this holy bullshit about teams and such," she said. "The reality is that I have about this much [pinches her thumb against her first finger] in common with the CEO. We don't exist on the same planet. We're in an adversarial labor-management situation." But she lamented the fact that worker solidarity had eroded. "You would think that people would turn to their peer group, but what has happened is they blame their peer group for their problem. We hear it constantly. 'The problem with work is the damn union.' "

Charlotte fought against NAFTA and now talked easily of revolution, tossing off images of violence: "Picture the Mexicans coming across the border, transporting materials into the United States. You can bet the Teamsters are going after them big time. I'll be out there in front with my gun. All your big unions are going to join together to make some big changes in this country."

Militantly protectionist and xenophobic, Charlotte wanted foreign investment limited and American companies to be forced to keep their jobs in America. If a product was made in the United States by a foreign company, she considered it a foreign product. And she reflected her politics in her purchases. Charlotte was a Buy American purist, a consumer vigilante who said she "razzes the heck" out of anyone with a foreign car, "tortures salespeople" until she finds American products, and "creates a revolution" in suburban stores, recruiting others to her cause.

She cited an example: "I needed a coat and a jacket. I'm in the store looking at all the leather coats, every color in the book. All made in Korea. I said to my husband, 'What the hell is this?' I asked the girl at the register for the name of the buyer in this store. She said, 'What's the matter?' I said, 'Ninety percent of your coats hanging on these hangers,' I said, 'are manufactured somewhere else, they are not made in the U.S.A.' I said, 'I'm not buying it if it's not made in the U.S.A.' If we start buying only coats manufactured in the U.S.A., coat companies are going to hire more people, and manufacturing is going to stay right here."

For coats, generically American would do. For shoes, Charlotte pushed a brand made in a nearby town: "When I go in a shoe store, I tell the parents, 'Don't buy them sneakers, they are being made in Indonesia for a dollar a day. They are shipping them to the States and selling them for $125. If you want to buy yourself a good pair of sneakers, go down to Canal Street, to New Balance. He will not move the factory out of Massachusetts.' "

Lou was an electronic technician active in Charlotte's union. He framed his opposition to the global economy in terms of conspiracy theories involving oil interests, "gross internationalists" such as Armand Hammer, Cyrus Eaton, and the Rockefellers, and secret deals he imagined between the shah of Iran and Israel in the 1970s. Anyone who wonders why the Gulf War did not boost George Bush in the 1992 presidential elections need only listen to Lou. "I don't know who runs this country," he said. "It's not our president, Congress, or senators. They are given some Play-Doh to play with, but somebody else controls the destiny of the world, somebody with a lot of money, maybe Arabs with millions of dollars. That's why we got involved in Kuwait. After we left, Kuwaitees defecated on their golden toilet bowls."

Charlotte, Lou, and their Millville companions felt invaded and exploited. "We are selling the country star by star, stripe by stripe," one said. Another believed that when Americans buy imported goods, the revenues go directly into the foreigner's bank account, "and they are making money over there." Several regularly called mail-order catalog outfits before ordering from them to see where their shirts were made. Linda, a professional laid off from a computer company, a single parent working two part-time salesclerk jobs while finishing college, wanted to close borders. She would work for a foreign-owned company only if it was her only choice to stay working, but she would hate it, she said.

Would relief come? They doubted it, having lost faith in their community and leaders. They said they trust only family and a small circle of friends—not their neighbors, not the church. They mistrusted politicians. "You start out with such enthusiasm, then they get there and are blocked," one said. And they felt surrounded by apathy, complaining about the inability to get a quorum for union meetings. On the biggest issues in the region, a local politician heard from one person out of every ten thousand.

The Millville group couldn't stop globalization; they knew too many economic interdependencies exist. Sam, an engineering manager, still bought from Japanese suppliers even though he considered Japan "the most racist nation on earth." Linda, the unequivocal "buy American" advocate, still looked for the best deal to stretch her budget as a single parent. Fred would grab a job with a foreign company in "Millville," just to have a job. But their attempts to fight globalization created a cycle of disadvantage for themselves and their community. Concentrating on the barricades meant walling themselves off from opportunity.

Joining the Millville residents in their protectionist, xenophobic, and domestic-preference sentiments were other local workers who have seen their prospects deteriorate and their company go downhill. At "Southway," pseudonym for a stagnating large defense contractor, some employees confessed to missing the cold war. During the cold war, enemies were clear. Tests of a country's strength were military, not economic. And Southway's cozy relationship with the government made jobs secure. Domestic preference was so important to some of them that they claimed to pay more and even sacrifice quality to buy American. They directed some anger to U.S. companies trying to manipulate their xenophobia. They talked about "frauds": American companies that send materials to Asia to be made into clothes, then do a minor procedure in the United States in order to slap on a "Made in America" tag. Unanimous that it is time to close U.S. borders, they focused on protecting jobs. They thought free trade was a myth and foreign aid should stop.

SEARCHING FOR SCAPEGOATS: THE PSYCHOLOGY OF "BLAME THE FOREIGNERS"

It is sometimes easier to blame troubles on outsiders than to see how one's own group might need to change. And when problems are complex and solutions difficult, protecting one's own through purchases or protests seems a simple daily act anyone can perform. Four social psychological processes are at work, causing such reactions.

The first is envy—the threat to self-esteem when outsiders, or foreigners, are seen to be doing better than insiders. Nationalism, theorists propose, with its promise of belonging, is a source of pride or self-esteem, and the pride people take in being American comes in part, some argue, from a feeling of superiority that accompanies that identity.[17] When members of any "in-group" encounter outsiders who are somehow different, their self-consciousness increases, and a heightened awareness of characteristics that distinguish in-group from out-group provokes comparisons.[18] If the others are seen to be doing better than one's own group, and the outsiders are people to whom the in-group can be reasonably compared, then the in-group's self-esteem is threatened. Members of the in-group may suppress their envy, but to enhance their self-esteem, they may overvalue the characteristics of their own group and devalue or denigrate the characteristics of outsiders.

A second phenomenon is scapegoating: displacing blame on others. People want to favor in-groups over out-groups, especially when they identify strongly with their group and see other groups as a threat. They expect in-group members to display more desirable and fewer undesirable behaviors than out-group members, remembering behavior that is consistent with their expectations and ignoring behavior that is not. To blame foreigners for economic distress is therefore easier and less threatening to self-esteem.[19]

A third phenomenon occurs when people explain their own behavior by the situation but others' behavior by their "character"—unvarying attributes.[20] People see themselves as individuals responding to particular circumstances, certainly not acting out a set of fixed group traits. But they see individual foreigners or foreign companies as representative of that entire category. They blame actions of individual foreigners on the entire group.

Consider two American facilities acquired by foreign companies. At both, American workers tended to attribute bad news inaccurately to their foreign parent (in other words, out-group members) rather than blame American managers. In one case, local American managers had frozen salaries and added four hours to the work week in an effort to impress their German parent with their tough financial decisions. Many employees assumed this unpopular policy came from bosses in Germany. But according to a manager, when the German leaders learned of it, they gave the American unit's president one month to reverse the policy. Similarly, soon after the American subsidiary of a Swedish company announced plans to transfer some of its manufacturing operations to Mexico, rumors began circulating on the factory floor that the Swedes were behind the decision. When the American president heard the rumors, he called an all-employee meeting and took full responsibility for the decision. But many blue-collar workers continued to blame the Swedes for unpopular moves.[21]

Anger at particular individuals or events can easily escalate into full-fledged country bashing when specific events are generalized as fundamental characteristics of whole countries. In the "Millville" group, Sam's discomfort with an uncommunicative Japanese supplier was attributed to a national characteristic—"Japanese arrogance"—rather than to a situational factor—the probability that the supplier did not understand English very well. The leap from single experience to national character encourages the next leap to xenophobia.

The fourth phenomenon is pressure to support one's own group. Once people's identities are defined in terms of in-groups and out-groups, they feel pressure to prove they belong to the in-group, including favoring fellow members of the group. Both "Millville" and "Southway" workers repeatedly voiced the need to take care of their own. This kind of solidarity can be a valuable form of communal responsibility. It can also pressure people to make decisions based solely on group membership.

Buy American campaigns have been associated with emotional pressure on people to show their membership through their purchases. By implication, such campaigns hint, those who do not buy American are less patriotic, less worthy of belonging, less concerned about their fellow Americans. Some of my focus group participants were tormented about their economic choices. A large company professional confessed, "When I first bought my Toyota, I was kind of ashamed to drive to work. I loved the car, but I was like, Oh, my God, I'm putting my fellow workers out of business." Pressures vary among cities, as a Hewlett-Packard manager reported: "People in the Boston area find it a little more embarrassing to drive a foreign car than, say, California, where half or more of the cars are not even U.S."

A fifth phenomenon involves trust and mistrust. Questions of trust are behind every battle between cosmopolitans and locals, as well as between in-group members and foreigners. Think about this chain of logic: If people are psychologically inclined and socially encouraged to form their identity on a national basis and show favoritism toward members of their own in-group, don't foreigners do the same thing? Therefore, can foreigners be trusted? Are their community contributions just an attempt to buy off the locals? Can their promises be believed? Will their commitments be honored? Will they pull out as soon as they have extracted all value from the locality?

It is not only foreigners who are mistrusted. Cosmopolitans, with their breadth of activity, multiple identities, and even multiple citizenship, cannot be trusted, some think, to act in locals' best interests. Therefore, nativists also mistrust domestically owned companies with international operations.

GLOBAL BUSINESS LINKAGES AND POLITICAL VIEWS

The economic health of a community moderates nativism, even in insecure situations. For example, in Spartanburg and Greenville, South Carolina, where substantial foreign investment has caused the economy to boom and unemployment to remain significantly behind the national average, people are highly positive about the global economy. They express less nativist backlash than in Boston, which was just coming out of a severe recession when our focus groups were conducted. Spartanburg managers and workers generally favor free trade and reject domestic preferences, despite the fact that Spartanburg's most influential and revered civic leader, Roger Milliken, chairman of Milliken & Co., opposed NAFTA and GATT and spearheaded Buy American movements.

But company differences are stronger than community differences. Even in Spartanburg, employees in aging American companies left behind by global competition echo the nativism expressed by the "Millville" and "Southway" workers. "Carolina Metals" is a pseudonym for a manufacturing facility owned by an investment company in the Midwest. Rocked by ownership changes and foreign competition, its workers are more nativist than others in Spartanburg or Greenville. They resent special incentives to foreign companies, fret that foreign firms bring their own people to fill the best jobs, and worry about foreign investors repatriating earnings. But mostly they want the workplace to be a homogeneous community where they can be among their own kind. One worker turned down a job with a Japanese company that would have doubled his pay because he couldn't see himself "bowing every day." Objective concerns are used to justify their choice of lower pay at a struggling American company over offers at foreign-owned firms; one worker declared, "I would rather work for America."

Attitudes are related to company cosmopolitanism: how much a company is linked to global networks and can offer benefits from globalization to people associated with it. Company differences were strong enough in my focus groups to transcend differences of position within companies. Although production workers in some companies tended to be more negative than managers about globalization, in others this was reversed. More interesting was the similarity of attitudes within companies. The most cosmopolitan companies tend to have the least nativist local work force. At firms possessing the three C's of world class concepts, competence, and connections, I found the greatest international awareness and the least backlash against globalism.

Internationalist or nativist attitudes are reflected in behavior. I compared the origins of cars in the parking lots of two facilities of similar size but differing most strongly in attitudes: "Southway," where nativism is strong, and Powersoft, a cosmopolitan software leader, where internationalist views prevail. On a typical midweek workday, nearly 70 percent of employee cars at "Southway" were from U.S.-owned companies (159 of 228); at Powersoft the pattern was reversed, with almost 65 percent of employee cars from non-U.S.-owned companies (194 out of 302).

Work experience has a powerful effect on politics, directly and indirectly. Active discussions in the workplace create a common perspective, as people debate current events. Managers communicate corporate values. People assess company interests, embracing them when that appears to bring benefits employees will share. And business situations provide opportunities for direct international contact, which also shapes perceptions.

The strongest support for internationalism and rejection of nativism comes from employees at large global companies. At Gillette, for example, which derives 70 percent of its sales from outside the United States, posts managers around the world, and is a world leader in its products, middle managers and professionals with deep Boston roots felt torn about economic problems in New England and described protectionism as a temptation but ultimately rejected isolationism and said they seek foreign assignments.

Hewlett-Packard is also noteworthy for the extent to which its people at all levels speak easily about "one world" across the globe. A production worker declared, "If headquarters were in Singapore, our worldwide divisions would still do things basically the same way." Some H-P managers can see circumstances under which foreign ownership of an American unit might even be preferable to American ownership, such as worldwide contacts and funding. They are less ready to jump on an American superiority bandwagon; when asked to name ten best products made in the United States, one demurred, saying, "I find equally good things made in Europe."

Hewlett-Packard production workers are well educated and sophisticated about the company's business. They praise the firm's training programs for keeping their skills up-to-date and its corporate communication efforts for keeping them informed. They feel reassured by the company's policy of flying employees with their families to other sites to consider relocation if work wanes in their area. They report that their fears regarding NAFTA were alleviated after listening to a manufacturing manager at an employee coffee talk predict net job gains in the long run.

H-P spreads a strong value system that transcends local identities. An associate explained why he could not subordinate quality to support Buy American campaigns: "Hewlett-Packard preaches that everybody out there is a customer and you're supposed to treat them with courtesy and be quick to solve problems. Yet car dealers don't care about you; they're just out to get your money. That's something that Hewlett-Packard doesn't breed, so for a lot of us it's hard to stomach."

Workers at Kohler in South Carolina are also internationalists because of their company's global linkages. They believe their company is the world standard setter in plumbing fixtures. Production workers enjoy a high degree of international awareness derived from observations of export products in the factory or trips abroad to look at manufacturing technology. Noting the extras Kohler puts into tank valves shipped to Japan, they recognize Japanese quality consciousness. Kohler workers credit foreign investors with bringing jobs, technology, and "culture"—a library and arts center—to their home community of Spartanburg. They are not protectionist and do not express Buy American sentiments. They want open markets abroad to help local companies sell and produce more. Although they miss public prayers at football games, their Southern morality does not include rabid in-group favoritism.

Large international companies are not the only cosmopolitans. Merlin Metalworks, whose objective is to make the best bicycles in the world, is a small company born global. Its thirty people make titanium bicycles, exporting some 35 percent of sales. Its work force believes strongly in the company's product—"We ride, we race," they proclaim. They are experienced outside the United States, dealing regularly with distributors in Taiwan, Hong Kong, Indonesia, Australia, and Japan. The open-minded learning orientation Merlin fosters enlarges people's horizons; a high school graduate aspires to move into design engineering because of his experience there. Workers often discuss issues among themselves, reinforcing internationalist views. A welder reported that watching the NAFTA debate on CNN with co-workers and discussing it at work swung him toward free trade.

As the locally owned affiliate of an international network, small A&A/Carey Limousine is also cosmopolitan. Encouraged by the benefits of its large referral network, horizon-expanding national conferences, and daily experiences with international visitors to its home city, its drivers, dispatchers, and managers expressed internationalist views. And at companies that anticipate increasing global activity, like Powersoft, associates talked animatedly about living abroad in the past and future: "I lived three years in Germany and loved every second of it." "Someday I'll transfer to Japan or Australia." "As long as there's a sink and running water, I'll go anywhere."

A company's market situation and economic interests also affect employee attitudes. The people most in favor of open markets and free trade agreements tend to work for companies that sell products into international markets. When employees identify with company interests, they understand that restrictions on foreign activities in the United States might be countered with retaliation in other markets, hurting their own company.

Company interests explain contradictory attitudes: pro-globalism in some respects and against it in others. At a large regional bank with international affiliates, employees support open markets because the bank finances trade through foreign offices, but they dislike foreign ownership because the bank is a possible takeover target itself.

Companies also create internationalists by providing direct international experience. Relatively few people get moved to other countries, but many more have contact with foreign companies on the job. For example, although high-tech EG&G sells primarily to the American market, it has ties with twenty-five countries. Its managers are well traveled and knowledgeable about the best products made elsewhere. Cosmopolitan in outlook, they feel the location of a company's headquarters makes no difference to their futures. They make no attempt to buy American. Similarly, Kohler factory workers who have been sent on work-related tours of Europe expressed more internationalist views than workers who have never left the country. And those who serve demanding international customers, such as the Kohler workers who produce in Spartanburg to Japanese specifications, also become more cosmopolitan.

The more international experience people have, the more likely they are to favor open markets. As direct contact with foreigners increases, people are less likely to invoke stereotypes. Ethnocentrism declines when people have more information about other countries.[22]

Not surprisingly, attitudes toward foreign owners and, by extension, foreign products and trade vary with the foreign parents' treatment of American employees. Production workers at Bull in Boston, for example, worried when the former Honeywell facility was bought by venture partner Bull in France, saying they felt invaded. They fretted they would be replaced by Bull's own people or that the new management would make everybody reapply for their jobs. None of these things happened, and people relaxed. When Hoechst bought American Celanese and a Spartanburg plant shifted from American to German ownership, associates saw their German owners bringing new investment and building a strong future, in contrast with previous American bosses who, they said, had let the company decline. In focus groups, these employees praised foreign investment and rejected Buy American movements.

The degree to which a foreign company preserves its own strong national culture influences some Americans' comfort level with foreign ownership. Complaints in focus groups were directed toward French and Japanese companies for difficult-to-penetrate hierarchies (such as a "rice-paper ceiling" for Americans in Japanese companies) or separatist cultural ways (special schools in the United States for Japanese and French expatriates' children). Generally, however, most people said favorable things about the country from which their own bosses came, reserving negative stereotypes for other places. An American executive at a Venezuelan-owned sporting goods manufacturer had highly positive views of Venezuelans, calling them "lovable, amiable, showing a high degree of concern for people." In contrast, he said, "The companies you don't want to have take you over are the Germans and the Japanese. They feel they know how to do it better and just come in and take over." Yet people at companies acquired by Japanese and German firms reported just the opposite—that Japanese and Germans are eager to learn from their American subsidiaries.

WHEN INTERNATIONALISM PREVAILS OVER NATIVISM

The United States has sometimes been called the first universal nation, building national identity around a set of diverse individuals who happened to occupy the same geographic territory rather than around particular cultural groups. Despite outbreaks of nativism throughout American history, an embracing of diversity has characterized much of American politics, especially after the Civil War. Many historians would argue that the United States was strongly isolationist until World War II (with Theodore Roosevelt and Woodrow Wilson among the exceptions). True enough, but within American borders, as Liah Greenfield proposed in an important study of nationalism, the primacy of the individual in the United States guaranteed that national identity would include a multiplicity of tastes, views, aspirations, and allegiances. Nativist sentiments were never widespread; ethnic pluralism was tolerated.[23] Individualism also biased U.S. policies toward consumers rather than producers, to give choices to individuals.

Internationalists do not think they help local and national economies by protectionism or favoritism. Although many in my focus groups said that "all other things being equal," they would like to "keep our own economy going" by "spending money here," internationalists believe four other considerations are even more important.

First is what might be called "qualitocracy," the desire to put quality first, to choose freely from among the world's best. Internationalists are more interested in the product itself than in its flag. If they consider country of origin at all in purchases, it is a proxy for quality, based on often stereotypical notions: choosing Canadian beer; French wine and cheese; Japanese electronics; or avoiding Third World products. Internationalists are happy if their high-quality choice nets them an American product, as long as they did not let national origin sway their choice. "It's okay to look at the label later. Just to check," one said.

Sustaining a qualitocracy is so important to some internationalists that they are upset by Buy American appeals to patriotism. They feel an obligation to spur change by deliberately avoiding inferior domestic products. They want the workplace, not the shopping mall, to be the determinant of economic strength; they say they will keep America strong by maintaining high quality in their own company's products, not by how they spend their paycheck.

Some people's internationalism stems from a second factor: blurred boundaries and the difficulty of determining which products are American made. Some laugh off Buy American campaigns as naive. In a focus group, a Gillette employee asked, "Honda is being put together in the U.S., Ford gets parts from all over the world. So what's an American car?" Lists solicited in focus groups of "best American products" included Wilson tennis balls and Michelin tires (made in South Carolina by companies owned in Finland and France, respectively) along with hamburgers and higher education. Internationalists said this proved national distinctions don't matter.

A third internationalist consideration is the desire to make judgments based on the particular actions of particular companies, rather than generalizing about a country. In forming opinions about products, internationalists look at the value they receive from that product, not even generalizing about the company, let alone the country of origin. In forming opinions of foreign investors, internationalists say that leadership at particular sites is more important than their ownership. They do not think it matters much where capital comes from, as long as there is strong leadership at the local site. "If a foreign company or individual buys a company and ruins it, obviously it wasn't a good thing," a Merlin worker observed. "But if they make it better than it is then, sure, I think the global community is the thing to do." What matters to internationalists is behavior and values, not passports.

The most sophisticated internationalist consideration is the desire to do not only what's good for the individual (the basis for free-choice qualitocracy arguments), but also what's good for others. Internationalists are able to put themselves in the shoes of foreign companies and consumers, seeing how U.S. products or direct investment overseas have looked to the rest of the world. They seek a level playing field, one with fair rules by which everyone plays. They feel that letting others into American territory is not altruism but self-interest, because American companies want the freedom to operate on others' territory.

This last consideration also helps cosmopolitans reconcile deep local loyalties with their global activities, as this dialogue among Gillette headquarters staff in Boston revealed. "As a company selling all over the world, we think that people should buy our products. But as consumers we think people should buy American," a manager said, pointing to an apparent contradiction. "It's the American way!" a colleague joked in response. Another continued more seriously, "When we buy a company like Waterman in France, we don't want people going nuts because Gillette is not a French company." The group concluded that Boston benefits from Gillette's acquisitions of companies elsewhere, so Boston, in turn, needs to welcome foreign companies to its territory.

Internationalists acknowledge that displacement occurs in the wake of globalization. But unlike nativists who want to stop the clock and close the doors, they prefer to help with the transition through worker retraining and industry reinvestment.

THE ELUSIVE BOUNDARIES OF IDENTITY

As companies globalize but cities and regions become more self-conscious about their own economic strategies, how does one define the boundaries of "local" loyalty, anyway? Who should be included in the "native" group? Some American companies are interested in moving production offshore, while some foreign investors want to create jobs for American workers. Who is "us" and who is "them" under those circumstances? asked U.S. Labor Secretary Robert Reich.[24]

Is community national, regional, or urban? Seattle is the home of many overlapping economic development efforts: on behalf of the city of Seattle, the Puget Sound area, the state of Washington, and a proposed region called "Cascadia," which encompasses Washington, Oregon, Idaho, and Alberta and British Columbia in Canada. Seattle is also active in APEC (Asia Pacific Economic Cooperation). When a European Gillette manager working in Boston said he supports a Buy Domestic policy, he meant either American or Western European cars; for him, "domestic" includes four countries. To many workers in our focus groups, "American" also includes Canada.

The boundaries of identity may also fall short of including the whole nation, centering around region, company, or even neighborhood—South Boston or East Boston, for example. Northerners tell me they are considered foreigners in the American South. In Seattle and Boston, anyone from outside of the area can be a "foreigner." A Hewlett-Packard worker feels a foreigner is anyone who would dilute the company's "California style"—a California flavor, by the way, that she feels Hewlett-Packard brings to every worldwide operation.

"It's more important for me to think about local production rather than what's produced in the United States," a limousine dispatcher said. "If I know a craftsman who makes something I need right here, why not buy one of those instead of a store-bought product?" When asked about America's best products, people in some Boston companies think about the Boston area's best products: aircraft engines made in Lynn, higher education and medical centers in Boston.

When the boundaries of identity are so elastic, it is harder to justify forming communities that exclude. Local loyalties can be positive, a source of community feeling that helps people take responsibility for one another. But excessive inward-focus slides into xenophobia, protectionism, and local favoritism at the expense of quality. Nativism eventually puts those espousing it at a disadvantage. It reinforces a spiral of decline, because it closes doors instead of opening new opportunities. It encourages people to erect boundaries rather than seek excellence.

Nativism limits choices. It closes people's mind to new ideas that come from outside their own group. It encourages people to limit their choices on emotional grounds rather than using their purchasing power to demand quality. And politicians arise to exploit nativism, feeding people's fears of foreigners as Ross Perot did in his opposition to NAFTA, offering to reassert local control, setting tougher rules for entry and exit, and thus maintaining narrow jurisdictional boundaries that prohibit collaboration across territories for mutual gain.

Ambivalence about the global economy, let alone outright resistance to it, keeps many Americans from being better prepared for it. Ever since victory in World War II gave the United States unprecedented economic dominance for subsequent decades, many Americans feel that others should adapt to America and not vice versa. In foreign markets, some American companies falter when they assume American products are admired everywhere, thereby losing market opportunities by failing to greet cultural differences as stimuli to innovation. Inside U.S. borders, inhospitality to the foreign at home—whether companies or people—locks isolates out of new opportunities. Those isolated from wider, more global networks—workers, professionals, or managers—are more likely to turn nativist.

Community solidarity can either divide people from the rest of the world or help them connect with it. The sense of one's own group and identification with one's own community can be a negative or a positive force in the global economy. Either it can be oppositional: mobilizing the people already here to keep others out, expending energy to build tidal barriers that will inevitably leak anyway. Or it can be collaborative: defining community by a mutual quest for quality and welcoming those who extend the boundaries of community to encompass ties with the world.

Locals can flourish when they expand their linkages to cosmopolitans. Rather than fighting globalization, businesses and communities need to use it to enhance local strength.

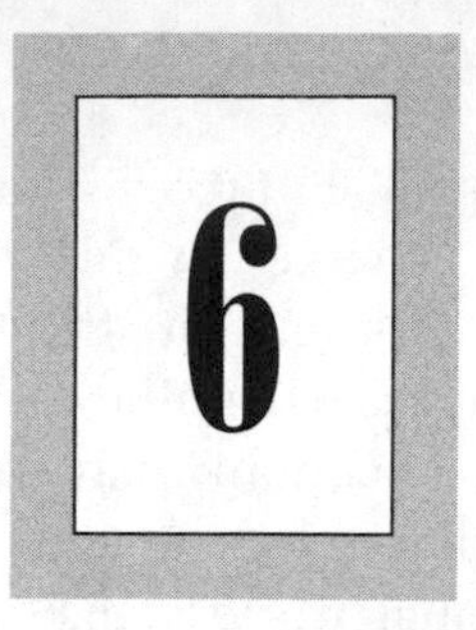

Workplaces, Careers, and Employability Security

"I don't believe any jobs are secure anymore," a limousine dispatcher said. "People in remote locations make decisions that drop the bottom out of the whole job market. That's true no matter what job you have. Somebody somewhere else can kill it." How do you feel about that? he was asked. "I hate it."

As cosmopolitan businesses extend their market scope, tap new and better supply sources, and link up with global chains, they inevitably loosen local ties and relationships. Decisions made by migrant managers disrupt the lives of stay-put workers. Cosmopolitan managers are comfortable moving operations—and themselves—anywhere. But the people who live and work in particular communities have dug in roots.

Most people in my focus groups say they would prefer to stay in the same company or community, even under debilitating conditions. One administrator fears the unknown: what if the next situation is worse? Others describe community investments—Little League coach, volunteer fireman, Arts Council chair, the new hand-built wing of the house, extended family nearby, a large mortgage and too low resale price in a declining property market. Even those with portable skills do not want to carry them too far. High-tech professionals who move readily from company to company do it largely within regions—on the Northern California circuit, the Seattle circuit, the Boston circuit. And most entrepreneurs start businesses where they already are.

Participants in the global economy may strive to hold on to community roots yet still find themselves unable to count on many other aspects of their professional world remaining fixed or stable. Even when viewed positively as a source of new market growth, the global economy is experienced by people across the occupational spectrum as a loss of certainty, a game in which today's success still does not guarantee the future; there is no letup, no stopping, in the pursuit of the next concept or skill.

In nearly every part of the world, the job-tenure ideal of the past is colliding with the job-insecurity reality of the present. Take Japan, the bastion of lifetime employment, where a high proportion of the country's millions of workers in large companies stayed with one employer throughout their working life; beginning in 1992, cutbacks and layoffs have shaken the social contract.[1] Look at Europe, where France and other European nations have loosened regulations to permit greater flexibility in hiring and firing. Or turn to China, still a Communist country; in the course of transforming large-scale government enterprises into share-issuing corporations, Guangdong province has broken the "three irons" of lifetime employment ("iron rice bowls"); managerial tenure ("iron chairs"); and protection against pay cuts ("iron wages").[2]

In America, "You can do everything right and still lose your job," people said in my national focus groups. The impact of corporate restructuring goes far beyond the numbers who have experienced it themselves. Everyone has a story to tell about a parent, a child, a neighbor, or a friend who had been laid off despite excellent credentials, like the many-patented project engineer from "Southway" now working in the produce department of a supermarket and trying to get a teaching certificate; he had to sell his house. Statistics show declining unemployment and continuing job creation. But the anecdotes stick in people's minds as a warning and a sign of change. A self-described "white middle-class professional woman" whose job was lost in a computer company restructuring expressed many people's sense of vulnerability and marginality: "What we're experiencing here is what minorities, black, whatever color, have experienced for many years. It's touching our doorsteps, and we don't like it."

The global economy threatens to create a class divide between cosmopolitans and locals. Cosmopolitans have portable skills, extensive connections, and wide opportunities. Those who are confined to particular places are more dependent and vulnerable.

Uncertainty now surrounds every workplace, but cosmopolitans are better positioned to cope with change because their linkage to wider networks also links them to wider opportunities. Workplaces in companies that are world-ready offer a new form of security, employability security. Companies that flourish, and thereby provide employability security, replenish their stock of the three C's of concepts, competence, and connections by investing in innovation, education, and collaboration.

Those companies least able to cope with change leave local workers anxious, vulnerable, and angry. The victims of change are found in insular, closed systems accustomed to a command and control structure, with limited employee education, involvement, or enterprise, and few external partners.[3]

THE SCOPE OF CHANGE

As experienced in offices and factories throughout America and the world, change is like an atomic reaction. Multiple changes are occurring simultaneously as one institution's strategy collides with another's. Changes in one industry trigger changes in adjacent industries, a set of local cascades following the globalization cascades. Industry transformation and upheaval are associated with organizational transformation and upheaval, which make new demands on the work force.

This is especially clear in cities dependent on industry giants. In Seattle, for example, in February 1993, Boeing announced plans to reduce companywide employment by 23,000 over eighteen months, with 19,000 jobs to be cut in Washington, 15,000 of them in giant batches in 1993 and 1994. Estimates of indirect job losses for the Seattle area were as high as 72,000, although historically after a Boeing layoff high-tech start-ups have picked up much of the slack within a year. Then, to make the situation worse, in late September 1993 GPA, the worldwide leasing firm based in Ireland, canceled seventy-one Boeing orders, although some of the difference was made up by a U.S.-assisted Saudi Arabian order. But there were questions about whether Boeing will produce its new models, the 787 and beyond, outside the area, to bypass Seattle's cumbersome regulatory process. Meanwhile the area's forest products industry was affected by the new federal forest management plan, McCaw Cellular was sold to AT&T, and Microsoft slowed hiring. The corporate giants were no longer sources of job security.

Continuing organizational change is not merely a matter of industry adjustments as corporate giants downsize one set of local operations while growing facilities elsewhere in the nation or world (such as Digital Equipment cutting tens of thousands of Massachusetts jobs while building a new plant for three thousand workers in Malaysia).[4] Changes in local jobs and careers reflect fundamental shifts in customers, suppliers, competitors, regulations, and technology. It is not simply a response to business cycles, nor is it confined to older, larger companies seeking revitalization in the face of losses.

In any city, pick prominent local companies such as banks, utilities, newspapers, and traditional industries and see how many simultaneous changes are occurring in every key relationship for the most profitable companies—all of them felt in the workplace. In one city

- a "top five" downtown bank faces industry consolidations and ownership shifts, leaving it the only locally owned major bank in the area, while competition increases from outside the region and the banking industry, large customers demand more customized treatment, and regulations require more small business and community service. Its responses include international expansion, reorganization to offer differentiated services in industry niches, reduction in suppliers, removal of management layers, a quality program, and new hiring standards.
- a major newspaper is sold to new owners from outside the city and faces stronger competition from new sources of information (both electronic media and local tabloids), a need for new production process technology, and a new customer base for advertising sales, because retail industry consolidation has moved retail headquarters out of the region. It too is developing new products, reengineering production, and looking for partners elsewhere while requiring more service to local readers.
- a manufacturer in one of the region's prominent industries is faced with heightened competition from Asia, severe geographic market shifts (90 percent of its regional customers are out of business), regulation that increases costs, and the need to use new production tech-

nology. Its responses include a merger with a local counterpart to leverage combined contacts; new products, including custom applications creating America's broadest product range in its field; consolidation of facilities; aggressive pursuit of new customers outside the region; product development collaboration with other mills; computerization of production; and a search for international suppliers and markets.

Across industries, forces for change are similar: industry consolidation, changing regulation, new technology, more demanding customers, and pressures for lower cost, higher quality, greater speed. The responses are also similar: a search for new markets (often internationally), acceleration of new product development, and implementation of a new organizational model, one that comprises fewer layers, faster processes, greater use of teams, employees educated to solve problems autonomously, deeper relationships (with customers, alliances, joint ventures, and suppliers), and greater reliance on outside suppliers to contribute to internal processes.[5]

Corporate downsizing is often the villain as workers discuss the uncertain future, but the main issue is changing job requirements and job dislocation, not downsizing. Large companies' downsizing makes headlines because of the vast numbers involved in one swoop. But equally important forces for workplace change are smaller companies losing their local business because of global supply chain changes, companies reengineering to fit industry consolidation, or the move of their customers' headquarters out of the city. More important are new requirements even where there is employment growth.

Change is a matter not of failure, but of success. The most change is occurring in the most successful companies. Companies with greater growth and international scope are more likely to have already initiated changes and to be continuing them, as the 2,655 responses to my survey showed. Knowledge-intensive services (hospitals, universities, professional firms) are catching up with manufacturing companies in making significant workplace changes.

THE NEW WORKPLACE AND ITS HUMAN IMPACT

The forces of change are redefining every organizational system and relationship, internally and externally. In every city in my survey, changes in customer, supplier, and employee relationships are highly correlated; they form a single statistical factor. At least a third of all companies are already making major changes of this kind, and more anticipate making them in the next three years. Even more companies plan changes in roles and rewards (training, reengineering, greater use of teams, new forms of compensation) in the next three years. Furthermore, organizational change is a long-term, ongoing process. Companies reporting change activities in the past three years tend to anticipate continuing these activities in the next three, with the exception of one-time changes such as new supplier contracts. All these changes are accompanied by continuing job dislocation, greater job insecurity, and higher job requirements.

OUTSOURCING

Companies increasingly contract out for ancillary labor-intensive services once performed in-house. Outsourcing occurs primarily in low value-added, labor-intensive jobs and services that remain local purchases while other high-ticket purchases are globalized. Low value-added services are outsourced and performed locally, whereas high value-added purchases of both goods (such as manufacturing components) and services (large contracts for consulting or advertising) come from national or international suppliers more likely to be outside the region than in it. For forty-two representative Boston-area companies, the most commonly outsourced activities are food services, payroll, cleaning services, building maintenance, incoming and outgoing mail, security, local transportation, travel arrangements, public relations, child care, training, technical writing, and printing. Manufacturing companies are also outsourcing parts of the production process to cut costs: metal fabrication, painting, die cutting, and even assembly.

Newer companies that rely on outside service providers because they are still too small to do everything themselves see little reason ever to bring those activities in-house. This means that growth companies that once could be counted on to create new high-wage jobs create them at a slower rate. According to a 1993 Coopers & Lybrand study of 392 companies identified in the media as the fastest-growing U.S. businesses, 65 percent of America's fast-track firms outsourced. Firms that outsource had the same number of total employees as those that did not, but their revenues were 22 percent greater, their growth rate 5.2 percent greater, and their capital investment slightly higher.

Greater reliance on outside suppliers to perform services as well as supply finished goods is both a cause and a consequence of outsourcing —one reason why changes in organization structure are so highly correlated with closer relationships with suppliers. But among the consequences for local workers who become independent contractors or employees of suppliers of outsourced services are lower wages, fewer benefits, continuing anxiety about employment stability, and more uncertainty about the future.

TEMPORARY JOBS

Temporary personnel agencies are among the fastest-growing companies in the United States and Western Europe. The greatest revenue growth on *Florida Trend* magazine's list of Florida's top 150 private companies in 1994 was enjoyed by Vincam Group of Miami suburb Coral Gables, a personnel provider, whose revenues doubled from the previous year. In 1993 there were no employee leasing or temporary staffing firms on *Florida Trend*'s list; in 1994 four of them were among the top group, and one, Creative Staffing, a Miami temporary service, also made the *Inc.* 500 list of America's fastest-growing companies.

Temporary employment is an example of how small numbers can have very large symbolic impact. For forty-two Boston-area companies, for example, workers with temporary status constitute no more than 1–2 percent of their work force; the highest estimate is 5 percent. But "temps" are increasingly seen as a permanent human resource strategy —so much so that a growing number of companies in widely varying industries, including hospitals, insurance companies, computer manufacturers, and software developers, have their own temporary pools, for which they recruit and train. This allows them to balance the flexibility to bring people in as needed with the ability to ensure their knowledge of the company and skill in its work. Companies with temp pools often provide vacations and health insurance, but not severance pay or pensions.

Temps from agencies are used in traditional ways, by small and large companies alike: to augment at peak seasons, for special events, for unusually large orders, and to maintain flexibility in an uncertain production environment. Some autonomous professional jobs are being performed on a contract basis by individuals or small companies (book editing, for example, or television production). In two cases out of a dozen interviewed, such contractors constitute a temporary force of up to one-third the size of the so-called permanent staff. Temporary labor is also being used by companies in areas in which they would once have simply added workers, because they do not want to promise permanent jobs. A large consumer products company plans to add temps more quickly than permanent employees, expanding its temporary work force from its current level of 2 percent to 5–7 percent of its permanent work force, concentrated in sales, service, and retail support areas. Managers and workers perceive that companies are afraid to staff up even in good times, because they fear a volatile economy.

More contingent employment is reinforced by tougher talk by managers in large companies that once promised de facto permanent employment. One executive characterized this as a shift "from a 'grow our own' civil service mentality to a focus on performance. We'll fire those who don't perform."

MORE WORK, LONGER HOURS

Those who remain on permanent work forces face extra work because of competitive requirements and the sheer pace of change. Work overload itself contributes to insecurity and uncertainty about the future, because it eliminates the time for planning to develop the next wave of innovation. Midlevel managers at downsizing firms complain about having to do many more mundane chores because of cuts in support staff. They report working more hours but getting less substantive work done. They have less time or mental energy to invent the future. A recent survey by Day-Timer found that the average American now works fifty-two hours a week—forty-six hours at the office and six on office work at home.

Workloads are growing:

- An engineering supervisor in a small semiconductor factory described his work pressures: "Today I have all functions, on demand, and I must respond immediately because I have a customer that has a need. I've never worked as hard, not physically but mentally. I'm just so afraid that if I don't respond to you as a customer, you may go someplace else, and I'm not going to get your business. We're always working, ten hours a day, but we don't get paid for it."
- A hospital accounts payable clerk whose hospital was bought by an out-of-state for-profit chain was angry about the short staffing that doubled her workload: "They're bringing in outside agencies to re-

place the men so they don't have to pay benefits," she said. "They leave, they retire, they're not replacing them."

- An audit clerk in a retail headquarters had a similar story of overload coupled with insecurity: "Just in my department there used to be five of us; now there are three, but the volume of work is growing and growing. Morale is just completely gone. And now they're considering putting all of the expense reports and documents on-line. So that changes my whole job to be data entry, eliminating my specialty, maybe my job. What do I do now? Am I going to have a job in three years?"
- A marketing professional appreciates the career opportunities that can follow downsizing but knows they exact a price. "Streamlining helped me in my position," she said. "A woman who worked for me had retired, and they streamlined her job into mine, which helped me get promoted and move ahead, although I do have twice the work."

Exacerbated pressures on employees open wide the possibility for error. An administrator reported: "Because it's very hectic in my department, there are a lot of errors now. Managers are running from meeting to meeting, things are late. Because you're rushed, you're answering the phones, you're taking messages, you're doing presentations, errors happen. Quality is starting to weaken."

An electronics company showed similar strain after restructuring to raise productivity, reducing job classifications from 1,300 to 32. Productivity rose all right but took its toll on employees who were at times subjected to unbearable workloads and pressure. One manager argued that workloads are out of control: "We tell people we value them, then they work seventy hours a week and are forced to change priorities four times. And no one has a policy that if you work one weekend, you won't have to work the next." Operating in an environment of overload, while reengineering continues, means that people stick with what they know and resist cross-training. Cross-training, once a career asset, now means more work. There are risks to trying new things when the poorest performers can be cut.

Management, too, carries bigger loads. At the electronics company spans of control have increased from the traditional twelve to one to eighteen or twenty-four to one. No time is left for mentoring. Nor is there sufficient time for the personal interaction essential to an organization's effective functioning. As one employee stated, "We have many exhausted, confused people. They are tired of parties and certificates that won't solve the morale problem." Factors within and outside the company undermine camaraderie: accelerated work schedules, the demoralizing impact of a stagnant economy, long commutes and shared rides that require employees to leave work without time to spare for socializing, decreased attendance at corporate events. And the flatter organization presents an identity crisis; gone is the order and status of numerous job titles that gave people feelings of pride and clarity about next steps.

ESCALATING SKILL REQUIREMENTS

Organizational change is reflected in both the nature and content of jobs. Better-paid, more secure jobs require both additional skills to perform the analyses required for quality programs and broader knowledge of technology and processes to participate in cross-functional problem solving to increase quality and speed. Routine job requirements now include involvement in process reengineering, quality programs, and work unit or cross-functional teams. For example, Bull used high-performance teams to reduce its computer production time from about two weeks to two hours, using new technology that involved greater integration at the component level. Ocean Spray's quality action team reduced the changeover process on a bottling line by about 900 percent—from 150 to 16 minutes. Both sets of teams needed skills above and beyond what it took for them to perform their regular jobs, and the result of their efforts was greater requirements for those jobs.

Pattern cutters, telephone operators, meter readers, hamburger flippers, and taxi dispatchers are among those now expected to use computers.

Newer companies design computer-savvy into jobs from the beginning: Merlin Metalwork's thirty workers producing titanium bicycles use a computer to schedule their work, track performance, and enter data about the product.

In production areas, narrow rote jobs are being replaced by more complex and demanding ones. At Gillette's South Boston factory, the jobs that are disappearing are low-skill entry-level jobs, such as manual assembly and visual quality inspection. "We begin now with jobs in which the operator controls several complex machines at high speed, controlling the product and outgoing quality levels," an executive said. "The work is numerically driven—extracting and using data, a constant reading of what's going on via the computer." Operators are entrusted with many decisions, asked to use their brains rather than simply show up. One example: reducing changeover time for shifting from five-packs of razors to ten-packs from three hours to ten minutes. The team videotaped the activity, watched its "home movie" with popcorn on a Saturday, and then brainstormed solutions.

For some workers, job satisfaction and autonomy increase dramatically as a result of the responsibility now bestowed upon them, even if workloads and hours increase. A production worker at the Kohler factory in Spartanburg, who doubles as suggestion program coordinator, reported happily: "Computerizing the warehouse gives me a new job. Before I loaded trucks, but now all I do is work with the computer, setting up everything that needs to be done, and keep ten different printers going. Plus I spend a lot of time on different committees. We talk about suggestions that are turned into plans. It's a lot of work, but we've had 76 percent of suggestions implemented. I even put in some extra hours off the clock to do all the paperwork and coordination." He said this is voluntary: "Kohler is not a pressure place to work. Nobody's honestly breathing down your neck every day. They place trust in you. If my foreman sends me to a job, he knows that's where I'm going. If I do him wrong one time, then he'll start checking up on me."

Because of constant change, many companies want newer knowledge more than the benefits of long experience with the company. If forced to choose between loyalty and learning, they would take learning. This is a matter not just of costs (newer, younger people cost less in wages and benefits), but also of assumed flexibility to keep up with rapidly changing fields. The head of human resources for an electronics manufacturer said that the company's current work force is a competitive disadvantage: "Our average employee has eighteen years of service. If you were starting a new company, you would not hire a fifty-five-year-old at a substantial salary who must be retrained and who comes with higher liabilities and insurance costs."

The new workplace thus involves more highly skilled workers operating on cross-functional teams with minimal supervision to solve problems in order to speed up the production cycle. Their very success at managing themselves, tapping into databases, solving problems, and doing things faster reduces the need for as many people, reinforcing uncertainty about future employment.

UNCERTAINTY: THE GREEN BANANA PROBLEM

When asked what they will be doing in three to five years, most people in my focus groups confessed that they haven't a clue. They said they cannot think beyond today. "Where am I going to be in three years? I don't even buy green bananas," a technician proclaimed.

Career uncertainty colors people's attitudes toward work. As one support staff member in a big company put it: "What do I hear all the time? Not only from managers here but friends of mine from outside work. Geez, you're lucky you have a job. You're lucky you have a job. It's like a mantra. I wake up saying, 'I'm lucky I have this job.' So I try not to bitch and moan, but make the best of what I've got."

Few incentives exist to build toward long-term goals within an organization or to invest too much personal meaning in a job that may be eliminated without warning. An employee defined a painful division between the desire to do well in a job and the likelihood that one's efforts will be futile: "I like what I'm doing, I like it a lot. But there's no telling whether or not next year, or the year after, this program is going to be there. One day, boom, see you later. Your job is eliminated. We don't want you anymore. That's scary. You just got to come in, and do the best you can, and hope that you go farther." Another acknowledged the realities of job dislocation but inured himself to its effects by pretending the issue does not exist: "I think if I worried about it, I'd be a basket case."

Corporate assurances carry little weight with jaded employees. As one reported: "Companies today promise you everything; with a snap of the fingers, it's gone." Nor is there any relief in sight. One employee felt his work situation was like being "in an earthquake, and you don't know if the door is going to come down." Whatever hope the future may hold could be illusory: "We don't know if the light at the end of that tunnel is sunshine or the train coming at us." To a greater extent than in the past, people suspect it's a train.

THE NEW SECURITY: "EMPLOYABILITY"

Traditional values are eroding: long-term employment security, the loyalty of employer to employee and employee to employer. Human resource policies must build new forms of security while embracing the emerging realities of flexibility, mobility, and change.

If security no longer comes from being employed, it must come from being employable. Large organizations can no longer guarantee long-term employment, and few people would believe such a promise anyway. But employability security—the knowledge that today's work will enhance the person's value in terms of future opportunities—is a promise that can be made and kept. Employability security comes from the chance to accumulate human capital—skills and reputation—that can be invested in new opportunities as they arise. No matter what changes take place, persons whose pool of intellectual capital or expertise is high are in a better position to find gainful employment—with the current company, with another company, or on their own.[6]

In newer firms in emerging technology industries, people already acknowledge this new reality, however reluctantly. They bet their future on continuing hard work and growth in skills that match changes in the industry, finding security in their own ability to generate income, perhaps as entrepreneurs themselves someday. Companies come and go, but technical know-how can still find a home. What makes the current company attractive are learning opportunities—chances to grow in skills, to prove and improve one's capacity—that enhance the person's ability to remain employable. Challenging jobs on significant projects are more important, in these industries, than promises about the future or benefits programs tied to longevity.

Even a promise of long-term employment is possible only because of programs aimed at ensuring employability. Companies can offer to invest in retraining and career counseling to upgrade people's skills continually so they will always be employable, although specific jobs might disappear and they might have to prove their ability to contribute to the company over and over again throughout their careers. Similarly, communities that encourage investment in human capital via continuing education, training, job-finding networks across companies, and support for new venture creation can help people feel secure even when they move across companies or invent their own jobs.

THE OPPORTUNITY ADVANTAGED

A new social contract based on the new realities is already emerging in leading cosmopolitan companies. Companies offering employability security invest in the three C's of world class concepts, competence, and connections. They are more

- *entrepreneurial.* They encourage employee ideas and lead their industry in innovation.
- *learning oriented.* They encourage their employees' involvement, give them opportunities to develop their skills, and learn from direct experience with customers or best practices in other companies.
- *collaborative.* They use teamwork inside and alliances outside.

In the exemplary companies, learning, entrepreneurship, and collaboration are "overdetermined"—manifested through multiple practices. These practices help people feel more valued and secure even in times of significant uncertainty and change, and they prepare people for future jobs.

For other companies, the laggards, insularity is associated with employee paralysis in a vicious cycle of decline:

- Insular companies operate without partners to extend their reach or provide a window on innovation. They stagnate.
- Stagnating companies cut budgets, especially for future-oriented investments. They fail to prepare their people for the future or empower them to seek and contribute new ideas.
- Lack of broad skills and absence of channels for contribution prevent people from innovating and contributing to solutions.
- Lack of faith in the future paralyzes the work force, lowers morale, undermines teamwork, and eliminates initiative.
- A dearth of entrepreneurial behavior limits those companies' ability to find new markets, products, or processes.
- Declining fortunes mean that such companies further reduce their investment in people, reinforcing the downward spiral.

Within the same industry, differences in investment in the three C's account for differences in opportunity for the local work force. Compare two high-technology instrumentation facilities, both units of large, multidivisional defense contractors whose military business is disappearing fast in the post–cold war era. "Southway," which was described in chapter 5, is caught in the downward spiral in which insularity reinforces decline. It lacks the concepts, competence, and connections necessary for success in newly competitive world markets. The second, EG&G, has long invested in technology innovation, extensive education and training, and partnerships.

"Southway" manufactures high-precision instruments for military aircraft guidance systems. Local managers feel increasingly powerless, with few local advantages remaining in their site. Corporate headquarters on another coast has taken over purchasing. Technological know-how once available only at a nearby university, which made the local site important, is now increasingly found in many technology centers around the world. The site is now a third the size it was four years ago.

Long insulated from the marketplace, "Southway" responded to military specifications rather than innovated. Its stifling atmosphere discouraged initiative. A noncollaborative mind-set made the company a laggard, missing out on the latest technology because it failed to partner with the newer companies leading technological advances. Competitors facing similar decline in defense spending have been able to bring new products to commercial markets faster. One senior manager jokingly suggested to my researcher that maybe it would be better if all of the longtime employees were gone, including himself. That was gallows humor.

In contrast, Massachusetts units of EG&G have maintained revenues despite military cutbacks, in part by looking aggressively for new applications for its technology internationally, in new commercial markets (such as autos and food service), drawing on significant alliances to help. Although almost all of its nearly $3 billion in sales through 1992 were in the United States, the company already operated in twenty-five countries. A Japanese partner offers market access. An Asian government partner helps develop micromachinery capability. EG&G also acquired several commercial businesses in Europe that dominate their market niche.

People at EG&G are just as shaken by change as the people at "Southway." But they look upon the future with more optimism because of the company's cosmopolitan outlook, international reach, and search for new ideas. The workplace is designed to help them increase in value to the company, through extensive training and cross-functional experience, while the company benefits from their greater skill and commitment. They recognize the relationship between their own security and what they are willing and able to contribute to the company's success. They see the value of global outreach.

EMPOWERED AT POWERSOFT

The new social contract is fully developed in the newest industries. At Powersoft employment is highly contingent, and people are wildly enthusiastic. Because Powersoft is world class in software, as described in chapter 2, it is a good example of how success breeds success—if the local work force finds employability security. "It's fun to work for a place that's on top of the world instead of from the netherworld," said a newcomer fresh from several moribund computer companies.

Constant flux and adjustment, coupled with tough industry competition, make the existence of any job highly uncertain and every job subject to continual change at Powersoft, as in numerous other companies in other industries. Some development and support staffers wish for a "moratorium on the tweaking" but recognize that the company's success depends on constant improvement, even if that means that "every three days we're changing the rules." This dynamic environment creates contradictory actions—for example, layoffs of people without transferable skills in a unit shutting down and a mad search for people to build new development operations. Human resource director Traci Weaver recalled a period when "I would be firing people in the morning and hiring people in the afternoon—a vivid example of how the constant changes in our business are reflected in employment."

To maintain flexibility, Powersoft has an in-house temporary employment department, Powersoft Temps, for about half the temporary pool the company uses. This gives Powersoft control over quality and fosters longer-term relationships with contingent workers. It helps Powersoft see the marketplace and make its own choices, rather than being dependent on whomever an agency has available. During a new product release in 1993, for example, twenty temps were used for a month for data entry, invoicing, and ordertaking. The company has since hired a number of people who started as temps.

Powersoft employees have flexibility to design three-day, four-day, or five-day altered schedule work weeks and can work from home, linked through computer, E-mail, and fax machines supplied by the company. Most human resource department employees work out of their homes at least half the time, including a full-time recruiter who spends most of her time on the phone in the evening, talking with prospective hires after their work hours. People reported in focus groups that they like being treated like adults who can come and go as they please. Furthermore, Powersoft provides opportunities for initiative. "If you see something that needs to be done, start doing it; it becomes your job," an associate said. "You can come in the door as one thing and in a short time end up as something completely different, because you chased an intriguing opportunity."

Powersoft people sound eerily like a manual for the new self-reliant career. Their comments are peppered with California-style New Age references—"the moon's in Jupiter," "I'm a Gemini." But it doesn't take long to realize that this is not a young or inexperienced crowd following the latest hip career cliché: the average age is thirty-five, and everyone my research group met had worked for other companies, giving them a reference point for their reactions to Powersoft. They talked about "earning the right to come back" because "no one is owed a job; sorry, pal." They reported that the challenge of a demanding technology provides "unparalleled opportunities to grow within my-self." They congratulated each other on their dedication, joking about the long hours. For example, when a senior manager in one of my focus groups referred to an "ethic that is far and above eight-to-five," a colleague quipped, "Only a half day?" The first replied, "That's 8 P.M. to 5 P.M." Another chimed in, "This is like a poker game. I'll see you your hours and raise you." Then a fourth made a serious point: "In this environment, second best just doesn't cut it. We all challenge each other. The long hours aren't because we want to outshine everybody; we want to keep up with everybody."

There is no guarantee of employment at Powersoft, but there is a promise of the best skills and connections to move on to the next position anywhere. An executive said, "The thing I always tell every-body is that while we want Powersoft to succeed in a dramatic way, because that is going to make all of our lives better, more important, we want the platform that we're running on to succeed. So if Powersoft crashes and burns, we can go somewhere else and leverage what we did here."

Experience has taught people to count not on the company, but on their ability to move. It's not that they want to be nomads; most express a desire to settle down. "It's an exciting environment, which makes you very attached to the company," a professional said. "You spend so many hours that it's hard to cut those roots and move on." But they will move if they have to. "I was at Digital when it was a fun place; I was at Prime when it was a prime place to work," another employee recalled. "Both times I got out before it was fashionable. I wouldn't hesitate to jump again if I see lifeboats being lowered."

Powersoft people's attitude about the future is strikingly different from the demoralized people living so day-to-day that they do not buy green bananas. Powersoft people agree that the next years are highly uncertain, but they can imagine a variety of possibilities with no ceilings or barriers. The banter among one group of managers about who would take whose job and who would be president stands in stark contrast with the hesitancy of people in other companies to name any position as a future possibility. They know they will be doing something different, something that uses the learning in which they are investing: for example, the front-line tech support staffer who thinks he'll be in a better job because he's also a part-time instructor at Northeastern University, or the administrative assistant who wants to work anywhere overseas for Powersoft.

They can joke about insecurity out of confidence, like this manager: "Security depends on the moment of the day. Whether my phone system just exploded. At that point my job security doesn't feel so good. When things are doing fine, I feel a lot better about it." And they tend to feel in control, that it is their own choice whether to stay or leave. Several said they hope they *want* to be at Powersoft in the future: "I hope I'm here, provided the culture of the company stays the same." Others indicated that the company has to continue to provide challenge and learning: "Boredom for me is fatal. It's why I left my last job. When I found that I had time to play video games in the course of an average business day, I knew I was in a lot of trouble."

Powersoft people say their best form of security is skills backed by transferable credentials and reputation, which enable them to move on if need be. One decided to become "the guru for a particular area of knowledge" after observing that leaders at Powersoft have "formal education, because you have to have the boxes checked off, training in various disciplines, extra courses in school, and knowledge of something inside and out." This means "your name gets known through the network."

Oddly enough, development of individuals to take responsibility for themselves stems from a strong collective commitment. A top executive described the responsibility he feels for the people around him who work so hard, which makes him feel he must execute "two hundred percent" in order not to let them down. Another said, "The moral investment in people in our organization is very, very high. We have a commitment to everybody to make sure that they are well trained and that they have the latest technologies within their grasp."

Numerous connections with Powersoft's extensive network of development partners, marketing allies, and industry collaborators not only improve Powersoft's products, they also improve its people's prospects. Dense ties among companies help guarantee that people's skills are portable—easily taken from one company to another—help ensure their horizons are cosmopolitan, and give them a large set of personal ties with other companies to serve as a job-finding network.

People at Powersoft can see their career routes extending throughout the industry, rather than confined to a single company. In emerging technology industries, a high rate of technical change produces a complex of interorganizational relationships, which requires companies in an industry like software to know a great deal about each other's human capital. When development projects spill across organizational lines, as in Powersoft's joint development work with Lotus in the Boston area or Attachmate in the Seattle area, engineers and managers may find that components of their career are controlled by different organizations: for example, jobs can be created by different organizations from those that actually employ the people to fill them, training may be done by still another organization, and multiple people working in multiple organizations assess a person's competence. As organizational partnerships and project teams change, people become acquainted with many different organizations outside their own.

Therefore, career development opportunities derive from relationships outside the organization issuing the paycheck as well as from performance within it. Sociologists Arthur Stinchcombe and Carol Heimer argue that these interdependencies among organizations create an improved labor market in which people feel more confident about finding future jobs.[7]

NETWORKING AND EMPLOYABILITY SECURITY

Security inside the company derives in part from outside ties. Replacing corporate isolation with collaboration enables individuals' horizons to become more cosmopolitan and makes employability security possible. When their workplace is a link in a global chain or a node in a global network, locals are vulnerable to remote decisions by cosmopolitans who do not necessarily put local welfare first, but they are also better positioned to cope with change whatever the decision. When I asked a Nynex telephone installer what he liked best about the company, he mentioned its operations in England—not because he would be sent to England, but because he felt the future would be more secure in a company expanding internationally. A Nestlé research manager in Ohio also understood the value of working for an international company: "When the American economy goes up and down, an international company rides through pretty evenly. We haven't had any layoffs. My job is very secure because we've got the best talent, and we'll be the one to survive."

At the Norton Company in Worcester, Massachusetts, some of the anxiety workers feel since its acquisition by St. Gobain of France has been offset by optimism about St. Gobain's international reach, which they see as enabling its investment in work force education and making its business units world leaders in their fields. Norton's education programs make the work force more knowledgeable both about what the company does and about customers and competition. As a result, workers on the floor making the product can talk knowledgeably about industry standards and what needs to be improved. All three shifts receive $4,000 yearly per person in educational assistance, a figure that has doubled from its level prior to the acquisition. Norton has spent $180,000 on just one nearby campus. It has also received federal grants to teach basic skills during lunch hour courses that educate people in groups of 150 for a half hour on company paid time.

One employee spoke enthusiastically about Norton's efforts to encourage employees to educate themselves: "People in this company feel that if you want to take the initiative to improve yourself, and at some point it can be of some value to the company, they are more than willing to approve it." Encouraging employees to take professional development seminars generates tangible benefits for the company. For example, a mechanic who wants to go to night school for a year to learn about refrigeration might subsequently be able to take on tasks currently performed by outside maintenance people.

Although uncertainty looms large and pay cuts have caused great anger, people at Norton are more optimistic than those in other companies in the area about the future and about the opportunities for advancement that hard work and learning can provide. Their confidence stems from ties to an international parent company with global reach.

GAPS IN THE NETWORK: THE CASE OF INNER-CITY MINORITIES

Where innovation, education, and collaboration flourish, and the links to global networks are clear, people's security increases. Where they are missing, economic marginality results. And concentrated marginality builds an underclass visible in inner cities everywhere, one populated largely by minority groups.

Inner-city ghettos in industrialized countries are a kind of new Third World, as the "Third World" tag increasingly applies less to countries than to life circumstances. Like Third World countries, inner cities are stereotyped, often wrongly, as harboring undereducated, less literate, dangerous populations, often newly arrived from underdeveloped places. Attempts to help inner cities often resemble foreign aid programs: charity grants, CARE packages to combat illiteracy the way they once went to feed the hungry abroad, missionaries and Peace Corps–type volunteers in inner cities, and "social work disguised as minority procurement," as a black executive put it.

If inner cities are the first destination for poor immigrants, those ethnic groups that escape tend to be the ones connected to networks in other places that help them join the world class. Cuban exiles in Miami started out with inherent network advantages that translated quickly into business advantages. Asian-Americans often possess ties to growing markets that can be leveraged for local success, the way Mochtar Riady built Lippo Group; Boston's small Asian-American Bank serves the local Chinese population and finances trade with the Far East.

Isolates, in contrast, are disadvantaged. Some companies with an inner-city base are less connected to the kinds of networks that create competitive advantage, lack the three C's and, therefore, cannot provide secure jobs. Consider two cases in two cities.

■ CASE #1: THE VICTIM OF MINORITY PROCUREMENT

An African-American computer parts producer remains isolated because this small company lacks the concepts and competence to firm up its connections. At its peak the company had eight large customers, but two accounted for most of its business. The company began over twenty years ago with a contract as the first minority supplier for a high-technology firm expanding in the area. After a period of growth, it has since shrunk significantly, as its low skill, low value-added work is easily replaceable; and its first and largest customer moved the process back in-house to keep its own staff employed during a business downturn. Moreover, the large customer had guaranteed a business base but also had a ceiling for minority vendors, so the minority company had never benefited from its customer's growth. "We only get the company's capillary business," the owner said, "that is, business where we can't hurt them if we screw up."

He suspected the minority vendor label hurt in other ways: "We did a great job for another customer, delivering eight thousand units J-I-T when they needed them. The engineer in that division loved us. He took me by the hand to another one. We couldn't get in."

The parts company is rooted in the African-American community; the CEO's commitments and relationships are strongly minority based. He is well known in the black community. He has been involved in numerous community projects, raising money and serving on half a dozen boards. Yet this high level of minority community involvement contrasts with a lack of involvement in business-related organizations that would begin to build other connections. "I don't join lobby or industry associations because they don't tend to do anything for us," he stated; and furthermore, he was "not a joiner." The CEO wondered whether networking is more difficult for African-Americans, for he felt that his city has tight neighborhoods that create exclusionary ethnic networks that make it hard for minority businesses.

Perhaps the company will survive through a new partner, with which it will share the facilities it uses to perform tests and assembly, as well as the training required to get quality certification from a large customer. Its aspirations involve work for foreign manufacturers. But unless it has partners that will open doors, its leaders perceive great difficulty in making the contacts necessary to enter global markets.

■ CASE #2: THE NEIGHBORHOOD BANK

In this case, in another place, the isolation of an African-American–based bank is associated with its focus on the minority community. Despite a smart, widely admired founder, the bank has had a shaky financial history characterized by a lack of competitive concepts, competence, and connections.

The company is dedicated to the social and economic welfare of the African-American neighborhoods that constitute its primary customer base; its employees derive a sense of mission from their community ties. But the company's operating capital and technology are limited. Despite efforts to automate and develop new products, the bank still cannot handle corporate accounts or sophisticated transactions. Not only does the efficiency of the bank's infrastructure lag behind its competitors', but it must invest a good deal of its resources in training its customers to perform ordinary transactions, such as filling out forms and understanding credit lines "so no one will dupe them," an associate said. Desire to help the community means offering high deposit interest, but that makes transactions less profitable, which further reduces capital. Reliance on a larger bank's ATM system diminishes the bank's price competitiveness, since it must charge its customers a usage fee.

Nonminority banks come to inner-city joint ventures with capital in hand, seeking neighborhood knowledge, treating their inner-city partners in much the same way that American companies treat partners in developing countries. But although this minority bank has great access to its neighborhoods, it has not been able to leverage its relationships with larger financial institutions to its own advantage. Any success the bank achieves in its domain invites in the competition, since success demonstrates that there is a market in the inner city for financial services.

The bank's difficulties in building a sustainable operation are compounded by its high staff turnover. Talented employees are plucked up by larger companies that are eager to find experienced minority professionals and offer higher pay and greater career opportunities. Isolation from mainstream and global financial networks has a discernible impact on opportunities for the bank's staff, exacerbating the insecurity of employees who feel blocked from advancement within the bank—and marginal outside their community. So some employees' dreams and hopes rest outside the bank, such as a would-be clothing designer or a part-time pastor who hopes his congregation can someday use him full-time.

Employees with career aspirations in business or financial services feel welcome at the bank but do not feel secure. Although the bank is forever scrambling to keep up with its competitors, it offers its employees many opportunities to learn, to "wear a hundred hats," in the words of one employee. The bank's minority culture enables minority employees to feel that they are judged on their performance, not on their color.

The bank's CEO, in contrast with the CEO of the parts supplier, makes a point of being well connected to his city's mainstream business community. Yet the results of his efforts, and those of other black professionals, have been disappointing. "We are all in the right groups," he said. "We get invited to luncheons and to serve as advisers. But when it comes down to getting business, it is still tough. We are part of the social network, but do not have real leverage. If they want a lawyer, they still go to the established law firm; if they want an architect, they go to the established big firm. Obviously, those firms are predominantly white."

Because mainstream businesses provide much verbal encouragement for new projects, but no commitment when it comes time for action, the bank plans to expand beyond the city it is currently located in, targeting black and Hispanic municipalities. In seeking out places where employees and elected officials may be receptive to a minority supplier with multiple products and diverse expertise, the bank believes it will overcome its isolation through networks involving its ethnic base —an ethnic strategy that has brought prosperity to Miami's Cuban-Americans and California's Chinese-Americans.

THE COSTS OF ISOLATION

In some cities African-American businesses are disadvantaged in two ways. Like the parts producer, they are isolated from cosmopolitan networks, and like the bank, they face competition for their local minority market from larger nonminority businesses better endowed with the three C's. Their problems are those of any small, local company that is isolated from the world class, with racial politics added.

In Miami an African-American politician and business promoter observed that segregation had forced the development of business competence—and protected markets—that was lost when black consumers and workers gained access to the mainstream. A black attorney blamed his ethnic group's problems on the Latin influx: "Blacks were left behind. Miami is the only city I've ever seen where blacks do not own a radio station, or a television station, or a car dealership, or a savings and loan, or an insurance company—anything! Blacks here have not only been manipulated out of the mainstream of the power structure, but, more important, they have been manipulated out of the economic mainstream of Miami." Echoing the desire to favor one's own group, an activist said: "If we are the main consumers in [an] industry, then the appropriate response is for us to become major producers of that which we consume."[8]

Lack of the three C's is self-reinforcing, creating a downward spiral for those minority groups whose natural ethnic network does not reach far beyond the community itself. A limited number of prominent African-American or Puerto Rican businesses, for example, means that there is little to no minority wealth to tap into and certainly no minority monies to use to influence and play major roles in major deals. Thus, strong personal relationships and support within the group do not translate into business assets such as access to capital, market leads, strategic alliances, or enduring supplier-customer partnerships. And ethnic networks establish demarcations that other people are hesitant or afraid to cross. A minority company that wants to stay in the inner city may find a stigma attached to the neighborhood that might make it hard to schedule meetings with nonminorities or get trucks to make deliveries. Thus, such companies cannot provide employability security for their work forces.

Many companies express a renewed interest in minority suppliers, but they target low value-added areas, such as office supplies in the case of an apparel producer or maintenance services in the case of a hospital. And as we have seen, the minority vendor designation is a mixed blessing. Dependence on a few customers makes the supplier vulnerable when customers change direction, unless the supplier is also capable of continuous change, constantly moving up in the value added to customers. Bill James, owner of C&C Information Resources, a Greater Miami computer services firm, is optimistic about the inclusion of black-owned businesses in state purchasing deals, as 80 percent of his business comes from schools and government.[9] But his optimism comes from his firm's high-tech competence.

Common efforts to improve American inner cities focus on bringing jobs to the community through increasing entrepreneurship or recruiting businesses in fields that take advantage of inner-city locations, such as food processors.[10] These are important steps, as long as they do not produce workers or companies unconnected to the wider economy. There is evidence that bettering the income of inner-city residents means looking beyond the neighborhood and establishing linkages with mainstream institutions. Community development corporations (CDCs) that have been successful in training and job placement pursue opportunities for placement outside their neighborhoods.[11] In short, employability security for disadvantaged minorities might be derived in the same way it is for nonminority locals: through linkages to cosmopolitan networks.

THE EMPLOYABILITY SECURITY AGENDA

Without the three C's pervading a company, local workers can too easily turn into a servant class, servicing cosmopolitans through low value-added activities. Small, marginal, and isolated companies cannot provide security for their employees by themselves. The gap that separates them from the emerging mainstream grows if linkages are not forged. World class workplaces provide employability security because they prepare people for jobs of the future and link them to opportunities that might lie outside the current job or employer. This makes employees better able to contribute to innovations that keep the company competitive, more competent at fulfilling customer desires, and more desirable as candidates for new jobs—either in the current company or elsewhere. For example:

- *Security for workers at Kohler's Spartanburg facility starts with world class quality and innovation.* The company has been first to market with more products than competitors, such as a toilet using only 1.5 gallons of water to flush, and the Spartanburg plant has led the company in quality since 1984. Kohler's large international market share translates into job security, but associates must be willing to upgrade their skills continuously to succeed in a company that has changed more in the last five years than in the prior thirty-five. Employee involvement makes people feel that their contribution is valued; a bright future is signaled by the company's investment in new technology at the plant.

- *Ricardo Semler grows Semco, his small marine and food service equipment manufacturing company in Brazil, and offers employability security by turning his company into a series of entrepreneurial networks.* Semco sets up its people in their own businesses, often using Semco's own fixed assets and working on Semco projects; entrepreneurial units partly owned by employees compete for outsourcing contracts. A variety of forms of compensation and ownership provide people with the opportunity to work both inside and outside the company while learning to run their own businesses. Two-thirds of Semco's new products are developed through its affiliate network; in 1990 and 1992 Semler was voted business leader of the year by fifty-two thousand executives.[12]

Education to support innovation and change lies at the center of employability security for both very large global companies and smaller, more local ones. Hewlett-Packard is among those large international companies setting the standard for employee education. A rival's benchmarking study found that among a set of leading technology companies, Hewlett-Packard rated highest in annual training hours per employee, devoting eighty hours per year; Motorola offered just above forty; Texas Instruments and Xerox, forty hours. H-P fosters employee development through extensive routine training at every level: management development, technical training, quality, diversity, and team building; retraining to help people move from disappearing jobs such as hardware engineering; structured development planning for supervisors and employees to create customized training plans based on individual strengths and weaknesses; tuition reimbursement; and a "no layoff" policy that includes relocation for anyone at any level if a site closes.

Emphasis on employee education and contributions can infuse smaller companies as well. Lau Technologies seems like a mini–Hewlett-Packard. A $50 million custom electronic systems manufacturer founded by Joanna Lau when she and other employees bought out their unit of a stagnating Massachusetts defense contractor, the company is owned by 21 of its 209 employees, and 48 others participate in a profit-sharing pool. Lau has moved from contract manufacturing of systems for the military to developing digitized identification cards for driver's licenses and other uses—a field new enough to provide room for a small company with innovative concepts and solid alliances. Lau designs the computer systems and machinery, teaming with partner companies to develop the necessary software, which helped Lau and partners win a major contract over a much larger international competitor.

Joanna Lau's associates feel their advancement depends on their own commitment to improving their skills and using them. Employees are provided seven days of total quality management training, extensive technical training in electronics and computers, and full tuition reimbursement for outside courses. They are cross-trained to perform multiple tasks: for example, workers who put components into boards also learn soldering and wire cutting, so they can move from mechanical assembly to board manufacturing as the need arises. Managers conduct an annual training analysis of each employee, which results in customized programs based on employee preferences. There is "buddy" training, in which a master trainer in each field trains others. Employees are urged to use the suggestion box and receive bonuses and recognition for quality suggestions. Slow periods between contracts are used for worker training; this takes advantage of downtime and assuages employee fears, as spending money on training is a sign that the company expects continuing work.

"I have bounced around a number of companies, small ones, large ones," a Lau Technologies manager said. "This is the first company where I have had some sense of security in twenty years."

JOINING INDIVIDUAL, BUSINESS, AND COMMUNITY INTERESTS

Exemplary companies that are learning oriented, entrepreneurial, and collaborative are best positioned to take advantage of rapid changes in technology, emerging international markets, and partnering in their own and related industries.

The new workplace pushes individuals to be more adaptable, as new skills are required and old titles and sinecures swept aside by rapid change. People must be encouraged to look beyond current tasks and local markets, even if this means looking beyond current employers. The implicit pact of guaranteed employment has been supplanted by a social contract marked by uncertainty as much as by global opportunity. Employers must continually develop people's ability to tackle new challenges, encouraging them to collaborate on teams ranging across the organization—and across industry and geographical lines.

Workers in the new global economy must earn not just their paychecks, but their jobs. And employers must provide not only immediate rewards, but preparation for the demands of the future—demands as likely as not to be made by an entrepreneurial spin-off, a current international partner, or an emerging industry competitor. As workers become more agile in meeting those demands, both they and their employers will benefit.

To enable workers to build their own employability security, companies and communities must work together. The scope of job dislocation and the framework in which employability security can arise extend beyond any one company and cannot be handled by a single company acting alone. Integrated actions by corporate, government, and educational institutions are necessary, such as

- *training and education collaboratives* that join several companies in "learning alliances," like the quality programs sponsored by Spartanburg's Chamber of Commerce or Nashville's Peer Learning Network: to offer training, compare best practices, share success stories, and provide internships across companies—to expand people's horizons and forge new connections.
- *abundant workplace learning opportunities*, from formal training to lunchtime seminars to work-site speakers, to expose people to new ideas and new fields, as occurs at Norton or Hewlett-Packard, with local colleges as partners.
- *human resource and job banks* linking networks of related companies, encouraging companies to see their network of suppliers, customers, venture partners, and industry counterparts as a resource for skills development, personnel exchanges, internships, or job placements, as occurs in the software industry for companies like Powersoft.
- *internal corporate entrepreneurship* around promising ideas that the established company cannot use—new ventures and spin-off businesses such as Ricardo Semco's satellites, which is the way Joanna Lau formed Lau Technologies. This helps people create their own opportunities for employment, resulting in new businesses that create new jobs.
- *intact safety nets* when dislocation occurs, such as portable pensions and benefits, retraining, or capital to start a business.

Employability security comes from the chance to accumulate human capital—skills and reputation—that can be invested in new opportunities as they arise and from the chance to make connections that link people to wider networks—the essence of cosmopolitanism. No matter what changes take place, people with more intellectual and social capital are in a better position to find gainful employment—whether it is with their current company, with another company, or on their own. In the global marketplace, a company's investment in the development of its people—beyond the immediate performance requirements of their current tasks—is an investment in its future bottom line. And a local community's employability security initiatives are an investment in a dynamic local economy.

Business Leadership in the Community

American cities count on business leaders for community projects and civic boosterism. In many cities private coalitions, such as Cleveland Tomorrow, Miami's Beacon Council, or the Trade Development Alliance of Greater Seattle, act as shadow governments, including public officials in the coalition but often transcending them in long-term importance. These groups can have greater organizational continuity than political regimes, their leaders can have greater longevity in their positions than elected officials, they can mobilize substantial resources or talent, and their activities are not confined to city limits.

Populist politicians and leftist critics have long railed against community "power elites" that dominate decisions in their own interest. But business leadership groups also get things done. As business cosmopolitans weaken their ties to particular localities, some locals must wish they had them back. Stanley Marcus, former head of Neiman-Marcus, complained that he can't get things done in Dallas anymore, like calling a handful of local business leaders to raise a quick half a million for a civic project. "Now the decisions are made in Tokyo or Hartford or Kalamazoo," he lamented.[1]

Where are the power elites when you need them?

Some of the forces changing the relationship between businesses and communities have a long history. Earlier in the century, corporate money gradually supplanted family money as the chief underwriter of social and cultural activities, and corporate chieftains became more important public figures than a city's heirs to family fortunes. As the dependence of locals on the largesse of large businesses increased, so did concerns about abandonment if ownership should shift outside the community—and shift it did. In recent decades large corporations started to abandon downtowns for suburbia and exurbia,[2] and booming "edge cities" mushroomed on the urban periphery,[3] eliminating the need for emerging companies or highly paid professionals to go downtown for services and thereby changing the political and social dynamics of central cities. At the same time, the dramatic increase of women in the work force decimated most communities' leisure class—that unpaid army of women volunteers who used to do good works.

Even more recently, competitive pressures have increased work hours for professionals and executives, reducing their availability for civic leadership.[4] Now, industry consolidations, mergers or acquisitions, and globalization of markets and supply chains undermine most cities' stable, rooted, homogeneous corporate elite, replacing it with more transient cosmopolitan leaders with a global outlook.

The new business cosmopolitans differ in their interests, availability, and perspective on social and political issues from those who have traditionally championed local causes. But this is not to say that they do not care about the place where they live and work. In addition to benefits they may gain from close proximity to industry peers, cosmopolitans find particular places attractive because of fundamentally local characteristics: a city's cultural ambience and quality of life. But globalization changes the terms of engagement around community issues, threatening to divide cosmopolitans with global perspectives from those pushing local causes.

SOCIAL RESPONSIBILITY IN THE GLOBAL VILLAGE

Assigning social responsibility to business is not a uniquely American idea. Around the globe, movements are emerging to get businesses to take more responsibility for solving problems once assumed to be government functions. An impressive corporate *Who's Who* is involved in international social service.[5] Prince Charles promotes international good corporate citizenship in emerging markets through the Prince of Wales Business Leaders Forum, established at a meeting in the United States in February 1990. Its premise: Governments are in chaos in newly developing countries such as the former communist nations, and only global companies are organized, competent, and rich enough to act.

Within the United States, a movement toward "caring capitalism" urges businesses to promote progressive social change. For example, Sherri Poe, founder of Ryka, a struggling women's athletic shoe company, started the Rose Foundation with the Lady Footlocker retail chain to help abuse victims regain self-esteem, pledging $10,000 a quarter and a share of Ryka's eventual profits. Caring capitalism is strong enough to have spawned its own trade association, Business for Social Responsibility, launched in 1992 by fifty-four companies, including two other Boston-based shoe companies, Reebok and Stride Rite, whose former chairman, Arnold Hiatt, sat on the founding board. By its first meeting in October 1993, BSR comprised over 750 companies.[6]

Across all five cities in my surveys, the 2,655 business leaders who responded are nearly unanimous in their strong verbal support for community responsibility. Eighty-nine percent agree with the proposition that businesses have a responsibility to contribute to their communities beyond the jobs they create. Almost 45 percent link community responsibility to business decisions by disagreeing that financial considerations alone should drive investment and location decisions. Almost half of the businesses report an increase in philanthropy during recent recession years and only 7 percent a decrease. Some large companies incurring financial losses report maintaining high levels of philanthropy anyway. All this should be good news for communities.

But actions are softer than words. Fewer act on community service values than espouse them. Many more companies encourage their employees to make contributions than engage in direct action themselves. And companies are more likely to encourage their employees to contribute time or money than reward them for doing so.

The level of community service is overwhelmingly a function of number of employees; larger companies do more. Community involvement more strongly differentiates between larger and smaller companies than does any other set of variables in my survey. Companies with greater local employment are more similar in their community service patterns than they are in any other aspect of their operations. The single benefit that communities can count on when organizations get larger is that they will provide more community service, regardless of industry, geographic scope of markets, or employment mix. This unremarkable fact is worth noting because it makes clear an additional vulnerability of communities when companies downsize: small companies replace lost jobs, but not community leadership.

Larger companies differ most from smaller ones in their ability to lend executives to community groups full-time and, secondarily, in whether they can provide summer jobs for youth or "adopt" particular social sector organizations, from schools to charities. Larger companies are also much more likely to give awards or recognition to employees for their community contributions. Larger companies can afford to do more, but they are also the ones most likely to be approached by civic groups as well as to reap benefits from philanthropy in attention, reputation, and political credit.

Verbal support for the increased responsibility of corporations to their communities has arisen in tandem with a growing mistrust of government, expressed in voting patterns and echoed in my focus groups. If government is unable to solve social problems and restore community values, many people say, business should accept the challenge. "One of the fundamental issues is a crisis in leadership, particularly in this country, and I suspect it recognizes no borders," said a middle manager at Powersoft, representing the views of many others. "I still think governments need to be guardians of the infrastructure, but the people best suited to do that—the best and the brightest—are smart enough to stay away from politics." Many people with a desire to serve their communities think they will do so through their companies. A production worker at Merlin Metalworks declared, "I'm interested in doing something through business, not through politics. There is much more potential to affect the world through business."

But here's the rub: Although locals think businesses owe contributions to their communities, cosmopolitans may be less available to make them. Without deliberate civic action, globalization can separate cosmopolitans with clout, for whom the local community is no longer the single most important arena in which they operate, from those who champion local causes. Global economic forces can potentially fragment a community's leadership while diversifying it to include outsiders from around the world.

Those with power and resources no longer share civic interests as a matter of course, as they did when communities were run by cozy groups of downtown bankers, utility executives, lawyers, and real estate developers with a common desire to see their local markets grow.[7] Newer industries in emerging technology fields are often found in edge cities on the urban periphery, not downtown, with business horizons and social interests that are often international, not local. As demands on cosmopolitan leaders multiply and their geographic horizons expand, heads of local cultural, civic, and service organizations don't bump into business power holders as easily. And local facilities are increasingly owned by outside companies that may not understand the community, nor be understood by it.

Three trends in the global economy are important to those committed to the viability of communities: the changing role of corporate headquarters, the new leadership entering communities from foreign and domestic investors, and a shift of business policy toward "strategic philanthropy."

■ TREND #1: FROM SKYSCRAPERS TO AIRPLANES—THE DISPERSION OF CORPORATE HEADQUARTERS

Business leadership for most cities was once found on the upper floors of downtown skyscrapers where corporate headquarters were housed. Locally headquartered national or international companies could be counted on to provide the lion's share of civic leadership. Cities still have some of those lions. In Miami it is Alvah Chapman Jr., former chairman of Knight-Ridder, the newspaper chain; in Spartanburg, Roger Milliken, chairman of Milliken & Company, the textile giant.

Traditionally, a home-city bias brought extra benefits to cities housing the headquarters of large, prominent companies. Even today, locally headquartered companies contribute more to their communities, standing out even among the largest employers, as my research group discovered. Allison Hughes analyzed the community involvement of 180 companies in Boston, Cleveland, and Miami, comparing the 20 largest employers in each city in three categories by headquarters location: local, nonlocal but domestic, or foreign. Locally headquartered companies do most for the community on every measure: the largest corporate contributions to United Way (averaging about $75,000 more per year), the largest average contributions by individual employees to United Way, and the most active involvement by their leaders in prominent local civic and cultural organizations. Foreign-headquartered companies give the least to the community, averaging $14,000 less per year in United Way contributions and less activity in civic and cultural organizations. Their local employees give slightly less per person to United Way, but this difference is not statistically significant, indicating that headquarters location may not influence employees' individual actions as much as it influences a corporation's.[8]

The home-city headquarters advantage extends to noncharitable domains with major community impact. According to *Miami Herald* investigations, out-of-state banks made fewer total loans in Florida than in their home states through 1993. Barnett, the only Florida-headquartered bank among the state's top four, had the best record of Florida-wide lending but showed a home-city bias within Florida; with its headquarters in Jacksonville in northern Florida, its lending in Miami and South Florida counties lagged behind. Regulators are working hard to erase the home-community bias; a 1990 Massachusetts law requires out-of-state bank buyers to set aside nine-tenths of one percent of an acquired bank's assets for affordable housing loans.[9]

Companies often have a larger stake in the qualities of their headquarters city than elsewhere above and beyond the numbers employed there (which can be small compared to places housing production facilities) because of who comes in and out of headquarters. In larger companies top managers and professionals are recruited on a national and international basis; companies need to make sure that their home city has maximum amenities and minimum problems in order to compete for talent in a global labor market. Civic amenities and services are important for those posted at headquarters, rotating through it, or visiting it for meetings. Companies often put showcase operations or pilot ventures in the headquarters region, for convenient visits by top management and customers. Headquarters is a frequent destination for customers or suppliers, so the home city needs to have attractive facilities, entertainment, and transportation.

A Gillette executive explained why his global company makes such large contributions to local cultural and social service organizations in Boston: "Management people are sophisticated. It is important that we can move people worldwide in and out of our headquarters, that they can educate their kids well, find good housing and cultural attractions here. It is important that we don't have slums or crime. For this reason, we are a major contributor to the Boston social structure, way beyond the proportion of our business here."

For larger international companies, the headquarters advantage can extend, in more muted form, to the city housing a broad regional headquarters, such as Michelin's North American headquarters in South Carolina or the Latin American regional headquarters concentrated in Miami. The Miami area's regional headquarters tend to have larger work forces than mere offices of other multinational companies represented there, with an average of 186 employees for headquarters companies compared to 140 for the others.

For newer or smaller companies, the headquarters city is the lead site, if not the only one. Employment growth begins first at home, then other sites are established, sometimes as dispersed outposts with relatively few people each, such as the international sales and service centers Powersoft has developed. Only 60 percent of a book publishing company's employees are near headquarters, but almost 100 percent of its charitable giving and community service is concentrated there, because each of its operations elsewhere has a very small staff. Migration of a company's functions and facilities out of an area still holding its headquarters eventually reduces local giving, but philanthropy moves out more slowly than operations. Conversely, new facilities moving in will not always fill the community service gap left by facilities moving out unless a headquarters comes with them.

Community groups like having corporate headquarters in their city because they can deal with executives who define strategy, determine budgets, allocate company resources, have control over their time, and represent the prestige of the institution. One company reported flatly: "Our causes begin at headquarters."

Ambitious managers know that being at headquarters means being close to power; a Bank of Boston middle manager explains choosing his current downtown headquarters job over a better-paid job at a remote location because of career benefits from bumping into top management. Managers far from headquarters are sometimes unable to do things for their business operations, let alone for the community. A manager at "Southway" attributes part of his division's difficulties to its distance from headquarters: "We have to go thousands of miles to get approval of anything, not only financially, but strategically." Another agreed, "There's very little visibility here." In contrast, Boston area EG&G divisions are power advantaged because headquarters is only a short drive away. Corporate resources are readily available—for example, services from corporate compensation and legal staffs or use of a corporate training facility; middle managers are more likely to sit on corporate task forces, giving them access to top management. Those divisions' leaders are more powerful assets for their local communities because of headquarters proximity.

A headquarters gets more attention. Community institutions consider chief executives a more attractive catch for boards and leadership roles than local facility managers, even if the facility contains many more employees and has more economic impact than a small corporate headquarters. Divisions of companies headquartered elsewhere complain that the local press gives more coverage to locally headquartered companies.

Some managers in newer growth companies acknowledge the home-city bias and think it is appropriate. A Boston high-tech executive argued, "It's more likely for a company that is locally owned to contribute right back into the local community than it is for somebody out in California to say, 'Okay, We've got a subsidiary out in Boston, we want to make sure that the Boston community is well taken care of.' Look at us. We have a large office in Chicago, and I doubt if we contribute to the Chicago symphony or even the Chicago United Way."

THE INCREDIBLE SHRINKING HEADQUARTERS

Communities have relied on their local corporate headquarters for large civic contributions, and locally headquartered companies have had instrumental and sentimental reasons to contribute. Now traditional corporate headquarters are declining in number and importance, as industries consolidate, control passes out of local hands, and emerging technology companies locate in suburban edge cities rather than downtown. Those headquarters that remain are shrinking. Downsizing, reengineering, outsourcing, and decentralization cut the size of staffs and number of functions concentrated at headquarters and reduce image expenditures such as huge office towers with fancy offices. Information technology reduces the need for as frequent meetings. Home office executives now travel outward as much as, or more than, field managers come to headquarters; for some cosmopolitan companies, "headquarters" is split over several cities, one for each set of key functions.

Headquarters is, in effect, wherever the CEO goes. Corporate leaders are more easily found on airplanes than in the office, and aircraft are increasingly outfitted as offices, with notebook computers and air-to-ground telecommunications. I had a longer conversation with Ned Johnson, Fidelity Investment's chief executive, on a flight to Los Angeles than in his Boston office.

Cosmopolitan Gillette's headquarters, for example, is so discreet as to be almost invisible. Its lead manufacturing facility in South Boston displays a gargantuan sign proclaiming it "World Shaving Headquarters." But actual corporate headquarters occupies a dozen upper floors of an office tower with Prudential's name on it, hardly a monument to corporate power: there are no Gillette signs in entry elevators and no main reception floor. Meanwhile, CEO Alfred Zeien spends a large proportion of his time at Gillette offices around the world. Corporate offices stay in Boston because executives like to live there, but many local issues are irrelevant to Gillette.

Even with a shrinking corporate staff and an invisible headquarters, Gillette is an important financial contributor to its headquarters community. But it is only recently that Microsoft, the world's largest software company headed by one of the world's richest entrepreneurs, got serious about contributing to Seattle, appointing a community relations director. Newer technology companies have different, more global priorities than traditional industries. And consider an electronics company founded in another city several decades ago, growing to several billion dollars in sales and expanding to twenty-five countries. Corporate headquarters is an unmarked building in a suburban office park where just 150 people work, out of 34,000 worldwide. Some business units housed nearby report to a division headquarters thousands of miles away. The company does little in its home city with respect to philanthropy and service. An important community charity is allowed to make a presentation to employees on company premises, but there are no payroll deductions for contributions. An executive said, "We don't think of ourselves as a company based here; we could be operated anywhere. We do not depend on a local work force or access to a local river. We are members of the Chamber [of Commerce], we pay dues, that's it."

When headquarters shrink in importance, headquarters advantages for a community decline. Texaco Latin America headquarters remains in the Miami suburb of Coral Gables because of close proximity to Miami International Airport, good communications links to Latin

America, and Miami's bilingual work force. But this regional headquarters, once a major supporter of Miami causes, downsized in 1993 from 250 to 180 jobs, giving more control to new field centers in Rio de Janeiro and Bogotá. As a consequence, Texaco's corporate giving to Miami-area cultural and civic groups was reduced considerably, upsetting local organizations anticipating continuing large contributions. Donations now go to Brazil, home to 1,600 employees. "From now on, we will make contributions in South Florida that are more in line for a company with less than two hundred employees in the community," president Clarence Cazalot said.[10]

Some cities face a civic leadership crisis with the loss of traditional headquarters. Downtown banks, utilities, newspapers, retail stores, and professional firms are being acquired by outside companies, and regional general managers for companies headquartered elsewhere are losing power as companies organize around product or customer type, not geography. In Boston this shows up in reduced contributions to charities such as United Way and a growing inability to find chief executives who can make significant commitments to civic causes.

There is a wide gap in interests between Boston's downtown banks and utilities whose markets are local and regional and Boston's Route 128 high-technology companies in the suburbs and beyond that are "born global." Newer technology companies are cosmopolitans that must be industry innovators and pacesetters, comparing themselves to companies everywhere in the world and planning expansions out of the region and into international markets. Local affairs and local recognition are much less important to them. They often complain about the local political and civic environment but are not really dependent on it. They have strong ties within their industry and with industry associations, but they have much less involvement with more general civic organizations. Their philanthropy is determined by their employees, and it differs from that of traditional downtown companies because employees tend to be younger. They are less interested in established cultural organizations and more interested in social causes, less interested in charity balls and more interested in charity runs.

Some cities cope with these changes better than others. Cleveland Tomorrow, an organization of CEOs of the fifty-six largest companies in the area, meets regularly to ensure that local concerns are high priorities for cosmopolitan companies. It has an active ambassadors program in which CEOs encourage their peers from outside the area to locate new facilities in Cleveland, including North American headquarters of international companies, which provides replacements for companies that disperse globally. Similarly, the Greater Seattle Chamber of Commerce can attract three hundred business heads, public officials, and civic leaders to off-site leadership conferences to create community development plans. But in other cities, civic leadership and community institutions have not caught up with the new realities.

▪ TREND #2: FROM FAMILIAR TO FOREIGN LEADERSHIP

In most American cities, business leaders were once a highly "familiar" group. They were often well known to each other and the community, because they were part of a stable, culturally homogeneous elite linked by long-standing relationships, knowledgeable about and committed to the community and active in shaping its agenda and norms. This leadership group was sometimes closed and exclusionary, as with so-called Yankee Brahmins in Boston or South Carolina's country club set. Foreigners in these cities were often blue-collar immigrants in ethnic enclaves.

Now globalization has changed the business composition of American communities, confronting local institutions with leaders who are unfamiliar—"foreign" in the metaphorical as well as the literal sense. Nonlocal ownership of major businesses continues to increase.[11] In some places new foreign residents include wealthy investors or expatriate managers. Foreign acquisitions of U.S. companies have increased dramatically since the 1980s, and international companies have built new operations in American communities. In 1990, 446 such acquisitions, valued at $46.2 billion, were completed, compared with only 126 deals valued at $4.6 billion in 1982. Foreign acquisitions of U.S. companies accounted for 28.1 percent of the total value of merger and acquisition activity in 1990, compared with only 7.6 percent in 1982.[12] In South Carolina, a great deal of new investment comes from outside the United States. In Cleveland, Sohio, a major community force, became British Petroleum America. What's more, much of this has been sought by local communities; cities and regions compete to attract new companies, domestic or foreign.

Now local workers as well as community residents must accommodate to leaders with far-flung ties, a distant headquarters, potentially different behaviors or expectations, and weaker attachment to this particular community. When German and Swiss companies started facilities in South Carolina, the heads of the American units had to convince European bosses of the need for budgets for local community service, something that was not part of European tradition. A Boston law firm acquired by an out-of-state firm had to fight to continue its $50,000 annual donation to a poverty law program; the other state had no such program, and the new parent was not accustomed to such donations.

Even when they strive to become insiders, cosmopolitans from outside the community confront it with new issues. The transition period following the entry of outsiders can be stressful. Uncertainties arise about commitment to local needs; expatriates may be transients. Opportunities for misunderstandings abound; cultural differences in work styles or ideas about the proper relationship between managers and workers become apparent. Curious, or suspicious, community residents scrutinize the actions of newcomer companies.

Whether or not companies signal community commitment affects their welcome; whether or not they are welcomed affects their community commitment. See this self-reinforcing cycle at work in cases involving French and Japanese companies, from cultures some Americans find most aloof and convinced of their own superiority.

ST. GOBAIN'S FIVE-YEAR PROMISE

The issue of foreign leadership is most contentious where it replaces familiar, homegrown leadership through takeovers of locally headquartered companies. Foreign acquirers of local companies are greeted more positively when they rescue a troubled business, save local jobs, know the technology, add new investment, allow local operational autonomy, convey respect for local traditions and know-how, and improve financial performance.[13] In short, reactions are positive if things don't change much, except for the better.

The "skyscraper" of downtown Worcester, just west of Boston, Norton Company was long the most important local company and a major contributor to the community, so locals aided Norton in its defense against a hostile takeover by Britain's BTR.[14] St. Gobain, a leading French company, acted as a white knight and stepped in to acquire Norton in 1990. Because community responsibility and protection of employee welfare were key concerns in the BTR battle, St. Gobain promised to honor Norton's commitments to the community even though this was not part of French corporate tradition. St. Gobain increased budgets for training and philanthropy and developed an innovative employee-centered approach to community service. Norton's new French expatriate chief, Claude-Alain Tardy, joined bank boards and Worcester community leadership. A Stanford-educated cosmopolitan, Tardy impressed locals with his ability to fit in with Americans.

Rather than dismissing the French as different, Norton employees display understanding of differences that could affect St. Gobain's sense of community responsibility. "Certainly over in France the government does a lot more for its people—more than our government might do," one said. Knocking on wood in a focus group, a manager praised St. Gobain for promising that it would not interfere with employee benefits or change Norton's charitable contributions to the Worcester area for five years following the acquisition.

Norton's extensive community volunteer program has been extended under St. Gobain. Employees are encouraged to volunteer their time to Little League, the Police Club, Worcester Fights Back (an antidrug coalition), United Way, disadvantaged children, or other local causes; selected employees are rewarded with thousand-dollar contributions to the organizations they support. "You can't always just take off from work," a professional reported, "but I've been encouraged to volunteer my time, and that hasn't stopped since St. Gobain took over."

Some are apprehensive, however, about the five-year contract's expiration and wonder whether community service will be reduced. Noting that philanthropy at Certainteed, another American company that St. Gobain has owned for over a decade, is less extensive than Norton's, a professional worries about whether this is a function of French ownership or Certainteed's relatively smaller corporate presence in its community.

HONDA IN OHIO

To get new cosmopolitans to contribute to communities, local leaders must bend to accommodate them, and locals must also learn to think beyond the boundaries of their particular neighborhood.

Honda of America began car production in the small town of Marysville, Ohio, near Columbus, in November 1982. The facility became a success story among Japanese auto transplants for its use of American workers and equipment to create a high-productivity factory, outperforming some Japanese plants and exporting over 40,000 American-built Hondas to seventeen countries a decade later. The Marysville factory produces 360,000 cars a year, more than any single North American plant. Year by year Honda has increased its American raw material and parts suppliers from 27 companies selling Honda $13.5 million worth of goods in 1982 to 320 companies and $3.21 billion; Honda also exports U.S. auto suppliers' products to Japan.

Honda has had significant positive impact on Marysville and the surrounding area, but it took considerable work to harmonize the interests of cosmopolitans and locals. Local politicians, seeing their power potentially eroded by the superior resources of an international company, were among the most threatened by the foreign influx, community residents reported. At first flattered to attract Honda, Marysville locals soon looked for signs that the newcomers valued community ways as much as the town valued the company. Many seemed to feel that welcoming newcomers should not entail changing local habits. "Early on they said we're building a new Kroger's supermarket with Japanese signs, because Honda was coming," one recalled. "And I remember taking real offense to that. When I lived in Switzerland a year, they didn't put up any English signs for me." Anecdotes underlining Honda's "foreign" culture and work pace circulated soon after the factory opened: about the man afraid to stop working even after an on-the-job injury or the woman who waited two hours until breaktime to return the call when her daughter was giving birth.

Because expectations were so high for Honda's community contributions, Marysville locals set themselves up for disappointment, even though Honda has done a great deal. Small businesses expected a dramatic increase in their sales, town officials thought downtown decay would be reversed, taxpayers assumed that the public schools would have a large benefactor to underwrite improvements. As in other places offering incentives to attract foreign investment, locals resented special treatment for Honda. Making matters worse, some local residents abdicated their own responsibilities. "Everybody thinks Honda is going to foot the bill, so they just sit back and won't vote for school levies," a community leader said. "I hear daily we're that rich school district in central Ohio that has Honda. And the only thing that Honda has done for the school system is increase the property value and taxation." Another commented, "Honda is resented for not fixing things. But without the economic vitality brought by Honda, the downtown infrastructure would have declined still further. We'd look like the inner city if not for Honda."

Marysville residents wanted Honda to do things for their schools; nearby Worthington residents saw their schools do things for Honda. Honda's Japanese expatriates and American managers from outside the area found school districts in Worthington able to provide Japanese-language classes, Saturday schools, English-language instruction, and other educational programs that Marysville schools would not or could not offer. Worthington schools had previous experience adapting curricula to the needs of children raised in other cultures or offering advanced language programs; this had influenced an American Nestlé manager's choice of Worthington when returning from Europe, where his children had become fluent in French. Worthington retail stores list prices in Japanese as well as in English.

The result of the Honda managers' preference for particular school districts is hardly academic. In choosing to live in Columbus suburbs like Worthington instead of Marysville, cosmopolitan managers commit more than their children's educations; they concentrate their own community involvement and the largesse of their company in the places they reside, diluting contributions to the place they work. A Marysville resident lamented, "Honda of America has contributed so much to the Columbus Symphony Orchestra's program in Columbus-area public schools, when they have a culturally deprived county in Marysville. Why are they shipping money to Greater Columbus? And then I realize that's where most of their children go to school."

During its early years in Ohio, Honda sent the Marysville school principal along with an administrator from each neighboring school district to Japan for eight days to sight-see and tour Honda's Japanese facilities but discontinued the program after managers were settled in other towns. Some local leaders think Honda, as a visible international company, wants to avoid preferential treatment for any one community; should Honda give its obsolete, Dumpster-bound computers to Marysville schools, one argued, it would have to give them to every town in the area. Others in a focus group found this a weak argument.

Marysville's locals are often hard-pressed to define an "appropriate" level of contribution. What is the metric—monetary value? Honda donates cars for raffles and motorcycles for the sheriff. Honda financed a new fire station and other public facilities, which also helps Honda, since now the emergency fire squad is routinely available and public buildings offer conference space. Is that what being a good neighbor means?

Or perhaps this foreign company's contributions lie not in traditional measures of civic giving to any one town, but in other forms of service. Honda has brought to Marysville an awareness of advanced manufacturing processes and management techniques, providing an opportunity for members of the work force not employed by Honda to enrich their vocational skills. A local vocational school won a multimillion-dollar Honda contract for customized training, proceeds from which support programs for non-Honda workers. Honda sends its associates to run its Total Quality Management courses for teachers and town administrators.

Locals can derive benefits from the presence of cosmopolitan companies, but not always the ones they were expecting.

INCLUSIVE OUTREACH

To help their cities win the competition for outside or foreign investment and to remain viable as leadership shifts from always "familiar" to sometimes "foreign," local community institutions must understand and cope with different expectations; they must be willing to change their process and priorities, perhaps adding programs, changing their approach to community service, accepting new kinds of contributions, or working in partnership with neighboring communities.

Leadership groups need to change the faces at the top and help outsiders become insiders. Community leadership needs to move beyond small groups of long established downtown companies that once formed the power elite. Unless outsiders or foreigners are welcomed into leadership groups, they cannot be expected to make decisions in the best interests of the community, nor can their global resources and international expertise be tapped. Business cosmopolitans, for their part, become insiders when they demonstrate commitment to the local community.

Traditional local leaders sometimes justify their exclusivity by complaining that newcomers, whoever they are, do not do enough, while not giving them the chance by excluding them from leadership circles. As Cubans became more prominent in Miami, for example, there were complaints that the Cuban-Americans did not contribute enough. An Anglo lawyer said, "The Cubans have been here over twenty years, they have made great economic strides, the kids play football and baseball, they go to the operas, they do all these things; why not give more to the community?"[15] At the same time, Cuban-Americans complained of exclusion to sociologists Alejandro Portes and Alex Stepick, who wrote: "In 1987, only two of the top twenty-five Dade corporations were run by Cuban-Americans. . . . Cuban-American managers also began to confront a serious 'glass ceiling' to advance in such local giants as Southern Bell, Florida Power and Light, Knight-Ridder, Ryder System, and Barnett and Southeast Banks. And Cuban membership in local establishment circles such as the Orange Bowl Committee were minimal."[16] Eventually this changed, but not soon enough for some people.

Instead of waiting to be admitted to elite circles, Cuban-Americans sought and won political power. Now other Miami Latins say that community service is an important responsibility. German Leiva, Colombian-born head of the Miami Free Zone corporation, explained: "Here we have a lot of people from different places in the world. I would like them to become more familiar with the community and more involved with it. Not everybody from Latin America wants to cooperate in the progress of the community, because the kind of community involvement that is here in the United States is not so normal in other countries. In many countries, they believe that they pay taxes so things should be done for them; they feel that the government should take care of everything. But here I have learned to work with the government. If you want to live in this country, you must do something for your community."

When newcomers foreign to community ways are welcomed, they can also be educated to the norms of the community. South Carolina's training network, for example, offers a course for foreign companies in "corporate community relations" that helps them learn how to become a local contributor. Equally important is that local institutions know how to include them, in light of shifts in the way all companies approach community service.

■ TREND #3: FROM UNFOCUSED CHARITY TO STRATEGIC PHILANTHROPY

Corporate community service was once a matter of signing up top executives for boards and boosterism supported by other top executives in the area, and corporate philanthropy was once an automatic form of noblesse oblige to any group in a company's neighborhood. It was largely diffuse or reactive; companies often gave small amounts of time or money to large numbers of groups, and executives dutifully showed up for the right civic luncheons and charity balls. Causes came looking for money more than companies went searching for causes.

Now globalization of business, dispersion of headquarters to more distant locations, and entry of foreign companies and outside managers join with business belt-tightening to make the old system harder to sustain. The head of a prominent financial services company had only scathing words for the old-style pressure to participate in activities he considers meaningless just to prove community loyalty: "I don't like the constant stream of foolish cocktail parties where you sit around 'doing good'—charitable events where you have to drink until after midnight. To say that's a social obligation is sick. I don't want to encourage our executives to do that." He mistrusts executives who seem to have the time to do all those "civic things"; why don't their businesses get their attention?

In the global economy, community service has become another set of weapons in the strategic arsenal, more intimately connected with the business mission, more highly integrated with a variety of business functions, and sometimes not even local in scope. This is one more blow to smaller, locally focused causes; they cannot count on support from cosmopolitan companies just because they are in the neighborhood. Cosmopolitan companies with national and international customers may look outside their local home for national or international causes to sponsor, detaching themselves from the needs of their home communities. Locals sometimes resent the contrast between the wealth some companies dispense elsewhere and the problems at those companies' doorsteps.

Community involvement has long been a source of political connections and goodwill. Companies still create a positive aura in the eyes of consumers, voters, or local government officials through community contributions and other forms of good corporate citizenship. To engender support for entry into a small town west of Boston, Wal-Mart established community credentials by paying for road improvements, buying half a billion dollars in products from Massachusetts vendors, giving almost $150,000 in charitable contributions to state charities, establishing scholarship funds, and working with local police on youth antidrug programs.[17] When entire blocks of businesses were burned and looted during 1992's Los Angeles riots, neighborhood residents protected McDonald's stores because of their franchisees' reputation for community service projects such as the Ronald McDonald House for sick children. Joanna Lau, CEO of Lau Technologies, noted a benefit to smaller companies from local community service: "Neighbors come to understand the business; if you need something, it's not the first time they've seen you."

Community service has also long had marketing benefits. The most significant local charitable givers are often those with the highest visibility in local consumer markets: banks, insurance companies, retailers, newspapers. For professional firms, pro bono service supports marketing goals; before lawyers could advertise, they could become known through civic and charitable involvement. "Cause marketing," which displays a company's altruism to consumers, is a new variant of this; one example is the advertising campaign by For Eyes, a Miami optical chain, to raise its profile by featuring its stand on homelessness, racism, oil spills, and gun control. But the visibility of community service causes other companies to seek "safe," noncontroversial charities.

Some companies see that community contributions build markets in the longer term. "Community service helps us cultivate customers. We will have no customers unless the community is vital," a prominent banker said. Alvah Chapman Jr., former CEO of Knight-Ridder in Miami, also linked community service to business interest in a vital economy: "You can't publish a successful newspaper in a community that's dying on the vine. If you want a successful company that's involved in the community, and a newspaper certainly is, then you have to contribute to that community's success, too."[18]

As the need grows to link community service to business strategy, companies seek more focus and impact. Just as they want fewer suppliers that can serve their needs in more places, they want more payoff from their ties to communities, especially when they face other demands on their resources from many more places. Most companies report increased scrutiny of their contributions to ensure that they support areas of concern for their particular business, do things that matter, and get recognition for their contributions. Ira Jackson, Bank of Boston's senior vice president for government and community affairs, said, "We want to make a difference, not just play a part. We were giving to too many causes at too modest a level. It didn't make much difference, and our dollars were undifferentiated. Now we want to leverage our investments. We want to support new initiatives with greater promise to have impact; nonprofits that are reinventing themselves; and replications, so we see a yield beyond one site. And we want recognition, like when we hire one hundred kids from an inner-city high school during a downsizing."

To ensure maximum impact, companies could form partnerships with counterparts to concentrate on a small number of projects, but because companies tie community service to their own strategies and business needs, interests and priorities may diverge and collaboration be made more complicated. Advocates for local causes must find a rationale that appeals to companies in diverse industries whose markets do not overlap. And strategic philanthropy can make civic collaboration more difficult when companies want to "brand" causes with their own name. As one executive said, "We would like to do more collaborating. But companies want to get the credit; they don't want to share the limelight and dilute publicity. Only the creator of the alliance gets the credit when others join."

Some companies concentrate on growing their own market by contributing products and industry expertise. A book publisher needs readers, so it sponsors literacy programs, essay contests in schools, and a children's library at a hospital, donating books as well as contributing cash. Telecommunications network companies need demonstration sites, so a set of Boston-area equipment manufacturers, including homegrown technology star Wellfleet Communications and global giant AT&T, teamed to donate technology, training, and engineering support to the New England Shelter for Homeless Veterans for a voice and data network eventually connecting homeless shelters nationwide.

Market-building goals are likely to take larger companies away from their local communities to the places potential customers reside. To help with entry into the South African software market, Lotus created a foundation to assist black communities with projects involving information technology, including internships for black programming trainees.[19] Strategic philanthropy can thus dictate a global, not local, context for giving, reinforcing a company's movement away from support of particular local causes. Corporations may find it in their interest to adopt national or international causes that transcend particular areas, to appeal to customers anywhere in the world, like Reebok's international human rights awards: global philanthropy paralleling global advertising campaigns.

It is easier to focus new cosmopolitans on local issues that affect business transactions. In Cleveland, where business leaders are particularly collaborative, William Butler, CEO of Eaton, long an international exporter whose founder, Cyrus Eaton, was famous for involvement in foreign affairs, heads the group that put together Cleveland's World Trade Center. But even in this domain, some communities find it hard to get consensus on priorities for civic improvements or raise money for them because industry interests are so variable. Traditional downtown CEO-studded groups are sometimes accused of losing relevance in the new economy.

The one goal for community service on which cosmopolitans and locals can agree is employee relations: supporting employees who live in a community in their service to it, making them feel proud to work for the company because of what it contributes to local quality of life. Employee interest now drives the philanthropic decisions of many companies; an electronics company has shifted its support from the symphony to rock concerts because of associates' preferences and from large downtown organizations to small local organizations in outlying areas where most employees live.

Job pressures and work overload drive some employees to rely on the company as the locus of their own community involvement. A software company marketer who works during holidays on new product launches misses the volunteering she used to do for food banks at Christmas and Thanksgiving and is grateful that the company offers chances to contribute toys or gifts when she can't give time.

Community service as an employee benefit is one way to engage, or reengage, cosmopolitans in local communities, as long as the definition of "community" is broad and inclusive, transcending neighborhoods and city lines. As in the Honda case, a corporate facility's location is not necessarily the community in which its employees reside or to which they feel attached.

CIVIC ENGAGEMENT: THE CITY YEAR MODEL

The new realities of the global economy challenge community institutions to think in more cosmopolitan ways: overcoming parochialism and isolation, bringing leaders together, pooling resources and effort, and involving employees at all levels in taking actions to enhance quality of life, solve problems, and ensure amenities and services that attract and hold cosmopolitan companies. Perhaps the very idea of business philanthropy and community service, which has connotations of arm's length noblesse oblige, needs to be replaced by broader notions of civic engagement: how to involve businesses of all kinds, global or local, in partnerships to take responsibility for communities in ways that respond to the shifts in business interests.

One creative model for civic engagement is City Year. Founded by Harvard Law School graduates Alan Khazei and Michael Brown in Boston in 1988 as a private-sector domestic Peace Corps, City Year has since expanded to Providence, Chicago, Columbus, San Jose, and Columbia, South Carolina. As a model for America's national youth service program, its impact resonates not only in improvements to the communities its corps members serve, but also through the lives of corps members, the involvement of employees of corporate sponsors, and the building of civic collaborations.

City Year's six hundred corps members, aged seventeen to twenty-three, earn $125 per week during their year of service and receive a $4,725 grant for college or a $4,000 savings bond on graduation. Corps members begin each day with calisthenics in a high-profile downtown location, then disperse with their team to work areas, where they might assist public school or day care teachers, serve meals to elders, run recycling programs, or create a health immunization tracking system. Privileged suburbanites serve on teams alongside inner-city youth, enabling friendships to form across class and race lines. In 1994, of the 606 corps members in six sites chosen from over 1,500 applicants, 49 percent were female, 43 percent white, 29 percent African-American, 16 percent Latino, and 7 percent Asian-American. To graduate, corps members must learn first aid and CPR, learn to write a résumé and file taxes, get a library card, and register to vote, and corps members without high school diplomas must participate in City Year's GED program. Graduate Stephen Noltemy declared, "City Year saved my life."

City Year's activities are performed in partnership with social service agencies, neighborhood groups, public schools, and other community institutions that define projects for corps members as well as for adult volunteers who turn out for Serve-a-Thons, periodic days of service. In Boston, the 1994 Serve-a-Thon included 10,000 volunteers washing 5,839 windows, painting 15 miles of walls and 53 schools, cleaning 465 elders' apartments, beautifying 35 parks, and salvaging 11 tons of food at 296 sites.

Corporate partners contribute service as well as money. Bank of Boston was the first company to sponsor a City Year team for $25,000 and eventually gave nearly $600,000, supporting teams whose City Year uniforms bear the bank's logo; in addition, five hundred bank employees regularly participate in Serve-a-Thons. "What could we lose?" senior vice president Ira Jackson recalled. "It had all the right elements: urban Peace Corps, kids, help the city." City Year also attracts cosmopolitan companies located far outside the city that have come back downtown to serve it, including Digital Equipment, Reebok, and Timberland, just across the New Hampshire line from Boston, which provides the outfits for corps members.

Jeffrey Swartz, Timberland's chief operating officer and City Year's board chair, feels that Timberland's partnership with City Year has transformed his company's culture. Timberland's personnel policies guarantee associates at least four service days a year on company time. Performing community service together through City Year is an important way Timberland develops its internal working teams; City Year staff have also run City Year's team-building sessions for Timberland employees. Other payoffs for sponsors include recruitment benefits; high-tech companies find that innovative programs allowing employees to volunteer help attract idealistic young engineers to Boston.

City Year not only brings edge-city companies back downtown, it draws companies into the service fold that have not traditionally contributed to local communities. This includes airplane-oriented consulting firms, whose professionals may be in their home cities only on weekends; now a set of Boston consulting firms jointly sponsor a City Year team. By encouraging active employee participation, rather than approaching companies only for fund-raising, City Year offers a model for engaging businesses in the community that responds to new realities.

Any number can sponsor teams, which allows many companies to put their brand on an activity or take pride in what their people do at Serve-a-Thons. Breadth of sponsorship is a City Year value, because it increases civic engagement. City Year has received federal funding from the national service program, valuing the model of a decentralized organization that matches public funds with local contributions. City Year operates a national program that is really "multilocal": communities concentrating on their own needs but learning from one another.

City Year is well endowed with the three C's that enrich the world class: its core concept is innovative, and staff are encouraged to be entrepreneurial in seeking new concepts; its organizational competence is built around constant learning; and its connections become the basis for three-way partnerships among public, private, and nonprofit sectors. The City Year model is successful because it concentrates the resources of many organizations on high priority problems, and it engages many organizations and many people in the work of their community. Similar models are at work elsewhere; in Great Britain, Prince's Trust Volunteers links community service to employability by offering skills training for unemployed youth as well as job holders through community project teams backed by one hundred large British employers.

THE NEW BUSINESS-COMMUNITY RELATIONS

The global economy compels a broader conception of community and of business leadership in it. The new conception should include greater local engagement while recognizing the needs of cosmopolitan companies. It should be equated not simply with money, but with involvement in activities that contribute to quality of life. It should include people at all levels from companies that differ in size, industry, and geographic scope.

As traditional sources of leadership dry up, communities must welcome and adjust to new sources of civic talent. Advocates for local causes must draw connections between their actitivies and issues of concern to cosmopolitans; strictly parochial causes diminish in appeal. Because business leaders who give time and money may expect more complex and collaborative relationships with objects of their largesse, small organizations operating alone are disadvantaged. Independent, isolated organizations will not have sufficient impact to secure resources and survive. Partnerships need to be forged among civic organizations, paralleling the business networks of the world class.

For communities to thrive in the global economy, locals cannot turn their backs on it; they must determine how best to convert global trends into local advantages.

PART FOUR

MAKING THE GLOBAL ECONOMY WORK LOCALLY

Cosmopolitan companies have the world as their playing field and their choice of the world's best places. Communities must determine how to attract, support, and hold them in order to ensure a viable economy and quality of life that links locals to global success, while meeting the challenges of encouraging cosmopolitan outlooks, providing greater employability security, and developing leadership for civic needs.

The best cities are places where businesses and people learn better and develop faster than they otherwise would, because they are centers of the three C's—the key global assets of concepts, competence, and connections. By concentrating on a particular asset, cities can become preeminent in one of three generic ways: as thinkers, makers, or traders.

As an archetypal thinker, the Boston area specializes in concepts—in knowledge-based industries that innovate, creating and developing new ideas and technologies that command a premium in world markets. As makers, Spartanburg and Greenville, South Carolina, specialize in operational competence—quality processes executed by a skilled production work force to manufacture goods or handle back room operations, attracting new foreign as well as domestic investors. Miami's traders specialize in connections; they preside at the crossroads of countries and cultures, brokering between them, moving commerce across borders.

I chose these places as models of emerging international cities because they are nearly pure types in their emphasis on one core capability. Each illustrates the elements for economic success as a thinker, maker, or trader, but each also has community problems and limitations that must be addressed if its success is to continue. Their stories offer lessons for businesses and cities everywhere about how to harness global forces for local advantage.

Thinkers: The Brains of Boston

Try this trivia question. Which of the following four schools was ranked number one in computer engineering by engineering school deans in a *U.S. News & World Report* survey: Stanford, Cal Tech, Carnegie Mellon, or Massachusetts Institute of Technology?

If you chose MIT, the correct answer, then you came out ahead of two teams of computer experts at the 1994 Computer Bowl, a competition sponsored by Boston's Computer Museum and reminiscent of the once popular television *G.E. College Bowl*. Both teams, one from the East Coast and one from the West, flunked the question.

It is appropriate that a city whose global strength comes from developing new concepts plays brain-oriented games. But this particular failure to get the answer right was a revealing moment for Boston and symbolic of a belief held by many who should know better, that Boston's high-technology time had passed.

In fact, Boston, with its rich history and knowledge-based economy, stands for one version of local success in the global economy: people and companies that flourish through the application of brainpower. Thinkers are preeminent in the first important resource of the world class: concepts. They are characterized by innovation, developing new ideas and products that set world standards.

Boston is a place where knowledge industries are key and economic success derives from knowledge-based innovation. Boston, with about six hundred thousand people in the city itself and some three million in the metropolitan area (which includes about three-fifths of the Massachusetts population and extends to New Hampshire and Rhode Island), is a patchwork of colleges and universities, hospitals and medical centers, software companies and consulting firms, surrounded by technology-based industries.

As is the nature of thinkers, Boston's commercial personality is more oriented toward professionals than business, more toward technology than mass production. The area is first in the United States in the number of physicians per capita and second in lawyers per capita.[1] The Boston area's best industries tend to be knowledge intensive, high quality, more customized, and also more expensive, because they represent new ideas. Many of the area's technology companies are defined by process, not product, and by technology, not market. One company, for example, uses the same fiber-optic technology to help surgeons look inside the body and to make street signs.

Boston is a magnet for brainpower and exports many knowledge-based products, but its vitality is often not adequately captured in statistics. Concepts derived from its thinkers command a premium in world markets; that is why Boston per capita income is among the nation's highest and income inequality relatively low. Expertise is also one of the area's large exports, something that is impossible to measure in its full financial impact in the global economy because trade in services is not tracked adequately by government statistics. Boston's education and health care are widely admired; on Cleveland's Citizens League benchmarking of Cleveland against thirteen other cities, Boston scored number one in "educational opportunities and work force preparedness" and in "caring people and healthy lives."[2]

As is also true of thinkers, an area dependent on innovation in concepts is only as good as its last good idea. Thus the Boston area has been characterized by comebacks; it is periodically written off, only to bounce back again. The city was hit hard by defense industry cutbacks in the 1970s, but when unemployed engineers left the state, an engineering shortage a few years later threatened to undermine an impressive renaissance in new high-technology industries. In 1988 the

Massachusetts comeback was dubbed a "miracle," but in 1990 the state was in financial disarray and the Boston area was soon hit harder by a national recession than other parts of the United States. Then it bounced back again, faster than most, with Massachusetts leading other industrial states in job creation in 1994.

The Boston story shows how a community whose global capability is thinking can continually renew itself. Cycles are inevitable but comebacks dependable.

THE COMEBACK CITY

From 1930 until 1980 the city of Boston experienced half a century of population stagnation and decline, but the 1980s brought a new wave of growth, immigration, and capital expansion. Several historical shifts marked the change, including the shift of the textile and leather industries to the South. In the 1950s and 1960s Boston had a garment manufacturing center in what is now a well-established medical area. In 1960 the city underwent extensive urban renewal thanks in part to a steady flow of federal money.

There was a shift away from manufacturing in the city, which was centered in outlying towns and in developing high-tech edge cities. In 1969 Boston's share of employment in service activities was out in front of the nation's thirty-four largest cities at 45 percent; by 1984 the number grew to 57 percent, with San Francisco and New York close behind. In 1993 half a million people were employed within the city limits, almost exclusively in services: 92,000 in government; 73,000 in finance, insurance, and real estate; 199,000 in other services; 68,000 in wholesale and retail trade; 31,000 in transportation, communication and utilities; and only 29,000 in manufacturing.[3]

The early part of the 1990s saw the end of the boom in the area a few years earlier described as the center of a "miracle." *Site Selection* magazine reported that from 1990 to 1992 only 48 new business facilities took root in Massachusetts out of nearly 12,000 nationwide. The state of Ohio, by contrast, had 770 new ones. Massachusetts lost a third of its manufacturing jobs between 1984 and 1994—213,000 in all. In 1991 Massachusetts ranked forty-fifth among states in capital investment per manufacturing worker; of the 277,000 jobs lost in Massachusetts between 1989 and 1991, a disproportionate number of losses occurred in manufacturing. Some argue that this loss of manufacturing jobs was due primarily to a technology shift in computers and cutbacks in defense spending and was not caused by a failure to modernize or by job displacement to lower-wage areas.

But whatever spin economic analysts put on it, the hard truth was indisputable: the boom ended as many well-known industry giants toppled. Perhaps the most poignant and visible symbol was Digital Equipment, which laid off tens of thousands of workers and lost a whopping $5.9 billion over a four-year period beginning with the fiscal year ending June 1991. But there were others as well. Wang Laboratories, which had reported almost $3 billion in sales and 31,000 employees in 1988, five years later declared bankruptcy and had 6,200 employees. The decline of the computer giants was reflected not only in the layoffs, but also in the fire sale price for which the Wang headquarters building sold. The cost of the building was between 55 and 60 million dollars; it sold at auction in February 1994 for $525,000, a paltry 35 cents a square foot.

Massachusetts had also been a leader in high-performance computing, especially in the advanced parallel-processing niche where it had a 50 percent market share, translating to 5.1 percent of a high-performance computing market projected to reach $5.7 billion by 1996. But by 1994 Boston's niche was looking shaky indeed. Kendall Square was mired in financial problems, and the much lauded Thinking Machines filed for bankruptcy.

A study done for the Massachusetts Taxpayers Foundation examined twenty-one national growth industries that sell to out-of-state markets and concluded that Massachusetts was losing its employment share in those industries. In 1976 the state accounted for 5.4 percent of national employment in growth industries that sell to out-of-state markets; the number rose to 6.0 percent in 1984 but by 1992 had dropped to 4.9 percent. Only money management, software, and the drug industry (including some biotech) increased. The study distinguished low technology, which can be located anywhere, from high technology, which is dependent on special science and engineering talent. Boston, with its wealth of universities and network of suppliers, is a perfect match for high-tech industry: the area supports custom job shops for specialized components and wholesalers who stock wide varieties of them, along with a highly skilled professional work force. But for low-tech companies, high costs of doing business can make it unattractive.[4]

There are also geographic explanations for the slowdown of growth in Boston: the entire region stretching from northern Rhode Island to southern New Hampshire simply ran out of room. When the economy was expanding, there were few good places left to locate growing companies and create new jobs. Then, as personal computers cannibalized minicomputers and defense spending declined, costs had risen to what some called prohibitive levels—the costs of energy, waste disposal, automobile insurance, and workers' compensation. Earlier economic surges boosted housing prices so high that growth was dampened; even at the height of the boom only ten thousand home-building permits were issued annually in the Boston area because of lack of land or restrictions.[5]

In 1984, Massachusetts, with 2 percent of the population, accounted for 15 percent of employment in computers in the United States. However, Route 128, the beltway that circles the city and embraces many of its technology companies, quickly lost ground to Silicon Valley, in part because West Coast companies like Hewlett-Packard and Sun adopted miniaturization and open systems before Massachusetts companies such as Digital Equipment. AnnaLee Saxenian, a bicoastal researcher, argued that Silicon Valley moved ahead of the Boston area because Route 128 had a rigid and closed business style dominated by a few giants, while Silicon Valley operated a flexible, fluid network where job-hopping, experimentation, collective learning, and risk taking were all encouraged. High-technology employment grew dramatically in Silicon Valley and began to overtake Route 128 beginning about 1975, according to census data. By 1990 Silicon Valley's high-tech work force numbered 260,000, while Route 128 had 150,000. By the early 1990s Silicon Valley housed thirty-nine of the United States' fastest-growing electronics companies, while Route 128 was fourth, lagging behind Southern California and Texas with only four such companies.[6]

Moreover, Silicon Valley was not Boston's only competition. The success of Silicon Valley and Route 128 spawned attempts to duplicate other high-tech hot spots in the United States, including Silicon Gulch in Austin, Texas; the Research Triangle in North Carolina; Silicon Bayou in Lafayette, Louisiana; and Robot Alley in Florida. Factors like low development costs, positive attitudes toward entrepreneurs, strong local school systems, and mild climate eventually led to both the rise of Austin, Texas, and the Research Triangle and to the decline of

Silicon Valley and Route 128.[7] Many of the federally sponsored megaprojects went to Texas, which landed the Microelectronics and Computer Center for Austin over Massachusetts's bid, and to Florida, which far outpaced the Boston area in space research. By 1989 New England had only 2 percent of the nation's space research dollars. Between 1987 and 1991 New England's share of total university research funding, long the highest per capita in the nation, fell by 14 percent, and MIT lost a federal magnet research lab to Florida State University.

Around 1994 a comeback began to be recognizable, and Boston became part of an economic renaissance that inched its way through the wreckage left by the bankruptcies, foreclosures, and layoffs of the early 1990s. Service industries continued to thrive. Small firms in such new industries as software and biotech saw growth and recovery while large manufacturers continued laying off workers, and those smaller companies created good jobs at an accelerating clip. Katherine Bradbury, an economist at the Federal Reserve Bank of Boston, found in an analysis of census data that despite the loss of manufacturing jobs, inequality was rising less in New England than elsewhere and that incomes in the Boston area remained high.[8] In September 1994 an industry newspaper reported that commercial real estate along Route 128 was experiencing a strong comeback driven by a resurgence in small-company growth. The area was in the midst of a transformation, through entrepreneurship, to technologies and industries of the future.

Boston's success in the global economy—and the success of cities everywhere that connect to the world through knowledge work and concept innovation—depends on several elements:

- institutions that attract and support the people with the talent and foresight to create new ideas;
- facilitation of entrepreneurship to commercialize concepts so that ideas, and the businesses based on them, grow in the area;
- industry networks that encourage interaction, stimulate further innovation, help develop specialized services to support area companies, and encourage cross-industry partnerships;
- cultural and social amenities constituting quality of life that motivate knowledge workers and the concept-based companies that rely on them to stay in the area.

■ SUCCESS ELEMENT #1: MAGNETS FOR BRAINPOWER

One clear reason for continuing high wages in Boston is its link to knowledge industries. The Boston area has sixty-five colleges and universities with approximately 250,000 students; 50 percent of the population attends college. The city also has thirty-five hospitals and three nationally prominent medical schools; the Longwood Medical Area drew more than $330 million in NIH research grants in 1992. College students represent one out of six residents.[9] Boston attracts some of the best talent in the country: in 1994 Harvard and Radcliffe Colleges reviewed a record 15,261 applications for the current freshman class. Fourteen percent of the applicants were admitted, and 75 percent of those admitted chose to attend, giving Harvard the highest yield among competitive colleges nationwide. About 35 percent of America's National Merit scholars enter college in Massachusetts.

The Boston area is a magnet for bright people. They attend school and then stay to start businesses. Among the leadership of 521 Boston-area companies who responded to my survey, 51 percent had spent the greatest portion of their childhood in the Greater Boston area; 65 percent completed their last formal education in Massachusetts, 54 percent of those in Greater Boston. Boston has one of the world's highest concentrations of college-educated people in its population.

All this brainpower is in turn a magnet for research dollars. Massachusetts, with about 2.5 percent of the U.S. population, receives about 10 percent of federal research funding. In 1989 the state received 7 percent of all National Science Foundation research grants, 14 percent of federal defense research grants, and 10 percent of federal energy research grants. In 1994 the Department of Energy awarded Small Business Innovation Research grants to thirty-seven projects in twenty-one Massachusetts companies with 2–175 employees, sending about 17 percent of the total awarded nationally to Massachusetts. New England, with about 6 percent of the United States population, received about 12 percent of the defense research dollars during this period (but less than 2 percent of the space budget, a specialty of other states such as Florida and Texas).

As one indicator of the importance of knowledge industries in the city itself, Boston's nonprofit, member-supported fiscal watchdog, the Boston Municipal Research Bureau, shows that almost 50 percent of the city's land area consists of tax-exempt property—including universities, hospitals, religious organizations, and the usual set of public buildings in any city that is also a state and regional capital.

Boston's brainpower is practical as well as intellectual. In 1990 Massachusetts institutions granted 13.5 percent of the nation's degrees in computer engineering. Between 1985 and 1992, the number of annual patent filings by Massachusetts firms jumped from 1,594 to 2,228, an increase of 40 percent, compared with 32 percent for the United States as a whole—although Massachusetts is still outpaced by California, where patents filed for the same time period climbed from 5,314 to 7,887, up 48 percent.

Industrial research dollars in Massachusetts increased by more than 245 percent from 1979 to 1989, compared with an increase of 166 percent for the United States as a whole. Research and development expenditures per capita were at least twice the national average at about $160 per person, but the state is also more dependent on federal funds than the United States as a whole; 71 percent of Massachusetts's research and development money comes from the federal government, compared with 58 percent for the United States as a whole. This strength, of course, is also a weakness when federal largesse declines.

Legions of laboratories are centered around Boston; the most distant one is seventy miles outside of the city, while most of the rest are clustered around the hub. They include the Army Research Laboratory, the Army Research Institute of Environmental Medicine, the Francis Bitter National Magnet Laboratory, the MIT Lincoln Laboratory, Navy Clothing and Textile Research Facility, NEMSC Woods Hole Laboratory, Philips Laboratory, Volpe National Transportation Center, and labs at the Hanscom Air Force Base. Hanscom's Electronic Systems Center released an economic impact study in March of 1994 that showed Hanscom base expenditures of $1.2 billion in New England in fiscal year 1994 and 11,500 employed at the base, plus 17,900 secondary jobs, practically all in the Boston area, and an estimated—but controversial—$3.2 billion total economic impact from this facility alone.

■ SUCCESS ELEMENT #2: FROM CONCEPTS TO COMMERCIALIZATION

Research and knowledge building are only the starting point. The next step is to translate knowledge into viable commercial concepts—a matter of technology transfer that allows entrepreneurs to run with promising concepts.

The MIT connection is a significant factor in Boston's business personality, especially in the high-tech arena. MIT has a long history of spawning companies, beginning in the 1880s with engineering consulting firms Stone & Webster and Arthur D. Little, which is now a global management consultancy. In the 1920s MIT helped create Raytheon and in the 1940s EG&G and Polaroid. In the 1950s came Digital Equipment, in the 1960s Analog Devices. By 1988 MIT's entrepreneurship guru, Edward Roberts, estimated that fully 72 percent of the new high-technology businesses established in the Boston area since 1975 could trace their origins to an MIT affiliation. A 1988 Bank of Boston study showed that MIT people and technologies were involved in 636 companies in Massachusetts alone; these companies employed over two hundred thousand people and had revenues of more than $40 billion. Looking nationwide, a 1989 Chase Manhattan Bank study found 225 companies in Silicon Valley with MIT roots, showing combined revenues of $22 billion. MIT-spawned companies are often world leaders in applying technology to a range of fields. For example, Bose Corporation, founded in 1964 by MIT professor Amar Bose, makes the best-selling high performance speakers in the United States, Europe, Japan, Canada, and Australia.

As public awareness of the need to nurture high-tech competitiveness grew in the 1980s, MIT became even more aggressive in encouraging entrepreneurship. In 1986 the MIT Patent and Copyright Office was renamed, shifting its focus from protection to transfer of technology. This led to a tenfold-plus increase in licenses and new company creation; during the last nine years John Preston's technology development team at MIT helped create sixty-seven companies and closed several hundred license agreements with existing companies. (MIT, Stanford, and the University of California account for half the university license agreements in the United States.) And over half of MIT inventions are licensed to industry within one year of the issue of a patent. MIT also participates in alliances and consortia, such as its venture with Kopin Corporation, a local manufacturer of flat panel displays, and Philips Electronics North America to commercialize liquid displays for high-definition television and multimedia computer systems, with the U.S. Commerce Department providing half of the $12.4 million funding.

INVESTING IN INNOVATORS

The Boston area pioneered in venture capital. The most famous investment is American Research and Development's backing of a young MIT-connected Lincoln Laboratory engineer, Kenneth Olsen, when he founded Digital Equipment in 1956 to produce the first commercial minicomputer. MIT president Karl Taylor Compton played a key role in the 1946 formation of ARD, America's first modern venture capital fund by General Georges Doriot, who taught at Harvard Business School, finding money from Boston insurance companies; ARD's first board included four MIT department heads.[10] ARD alumni launched similar firms, starting with Boston Capital in 1963. Bank of Boston became involved in loans for technology-oriented businesses in the 1960s. "We have a long tradition of being bankers to innovators," a senior executive observed. "We financed the wool trade with Argentina for the textile industry starting a century ago, gave Ray Kroc of McDonald's his first loan, and provided help to Raytheon and Wang in getting started." Bank of Boston maintains strong high-technology financial expertise, updating the industries it supports; it was the first bank to offer a specialty in environmental technologies.

When venture capital became a major force in the United States after a 1978 reduction in the capital gains tax, America's venture capital pool grew from under $3 billion in 1978 to over $16 billion in 1986, about 12 percent of which was concentrated in New England.[11] Venture capital is a still flourishing industry around Boston, although young companies offer mixed reviews, arguing that more money is available in California or that venture capitalists have retreated from offering risky start-up funding. Lack of capital is a perennial complaint; Greater Boston businesses in my five-city survey pointed to this problem and also blamed banks for cutting back on small business loans as the economy went into recession and the banking industry consolidated, leaving few major Boston-area banks that were not owned out of state.

Recognizing the value of technological entrepreneurship, state government leaders helped fill part of the gap. In 1969 Jerome Weisner, then president of MIT, helped establish the Massachusetts Science and Technology Foundation, which argued that new technology companies are critical to the state economy. Then, under Governor Michael Dukakis, a task force on capital formation found a gap in capital for early-stage financing and recommended that the state step in. Massachusetts Technology Development Corporation (MTDC) was established in 1978.

MTDC's mission is to address the capital gap for start-up and expansion of young technology companies. The corporation quickly became self-supporting and is considered an international role model for astute investments. Limited to $250,000 per investment, from 1980 to 1985 the MTDC made investments of over $7.3 million in thirty-three companies; then in 1986 it began investing $2 million of state pension funds in later-stage financing.

Through June 30, 1994, MTDC made cumulative investments of over $25.7 million in seventy-one companies. The first fifty-nine investments were said to have created nearly five thousand new high-tech jobs in the state. Success stories among publicly traded companies include Powersoft and Interleaf in software, Xylogics in computer equipment, Kronis in industrial automation systems, Endogen in biotech, and Spire in material sciences. MTDC's start-up $200,000 investment in Interleaf netted a gain of $3.4 million when MTDC liquidated its position in 1987. Interleaf continued to grow as a world standard setter, entering the Japanese market in 1992; Interleaf 5, document creation software, was named product of the year by the Japanese Association of Graphic Arts and Technology.

Powersoft (then called Computer Solutions) received $150,000 from MTDC in 1983 and again in 1984 when it had developed manufacturing automation software out of its original programming business and needed a national sales effort. MTDC connections helped the company raise an additional $750,000; Powersoft eventually needed over $6 million, which it raised through venture capitalists introduced by MTDC. That boost enabled Powersoft to become the leader described earlier in this book; Sybase's agreement to buy Powersoft for $904 million in stock in 1994 was one of the software industry's largest deals to date.

State officials explored how to further the area's success in innovation. In 1985 five centers of excellence were established to unite business, academic, and government leaders around a particular technology and to find or create a flagship facility to serve as a rallying point for each center, in places where the technology was already rooted and could build on strengths of public universities, which had always been the poor stepchildren to the area's wealthy private universities. Some of the centers worked better than others; the microelectronics center waned when federal support went to Texas instead of Massachusetts. In 1994, under Governor William Weld, the Massachusetts High Technology Park was revived as a force to stimulate technological innovation.

Meanwhile, however, networks of thinkers in the area were already inventing new concepts that would produce dynamic companies and job growth in industries of the future.

■ SUCCESS ELEMENT #3: INDUSTRY "SCHMOOZING"

If all it took to produce knowledge-based growth companies were research labs and government support, then many places would already have the next high-tech success story. After all, they try to duplicate Boston's and Silicon Valley's success by putting together a similar combination of resources, often at public expense, through research parks connected to universities.[12] But an environment for entrepreneurship rests on voluntary social ties, the quantity and quality of interactions among people and companies in an industry. These ties and exchanges not only stimulate greater innovation, they also keep people focused on the entire community as an arena for innovation, as new spin-offs emerge from established companies (for example, at least ten software companies were started by people leaving Apollo Computer), as service companies grow to provide specialized support for the industry, and as companies hire each other's people, the way Powersoft recruited programmers from the remains of Cullinet.[13]

Some say that Silicon Valley rose and Route 128 fell in the 1980s because Northern California offered more opportunities for "schmoozing"—the human interactions that cause ideas to circulate and creativity to be enhanced. Without schmoozing, thinkers can become closed-minded and miss new ideas or opportunities. But the critics who decried Boston's closed culture were looking only at its ailing computer and defense electronics giants. In Boston's most important new industries, there is abundant organized or serendipitous schmoozing, some of it part of a strategy by Governor Weld's Council on Economic Growth and Technology to strengthen key industries.

The MIT Enterprise Forum, begun in 1978 after a series of informal workshops for MIT alumni in 1976 and 1977, is the mother of networks for Boston-area entrepreneurs: a way to make contacts, boost know-how for new ventures, and get practical help in producing business plans. For example, Eric Giler, founder of Brooktrout Technologies, a producer of voice and fax messaging equipment, first discussed his business concept in a start-up clinic at the forum in 1984; ten years later Brooktrout had about $25 million in revenues. The Enterprise Forum, a revenue-producing venture for the alumni association, has fifteen chapters in the United States and four international ones in areas with a significant MIT alumni population, including Israel and Russia.

Opportunities for making contacts abound. The 128 Venture Group, for example, was founded in 1983 as a monthly forum for people interested in creating new high-technology ventures, including entrepreneurs, venture capitalists, professional service providers, and job seekers. It was created by Michael Belanger, a consultant and venture capitalist who had been involved in a venture capital group in Connecticut. Over eighty people attended the first meeting, and the three-hour morning sessions continue to attract up to two hundred participants, from a mailing list of about eight hundred. About once a year, joint programs are held with other groups out of the many networks for technology entrepreneurs in the area: the Boston Computer Society, entrepreneurship clubs at local universities, and so on. My colleague Nitin Nohria interviewed 103 participants, finding that 59 percent generated significant leads via the meeting (with potential investors for example, or with management candidates).[14]

GROWTH THROUGH OPEN NETWORKS IN SOFTWARE

Software's roots in Boston reach back to defense contracts in the 1940s at Harvard and MIT. Harvard developed two of the pioneering computer languages, and research at MIT led to the first time-sharing system, computer graphics, spreadsheets, and the first database system developed in the state. Bolt, Beranek, and Newman's Arpanet was a precusor to the Internet. By the fall of 1994 there were over 1,800 software companies in Massachusetts employing over 62,000 people, with another 33,000 working in software units of hardware companies. At $5 billion in combined sales, almost 8 percent of America's total for the industry, Massachusetts companies enjoy the highest incidence of profitability in the country and have the highest-paid and most productive employees in terms of revenues per person. It is a good industry for an area of thinkers; almost a third of all those employed in software are in the knowledge-creation functions of research and development.[15]

The vitality of this Boston-centered industry, which averaged 20 percent annual employment growth from 1989 to 1994, was easy to miss during the crash of the "Massachusetts miracle" and the deep recession that followed, because it rests on small companies not visible to consumers or analysts—90 percent are still privately owned. Lotus Development Corporation, begun in 1982, is among the few giants and founder Mitchell Kapor a local rags-to-riches legend. Kapor, a teacher of transcendental meditation, left Lotus in 1988, starting a foundation for electronic free speech. Together with Boston's Open Software Foundation, this was emblematic of the real meaning of the transition from computer hardware to software in Massachusetts: the culture of software is more open, and consequently the people and companies are densely networked.

In 1985 the Massachusetts Software Council was formed to promote the industry domestically and internationally, but it soon became a source of schmoozing. Richard Rabins, head of Alpha software, and Eric Vogt, founder of MicroMentor, had begun to have dinner once a month to talk about issues they faced in running their companies. They invited other software CEOs to join them for their monthly meetings and soon discovered that they were both fulfilling a need and helping each other. An organizational meeting was held in November of 1985, and Vogt became the first president. Executive director Joyce Plotkin recalled how she came on board: "I heard about this fledgling operation and contacted Eric. He interviewed me over cocktails at a fund-raiser, then asked me to draw up my own job description, since he wanted a creative approach to the task. His only directive was that he wanted me to market Massachusetts software the way Florida markets oranges."

From March 1986 to the fall of 1987, Plotkin worked out of Micro-Mentor's office near Harvard University, close to the center of a software industry that was growing quietly primarily in urban areas of Boston and Cambridge, while high-tech manufacturers were more visible out on the periphery around Route 128. After interviewing the board, Plotkin concluded, "It was clear to me that the last thing these very small companies needed was an indirect marketing campaign. They needed more direct services."

Today the Massachusetts Software Council runs twenty-seven meetings a year for its three hundred members on international opportunities, legal issues, sales and marketing strategies, or CEO-to-CEO advice. Three times a year large membership meetings are held with industry superstars such as Bill Gates, Philippe Kahn, and John Sculley. But the council also knows that to make schmoozing attractive to overloaded entrepreneurs, it must be fun. The council is the only trade association in Boston with its own rock band, made up of several board members who like to get together and jam.

The software council links people and opportunities. Its pioneering fellowship program, featured on national television news, is a public-private partnership with MassJobs that offers retraining in the software industry for seasoned professionals who have been laid off from hardware, defense, or electronics companies. The program includes an extensive orientation to the industry and a five-month work assignment in a software company. To promote new careers, beginning in April 1994, résumés were circulated in a book that included testimonials about each candidate. For example, Zena Thomas, who had been a project manager and systems analyst at Wang Laboratories, took an assignment as quality assurance consultant for Relational Courseware of Boston; another Wang veteran, Sandra Hayes, created a company identity and marketing materials for Coptech.

Extending networking beyond its membership and contributing industry expertise to the community, the council produced *The Switched-on Classroom* in 1994, an educational planning guide promoting the use of information technology to enhance learning. Distributed free to all K–12 school principals, superintendents, and school committee members in the state, it was so well received that it stimulated an even more innovative concept, the Mass Tech Corps. Beginning in twelve pilot school districts in 1995, volunteers work on an electronic infrastructure to link schools to the information highway, "the way the Peace Corps built roads for the Third World," a participant said.

One of America's first local software industry collaborations, the council today is considered a model worldwide for the ways it directly affects companies' success prospects by giving them specific, concrete learning opportunities. "I don't think networking is enough. It's important, but not enough to justify paying dues year after year," Plotkin said. "Instead we ask lots of folks to talk about their practical approaches to business problems. It's not a best practices model, because we do not really have any way of knowing who does what in the best way possible. What we do is ask the larger companies to share their experiences because they generally have tried a number of approaches and have a wider range of experiences to share. They have also been pretty willing to talk about things that haven't worked." This exchange of experience is especially important for an industry composed of small companies that are just emerging as well as for larger companies that are reinventing themselves—such as Wang, for example, from hardware to imaging software; Prime from hardware to computer-aided design in its new incarnation as Computervision.

Powersoft's founder, Mitchell Kertzman, chairman of the Massachusetts Software Council, feels that Powersoft takes advantage of dense local industry networks to identify good people and good ideas through contact and conversation among companies, facilitated by the software council and led by chief executives. "I am Powersoft's chief schmoozer," Kertzman said. "That is a big part of my job, schmoozing officer. I have to get out and meet people. The area serves me mostly for the quality of employees, which for the software business is critical. I think Boston has the highest caliber of employees in technical areas and a critical mass of talent in software." Indeed, so much "schmoozing" and networking goes on in this densely clustered industry that some Powersoft managers complain it eats into their private lives.

TELECOMMUNICATIONS INDUSTRY INTERCONNECTIVITY

While computer and defense company layoffs made headlines during the recession of the early 1990s, smaller companies in other important emerging brainpower-based industries were discovering each other and forming networks.

A 1991 Bank of Boston study found that Massachusetts was already a world leader in the internetworking equipment sector of the data communications industry; fifteen independent regional companies had nearly 50 percent of the market share worldwide in a rapidly growing market. Discussing these findings at a conference that year at Harvard's

Kennedy School of Government, where telecommunications policy is a specialty, a group of industry leaders decided to form the Massachusetts Telecommunications Council, perhaps the first private broad-based council in the industry. Begun in 1992 and chaired by Sidney Topol, retired chairman of Scientific Atlanta recently returned to his native Boston, the council grew to 115 member companies in a position to achieve Congressman Edward Markey's dream that Massachusetts companies would be "general contractor for the information highway."

The primary objective of the telecommunications council is to make Massachusetts the telecommunications capital of the world, attracting global companies. The council has made strides in creating a network within the industry, generating business deals, helping to plan for the information highway, and sponsoring an investor conference that showcased thirty-two companies to three hundred investors from Wall Street and nationally. It is also publishing the first ever Massachusetts telecommunications directory, which will contain listings of companies and people working in the industry and explanations of the work they do, and establishing the Commonwealth Exchange, a business communications network like Commerce Network in Silicon Valley.

While giants such as AT&T in North Andover are downsizing, smaller companies such as Wellfleet Communications, Proteon, Chipcom, or PictureTel are growing. Communications equipment produced in Massachusetts, mostly in the Boston area, has 32 percent more value added than the national average and is second only to Colorado in volume, according to industry figures.

With common roots in software, Boston's telecommunications industry shares with that industry a set of dense ties that link smaller companies to wider networks. In fact, alliances and partnerships bridge all three of the Boston area's major emerging industries: software, telecommunications, and health technologies. For example, telemedicine, in which physicians view patient records or test results and make diagnoses over video networks, originated at Massachusetts General Hospital. Or take PictureTel, founded in 1984 to make videoconferencing systems. In 1994 PictureTel joined with the United Medical Network and MCI to create an independent visual communications network for health care delivery. The company also unveiled new application-sharing software in the form of low-cost desktop videophones.

Some local companies are joining forces to quickly turn global. Chipcom, founded in 1983, had 40 percent of its revenues outside of the

United States by 1991; the company then merged with a neighboring company and signed a technology agreement with another. By 1994 total revenue was near $200 million. Companies are also collaborating locally to apply industry resources to community service—consider the alliance of Wellfleet, AT&T, Anixter, and LCN to provide telecommunications networks to homeless shelters (described in chapter 7).

TURNING SCIENCE INTO HEALTH TECHNOLOGIES

Medical technologies spring from the Boston area's medical and scientific brainpower and help cross-fertilize concepts as well as renew innovation. Boston's laboratories have long been world centers of medical innovation. Massachusetts General Hospital's distinction in the medical field dates back to 1846, when it was at the center of the development of anesthesia. Reflecting the endurance of health industries while others wane, the hospital has extensive research facilities located at the former Charlestown Navy Yard, which closed in 1974. Other hospitals are equally distinguished innovators in science and organization; Beth Israel is a national role model for professional teams and patient-centered care.

Boston hospitals are big employers and also big consumers. Although they are typically classified as services, and in most cases nonprofits, hospitals closely resemble manufacturing companies in their purchasing patterns, spending hundreds of millions of dollars on equipment and disposable items. These purchases are more often local than the purchases made by high-tech or biotech companies because of local manufacturing of relevant supplies. One distinguished teaching hospital, for example, buys $30 million of monitoring equipment a year, much of it from a Massachusetts operation, plus surgical gloves and bandages from Massachusetts producers.

Medical instruments companies are a significant force in health technologies—one that draws on many of the high-tech fields around Boston, including software, and takes advantage of local partnerships—as with a venture linking Brigham and Women's Hospital and BioSurface Technology in Cambridge for tests of cartilage replacement products. By various measures, Massachusetts ranks second in production of some categories of medical devices and third nationally in the medical instruments industry, falling behind only California and Wisconsin, the latter because of a single large company, General Electric. The Boston area's own world star is Hewlett-Packard.

H-P got involved in medical devices because co-founder Bill Hewlett's father was a doctor. When he started the company with David Packard in 1939, he thought that the measurement business could be applied to the medical area. In the 1950s H-P began to look for companies with which to partner, finding Sanborn Medical Electric Products in Waltham on Boston's Route 128; H-P bought Sanborn in 1962. Now H-P's medical products group is a world leader. Group head Ben Holmes said proudly, "No one else has the combination of computation, measurement, information management, and medical experience working with clinicians." Manager Susan Schettino said simply: "We set world standards."

In 1994 H-P consolidated all Boston area operations in Andover, north of Boston, where the medical products group also oversees facilities in Oregon, Germany, and a start-up final assembly operation in China, laying groundwork for eventual manufacturing there. The group makes ultrasound equipment, fetal monitors, patient monitors, and other medical devices, reaching $1 billion in revenues in 1992 and $1.14 billion in 1993. The company has a wide range of international alliances, including third-party software companies, production partners in Germany, marketing partners in Japan, and some that could not be disclosed.

One product joint venture involves Boston Scientific, a leader in its field, which makes catheters to look into heart arteries. Combining H-P's products with Boston Scientific's means that information from the arterial scan can connect directly with an H-P ultrasound machine. The fact that this partner is in the Boston area is "convenient, but not a deal maker," Holmes said. Still, it is a reflection of the cross-fertilization and collaboration that can occur for knowledge industries drawing on Boston's thinkers. And H-P contributes to Boston in industry-specific ways as well as taking advantage of the area's strengths—$7 million to Harvard Medical School, equipment to Boston University Medical School, partnering with major teaching hospitals to develop an electronic medical record card. "A lot is going on here in health care," Holmes said. "The area has the premier set of teaching hospitals. We have access to leading physicians and can talk to people who make a difference in the health care field. It has more universities per capita, and MIT is interested in working with industry." Furthermore, "People like to live here."

Biotechnology is a newer field, full of as yet unrealized promise, but just the sort of industry in which a community of thinkers can excel. The Boston area and eastern Massachusetts are home to a significant share of U.S. biotechnology companies, with 172 companies out of 1,000 identified in industry reports, number two in the nation. By comparison there are 192 in the San Francisco Bay Area (ranked number one) and 114 in the mid-Atlantic (ranked number three), the traditional pharmaceutical industry stronghold.

The American biotech industry had $7 billion in 1992 sales, with Amgen the highest at just over $1 billion and Boston's Genzyme third with $180 million. The industry is dwarfed by the pharmaceutical industry's $114 billion in 1992 sales, but biotech is seen as the industry with growth promise and one still in the thinking stage, so Boston's strengths are an asset to emerging companies. "In biotech and medicine, U.S. companies set the standards," Genzyme CEO Henri Termeer observed. "The strongest driving force in biotechnology is technical factors, university research, clinical research at medical institutions, rather than environmental factors such as business climate. As we get larger, this will be less true. Vendors, regulatory bodies, and the labor force will become more important."

Some trace the field now called biotechnology to a commitment by Harvard and MIT to molecular biological research. In the early 1980s recognition and a name were conferred on a set of new companies producing drugs using biology rather than chemistry. "Nobody called it biotech in the late 1970s and early 1980s; science was just coming to the forefront," recalled Ron Kessler, managing partner of law firm Palmer and Dodge. Palmer and Dodge became involved in this area of law in the late 1970s because an associate whose wife was a scientist developed an interest in it. "We were there when it started," Kessler said, noting that the legal risks in the industry make it a good market for lawyers.

In 1985 Massachusetts targeted biotechnology as a key industry for the future as part of its Centers of Excellence program. The state's Biotechnology Research Park in Worcester is now one of the largest biotech parks in the world. Its Biotech Research Institute, with facilities in Worcester and Boston, also retrains laid-off defense workers for biotechnology jobs.

Genzyme is one of the success stories. Henri Termeer, a Dutch executive with Baxter Diagnostics, joined Genzyme as CEO in 1983, when the company was still relatively new. Genzyme used many innovative financing mechanisms, including public offerings for research and development partnerships, to fund research. Genzyme's research to develop a therapy for cystic fibrosis was financed by Neozyme Corporations I and II, for example, and $85 million was raised in a public offering in May 1992. By 1993 about 16 percent of Genzyme's sales came from outside the United States, projected to rise to 40 percent in the near future.

The biotech industry spends an average of 81 percent of sales on research and development, compared with 16 percent on average for the pharmaceutical industry. Still, executives report an uphill battle to convince politicians and the public about the value of the industry and to explain why initial therapy costs are so high. Genzyme's Ceredase, an enzyme-based treatment for Gaucher disease, became a focal point, and Termeer found himself in Washington, defending what the company says is the first safe and effective treatment for this genetic disorder that afflicts an estimated five thousand people worldwide. "I think the spotlight on Ceredase has been helpful to the industry as a platform to examine pricing issues," Termeer said later. "It allowed me to invite Congress's Office of Technology Assessment into the company. They now see that Ceredase is expensive to produce." Termeer also works on public policy affecting the industry in Massachusetts; in 1991 he became the first chairman of the subcommittee on biotechnology and pharmaceutical development of Governor Weld's Council on Economic Growth and Technology, with two Palmer and Dodge law firm partners contributing expertise.

Biotech is a young industry just getting organized on a national level; in 1994 two smaller organizations merged to create the Biotechnology Industry Organization, with 520 members from forty-seven states. But it is already organized in Boston, lending strength to the infant companies clustered there. The Massachusetts Biotech Council began as informal discussions over coffee and doughnuts among a handful of industry leaders about a decade ago and now includes in its membership about eighty biotech companies, from tiny to large, and forty service companies considered associates to the industry. Extending schmoozing beyond formal meetings, it has an active softball league.

Early members included Peter Feinstein of Biogen, Mark Goldberg, now president of the Massachusetts Biotech Research Institute, and David Glass, formerly with Biotechnia and now with Massachusetts General Hospital. "As you can see, this is a very dynamic, constantly changing industry, there is a lot of evolution, changes, and people are always moving around," said Alison Taunton-Rigby, chairman of the council and former president of Mitotix, who is herself a veteran of Genzyme, where she was senior vice president for six years, and several other companies. "A major strength of Boston is the hospital system. You always want the best clinical investigations. It is obviously much easier if the best hospitals are local."

Taunton-Rigby, a U.K.-born scientist with a Ph.D. in chemistry from England, recognizes the industry's vulnerabilities. "A major issue biotech companies face is survival," she said. "Our issues now are much more geared toward public awareness, so the public will be aware of the importance of biotech development. Health care reform has made investors much more cautious, and it could shut down investment. People do not realize that every future drug will come out of biotech, that 20 percent of Massachusetts people are employed in health care. Biotech is significant as a critical industry in Massachusetts." Its riskiness, however, is underscored regularly, from Biogen's 1994 decision not to seek regulatory approval for its anticlotting drugs, angering its public shareholders, to the arrest of two scientists in December of that year on espionage charges as they allegedly tried to sell a genetically engineered organism to an FBI agent posing as a Russian black marketeer.[16]

MORE SCHMOOZING: INNOVATION IN OLDER INDUSTRIES

Another kind of collaboration is aimed more at revitalizing established companies and helping them compete in global markets. The Center for Quality Management in Cambridge was started in 1989 by seven companies who wanted to learn together: Analog Devices, Bolt, Beranek and Newman, Bose, Digital, General Electric Aircraft Engine, Polaroid, and Teradyne. Most of the companies had extensive experience in Japan. Working with MIT and a visiting Japanese professor from Tsuukuba University, the center developed courses and built links with leading Japanese practitioners and also formed a networking committee with CEO roundtables and networks for people in other functions. The center arranged a visit to NEC in Japan and developed university affiliations with Bentley, Babson, Lesley, Boston College, Boston University, MIT, Tufts, Wentworth, Worcester Polytechnic Institute, and Harvard Business School.

Aware of the latest knowledge, area companies are quicker than most to apply it. A 1993 study of 123 manufacturing executives in New

England found that 10 percent had already attained certification under ISO 9000, the emerging international quality standard, compared with only 1 percent of companies nationally; 13 percent planned to register by the end of the same year; and 39 percent planned to register by the end of 1994. The study found that 80 percent of the executives said they were doing it to improve their competitive position, 63 percent to improve quality, 52 percent to help with exports, and 47 percent to satisfy major customers.[17]

Small and midsize companies in other technology-intensive industries are also flourishing, in part because of continuing innovation that sets world standards. Analog Devices, after ten years of development work, much of it in concert with MIT, is one of only forty-one companies to win a federal advanced research grant out of three thousand applications; the grant was for surface micromachining, which etches smaller and more complex systems for controls. Informed observers say Massachusetts is in a position to become a world center of excellence in this new technology.

Thanks to thinkers who innovate, Massachusetts still has a toehold in older industries. The textile industry has discovered niches for survival, including high productivity and fast turnaround time for exporting. Buckley & Mann, a manufacturer of nonwoven fabrics founded in 1856, merged in 1994 with Draper, a textile manufacturer in a neighboring town. The consolidated company now considers itself one of the most innovative small mills in the country. Another regional example is Quaker Fabrics, a large manufacturer of upholstery fabric that has built a big business in Mexico. The entire industry has become a network, with hundreds of companies tied together like a large family, calling on each other frequently for support and information.

Industry ties are strong in the Boston area. Community ties are equally critical, but more problematic. Thinkers need what the community provides for quality of life, but they often do not cooperate in creating it.

■ SUCCESS ELEMENT #4: THINKERS AND THE QUALITY OF LIFE

The brains of Boston come to go to school or are lured by job or business creation opportunities. They stay because they enjoy the quality of life. As a software executive said: "The opportunity for money got me here, but that brass ring, those stock options, could go away just like that. At this stage, only quality of life counts. I've spent a lot of time in Europe and Southeast Asia, and there is no way I would ever live there. And Mexico? Pff. South America? When you come back here, man, you kiss the ground. We are very lucky."

What knowledge-oriented companies need most is talented people; companies will locate where knowledge workers want to live. The founder of a large financial services firm explained, "Our headquarters is here because I live here. For people in the analytical part of the business, they like to live here, so they can afford to pay the taxes. Thank God New York is so bad. If not, Boston would have a major problem because New York would absorb most of the financial services business." Nader Dareshori, CEO of Boston-based publisher Houghton Mifflin, also said that his company needs bright young people who can communicate and design creatively; Boston is attractive to them, he claimed, for its "superb social and intellectual environment," including free concerts nearby at the New England Conservatory.

But Boston's brainpower advantages can erode easily. Ideas are easily portable, and they can be carried away by the people who develop them. Ownership of many publishing companies has shifted to New York, including the purchase of the leading daily newspaper, the *Boston Globe*, by *The New York Times*. Biotech companies are takeover targets by large pharmaceutical firms from outside of the region. And several Boston mutual funds companies now maintain a second headquarters in New York. Some knowledge workers leave the area in the wake of change; our focus group discussions with midlevel managers and professionals and direct production services workers suggest that skilled professionals are more willing to move out of the area than are less skilled workers. It is a matter not only of job opportunities, but also of lifestyle. Some high-tech executives worry that skilled software engineers, for example, are already gone from the Greater Boston area. The head of a start-up company recounts difficulties raising venture capital because of a perception that Boston no longer has the talent base it once did.

Boston faces growing competition from other knowledge centers. "My biggest fear is of a brain drain in which technology expertise will move outside of Boston," a top executive in a leading software company said. "We haven't yet experienced it, but there are more jobs being lost in technology than there are being created in the Boston area. The software industry and the biotech industry aren't at the scale of all the hardware companies. I think there are a lot of people leaving this area; I hope we don't get below the critical mass of the type of talent we need to sustain an industry of the size that we would like it to be. It's taken Atlanta twenty-five years to grow their technology practice; they are just getting the critical mass now and are beginning to describe themselves to the world as a technology center of excellence, hoping to bring more industry there."

To continue preeminence as a center for thinkers, an area must stay vigilant, investing in the latest education, because knowledge can erode, and expertise in one field is not necessarily interchangeable with others. Powersoft's operations head Bill Crich worries about the transition from hardware to software engineering. "We are desperate to hire really good people," he said. "What we see here in the area is people using older technologies from Wang, Data General, and DEC. If we were on the West Coast, people from Sybase, Oracle, Informax, and Microsoft would be more appropriate for what we are looking for." That's why the Massachusetts Software Council's retraining program is so important, but it reaches only a handful of people a year.

Knowledge workers can demand quality of life and generally can also pay for it, but quality of life is dependent on whether the community works. Boston has obstacles to overcome; weather is only the first aspect of climate, as a high-tech professional made clear: "It's very hard to live here, very hard. There's nothing convenient about it; we are ten years behind California in almost anything that we do. It's very difficult to drive out here. It's very difficult in some ways to have children, because you have to find a way to take them places. People tend not to be able to live really close to work, with some few exceptions. And in the wintertime your commute can be particularly difficult."

Since many of the knowledge workers in the Boston area stay because of quality of life, community amenities—or problems—become business issues. Fortunately for keeping its thinkers, Boston is rich in amenities. Many other cities have cultural attractions of a traditional sort that now equal or surpass Boston's outstanding museums, musical groups, and theatrical performances—although Boston was often the first to invent new genres such as its nationally acclaimed Children's Museum and its Computer Museum. But on other social fronts, many would bet that few other cities of its size have as much social innovation or as many creative new concepts for making a community more livable in ways that are attractive to younger knowledge workers whose brains power industries of the future.

Social entrepreneurship abounds in Greater Boston, home base for national and international role models such as City Year, described in chapter 7. The thinkers of Boston are continually hatching new concepts. Consider just a few that reflect the new community service model of civic engagement:

- Gang Peace, an antiviolence youth service agency in Boston's Dorchester neighborhood, has provided information to twenty-seven cities seeking to replicate its model. Teen Empowerment, in another neighborhood, involved seven hundred youths in a 1994 "peace conference."
- First Night, a well-known public New Year's festival, started in Boston; its founders eventually helped other cities develop their own family- and community-oriented New Year's events.
- WGBH, one of 350 public television stations in the country, produces about a third of all national public television programming that is made in America, including widely praised documentaries.
- Boston is the pilot for CARE packages to combat illiteracy by distributing books through social service agencies.
- CityACCESS, sponsored by the Boston Company, is an alliance of many social service organizations such as the Boys and Girls Club and the Asian American Civic Association to help low-income residents visit Boston's major museums and attend performances.

Corporate social innovation is also widespread. Stride Rite, often regarded as America's most successful children's shoe company, introduced in 1971 America's first in-house corporate day care center for both employee and community children at company headquarters in Cambridge. In 1990 the center became the nation's first in-house intergenerational day care center, expanding to include elderly people who needed daytime supervision. Stride Rite has been a trendsetter in other ways as well; it was the first American company to implement a corporate "no smoking" policy. And Arnold Hiatt, then CEO of Stride Rite, helped found Business for Social Responsibility. (But Stride Rite later abandoned its inner-city facility for a new one in Louisville.)

Bank of Boston's First Community Bank is a model mixture of business and social entrepreneurship. Led by Gail Snowden, a twenty-year banking veteran who grew up in Boston's African-American neighborhood of Roxbury, First Community Bank is a fifteen-branch operation across several states with a full range of products and services for inner-city residents. The bank has its own product line called First Step for first-time home buyers, first-time bank users, and first-time borrowers. Early in 1993 the bank opened a branch in the Grove Hall section of Roxbury, a neighborhood of thirty-eight thousand people who had had no bank branch for twenty-three years. The local community development corporation helped put the package together that developed the Lithgow Building as a site for the bank, eventually attracting thirty-eight businesses. Ira Jackson, Bank of Boston's government and community affairs executive, reported: "Previously it was Siberia for Bank of Boston people to be in retail, and certainly not in the inner city. Now Dudley Square is the hottest place to be." Other banks from around the country have come for a look, and many hope to replicate this model.[18]

Bank of Boston is involved in other innovative business-community partnerships. In 1994 its mortgage subsidiary teamed with Organization for a New Equality, headed by black minister Charles Stith, to counsel those in danger of foreclosure and sell foreclosed properties to low-income families in Boston and three other New England cities.

THE LIMITS OF THINKERS: WHEN WORLD CLASS CONCEPTS ARE NOT ENOUGH

Despite the area's strength in industries well positioned for the future, there are clear weaknesses; according to recent Census Bureau projections, Massachusett's population growth is the slowest in the nation.[19] It is hard to know whether Boston's economic glass is half empty or half full. In 1994 Massachusetts fell from thirty-third to thirty-seventh on David Birch's ranking of places friendly to small-growth firms, but thirty-three Massachusetts companies made the *Inc.* 500 list of fastest-growing private companies, beating all states but California and Florida.

Boston's knowledge is both its strength and its vulnerability. The Boston area's connections to the global economy are primarily through its thinkers. Knowledge-based companies export a high proportion of their output. Knowledge-intensive service industries such as universities, research labs, consulting firms, and even hospitals sell their knowledge in other markets; embed it in products through linkages with entrepreneurs and manufacturing firms; or lure people to Boston to obtain Boston-centered knowledge firsthand, through educational programs or medical consultations.

Thinkers not only must keep innovating, but the individuals populating brain centers are sometimes individually oriented entrepreneurs who are hard to organize, arrogant, or elitist. There is often a wide gap between techno-cosmopolitans and a less skilled local work force. For locals who are not part of the brainwork industries, opportunities are harder to find. Specialization in concepts provides ample work for techno-cosmopolitans. But capitals of thinking can all too easily neglect the other two C's of competence and connections.

■ DANGER #1: LOSING MANUFACTURING AND OPERATIONS COMPETENCE

Manufacturing industries that employ large numbers of less skilled workers are shrinking in size and importance; loss of routinized production jobs continues. Boston is losing ground not only in manufacturing, but also in processing operations that support knowledge industries, from routine computer programming to telemarketing. A mutual fund CEO reported that his firm is growing, but most job growth is far from Boston headquarters; the result will be a narrowly focused group of high-end people in Boston and more employees elsewhere. His company recently opened a service facility in the Southwest, seeking a lower-cost but also experienced clerical labor pool with a strong work ethic. He said his company considers itself a "great example of how globalization is benefiting Boston," but he added that what this brings into Boston is wealth for the principals and very little in the way of new jobs. "We do not identify ourselves with the city that much," he confessed.

Cities whose core capability is conception can all too easily lose sight of execution. Operations functions can disperse away from a company's brain center to other places with competence as makers—such as the biotech firm that kept research in Boston but expanded manufacturing jobs out of state. Boston is lucky to have Gillette, a world class manufacturer committed to maintaining technology-infused manufacturing at its South Boston plant in the heart of the city. The same interest in expanding operations in the area is not true in other consumer manufacturing companies.

A large shoe producer, for example, was born and grew up in a traditional shoe industry center just outside of Boston. Five years ago 18 percent of its sales came from outside the United States; today the figure is 50 percent. Most of its future growth will come from outside the region and even outside the country. Nearly a third of its current employment is centered at its headquarters and distribution center, but that percentage is declining in number and proportion. The company's edge is shifting from product design, a headquarters function taking advantage of Boston's brainpower, to dealer service, a dispersed function that does not require high-priced knowledge workers. Executives claim they now get as many ideas and role models internationally as they do locally, and their major competition is not with other local shoe companies like Stride Rite, because they compete in different niches. And as the company diversifies into other lines, like apparel and equipment, skills are needed that can be found in greater numbers in other regions like New York and California. Because there are few consumer product companies in the Boston area, this one cannot find a ready source of managers and marketers and must recruit from other areas.

Even in knowledge industries drawing on Boston's brainpower for innovative concepts, leaders warn that once products are designed, their production could move out of the area, taking with them good manufacturing jobs. As the biotech industry matures, a report in 1991 predicted, Boston could no longer have a corner on the intellectual side; and as it moves toward manufacturing and selling of products, Boston's research-driven competitive edge could diminish. Genzyme's Termeer commented, "The biotech industry has 270 products in the final stages of trial. Each will need a manufacturing plant. Right now there are only one or two suitable facilities in the state." Genzyme itself had considered moving its manufacturing out of Boston, receiving attractive offers from other states such as Oregon. It stayed out of loyalty, Termeer said, to those with MIT and Harvard ties who wanted to remain in the area. It made economic sense to continue to build on the skill base it had established.

■ DANGER #2: NEGLECTING INTERNATIONAL CONNECTIONS

International trade and exporting play a comparatively minor role for smaller companies outside of high-tech networks; according to my five-city survey, only a small proportion of businesses in the Greater

Boston area are involved in international markets. And the same ideas keep recycling in every examination of export issues for smaller companies: more market leads, more ways to find international partners.

Greater Boston technology-based companies succeed well in international markets, especially in global industries that American companies dominate. The 63 percent of Massachusetts software companies that produce packaged software, for example, are heavy exporters; 32 percent distribute their products outside the United States, and 23 percent earn more than 30 percent of their revenues from international customers. Overall, 19 percent of the revenues of area software firms comes from sales outside the United States, compared with 11 percent average international sales for software companies nationwide.[20]

By and large, however, the area's emerging companies have relied on superior concepts to guarantee desirability to international distributors; trade links that could boost sales or include lower-tech companies have not been as actively cultivated as in other cities until recently. Boston has many of the same pieces of a trade infrastructure as international trade giants such as Miami: a World Trade Center; thirty-eight international consulates; an array of consultants, matchmakers, and associations; many international Chambers of Commerce; a growing number of governor-led trade missions, including one in December 1994 to Ireland and Britain, places where Boston's residents have ethnic ties and that serve as entry points to Europe. But Boston's international trade initiatives are fragmented, outpaced in quantity and quality by other cities, and, some say, underutilized.

Boston has major resources unavailable to many other places: a large number of foreign students among the city's huge college population, many world-renowned international experts among the university faculties. Boston is above the national average in the percentage of degrees its colleges and universities confer on foreign students. But simply having resources located in an area does not ensure that they help build economic strength.

Foreign investors play a limited role in Boston; the city's strength still lies in its own ideas—and foreign investors often come to get those ideas, such as Japan's NEC, which has a major research lab outside of Boston. Occasionally companies contribute ideas to the community they have gained from operating in foreign countries, but this is rare. Gillette, for example, brought the German apprenticeship model to the Boston Private Industry Council, which in turn helped stimulate

Project Pro-Tech, an innovative school-to-work program that became a prototype for a national initiative. Many Boston companies are so locally focused and so sure that the best knowledge lies nearby, they do not take full advantage of their own international connections, let alone contribute them to the community. There are exceptions: Bank of Boston, with its extensive holdings in Argentina, Brazil, and Chile, announced in May 1995 a program to boost area exports: free online market data, local export schools, and "trade outposts" (use of its Frankfurt, Hong Kong, and South American offices).

Despite extensive export and international trade activity on the part of Greater Boston–area companies, there is little international "presence" in the business community, especially when compared with the visibility of an international business community in other metropolitan areas. In interviews my group conducted with international companies, executives indicated that they move people in and out of foreign assignments infrequently and that only recently have they begun to explicitly share learning between domestic and foreign operations. Very few expatriates are brought to Boston; those who are deployed to the city come because of special technical skills, not to bring international experience, and they often do not form a community with any visible international presence.

Consultants helping local businesses with their international connections point to the low priority placed on cultivating foreign relationships, even for export purposes. Some of them, like Fabrizio Alvarez de Toledo, are consummate cosmopolitans themselves. De Toledo, managing partner and founder of Actinvest Technologies, affiliated with a company based in Milan and London, points to a domestic bias that could someday hurt Boston companies. A quadrilingual engineer and physicist educated in Europe, MIT, and Harvard Business School, de Toledo worked for Stone & Webster Engineering in international marketing for Europe and the Middle East and served as head of science and technology for the OECD in Paris. Now he is trying to build a business helping emerging American technology companies, such as an advanced robotics company, expand sales and establish strategic alliances in Italy and the rest of Europe.

De Toledo describes how hard it is for small Boston-area companies to do what is necessary to build export markets. "The companies I am working with in the United States are busy doing their thing in the American market," he said. "They spend their time doing things that will make them successful here and cannot seem to find the time to go meet companies and people in Italy. And they don't have the money to pay for all the travel that it takes to establish rapport and relationships. The added hurdle in international marketing, the added gap, is cross-border contact. You have to get on a plane, land in the country, and meet people."

■ DANGER #3: ARROGANCE

"People in Atlanta think we're like the French. We have arrogance and don't deserve it," commented Paul O'Brien, former chairman of Nynex New England. A study done by Robert Levine, a psychologist at California State University, ranked Boston twenty-eight out of thirty-six cities on several measures of kindness to strangers.[21] Although the researchers attributed low scores to population density, participants in my focus groups sometimes pointed to elitism on the part of cosmopolitans and unhelpfulness on the part of locals. A worker at Carey Limousine said, "I think for the most part Boston has the worst customer service you'll come across. I go to the Midwest a lot; out there people are a little bit more concerned about providing a higher quality of customer service. In the Boston area a kind of take-it-or-leave-it attitude prevails." A manager from another company concurred: "I am making a sweeping generalization, but the people who tend to live in Massachusetts have not lived anyplace else, so they don't know that there is a good life to be had elsewhere."

The press takes the brunt of the criticism; 57 percent of the 521 Boston-area companies in my survey rated the media a hindrance to their business, well ahead of the next most negative city, Seattle, where 31 percent found this a hindrance. One CEO blamed the press for "too much cynicism and negativism," he said. "The press can help by being more of a booster for the area. We need to provide a forum for business people to share their views without the threat of being raked over the coals by the press." But some also think that arrogance begins with knowledge industries themselves. Long confident of Boston's superiority, they have not felt the need to reach out to other places, for learning or marketing.

"Massachusetts does not do enough to take advantage of its greatest asset: university research," a business leader observed. "We need to do a better job of promoting one of our only world class assets. Since Massachusetts already thinks so highly of itself in this regard, it makes no effort to promote itself. Meanwhile, other states are more aggressive." Another high-ranking manager in an important utility reported, "Selling is not part of our culture. We are smug and arrogant. People don't think they have to sell Massachusetts, yet the number one problem is finding prospects. The roadblock is getting other groups to help stimulate being proactive. The truth is that Massachusetts is not on anybody's screen to investigate for manufacturing and industry. It is a big, big problem. Even telecommunications, biotech, and software are losing their edge."

■ DANGER #4: POLITICAL FRAGMENTATION AND COSMOPOLITAN-LOCAL TENSIONS

"I am a big believer in globalization," a Boston politician said at a civic event in 1994. Then he went on to explain how narrowly he defined it: "I support a rail link between Boston and central Massachusetts."

It is ironic that Boston, a center of excellence and innovation containing many national and international role models, is at the same time historically and traditionally a balkanized city with a history of tensions between the cosmopolitans of its knowledge industries, who think globally and are often on airplanes to dispense expertise anywhere other than Boston, and the locals, who have made politics a cottage industry and a career path. Cleveland's Citizens League rated Boston near the bottom of fourteen cities in "political participation and accountable leadership."[22]

My survey of 521 area companies showed that important aspects of the business climate are in fine shape; Greater Boston's brainpower and cultural attractions carry very high positives and almost no negatives. But the situation is reversed with respect to political institutions and the press. Rating twenty-eight local resources, survey respondents gave the highest "helpfulness" and lowest "hindrance" ratings to skilled labor, universities, hospitals, research laboratories, and cultural events. In contrast, the highest "hindrance" and lowest "helpfulness" ratings went to the legislature, federal agencies, state agencies, Congress, and the press. The community is viewed positively, and government is viewed negatively. The legislature takes the most knocks for being perceived as unreliable and antibusiness. Larger companies report they have had to make threats to stop business-unfriendly political moves. A manager in one large company tells a story about the head of another significant Boston company who learned of a proposed bill to tax the profits on service industries. That CEO "went down, sat in front of the office of the key politician, who made him wait an hour. He got in there and said, 'I employ 5,800 people in Boston. You pass that and I'm moving them all to Dallas. Good-bye.' Bigger companies like us, we can push back. But for other, smaller companies, I think it's a problem."

Politics is highly territorial. The Boston metropolitan area comprises scores of cities, towns, and neighborhoods, each one infused with highly protective attitudes about "my little patch." This phenomenon dates back to 1873, when adjacent Brookline became the first place in the country to reject annexation by a major city.[23] Today the president of the North Shore Chamber of Commerce describes his area as consisting of thirty towns, each one of which thinks it is the only place in the world. Company heads in my survey sometimes described the operative "community" for their community service activities in specific geographic terms that included only the few blocks on either side of their building. "Local" was taken quite literally.

"Instead of everyone thrown together, Boston's history is more like the Balkan states; people tend to live in feudal domains," one manager said. Ethnic succession accounts for some of this: "You have an Italian section of Boston, you have the Chinese section of Boston. In Houston, you don't have that. We're all mixed up. There are no real barriers. So there isn't a real culture, so to speak, as there is here. In this part of the country there is definitely an Italian culture, a Jewish culture, a Catholic culture, and those groups have been here a long, long time. In some ways there might be more prejudice here than in the South, but it's not always spoken." There is also a downtown professional culture, a Cambridge-based academic culture, a medical center culture, and a State House culture.

The balkanization of Boston is also reflected in the split between the city and its surrounding communities; for example, there was historically little contact between the high-tech community on the periphery of the city and the professional or financial community downtown. This was exacerbated by downtown real estate trends in Boston in 1993; the city lost IBM, parts of Nynex, and AT&T, all of which were consolidating their space. The replacements came from financial services: Fidelity, Scudder, Bank of Boston, Peat Marwick, and State Street Bank.

Politics has been called an industry in Boston. Former mayor Kevin White said, "Irish gravitate [to politics]; politics is a natural environment for them."[24] In Greater Boston there is a wide chasm between business and politicians; there is also a long-standing split between cosmopolitans and locals. The people who populate the world class institutions like Harvard and MIT advise national governments in Washington and around the world but do little at home. There is a widespread belief that Jesuit-run Boston College has produced more local politicians than any other area college or university. A bank president comments on the Yankee Brahmin–Boston Irish split; Brahmins, he said, go to Harvard and become cosmopolitans, while Boston Irish go to BC and have local political or downtown business careers.

Until the 1990s, when more business-friendly politicians were elected to executive offices, public officials almost specialized in populist disinterest in business. A bank executive told me about his response to former Boston mayor Ray Flynn's request for advice about economic development. The executive urged him to visit the Gillette plant in South Boston, a significant employer in Flynn's home neighborhood. The executive suspected that the new mayor didn't even know the CEO's name, let alone the man himself. Flynn, self-styled candidate of the neighborhoods and the working people, said that was something he could not do.

"There is still an attitude in Massachusetts that business is bad," another executive said. "The press, the legislature, and the public believe that big businesses are polluters and thieves. They do not fully appreciate that business creates jobs."

The private sector bears some responsibility for the distrust that appears to flourish between business and politics. Cosmopolitans of the high-tech industries, secure in their world class status, have often turned their backs on local concerns. Traditionally, many high-tech companies concentrated on their own industry first and paid little, if any, attention to social responsibility. Their only politics were politics of opposition, largely to taxes, not of vision for the community. Many of them lived on the periphery of Boston in pristine rural areas and new edge cities; others simply escaped across the border to New Hampshire. They contributed little to public education, which deteriorated, even in the suburbs, and they fought taxes that would have benefited schools.

By the 1980s, "the affluence and dynamism of high technology companies contrast starkly with the pauperism and deterioration of public educational institutions," Elizabeth Useem wrote in 1986 after studying schools in the Silicon Valley and the area around Route 128. Useem found that companies seek relationships with higher education, but not with secondary education. She wrote: "Educators are preoccupied with managing decline while neighboring corporate executives plan innovative products for growing markets. . . . The disparity between the capacities and goals of education and industry has widened and threatens the welfare of workers, companies, and the U.S. economy as a whole." Indeed, in more recent years Massachusetts spent a smaller percentage of state government resources on K–12 education than any state but New Hampshire.[25]

REPAIRING THE INFRASTRUCTURE FOR COLLABORATION

The recession of the 1990s and the new challenges posed by the global economy pushed Boston's leadership to work on its crumbling social infrastructure. While industry collaboration was strong in emerging industries, social entrepreneurs flourished, and networks such as those formed by women in leadership positions were growing in strength, civic cooperation overall was weak, a legacy of earlier neglect.

One attempt to produce a united front was Challenge to Leadership, a civic forum begun in 1984 by Cardinal Bernard Law and William Taylor, publisher of the *Boston Globe*, to promote cooperation among leaders from all sectors. For 1992–93, under the chairmanship of John Hamill, president of Fleet Bank Massachusetts, the topic was economic revitalization. A variety of civic and business organizations, including the Private Industry Council, the Massachusetts Business Roundtable, Associated Industries of Massachusetts, and the Greater Boston Chamber of Commerce each took ownership of one initiative with the help of Boston-area consulting firms. There was a lot of cynicism to overcome, like this comment from a battle-weary executive who doesn't believe anything will change: "Civic associations are like chemotherapy for cancer. They do the best they can under hopeless circumstances." A decade after Challenge to Leadership was formed, many still missed a single voice speaking for the business community since Richard Hill left his post as chairman of Bank of Boston in 1982.

A Council on Economic Growth and Technology was one of newly elected Governor William Weld's first initiatives in 1991 and a catalyst for a strategic vision for the state that Michael Porter helped create. Industry subcommittees have identified policy barriers and stimulated actions to remove them, as well as recommending ways for the area to become more business-friendly. At the same time, the New England Council, a six-state business association, has been an effective voice for the entire region in Washington, the source of so much funding for Boston's brainpower. It has also been a force for cooperation on matters that cut across the relatively small New England states. In April 1994 the council brought together representatives of the major airports in the region to begin talks about a regional strategy. The *Boston Globe* called it an overdue overview. For 1995, the council vowed to regain lost manufacturing jobs by boosting exports, a priority also of Associated Industries of Massachusetts. AIM formed a new leadership group on trade, further strengthening civic collaboration.

But the area is a latecomer to some economic development efforts. It has often taken new blood from out of state to bring leadership and vision. That is why all communities benefit from outside or "foreign" investment even beyond the capital infusion. The Greater Boston Chamber, for example, was considered moribund until new leadership took over in the early 1990s.

Efforts are accelerating but are still fragmented around industry interests. The Alliance for Economic Development started in April 1993 as a consortium of electric, gas, and telephone utilities, a railroad association, and the state Office of Business Development, to foster business development by operating a computerized site-finding service. The idea came from Bernard Reznicek, who moved from Oklahoma to head Boston Edison in 1990—and left Boston again in 1994. Reznicek knew that other states' utilities and governments were much more active.

In 1991 Reznicek also took over an embryonic Massachusetts Ambassadors Program from an organization to stimulate high-tech growth that never really got off the ground until 1993 or 1994. About 250 CEOs and senior executives have promised to sell the state to their peers and contribute intelligence about likely prospects. For example, after the California earthquake, the head of a Boston electronics company learned that a sister company was thinking about moving its headquarters and a computer assembly plant out of California. The company was approached about sites around Boston, including a vacant retail warehouse, but its 2,500 jobs eventually went to Sacramento. It is not clear whether Boston ever became a front-runner.

"We can't compete with other states for manufacturing," an influential journalist said, perhaps implying that no one should try. "We don't want to be Alabama." But if not manufacturing, then what about knowledge functions? An executive lamented, "Boston *should* be attractive as a headquarters, especially for European companies. Flying into here is easier than into New York. You arrive earlier. Why aren't we doing anything to make it happen?" He, like others, said it was time to get working.

More companies say they are active in their communities and take their civic responsibilities far more seriously. But Boston's leadership has been particularly decimated by the kinds of shifts outlined in chapter 7. Not only have the number of CEOs at the top of skyscraper headquarters declined because of industry consolidations and ownership shifts to outside the area, but Boston's growth industries are just the kind that care much more about industry collaboration than civic activity. Professional firms abound in Boston, including four consulting industry giants headquartered there with over $200 million in revenues each (Boston Consulting Group, CSC/Index, Arthur D. Little, and Bain), but consultants on the road rank among the least involved and the least interested in the community. In one company with a high concentration of professional talent, community involvement is actually discouraged; the CEO sees it as a time-wasting productivity drain, equating it with late night charity dinners.

There are a growing number of efforts to get Boston's brainpower working for Boston as well as for the world. One model is Boston Management Consortium. Begun in 1984 as an in-house organization consulting unit for City Hall, in 1989 it became a city program with a private-sector advisory council and in 1990 was spun off as a nonprofit public-private partnership between city government and over one hundred corporations and consulting firms. In 1993 more than one hundred volunteer consultants helped the city improve operations; the city paid fees of $400,000 and received over $1 million in services, not including cost savings netted by the projects. Smaller firms donate four to ten days a year; larger firms such as Price Waterhouse or Bain donate more.

One accomplishment of the consortium significant for improving Boston's quality of life is a safe neighborhood plan developed after a neighborhood summit that included gang members and housing project tenant leaders. The plan was credited with helping Boston reduce its violence rate by 23 percent between 1990 and 1992, more than any other major U.S. city.[26]

Still greater public and private cooperation is considered the highest priority among a large segment of the business community. Business and civic leaders who engaged in dialogue on these issues at my forum at Harvard Business School in April 1994 felt that if trust and communication could be increased, work could proceed on other matters important to business. As the head of a midsize manufacturing company put it: "I feel that I am doing everything I can to keep myself competitive. I am networking, I am innovating, I am globalizing my business. My challenge is not the marketplace, because there is more than enough business. My challenge is overcoming obstacles government seems to set up."

Breaking the cycle of cynicism and adversarial relations requires rethinking how cosmopolitans and locals interact as a community. One CEO issued a call to action: "We must reverse the negativism of the media and enlist their support in building a positive business climate. We must find courageous leaders to replace cynical politicians who pander to public whim merely to preserve popularity. We must recognize that to preserve Boston's preeminence as a business center, we must be bold and creative."

There are signs of greater public-private cooperation. By early 1995 Boston mayor Thomas Menino's outreach to the business community was paying off. Reebok Foundation, for example, gave $1.5 million to the city for after-school programs, even though Reebok's base is far outside the city. Governor Weld continued to streamline regulations, at business leaders' urging, to protect jobs.

Paul O'Brien, influential former chairman of Nynex New England, the Greater Boston Chamber of Commerce, the CEO group known as the Vault, and, it seems, nearly every important civic activity, feels the community can come together: "I see the Boston leadership community as far more effective than they think they are. I chalk it up to native New England self-criticism. But the city of Boston has run in the black for the last twelve years, unlike most cities around the country. Boston has relatively decent race relations, relatively small institutionalized poverty, and with a new teachers' contract, the school systems have got a chance of being at the leading edge of reform.

There probably are better leadership models for how businesses work together elsewhere. Cleveland and Minneapolis come to mind. However, one of the charms of Boston is that everybody does not agree with each other, it is not lockstep."

The challenge for thinkers, it is clear, is to extend a cooperative hand without giving up independence of mind.

LESSONS FOR OTHER CITIES: THINKING YOUR WAY TO SUCCESS

Nurturing an area's core capability in developing new concepts, its skill at innovation, can bring enormous rewards: products and services in demand in world markets because they set world standards, institutions that are centers of knowledge and attract still more brainpower, higher average incomes for knowledge workers and secondarily for the area as a whole, and the ability to generate new industries as old ones decline.

To become a world class city rich in concepts requires educational and research institutions that attract brainpower and put it to work creating new ideas or developing the next generation of technologies. It requires a support system for entrepreneurs: sources of capital and encouragement from both the private and public sectors; ways to transfer promising ideas from laboratories to businesses; professional service providers, whether legal, banking, or marketing support, that are familiar with industry requirements and the needs of fledgling businesses. It is aided by dense networks within and across industries, ranging from industry councils to informal interactions among leaders. Those dense networks encourage a flow of people and ideas; they facilitate alliances and partnerships between organizations that take advantage of local connections to create productive new ventures that combine technologies or capacities. And status as a world class knowledge center is maintained because of community amenities attractive to knowledge workers, including educational excellence, cultural events, and innovative social enterprises, all of which require active civic engagement.

This final factor, quality of community life, points to one of the problems of areas preeminent in thinking but undistinguished in making or trading. An entrepreneurial, innovation-driven economy sometimes undermines community collaboration because it tilts toward arrogance, widens the gap between cosmopolitan knowledge workers who think globally and less educated blue-collar and personal service workers, values attention to industry ties more than civic ties, and rewards originators of ideas more than those who cooperate in adopting them or marketing them.

It is risky to rely excessively on new concepts for an area's success, because knowledge development functions occupy only a fraction of a business's work force once a new business grows. Unless places emphasize the other two C's of operational competence—a cost-effective routine production base—and international connections, they will fail to retain the companies they hatch or attract new ones. If companies in search of manufacturing competence and trade connections disperse processing activities to other places, a community loses an important source of jobs and vitality.

One way communities can make the global economy work locally is to encourage entrepreneurs to build innovative products that incorporate the newest and best knowledge and command a premium in world markets. But for the community to thrive in the long run, there must also be collaboration among leaders for active economic development and civic improvement.

Makers: Foreign Manufacturing in South Carolina

Spartanburg and Greenville, in the hill country of South Carolina, make an unlikely center for international industry. Yet these sister cities are the site of the largest per capita diversified foreign investment in the United States. The Spartanburg-Greenville success rests on the second C: competence. By systematically upgrading their ability to meet the needs of manufacturers, these cities have derived local benefits from the global economy.

As in other American cities, the center of action has shifted from downtown to the shopping malls and industrial belt on the periphery. But what is found on the outskirts of Spartanburg, Greenville, and throughout the seven-county area called the "upstate" is unusual: an impressive concentration of foreign manufacturing companies on I-85, the interstate highway from Charlotte, North Carolina, to Atlanta—a highway familiarly known as "the autobahn" in honor of the large number of German companies in the area.

For decades business leaders such as Roger Milliken, chairman of textile giant Milliken & Company, and Paul Foerster, a German retired head of Hoechst Celanese's Spartanburg facility, have been prime movers of economic development, shaping an industrial policy that is also a foreign policy; Foerster recently established South Carolina's office in Frankfurt, Germany, and served as the state's unofficial ambassador to Europe. Business leadership has constituted a kind of shadow government, more cosmopolitan and more enduring than most local politicians. As an insider observed, "In South Carolina there's an incredible network, a fairly small network, of people who get things done and make decisions." Another said, "In South Carolina, there's a very blurred line between political decisions and any other kind of decision."

For Spartanburg and Greenville, foreign investment has been a positive force, bringing benefits to local businesses, workers, and the community well beyond the usual measures of capital infusion and job creation. The presence of international companies has created and spread the concepts, competence, and connections world class companies need by unleashing and renewing entrepreneurship and innovation; bringing an orientation to learning from well outside traditional boundaries and an awareness of world standards; and connecting local companies to international networks and civic collaboration at home.

"The modernization of the American textile industry here could not have taken place without the foreigners who brought machinery and helped revitalize the economy," according to Olin Sansbury, chancellor of the University of South Carolina at Spartanburg. Foreign companies have stimulated improvements in American companies. "There has been signficantly more reinvestment and fresh investment on the part of American companies as a result of the courage factor provided by the foreign investors. If those folks are coming in and making major investments in this growing area, then there is some reason for us to think about that, too," observed James Barrett, head of the Spartanburg County Foundation. "The mood that has been set over time has created a welcome environment. One success seems to follow another."

THE ECONOMIC TRACK RECORD

The cities of Spartanburg (population 230,000) and Greenville (population 345,000) and the seven surrounding counties of the upstate form the largest metropolitan statistical area in South Carolina and house a joint airport. U.S. Foreign Trade Zone 38 is located near interstate I-85 in Spartanburg County. The entire I-85 business belt contains almost a million people and boasts, Greenville boosters say, the largest number of engineers per capita in the United States and the country's lowest work stoppage rate (zero days over a five-year period). The state's largest manufacturing employer is Michelin Americas, subsidiary of Michelin Groupe of Clermont-Ferrand, France, the world's number one tire maker in sales, with three facilities in Greenville, Spartanburg, and Anderson Counties, a total investment of $1.5 billion, over nine thousand employees in South Carolina, and high factory wage rates of $15–$16 per hour. R&D for Michelin Americas is also in Greenville, and a test track and distribution center are housed nearby. In 1985 Michelin moved North American headquarters to Greenville.

The upstate has a diversified economic base, shifting successfully from the textile industry, which was once based largely on muscle power, to high technology, computers, metalworking, plastics, and automotive industries. Unemployment is well below state and national averages; Spartanburg has consistently led South Carolina in new job creation. In 1992 average unemployment in Spartanburg County was only 4.8 percent, compared with 7.4 percent in the United States; Greenville County was not far behind with a 5.2 percent rate. Throughout the 1980s there was a net increase of 11.6 percent in total employment (with a population increase of 11.2 percent), despite significant job losses in the textile industry. By November 1993 unemployment was down to 4.5 percent in Spartanburg County, 4.8 percent in Greenville County. Almost two-thirds of the 378 Greenville- and Spartanburg-area business heads responding to my survey had added jobs in the past three years, the highest proportion of any of the five places.

Spartanburg's employment base is skewed toward manufacturing, which accounts for 38 percent of its employment; Greenville has a lower proportion of workers in manufacturing and a larger proportion in service-related jobs. Only 0.5 percent of the area's industrial workers are unionized; South Carolina is a right-to-work state. South Carolina's nationally recognized worker training has upgraded the whole work force, and the average wage across the state is rising.

For the thirteen years from 1980 through 1992, Spartanburg enjoyed over $2.5 billion in new capital investment directly creating twenty-four thousand new jobs, not including additional jobs in construction trades to build plants, or in service industries, warehouses, or wholesale and retail trade; during the 1980s decade gross retail sales more than tripled. In 1992 Greenville-Spartanburg ranked seventh in the United States in the number of commitments to new facilities in *Site Selection and Industrial Development* magazine's annual listings; it was tenth in 1991.

In 1994 the upstate was home to over 215 international firms from eighteen countries, and over 50 have their U.S. headquarters there.[1] Most of them have expanded continuously; according to a Greenville Chamber of Commerce survey of 87 foreign-owned companies, 80 percent have expanded since their arrival in the upstate, and about 55 percent are planning a capital investment project in the next three years. Fourteen international flags fly above the new Spartanburg Chamber of Commerce building, on behalf of Spartanburg's 83 international companies from fourteen countries.

The 1992 announcement that BMW would locate its first-ever manufacturing facility outside of Germany in Spartanburg County, just over the line from Greenville, put the area in the world limelight. Newspapers and magazines noticed the "boom belt" in the Southeast along I-85. The BMW facility promised to bring two thousand direct jobs and create perhaps ten thousand more, at a time when the U.S. auto industry was only beginning to emerge from recession and U.S. cities were desperate for sources of new jobs.

The BMW announcement made international headlines and created a local stir because BMW is a well-known upscale consumer product, a household name. Local pride and local humor went hand in hand, as T-shirts proclaimed that BMW stood for "Bubba Motor Works." But behind this highly visible large investment stood several decades of international manufacturing and foreign investment in Spartanburg-Greenville, by companies that were not household names. These companies produced machines and materials not visible to the public eye but fundamental to the global competence in industrial skills that brought BMW to the area. The history of economic development in Spartanburg-Greenville is an object lesson for other communities: the importance of a solid base of midsize entrepreneurial companies with international connections and continual innovation in basic manufacturing, employing a work force whose skills are upgraded continuously against world standards.

Spartanburg-Greenville not only attracted foreign investment, it held it and grew it. Companies that set up an office in the area tended to bring more functions, more jobs, more skills, and more benefits to the area over time. Of 215 companies in the upstate with foreign affiliations in 1994, 67 percent are engaged in manufacturing, 24 percent have their U.S. headquarters there, and 68 percent were Greenfield start-ups, infusing new energy into the community. And it was not just any foreign investment. The area first attracted companies from Germany and German-speaking Switzerland and Austria, whose cultural style was to sink roots and assimilate; expatriates became long-term residents and even citizens.

Many companies were small and midsize; their only edge was innovation, and they could grant considerable autonomy to their American operations to act entrepreneurially. The companies first came as part of an industry cluster centered around textile machinery and fibers.[2] A core capability in textile machinery was extended to other kinds of machinery, which then diversified the industrial base and reduced the area's vulnerability to downturns in the textile industry. An innovative worker training scheme created as the first foreign companies entered the area produced a world-ready work force. And as the population became more cosmopolitan through the influence of foreign companies, a second capability developed: creating a hospitable atmosphere for additional foreign investment unrelated to textiles.

The development of Spartanburg-Greenville as an international manufacturing center happened in waves. It started with sales, distribution, and service offices of central European textile machinery makers and later broadened into manufacturing. Gaining further German and Swiss investment was convenient because there were companies from those countries in textiles. Community and political leaders did not set out to concentrate on those countries, but that is where the manufacturers were and where people already in the Spartanburg area had contacts. German and Swiss businesspeople happily settled in Spartanburg invited their colleagues and friends from Europe. European growth looked limited, the U.S. market seemed to be open territory, and many Europeans found the American quality of life attractive.

As time went on, selling the upstate became easier, because prospective investors could talk to people from their country already there. When one wave of immigration and foreign investment was exhausted, another formed. The Swiss wave, for example, came between 1960 and the early 1970s; then Swiss companies stopped coming, but by that time companies from other countries were attracted to the area. When textiles began to sag, there were deliberate attempts to attract other kinds of industries to supplement textiles, and many of the equipment manufacturers found additional applications for their machinery and skills. With the exception of Hoechst, large manufacturers came quite late in the day. The area first attracted entrepreneurs rather than branches of large companies.

Contrary to popular belief, low wages or tax incentives were not the primary reason foreign companies were attracted to South Carolina's upstate region. Indeed, recent studies have shown that state and local tax incentives play little or no role in the location of business activities by foreign companies in the United States. Patterns of location choice do differ depending on whether foreign investors get tax credits at home for state tax payments,[3] but generally, business-related factors play a larger role. South Carolina's principal incentive was business related: its innovative job-training program guaranteed a custom-trained work force at no expense to employer or employee.

Foreign companies were also attracted and kept because of the area's hospitable attitudes toward them, but this was a mutually reinforcing interaction. The commitment of foreign companies to the area is among the reasons the locals' response to them was so positive. Very few foreign companies have left the area; they have expanded their investment over time. Charles Boone, president of the Spartanburg Hospital system, observed: "They're very community spirited. They are interested in integrating themselves into the community and not living in a ghetto here. Our Swiss neighbors in the 1960s loved to visit Switzerland, but they had no interest in going back permanently. They said there are so many things available in this country that you've got to go outside of Switzerland for. Here you can go from state to state and not have to stop to show your passports."

The locals' view is also generally positive because foreign and outside investment helped keep—and expand—home-grown companies in the area. For example, Hersey Measurement, which is perhaps Spartanburg's oldest company, was founded in 1859 to manufacture rotary pumps, bolts, and general machinery and was kept going by new owners from Atlanta in a joint venture with a German company. Its acquirers decided to keep Hersey in Spartanburg because of an excellent work force, building a new plant that doubled the size of its local facilities. Lockwood Greene Engineers, one of America's oldest engineering services companies, was reinvigorated by its acquisition by a German company after a difficult management buyout. Metromont Materials, a leader in concrete, was rescued by a British company after large American companies abdicated the industry. Prym-Dritz, a maker of sewing notions, was saved by a German company after a series of ill-fated changes of ownership; the new German parent consolidated all of its U.S. operations in Spartanburg.

The area also has homegrown entrepreneurial companies in service industries, such as Flagstar, founded in 1961 and growing to nearly $4 billion in sales, which have been important to the area—in the way the new Flagstar urban headquarters helped Spartanburg's downtown revitalization, for example, or by the economic windfall caused when CEO Jerry Richardson won the National Football League's latest franchise for his Carolina Panthers—but Flagstar has also caused problems, by initiating abrupt layoffs, for example, or provoking a lawsuit for racial bias, as with the Denny's chain restaurants. But foreign manufacturers have been among the most innovative and progressive forces in the region, as we shall see when its remarkable success story unfolds. They have built world class manufacturing skills and turned locals into cosmopolitans.

Four factors lie behind the area's success:

- visionary leadership, from lead companies that built a foundation for later successes, working actively to recruit international companies to bring new resources to the area;
- a hospitable business climate and positive work ethic attracting innovative manufacturing companies making long-term investments and helping foreigners feel welcome;
- customized training and continual upgrading of worker skills through educational improvement;
- collaboration within the business community and across sectors to bring world class quality, improve operational skills and practices, offer mutual assistance, and act in concert on community priorities.

■ SUCCESS ELEMENT #1: ACTIVE OUTREACH

"Foundation" or "lead" companies often account for how a community connects to the wider economy. They are the platform from which later growth develops. The first major businesses in a region provide the leadership—or not—for community building. Their industrial base and their character as companies shape the prospects for those that come later—and, indeed, for those that are attracted to come at all.

In South Carolina's upstate, foreign investment began in Spartanburg, the foundation was large textile companies, and the generally acknowledged leader among those companies was Roger Milliken, chief executive of Milliken & Company. A community leader said, "Being a Southerner, I think the first big 'foreign' influence was the Millikens—Northerners. Their influence has been stronger than all the international people combined."

MILLIKEN AND THE FABRIC OF A COMMUNITY

One significant action in 1954 set in motion a number of forces that eventually brought economic strength to the region as a major player in the global economy. In 1954 Roger Milliken moved the company headquarters and his family from New York to Spartanburg. Milliken saw the need to compete with cheap imports by modernizing equipment to bring labor costs under control and improve quality. So in the late 1950s he started systematically encouraging German and Swiss manufacturers that supplied the textile industry to set up shop in Spartanburg to be close to their customers. Richard Tukey, executive director of the Chamber of Commerce, got on board very quickly to make it happen. Other suppliers, such as Hoechst, which sold fibers to the industry, got the message, as Paul Foerster recalled: "We knew thirty years ago that we had to be close to our customers—and if we didn't know it, people like Mr. Milliken made it clear."

Milliken & Company roots date to 1865 in Portland, Maine, where Deering Milliken Company was founded, soon establishing a New York headquarters. Its first plant in Spartanburg, among the oldest continuously operating there, opened in 1884. With current sales of nearly $3 billion, Milliken has long been a valued industry innovator. In 1981 Milliken instituted a pioneering internal quality program, leading to a string of awards: the American Malcolm Baldrige National Quality Award, the British Quality Award, Canada Awards for Business Excellence, and the European Quality Award. It was the first, and in some cases the only, fabric supplier to receive the highest quality awards from General Motors, Ford, and Chrysler. Milliken Research Center is the largest private research organization in the world and conducts over 70 percent of American textile research. Milliken is environmentally aware, and its headquarters on I-85 regularly gets awards from the local garden club. Milliken has school partnerships in every U.S. plant location. Its Innovators Hall of Fame, begun in 1984, recognizes innovations among its fourteen thousand associates working in fifty-five manufacturing locations worldwide; Milliken University polishes their managers' skills.

The surrounding area had a history of progressive—some would say paternalistic—textile companies; nationally, about 70 percent of American textile industry was within a hundred miles of Spartanburg. Inman Mills was the first industrial firm in South Carolina to offer free infant immunizations on-site. Mayfair Mills joined Milliken & Co. as a founding member of the "Crafted with Pride in the U.S.A." Council described in chapter 5—Roger Milliken was the council's first chairman—and started studying W. Edwards Deming's quality principles in 1980, well before they caught on elsewhere. Walter Montgomery Sr., the retired chairman of Spartan Mills, named one of the twenty-five most important leaders in industry history, now in his nineties, founded the Spartanburg County Foundation in 1943, the oldest community foundation in the state and one of the oldest in the Southeast, with assets exceeding those of any other foundation south of Washington except the one in Winston-Salem.

But it was Roger Milliken who brought cosmopolitanism to Spartanburg. Milliken relocated a portion of his staff from New England to South Carolina; they focused attention on education even before international companies became a formidable presence demanding better education. "When Milliken came down they brought a lot of executives and provided executive-type positions," recalled a woman active in the community. "Those people had higher expectations of the school system and were willing to make more of a commitment to education." Milliken led the group founding Spartanburg Country Day School, a private school that attracted children of expatriates before the public schools improved.

Milliken helped make the area hospitable to foreign companies and ensured that the area reaped the benefits. With Boone, the hospital chief, and others, Milliken established the Carolinas Country Club for foreign companies at the request of the Chamber of Commerce. He chaired the Greenville-Spartanburg airport authority. And Milliken's international contacts became the first source of foreign investment in Spartanburg.

THE TUKEY TURNPIKE: HIGHWAY FROM EUROPE TO SPARTANBURG

The primary activist luring foreign investment to the area was Richard Tukey, executive director of the Chamber of Commerce from 1951 until his death in 1979 and now much honored in Spartanburg—his initials grace the local public broadcasting station's call letters, WRET; I-85 is sometimes called the "Tukey turnpike."

Tukey went overseas to textile machinery shows as the natural place to find investors, eventually developing a wide network in Europe. People in Spartanburg were open to foreign investment because the alternatives for them were poor jobs in textile or poultry plants or no job at all. Tukey was a visionary who realized that there were very few, if any, American textile equipment companies left. He saw that as an opportunity for this area, but one that had to be cultivated. "Dick saw international trade coming," Boone recalled, "and he felt it was going to be important to have that here in Spartanburg. He was criticized, as are all people with foresight, for dealing more with foreign companies than with local industry already here."

Tukey was a consummate politician and salesman. His allies included South Carolina's governors and lieutenant governors, starting with Fritz Hollings and enhanced by every succeeding state administration. "At Tukey's urging, the state did all kinds of things to make this area attractive to Europeans," commented university chancellor Sansbury. "For example, he got the legislature to amend the alcohol laws so that Germans, Swiss, Europeans, could import wine on a more convenient basis."

Tukey tales abound. In 1965 he helped establish the U.S. base for Menzel of Germany off I-85 in just four days, including housing for the manager and articles of incorporation for the company.[4] When Kurt Zimmerli, CEO of Zima, first explored moving to the area, Tukey shepherded him to banks and presented him to community leaders, introducing him as a source of new employment and paving the way for a warm welcome. A German executive recalls how Tukey lured his company to Spartanburg in 1978. He had chosen South Carolina because of the climate and a relationship with a Columbia company. He went to Columbia and within three days had a lawyer, a bank account, and a building, although nothing was signed. Then, through a banker, he was introduced to supersalesman Tukey, who talked him out of Columbia and into Spartanburg not only for its advantages, but also because Tukey would help him personally.

"He was an introducer and an icebreaker," another Spartanburg leader said. "He was really awful looking; he didn't have vast personal resources to wine and dine people, either. But he had a wonderful personality." Called a "miraculous individual," he helped establish a variety of institutions that reinforced Spartanburg's international look and upgraded its educational and cultural amenities. He started a German-style Octoberfest. He saw the need to strengthen education as a companion to strengthening the economic base. He helped establish a top-ranking state educational television capability broadcasting courses throughout the state. "South Carolina ranks forty-ninth in a lot of things," said Elaine Freeman, executive director of the ETV Endowment, "so it's a special source of pride for us to have this fabulous educational TV."

■ SUCCESS ELEMENT #2: HOSPITABLE BUSINESS CLIMATE AND POSITIVE WORK ETHIC

Spartanburg was first to catch the foreign wave, making innovative companies feel welcome and enabling foreigners to become community leaders. The business climate was hospitable to long-term foreign investment, and the indigenous work ethic was attractive to innovative companies.

THE FOREIGN SURGE

The foreign wave started in the 1960s, with a set of homegrown midsize international companies that established their own greenfield sites rather than acquiring American companies. Then they stayed and expanded, often because they sent entrepreneurs who committed themselves to growth in Spartanburg; some expatriates became citizens and community leaders. Several aspects of the area's foreign investment are noteworthy:

- *Industry diversification based on core skills.* The textile industry provided a customer base, but the technical skills and capabilities of the companies that came were not confined to one industry; they could be extended to many other industries.

• *Expansion and upgrading.* The foreign companies gradually expanded the functions and skills located in the area. Functions tended to expand from sales and service to manufacturing. Markets tended to expand from regional to North American to export markets. A regional office often became the North American headquarters. Initially the companies transferred technology, quality, and skills from the foreign parent; but eventually many of the U.S. units outperformed them and taught them.

• *Entrepreneurship and innovation.* The first companies were generally midsize, sending entrepreneurs who could build new ventures from scratch and granting them considerable autonomy to do so. U.S. operations were thus highly independent, rather than subordinate branches of multinational giants; foreign managers in America were entrepreneurs committed to growing the local business, not expatriates on short career rotations. Survival depended on a high degree of technological innovation.

• *Easy local assimilation.* Companies generally sent only a few foreigners, some of whom took U.S. citizenship; the large number of American hires gave the companies an American flavor. The first foreign company representatives were well-educated, English-speaking, cosmopolitan Europeans who could easily blend into the local population —there were no observable physical differences—and join the leadership class. They came from middle European countries less concerned about maintaining language purity or separatist traditions than Japan or France. (To many Spartanburg locals, the "real" foreigners are poor non-Europeans, such as more recent Asian immigrants.) Moreover, the original companies were not household names, not particularly visible or publicized, and not of particular interest to average citizens —so they could blend in without notice.

According to local leaders, it took a long time for most people to realize just how many foreign companies there were in Spartanburg, which caught the wave before Greenville. In my research group's interviews, so many took pains to tell us that there was *not* a "foreign invasion" of the upstate that we understood how invaded the locals might have felt. A college official recalled, "They were coming from Germany and Switzerland and Austria, this company and that company and another company. They weren't coming as groups with an invasion plan." A local businessman said, "For all the other Swiss and German, European companies that would locate in Spartanburg, there might be one or two or five foreign nationals in a company, then the rest were all Americans. I'm sure it's not by accident. They have been really careful in making sure it didn't appear like an invasion."

One of the first European textile equipment sales offices was opened in 1959 when Brian Mackey Lyttle moved from Ireland to Spartanburg to start Hobourn Sales, a division of Hobourn Aero Components of Rochester, England, which made machinery for texturized hosiery yarn. A few years later, facing a saturated market, Hobourn made plans to close its American operation. Lyttle bought the company in 1964, changed its name, developed relationships with other manufacturers, and introduced new products. When double-knit fabrics went out of style almost overnight in 1970s, and the textile industry was in a downturn, Lyttle diversified into screen printers, water purification systems for pools or hot tubs, and acrylic building blocks.

By far the dominant culture represented in the first wave was middle European—Swiss, Austrian, and German. Also among the first new foreign facilities in 1959 was the sales and service office of Rieter Machine Works of Winterthur, Switzerland. Rieter, whose initial U.S. chief was a friend of Roger Milliken, located in Spartanburg after the Milliken move because the U.S. textile industry was 30–35 percent of its market (now about 20 percent). Rieter gradually expanded into manufacturing, increasing its investment in South Carolina. And over time, Rieter's U.S. operations became more independent, less controlled from Switzerland, especially in terms of technical and personnel decisions, and the parent company itself became more international, with more foreigners on its management board. Ueli Schmid, the current CEO, joined Rieter in Switzerland in 1970, moved to the United States in 1980, and became an American citizen.

As a Swiss company operating in the United States, Rieter discovered numerous areas of difference. A conversion from metric standards was the least of the issues. With respect to quality and procedures, Europeans were more precise, even "rigid," Schmid said. For each new product, Rieter brought a very small number of Swiss over for a six-to-nine-month tour, then moved them back. "It was never planned to have too many Swiss in the operation," Schmid recalled. Sending American workers to Switzerland for one to six months to learn Rieter ways did not work out very well because they were not adept at languages or adapting to foreign environments.

But Rieter could blend American entrepreneurial risk taking with Swiss technical precision to achieve outstanding results in the United States. Its American plant is one of the most competitive in the company, usually beating the Europeans by over 15 percent in productivity. Because the plant is close to the market, it does things technically "they would hesitate to do in Europe," Schmid said. "It's the American approach that is much more Let's try it, let's go for it. We had a very nice market leader, but the machine didn't fit in a customer's plant. In Europe you would have a few commissions to study it to see what can be done. We in America did it between production runs. We adapted the machine together with the customer, super cooperation. The machines arrived at the plant, and they fit in." Initially technology transfer was from Europe to the United States, but "these days the plant has as much impact on how they do business over there as the other way around," Schmid reported.

In his view, the U.S. market is one of the toughest, because American companies put the highest demands on equipment and have one of the least trained work forces. "A mill in Europe runs, let's say, six thousand hours in a year," he said. "Here in the United States you are usually above eight thousand hours for the same equipment. In Europe plant management depends more on in-house expertise to maintain equipment. Here in the United States, the plants call the supplier to come and fix it." But, Schmid felt, those who work with European companies in the United States are exposed to different, often higher standards that exert a positive force in improving U.S. competitiveness. "The ideal work force," he said, "will combine American flexibility, American drive, with a Swiss education."

Other German and Swiss companies soon followed Rieter. In 1963 Sulzer Ruti, Swiss manufacturer of weaving machines, also established a sales and service office. Proud of both its Swiss and its textile roots, the company hosts an annual celebration of Swiss Independence Day through the Swiss American Society of the Piedmont and, in 1988, gave the Spartanburg Chamber of Commerce a six-foot globe made of textile machinery parts.

With a base in the area, the conversion from sales and service to manufacturing began. Menzel, from Bielefeld, West Germany, established its office in 1965 but soon realized it was more practical to build machinery in Spartanburg, the first European firm to do so. It is an industry leader and a demonstration of the multiplier created for Spartanburg as competence grew there. Menzel created an innovative material handling system for large-roll batching used in plastics, fiberglass, rubber, and other applications besides textiles. Now three times its original size, it produces in America machinery not built in Germany and derives under 40 percent of its revenue from textile industry. But German roots are still clear; two sections of the Berlin Wall are kept on display outside its Spartanburg corporate offices. The president of the German parent, Gerd Menzel, was made an honorary citizen of Spartanburg and received the Order of the Palmetto from former South Carolina governor John West.

Cosmopolitan entrepreneurs came with the middle European wave. Kurt Zimmerli, Swiss German head of Zima/Kusters/EVAC, observes that "the class of Europeans that come to the United States joining these foreign companies—well educated, cultured, and high income —are very demanding in terms of education and amenities in the city." He was one of them. He first came to the United States in 1957 and worked as a chief engineer for a Massachusetts company that supplied Milliken, later becoming a vice president for international activities for Gulf + Western, living in Philadelphia and New York. He was familiar with the area through Milliken, and he liked its international flavor and the local people.

Once in Spartanburg, he established Zima in 1969 as his own engineering-oriented equipment contractor representing a number of European manufacturers, created a joint venture with Eduard Kusters of Krefeld, Germany, to establish its U.S. base on I-85 in 1974, and acquired EVAC, a local company, in 1991. Initially Zimmerli imported most of the equipment, but then he started manufacturing in Spartanburg. Today, he says, "the majority of the equipment sold is local production and in the area of carpet machinery. Our joint venture partner discontinued its own manufacturing of this product based on the fact that we introduced new technology and outsold the German plant by a factor of ten to one. Today, 90 percent of all carpet dyed continuously worldwide is processed on our Kusters equipment."

Zimmerli became an American citizen early in his stay and became active in the community, helping found a bank and the Friends of Music, and serving as chairman of the Chamber of Commerce's international committee for twenty years. He serves on the board of trustees at Converse College and is the current chairman of the Spartanburg County Foundation. His employees are American, and most of his contact with other internationals is because of mutual business or civic interests, not shared national culture.

Like Zimmerli, Hans Balmer liked what he found in Spartanburg. Sent in 1972 from Switzerland for two years as Leepfe Brothero Ltd.'s U.S. representative at the age of twenty-five, he married an American and stayed. In 1985 he founded his own business, Symtech Inc., which he has grown to nearly $50 million in sales, using the best models of supply chain partnering, as described in chapter 4. Symtech integrates equipment from many European manufacturers to provide a complete manufacturing process for its customers. Balmer, a big believer in synergies and collaboration, has brought other foreign companies to Spartanburg, such as LTG Technologies, which makes a variety of air-conditioning, waste handling, and pollution control systems. Balmer succeeded Zimmerli as international committee chair for the Chamber of Commerce.

FROM MIDSIZE INNOVATORS TO GLOBAL COMPANIES

The area attracted innovators, derived from the *mittelstand* or midsize companies that constituted much of the industrial strength of Germany. Their innovations brought technological expertise to the area and made expansion possible for the companies. For example:

- Zimmer Machinery, holder of hundreds of patents, which came in 1969, makes high-precision split-second printing equipment, the parent company's only manufacturing facility outside Austria.
- Saxonia-Francke of America, which came a decade later, is a pioneering metal-stamping company extending the European fine-blanking process and is expanding into laser processes.
- SEW-Eurodrive is one of the world's largest gear producers; its Spartanburg unit exports to twenty-six countries.
- Staubli, which has been expanding its manufacturing of pneumatic and hydraulic coupling products in Spartanburg, bought Westing-

house's robotics division in 1988 and recently signed a global cooperation agreement with Cincinnati Milacron, bringing still more opportunities to the area.

Greenville and Spartanburg also house America's largest silicon wafer plant (German-owned MEMC Electronic Materials), the world's most advanced tennis ball manufacturing facility (Wilson, owned by AMER Group of Helsinki, Finland), and the largest supplier of software to the pharmaceutical industry.

An exception to the predominance of small and midsize companies in the initial foreign surge was German chemical giant Hoechst. Hoechst traces its local origins to 1967 and a joint venture with Hercules, which it acquired, then merging in 1987 with Celanese to form Hoechst-Celanese. The company has both raw materials and fiber plants in the area; in the chemical plant alone equity investment totals close to half a billion dollars.

Besides bringing jobs to Spartanburg, Hoechst brought another important local leader in Paul Foerster. Foerster moved to Spartanburg from Germany with his family in 1967 to run the fibers facility on a four-year contract, which was extended until his retirement in 1990. A cultural cross-fertilizer, he turned Hoechst-Celanese into an important charitable contributor to the area despite the lack of a charitable tradition in Germany. "It took me about three years to educate the guys in Frankfurt," he recalled. After retirement Foerster became honorary consul for Germany, liaison to Europe for South Carolina, chairman of the Spartanburg Chamber of Commerce, and responsible for much international company traffic through Spartanburg.

As a global company, Hoechst-Celanese is a cosmopolitan force in Spartanburg. It manages its American business relatively autonomously but coordinates with similar businesses in Germany, especially for frequent technology interchange, accomplished through visits, temporary assignments, and increasingly, information systems. It concentrates on the North American market but expects to grow its modest exports—now under 10 percent. There is a great deal of cross-flow of information among Canadian, Mexican, and American plants. Foerster's successor, Bill Mayrose, said that German ownership brings only advantages: "We run basically as a U.S. corporation, but because Hoechst is a large, technological company, we can utilize that whole technological resource from anywhere in the world."

WELCOMING FOREIGN COMPANIES

In the 1980s attracting foreign investment became an explicit strategy for Greenville as well as Spartanburg. By 1994 German companies still dominated, with 65 of the upstate's 215 foreign-affiliated firms, but British companies were second with 43 and Japanese third with 29. While there were only 16 French-affiliated companies, employment in them was almost as great as in German companies because of Michelin. Service companies were foreign owned, too; supermarket conglomerate Ahold of the Netherlands, a member of the European Retail Alliance mentioned in chapter 3, employs four thousand people in the upstate through its Bi-Lo chain headquartered in Greenville.[5]

From the start of the foreign surge, European managers were welcomed by the community, which exemplified the reality of "Southern hospitality." Betsy Teter, former business editor of the *Spartanburg Herald Journal*, recounted girlhood memories of the 1960s, when her neighborhood had welcome wagon parties for the new foreigners who were moving in. But established business leaders were also selective, wanting companies that would not threaten existing business practices or attract a different class of worker. Kohler, a leading manufacturer of plumbing supplies from Wisconsin, was one of the first nontextile industries to come. "The textile industry was real jittery about that," a community leader recalled. Several people told us the Toyota story, although others denied it: "Toyota tried to come to this area a few years ago. A lot of people came out against it, especially the textile industry, which got such bad press for this." Another said, "I think the textile people fought Toyota because of unions. We are a right-to-work state, and people here pride themselves on that. Auto companies might be wonderful, but what about the workers who come with it and bring in crime?"

THE SOUTHERN WORK ETHIC

Locals could express their concern about new kinds of workers coming to the area without sounding unduly prejudiced—to their own ears, at least—because the area had long enjoyed a tradition of hard work. Over lunch at the Carolinas Club and dinner at the Milliken Guest House during my research group's first visit, executives and community leaders sounded the same positive note: "It's a real big-time work ethic around here." "It's all business." "Everybody goes to work at eight A.M."

The upstate work ethic is said to be rooted in religion and a tradition of independent farmers, not slave owners, who were ingenious, resilient, and hardworking, even if not literate or well trained. The religious connection is particularly clear. Greenville and Spartanburg had the highest proportion of business heads in my five-city survey reporting that churches or other religious institutions are helpful to their business (61 percent, in contrast with the next highest area, Boston, at 37 percent) and the highest percentage of companies reporting moderate to substantial levels of charitable giving as a company (77 percent). Steve Spiller, British head of Sagem-Lucas, a British-French joint venture, described his reactions: "One of the things that astounded me when I came over was the work ethic of people who work for me. I came from Europe, where the work ethic of the Japanese had been battered into me all the time—the 'last grain of rice' story, that the Japanese worker pays so much attention to detail when he's eating his lunch that he will take the last grain of rice out of his lunch box before he's finished. And I found it here. It is significant that a lot of my people attend church on Sundays; I think that brings them into a morality all their own. It's amazing when we look at the payroll, how many people tithe portions of their salary to their church. When we finish work here at five-thirty, you don't see a crowd of people charging out the door. People leave after five-thirty when they finish doing the job. And we're all salaried here; that has never been abused."

Other international managers also praise South Carolina workers over Europeans. Ueli Schmid of Rieter: "The flexibility of an American work force is absolutely incredible." Hans Balmer of Symtech: "The human 'product' is right in Spartanburg. The labor force has a very good attitude of wanting to work, doing a good job, respecting what a company is doing for them, and being thankful for it, not taking it for granted."

■ SUCCESS ELEMENT #3: IMPROVING TRAINING AND EDUCATION

Good attitudes are not enough. The work force needs skills that meet world standards. For over thirty years a collaboration led by the state has provided outstanding technical training and has been a vital factor in expanding high-wage manufacturing jobs in the Greenville-Spartanburg area.

WORLD CLASS TRAINING: TECH SPECIAL SCHOOLS

Spartanburg and the upstate first attracted foreign companies for marketing reasons—to be close to their textile industry customers; but the area's leaders enticed them to expand manufacturing and then attracted still other nontextile industry manufacturing jobs because of an innovative job training system, a national model devised as a "crash program" to deal with economic desperation in 1961.

The South Carolina State Board for Technical and Comprehensive Education training system offers free, customized technical training of prospective workers and supervisors to companies bringing new investment to the state. The board assigns staff to prepare manuals, interview workers, and teach classes—tech special schools—based on technical requirements established by the company, after work hours, at no cost to trainees, either. The company has no obligation to hire any worker completing the training, nor does the person have to accept a job offer. In some cases the state will pay to send first-line supervisors for training elsewhere, even in a foreign country. Training benefits apply to major facility expansions as well as to new sites.

A network of sixteen technical colleges runs the tech special schools, including Greenville Technical College, rated by *U.S. News & World Report* as one of America's best technical schools. The network has trained over 145,000 workers for about 1,200 facilities since inception —31,521 for the textile industry; 34,005 for metalworking; 17,647 for electrical and electronic machinery trades. In fiscal year 1992–93, 6,445 people (42 percent black) were trained for 121 companies, including U.S. companies such as Tupperware and Perdue, at a cost to the state of about $6.4 million; the 1993–94 budget is $10.8 million.

The training board helps upgrade skills for the global economy in other ways, offering courses for companies such as "World Class Concepts," developed by the "World Class Training Center" at Tri-County Technical College, or corporate community relations guidance for international companies moving to South Carolina. Accompanying this is a Buy South Carolina program to support just-in-time inventory systems by finding local suppliers.

Companies can also draw on training from the Quality Institute of

Enterprise Development Inc., a private nonprofit venture spun off from the state's Economic Development Board, which partners with upstate technical colleges, University of South Carolina at Spartanburg (home of one of six national manufacturing quality institutes), and the local Chamber of Commerce. (Its funding from the Appalachian Regional Commission is an acknowledgment that economic development means more than roads and bridges.) Its recent emphasis is on ISO 9000, the European quality certification—for example, a one-year assignment to train associates for Milliken & Company so that its U.S. work force meets world standards. Executive director Randy Garrison observed, "The majority of the businesses pushing to get ISO 9000 registration are pretty much American-based corporations. Some originally thought that if they didn't do it, they wouldn't be able to trade in Europe, but quickly found that was a misconception. Now they do it for the proper reason, which is to better their operation."

For German and Japanese companies with extremely high technical expectations and quality standards, South Carolina's training benefits and the upstate's technical education resources are major incentives. Mita South Carolina, for example, a Japanese toner manufacturer, used the tech special schools to build its U.S. work force after coming to Greenville in 1991 to manufacture for the North American market. Of its 150 current employees, Japanese constitute only the top dozen managers (the heads of engineering and human resources are Americans), with Japanese technicians working at start-up on installation and troubleshooting. Japanese managers found the first supervisors and agreed upon a curriculum with the state training board.

Hiring for Mita began in earnest when Rick Teal was recruited as human resource director in October 1991 to get ready for a March 1992 opening. Mita had 1,200 applicants for the first 80 jobs, despite uncertainties about pay structure or even job content because of state-of-the-art equipment new to Mita and proprietary. "The initial hiring plans were for about eighty hourly people," Teal recalled. "We went to the Employment Security Commission and started to interview people for the special schools—for two weeks, interviewing one about every fifteen minutes during the day, and then I came back to the office and worked during the night. I made a conscious decision to stop hiring after we found about forty good people, because I really didn't know if I should have been hiring tool and die makers or if I was overskilling because all I needed was simple assembly. So those forty enrolled in the special schools program, some for toner, some for molding. It turned out it didn't really matter which program they were in, because the basic skills were very helpful—math skills, communications, metric system, and so on."

The tech special schools provide an increasingly world-ready work force, but some international managers want the work force to meet even higher standards. Hans Balmer, clearly reluctant to sound critical, said, "We lack technical training; the absence of apprenticeship programs is a big drawback." German-style apprenticeships are on the agenda for South Carolina. Journalist Betsy Teter said, "They are concerned about education, that the workers applying for jobs don't have any thinking skills, can't read and write. The new collaboration between German companies and technical education institutions will hopefully provide a cushion between public school secondary education and business."

UPGRADING PUBLIC SCHOOLS

Improvements in public K–12 education came concurrently with the early foreign investment surge in Spartanburg. Spartanburg legend has it that many years ago, when the state distributed a windfall to the towns, Greenville used its money for sewers, so it attracted big American industry, whereas Spartanburg used its windfall for education and landed the foreign companies.

The primary impact of foreign investment in the upstate was economic—a sound tax base. But foreign companies also helped strengthen a vision of what education should be. "Since these companies moved in," a German executive noted, "German, Swiss, or from the North, they raise standards for worker knowledge."

The presence of international companies was an excuse for change, not a cause of it, according to educators; it helped them make the case for educational spending to raise the standards everywhere. Most foreign investment was on I-85, outside of Spartanburg District 7. An educator said, "I've been in the county office ten years, and because of foreign investment, on a per pupil basis the richest district has changed four times in ten years. Then even the poor neighbors use that as an excuse with the school board to have the same thing everyone else does." A school superintendent observed that foreign managers' "higher expectations for education gave us a golden opportunity to do some good things with our system." Another reported, "In our outlying district, we've tripled the foreign language enrollment, and it didn't have a thing to do with a single company in Spartanburg County. But the international presence helped me politically justify what I secretly wanted to do anyway."

School reform efforts began in Spartanburg in the 1950s when leaders wanted to lessen the disparity among districts. Since the 1960s, local leaders recalled, Spartanburg "taxed ourselves high compared to the rest of the state." Improving education was a state priority in the 1980s. In 1984 South Carolina, with private sector help, created a sales tax–financed 30 percent increase in school budgets, which led to a rise of 128 points in average SAT scores;[6] Richard Riley, then governor, would later join the Clinton cabinet as U.S. Secretary of Education.

Spartanburg's District 7 High School has been consistently excellent through the decades, setting a tone for the area. It was one of the first in the United States to offer advanced placement courses and continues to receive White House Achievement Awards—the only high school to have won three times. Spartanburg's nationally recognized, ranked championship academic team now gets its photo on the front page of the *Spartanburg Herald Journal* the way the football team once did if it scored five touchdowns.

Greenville also responded to its growing international flavor. Greenville's Southside High School is the only high school in South Carolina, and one of a handful in America, awarding the International Baccalaureate Diploma, based on a 1963 project in Geneva, Switzerland, to alleviate the difficulty children of diplomats experienced when returning to their own country after living abroad. The program, which requires special admission, offers an education on a par with European schools enabling entrance to European universities. Currently about two hundred students are enrolled in grades 9–12, most of them Americans.

An educator from Dorman High School summarized the surprise outsiders have at finding such good schools in the upstate: "We have an in-house joke that's not so far from the truth. If we have a student transferring in from north of the Mason-Dixon line or west of the Mississippi River, their parents are going to immediately want them enrolled in the honors classes. They think that we are so backward that no matter how poorly their child might have been doing wherever they were before, they are honors material here. They stay about two or three days, then they are back over here saying 'I think maybe we need a level change.' "

One reason educators consider foreign companies incidental to school reform is the minimal foreign presence in upstate schools until recently. The first foreign companies sent a relatively small number of expatriates, and there were few foreign students in the public schools. Initially foreign expatriates' children tended to go to Spartanburg Country Day School, a private school described by a resident as having a "German-centric education." Foreign educational aspirations were often satisfied outside the public schools because several nationalities established their own after-hours and weekend schools. Greenville's international offerings include the Michelin School, established in 1975, where twelve teachers educate about fifty-five children of Michelin employees entirely in French following the French school curriculum; Deutschschule für Kinder, operated by Greenville Tech; a Chinese school; and a Japanese Saturday school.

Furthermore, because most of the first migrants were middle European, they generally came with an outstanding previous education and excellent English. Only recently have younger families moved in from France, Germany, or Japan and put non-English-speaking children into the schools. An educator recalled that "the first time I heard people say we need to have English as a second language is when the Laotians came in the 1980s."

The BMW announcement generated greater interest in learning German, the way Michelin's arrival did for learning French. But another educator said, "The emphasis on foreign languages has not necessarily come from international companies moving into Spartanburg County. It is much more of a global issue, like turning on CNN at any time and seeing what's going on across the world. I don't think taking German is necessarily going to get somebody a job at BMW, but there is more awareness that some knowledge of a foreign culture or language will make you more competitive in the international arena."

Around 1988 the Spartanburg schools added a required course on world geography to, one of its teachers said, "make our kids competitive, an internal curricular decision, not something imposed by Michelin or BMW. In the world cultures course, the foreign students are much more comfortable because they feel at home, they feel that people are interested in them. Our local children get to see what these people they've heard about and read about are really like, and that they are just like them."

The area's international companies offer opportunities for public school students. In 1992 the District 7 orchestra went to Germany and were special guests at one of the BMW plants, giving a concert for workers as "the official BMW orchestra." A school official compared this with the past: "When I started to teach twenty-five years ago, 80 percent of my kids hadn't been outside of Spartanburg County, even to go to Greenville."

International awareness and world class skills are now a priority in Spartanburg and Greenville, not only for K–12, but also for the upstate's colleges and universities. Skill improvements in math, science, computers, and technology are especially important because of the industrial base. Educators are upgrading language training—at USC at Spartanburg French classes are held at eleven A.M. so they can tie in by satellite to the French evening news from Paris—and significantly expanding exchange programs and internships abroad. For the latter, in particular, foreign companies are a key resource, connecting locals to many parts of the world.

Improvements in public education and a greater awareness of world standards mean that schools are helpful to businesses; Greenville and Spartanburg business heads were the most likely of those in the other places in my survey to find public schools helpful (60 percent indicating this) and adult training even more helpful (80 percent). But business leaders want the schools to do an even better job. The largest number of open-ended suggestions from business heads in the area involved educational improvements. International managers fault the American work force for poor skills, stemming from inferior education, which shows up in both white-collar and blue-collar jobs. "Sometimes we have to screen a lot of people to find the right one," a German executive said. "American schools are lacking discipline totally, so what do you expect? My children went to public school here. I would be stricter; I would enforce what they learn so they still know it after two weeks or two months or two years." He illustrated his criticism with an example of an office worker who wondered why there was no reply from a letter she had mailed; she did not know that Santiago was in Chile, not California, and required more than a thirty-two-cent stamp.

■ SUCCESS ELEMENT #4: RAISING QUALITY THROUGH COLLABORATION

Companies entering the upstate from outside the region discover strong cross-business and cross-sector collaboration that strengthens the area's economy in numerous ways. In smaller cities and towns, it is natural for the same people to get together for many activities; but not every small city has the level of active, formal, and strategically focused collaboration that characterizes Spartanburg and Greenville.

Timothy Weibel, southeastern district manager for R. R. Donnelley, summarized it: "Donnelley's been here about fourteen years. The presence of international activities was essentially irrelevant to us, because our customer base is domestic. But what struck me when I moved here two years ago was the unbelievable cooperation between business leaders and local and state governmental officials to bring BMW to Spartanburg. I see very strong networking, with a very positive impact. And the international community has had a tremendous impact on Spartanburg's openness to diversity. There has been a tremendous amount of learning on the business side that's taken place within the community. Donnelley has learned a great deal from our counterparts; we have a very strong apprenticeship program modeled on German systems."

The business climate is praised in South Carolina's upstate, especially cooperation between government and business. More than in any other place in my five-area survey, business heads in Greenville and Spartanburg agreed strongly with the statement that laws and policies create a favorable environment for business (69 percent agreed, compared with Seattle's low of 11 percent or the quarter who agreed in Boston, Miami, and Cleveland). Two-thirds of South Carolina respondents reported that state economic growth programs were helpful, also outpacing the other places. Half indicated that they found state legislators and local officials helpful for their businesses, compared with only 39 percent in Miami, the next most positive about government, and overwhelming negativity elsewhere.

Strong, active Chambers of Commerce are catalysts for much of the positive spirit and cooperation, making the connections and mounting the programs that serve as the infrastructure for collaboration. In Spartanburg, the Chamber of Commerce has 1,800 members from thirteen municipalities forming seven area councils; in 1989 it moved to a new building in the Plaza of Nations area of downtown Spartanburg, proudly displaying flags from the fourteen countries represented in Spartanburg's international business community. One of its achievements is the creation of vehicles for joint problem solving by the community. In 1989 it joined with the Spartanburg County Foundation and others to launch the Consensus project, a community priority-setting activity based on a set of critical indicators of Spartanburg's community "health," starting with about seventy-five leaders and eventually getting input from many citizens. The Consensus project has led to adult education, actions for teenage pregnancy, and Leadership Spartanburg to train leaders.

The Spartanburg Chamber of Commerce's programs have directly improved business performance. The Spartanburg Chamber has a "vice president for quality," an unusual office signifying the Chamber's activist role in industry. Its Quality in the Workplace program was created by a committee on quality in 1983 and launched in 1984, very early in the total quality movement in the United States. It extended quality principles in use at local companies such as Milliken; when Milliken won the Baldrige Award in 1989, the program became even more widely used in business, including in forty companies such as Hoechst and Michelin as well as in smaller companies without internal quality staff and in charities such as the local United Way.

The Chamber of Commerce is also a spark plug of many initiatives to improve education, such as Spartanburg 2000, in which business and education leaders work toward attaining national goals for educational improvement; Cities in Schools, a dropout prevention program; and Top Priority, which encourages local businesses to commit to practices to support education such as Tech Prep, creating a vocational track in the schools under a federal grant.

With three thousand members, the Greenville Chamber of Commerce is the largest in South Carolina. It has had a successful headquarters recruitment program since 1985; in 1993 fourteen companies made headquarters-related announcements in Greenville, to open new regional headquarters offices or add more people to existing regional headquarters, including Michelin and Lockheed Aeromod.

Greenville's Chamber of Commerce also facilitates collaboration among companies, to exchange best practice ideas, screen employees for jobs, encourage new companies to come to the area, and solve each other's problems, sometimes lending staff. A monthly Chamber-sponsored manufacturers' discussion group helps with employee relations problems—something particularly beneficial to foreign companies employing an American work force—and serves as a job-finding network circulating résumés and lists of names. When Sara Lee opened a plant, Fuji's plant manager helped Sara Lee develop team management concepts. At a "prospect" dinner the Greenville Chamber of Commerce held for a smaller company being enticed to the area, its representative mentioned that the company could not afford a human resource function right away. The other manufacturers present, including the Japanese company Mita and American companies, volunteered to build a team of three or four of their own people to serve in the interim, to screen résumés and hire the company's first staff.

Collaboration increasingly extends beyond city limits. Spartanburg and Greenville discuss an occasional joint project, but battles over turf are still a sore spot. Although there is competition for business investment among these friendly rivals, there is also a great deal of cooperative and overlapping activity; Greenville takes credit for things that are in Spartanburg and vice versa. The joint airport helped break the barrier between the two cities, and the wooing of BMW involved still more cooperation. Greenville's and Spartanburg's hospital systems wrote a joint proposal for BMW, encouraged by a call from the governor's office.

Leaders of the region increasingly acknowledge their shared fate. Many Spartanburg small-business proprietors and larger-company managers responding to my survey called for greater Spartanburg-Greenville regional cooperation, still more business-government cooperation, and even merger of the cities and counties into one metropolitan area. A Greenville-Spartanburg-area joint development plan was issued in November 1993 because of a projected ten thousand additional people living in the area by 2010, with implications for the airport, water, and sewer systems.

Now there is a regionwide effort for all I-85 companies, especially with respect to infrastructure needs. Twelve Chambers of Commerce representing the seven upstate counties are moving toward common upstate messages and publications. This is a recognition that the whole area benefits when one portion of it attracts a new company. For example, the Greenville Chamber of Commerce has had an international economic development officer for six years, Tamara Cope—the only Chamber in South Carolina that does this. "I sell the whole upstate when I go to Europe or Japan," Cope said. "The county line is not meaningful. Companies can be successful anywhere in the Carolinas."

Some leaders attribute this increase in regional collaboration to the global economy. "Foreign industry has created regionalism more than the Greenville Chamber or the Spartanburg Chamber," one said, because international companies in the area, such as Michelin, spread their activities and use suppliers across many counties. Whatever the cause, a strong infrastructure for collaboration has been reinforced and extended from small jurisdictions to the wider area.

THE BMW DECISION: ATTRACTING "BUBBA MOTOR WORKS"

The four elements—leadership, a hospitable business climate and work ethic, work-centered training and education, and an infrastructure for collaboration—meant that when BMW considered Spartanburg as a location for its first manufacturing facility outside Germany, the entire upstate was ready. Between March and June 1992, the Spartanburg Area Chamber of Commerce worked with state and local leaders to win what has been called South Carolina's biggest economic victory.[7] Then-governor Caroll Campbell reported that he made the first "clandestine contact" in Germany on his way home from a trip to Israel and worked out the first details with BMW representatives around the pool at the Governor's Mansion. Almost without exception, every international firm in the area wrote a letter to the chairman of BMW. Roger Milliken, I was told, sent Milliken staff to a competing midwestern site BMW was considering to photograph it and show its flaws.

BMW took 1,039 acres of land on I-85, with easy access to the Greenville-Spartanburg airport. The state and local governments spent $36.6 million to buy 140 properties and move about seventy families from the land to woo BMW. According to Betsy Teter, "The people who had to move were mostly cooperative because they felt they were doing something good for the community and were paid three times the value of their homes. Only a few resisted, holding out for a better deal, but they moved in the end, including a family that had just finished construction a few weeks earlier. Most people moved about two miles away." Indeed, in general, she said, "the town was very supportive of the county's actions. There is a real attitude here that manufacturing jobs are good for the community. I don't see a time ever coming when people feel there is too much foreign investment; there can't be too much. Every time we've raised that issue in the newspaper, people get upset."

Jim Johnson, president of American Rental Centers and chairman of the Spartanburg County Republican Party, recalled looking forward to the BMW entry as a stimulus to community and educational improvements even before he had any idea that "I'd do the first nickel's worth of business with them" in the form of supplying materials for a BMW party the day after the annual Spartanburg international festival. He said that the BMW groundbreaking ceremonies showed how welcome the community wanted the company to feel: "There was a horde of volunteer people who went out there and just did it and worked and wore their T-shirts and ushered people, or whatever, in a spirit of volunteerism. It was a Spartanburg community event. Many people did it just for the spirit of it. It was one of the better things that happened in the community in quite a while because it was a cohesive kind of thing —cheering crowds up and down in the little towns when a parade of a hundred sixty BMWs drove through." Much hoopla surrounded the move. BMW gave a car to the state highway patrol "so you get the pleasure of being pulled over by a $45,000 BMW," a leader said, laughing.

But there was also some "carping" from what local leaders called "narrow-minded people": for example, "Why is the government giving BMW all that money when they could be helping poor folks?" One rumor had it that if workers applying to BMW had a unionized company listed on their résumé, it went in the trash; another alleged that some managers turned BMW down because of its open office plan. It was hoped that BMW was committing to the upstate in the long term, an area that has never experienced massive plant closings or industry exits. "BMW is different from a lot of the other international companies in that it is truly foreign owned, and the owners aren't part of the community," a local leader observed. "Other than Michelin we haven't had a whole lot of those where they just put a manufacturing plant here. This is a big one; it's different from what we have had, and I don't know what that's going to bring." Still other concerns focused on the problems of growth in general: traffic congestion or overload on physical infrastructure. Even those who are enthusiastic about BMW's presence want to make sure the area gets sufficient benefits, recommending that BMW be used to promote the area: "We paid enough for it, after all."

The overwhelming feeling was excitement and pride. BMW is expected to create at least two thousand jobs directly at starting wages of about $16.50 an hour, the largest new manufacturing facility announced in the United States in 1992. *Site Selection and Industrial Development* magazine called it the fourth largest single creator of new jobs in the world, behind Euro Disney in France, relocation of a drug company to California, and expansion of a Texas plastics plant. A rumored sixty-six thousand people applied for the first six hundred jobs, just from the fifty-mile radius agreed to by the company for traffic reasons. Leaders report that the sense of excitement extends to teenagers who dream about working there.

Another eight thousand indirect jobs are attributed to the BMW facility. Many local companies started to benefit immediately, such as Fluor Daniel (the Daniel part was indigenous to Greenville), BMW's general construction contractor. Auto suppliers planned to open facilities. But what many of the newspaper accounts at the time failed to mention was that there were already a number of innovative world class suppliers in the area, such as Milliken, a major fabric supplier to the auto industry, or SEW-Eurodrive, one of the world's largest gear producers. Sagem-Lucas in Greenville, a joint venture of giant Lucas Industries plc of the United Kingdom and Sagem S.A. of France (makers of most of Europe's fax machines), produces diesel and gasoline injectors; it already had a substantial contract with BMW as well as with Rover, Jaguar, and Saab. Helima Helvetion International, a German producer of window spacer bars to hold glass windowpanes in place as well as other forms of customized aluminum tubing for the world auto industry, started a manufacturing center in Spartanburg in 1991 that distributed throughout the Americas and exported some products to Europe.

BMW intends to use the latest global concepts while maintaining a thoroughly local North American presence, explained Carl Flescher, vice president for community and corporate communications. "In thinking about ourselves globally, BMW has realized that thinking about a specific group such as the Japanese or the Americans or even the Europeans as a unified national force in the car business doesn't get you anywhere," Flescher said. "What's really at issue is our ability to understand which competitive forces other corporations are exerting, and how they are strategically positioning themselves on a global basis in order to survive in the long term. The manner in which these corporations connect with the countries and communities in which they operate is also critical to their survival. This requires plenty of local integration. A company here in the United States, whether it's German or French or whatever, is going to be Americanized. Our previous chairman, Mr. von Kuenheim, will tell you that Opel of Europe, while being a General Motors subsidiary, is at the same time European through and through. So it is for BMW. We came to the United States, and we wanted to represent the best in the industry. And the best have shown us that when you enter a market, you become that market."

"BMW did not care that other foreign companies were here," Betsy Teter argued. "It was attracted by the same things that other companies were: low wages, hospitable environment, vibrant economy. They only found out other foreign investment was here after they became interested in Spartanburg for other reasons."

Local leaders feel that the BMW site means social and educational development as well as more narrowly conceived economic development. They think it will spur additional improvements in the community. "We've had so much press about BMW coming, we've got to improve," a local leader said. "We don't want them bad-mouthing us, saying 'Darn, we made a mistake going to Spartanburg, South Carolina, their system stinks.' "

LOCALIZING THE GLOBAL ECONOMY: FOREIGN IMPACT ON THE COMMUNITY

The world came to Spartanburg and Greenville, rather than members of the community going out to the world. The initial international base consisted of importers, not exporters, and then manufacturing grew for North American markets. The area's companies responding to my five-city survey were more likely to see their scope as national rather than international; the smallest percentage of any of the five places envisioned increasing international sales, since the world outside North America is handled by parent companies elsewhere—although some notable companies like Milliken and SEW-Eurodrive supply the world from South Carolina. Recently, more Spartanburg families are starting to do a tour abroad with their parent company or to go for training, as the BMW workers are. But for the most part the area connects with the global economy at home. With the exception of employees in a few companies, locals are not part of a global work force; there are relatively few rotations in and out of the area and country. As Hans Balmer explained, "Ninety percent of the international contact for people who work for Symtech is through Europeans coming here to meet with our people. Rarely do our people travel to Europe—maybe three or four per year—and some of our sales staff have never been. We are importers, not exporters. When you export, it's a different thing."

Ask people in Spartanburg and Greenville about the influence of foreign companies on their area, and they immediately turn to culture and cuisine. To many people, "culture" means food. Indeed, Japanese firms ask about food on questionnaires the Greenville Chamber of Commerce sends to companies considering the area (although they are the only foreign group so explicitly food conscious). Locals point out that the deli is run by German expatriates' wives, or that Spartanburg has more gourmet stores than comparable-size towns, or that the hospital cafeteria has more international dishes. People in Greenville describe the foreign flavor on Main Street, including authentic Dutch or northern Italian restaurants, although one complained there are "not enough Italians to have great restaurants like in Manhattan." There are some subtle differences in consumer preferences, too; Europeans buy more bicycles and wallpaper, shop owner Allen Funk reported.

Every fall beginning in 1985, Spartanburg has an international festival, with activities, displays, and food from many cultures; this is an important symbol that was mentioned often by the leaders we met, even though some of them had not attended personally. Like professional sports, it is a community-defining event with meaning far beyond its attendance. In honor of Spartanburg's concentration of German and Swiss companies, there is also a Dezemberfest arts festival, which a German Volkswagen dealer was instrumental in starting. Greenville, which has more Japanese investment, houses Nippon Center Yagoto, a cultural center and five-star restaurant (the only one in the state) given to the community by Kiyohiro Tsuzuki, president of TNS Mills. It includes a Zen rock garden and a genuine tearoom, one of only two in the United States, Greenville claims, along with the one at the Japanese embassy in Washington.

"The presence of foreign companies offers a lot of cultural things out of proportion to such a blue-collar, small Southern town," a Spartanburg leader commented. "In thirty years this has become a much less parochial, chauvinistic community," observed Charles Boone, president of the Spartanburg Hospital system. "The internationals bring in other ideas and customs. There's always a German night or a Greek night—delightful events, they really are. People have come to understand that there is life outside of Spartanburg County, South Carolina."

The upstate area is home to a large number of international organizations for a relatively small population: Alliance Française du Piedmont, Canadian Club, Cara Club (Irish), Chinese Landsman's Association, Dutch Club of Greenville, English Speaking Union, Friends of Internationals, German American Business Forum, German American Club, India Association, Japan America Association, Philippine American Association, Polish American Club, Swiss American Society of the Piedmont (one of the oldest, twenty-nine years old), Western Carolinas Associates of American Scandinavian Foundation, and the Western South Carolina International Trade Association. Greenville Sister Cities International Inc. was formed in mid-1980s to join a program started by the National League of Cities, which resulted in Piazza Bergamo in downtown Greenville, honoring the first of many sister cities. The organization Friends of Internationals in Greenville operates an International Language Bank, a listing of translators and interpreters.

But the foreign presence is subtle, its visibility relatively recent, and the little things that people point to are not always entirely what they seem. In Spartanburg, the deli run by German wives is now Mexican, and the Italian restaurant, Patelli's, is run by Indians. Foreign film festivals, a good symphony, and an arts center came to the area because of economic affluence and growing sophistication of the population, not because of the presence of foreigners, even though many locals assume that these occurred to meet the "higher expectations" of internationals. Stores stock a greater range of items that they attribute to Europeans, such as cheeses, wines, or sausages, but those items, and many exotic Japanese ingredients, are now widely available everywhere in America as a result of globalism.

It is assumed that "international people" brought higher expectations with regard to the arts, which built a good symphony and other programs: "The quality of the arts is extraordinary here, partly because of the expectations of the international people, especially the top level, who come in expecting to have good symphony, good theater, good everything." But it was Milliken executives who first brought a demand for high culture, and the locals' assumptions about who or what is "foreign" are sometimes wrong. Kurt Zimmerli pointed out, "We talk about international companies all the time, but this usually refers to those companies known to be foreign owned or headed by foreign nationals even though they actually have few foreigners working there. We also have many companies in South Carolina that no one considers foreign or international companies because it is not common knowledge that they are in fact totally foreign owned. The cultural impact comes from the exchange between the people who live in the communities, not from the source of capital."

Although children can hear German and French at the community swimming pools, English is the preferred language for many Europeans, even among themselves. And those nationalities are so common —perhaps about 6,000 Germans and 450 Swiss—that they are no longer an "attraction" because of their strangeness, according to Hans Balmer, who said that "we German/Swiss consider it discourteous to speak our native language in the presence of someone who doesn't understand the language."

Spartanburg and Greenville have not been turned into foreign colonies, but the locals have become more cosmopolitan, with extended horizons and higher standards. Roger Milliken was perhaps the biggest influence on the quality consciousness of the community, but suppliers to international companies also credit them with raising standards to world class levels.

One business executive told this story about working with a Japanese company in the area: "They have very high standards and high expectations of all their vendors, different from dealing with a traditional American company. They expect more, they demand more, and at first they're a little intimidating. They're not as forgiving as American companies. Our company has very stringent quality standards, yet even as quality conscious as we were, we learned we needed to be even more so. At first I didn't like it, but then I thought they were really right and have taken steps. Last week we had an entire truckload of material for the packaging products we make for them come in from a company in Virginia. We began to ship to them, but they sent some back because a large sheet had drops down the middle, looking like water drops. For their use, it doesn't matter if it has water drops on it or not, but they make the Cadillac of the industry, so why should they accept it? So we sent the skids back to the Virginia place, the entire truck, $10,000 worth of material. At first they didn't want to take it back, but eventually they came around."

James Barret of the Spartanburg County Foundation agreed: "Creating new plants and new centers of operation has raised everyone's expectations about how plants ought to look and operate. International companies evidence a tremendous degree of care. There has been a ratcheting up of corporate understanding of worker participation and worker needs. The total quality issue was speeded along by the presence of new international actors."

The presence of foreign companies undoubtedly raised the adrenaline level of the business community, providing an external perspective that increased dissatisfaction with traditional practices and motivated them to do things systematically better. It was impossible to sustain sleepy local companies in an environment in which world class cosmopolitan companies came expecting, or looking for, new or better ways in terms of technology and skills. Business leaders and the work force are more aware of global standards. This shift of sensibility is much more significant than the trivial number of people studying foreign languages. And awareness has spread throughout the population. Barret reported: "The foreign presence is not an item of talk at the gas station. But even folks who know very little about the global economy know that there are places with strange-sounding names that print paychecks, that we are part of a global complex."

The extension of mental boundaries raises aspirations. Paul Foerster said, "The presence and activity of international companies in our community has significantly increased respect for them and the slate of options for people in all walks of life who are willing and able to acquire the skills and knowledge critical to perform successfully in a global business environment." An educator born in the area saw how this affected students: "Within the last five years, the international flavor of the community has helped raise some potential career expectations and aspirations of our students. When I grew up your competition was in your same classroom. The next generation felt competition across the school district. Then it became state-to-state competition with California. Now it is with the Japanese or the Chinese or the Europeans or the South Americans. Our students know they have to compete with students from foreign countries. This has raised the whole expectation level, like it or not." James Talley, mayor of Spartanburg, called the international presence "a learning experience for our younger kids who won't ever get to travel those distances to see those different cultures and just hear the language and see how they act. We're more conscious of what happens in other places because we have firsthand knowledge by talking to foreigners here." It is not surprising that Greenville and Spartanburg showed the most support of any of the places in my survey for active government strategies to seek foreign direct investment in the United States and foreign markets for U.S. products.

At the same time, the main concern about international companies, voiced reluctantly but consistently, is whether they will give money or leadership to the community—with some notable exceptions. Among the givers, Kurt Zimmerli, Paul Foerster, and Hans Balmer are mentioned frequently as examples of foreign nationals who have become community leaders; Zimmerli and Balmer are also naturalized American citizens. Foerster spent several years "educating" his management in Germany about expectations for corporate citizens in the United States; Ueli Schmid, too, secured a pool of dollars from Rieter to spend on contributions at his discretion in the United States.

Foreign business investment has not been matched by direct contributions to community charitable and civic causes. The state educational TV network has trouble getting international company support to fund speed teaching of German, despite sixty-five German-affiliated companies in the upstate. A private school found that its solicitations for contributions were received negatively by some European families, who felt very uncomfortable being asked. An activist in the United Way said that most foreign companies "do not give like the Americans." The consensus among the people I met was that it takes time to educate foreign companies from countries where the social network is established by government about America's self-help volunteer and charitable tradition. "It's the mentality of Europeans," a civic leader said.

Some leaders understand the differences among European, Asian, and American societies in community institutions. As one commented, "Foreigners have not attended our schools, public or private, they are not tied to any of our social service systems—the Red Cross, the Salvation Army—which are outside the range of their experience. They understand the United Way fairly well because its principal marketplace has been in manufacturing establishments, and United Way has made sure that the foreign investor community has been represented in the local drive." Some expatriates also keep themselves apart from the social events that knit a community together. "They're not hanging around the card room at the country club," an American executive said. "They're out working."

The impact on Spartanburg and Greenville residents not working at foreign-owned facilities is mediated through the area's economic growth, spreading a general feeling of prosperity that increases security and permits generosity of spirit. Jobs are better quality and better paid ("which clashes with some of the business community's desire to keep wages low," Betsy Teter said). The community has willingly opened its arms to different ethnic groups, as community leaders said repeatedly, including the seventy Indian refugee families from Uganda brought by a Spartanburg group. Focus group discussions with managers and workers at four Spartanburg-area companies confirmed the welcoming of foreigners and a widespread feeling of security, even in companies that faced restructuring and downsizing.

Take the case of employees at Lockwood Greene Engineers (LGE). One hundred sixty-two years old, the company is one of the oldest firms of professional engineers and architects in America and another example of a firm that moved its headquarters from New York City to Spartanburg. After a leveraged buyout, LGE was sold in 1981 to the German firm of Philipp Holzmann AG of Frankfurt, but there is no visible German presence, and a legacy of employee ownership from the buyout days creates a feeling of commitment that still permeates the company. Focus group participants at LGE find foreign ownership a positive force for the community and irrelevant to their daily lives. In the late 1980s, facing heightened competition, the company worked on becoming more "businesslike" and mounted a quality leadership program; it wants ISO 9000 certification to satisfy its *American* customers, not because of the European connection.

"We don't care who owns a company," associates told us. "We care about the quality of management." This is a theme echoed by workers in all the Spartanburg companies my research team visited. If foreign ownership of LGE makes some government contracts difficult to obtain, that is balanced by the boost to the economy of the region from foreign investment. "As long as I don't have to live there," foreign ownership is fine, declared one LGE professional.

There is no real domestic preference in the LGE group, "despite Mr. Milliken," they said, a leader they all admire, who argued against NAFTA and GATT and for Buy American—although one woman went on an "American binge" three years ago and now proudly drives American cars. As an associate said, "This is probably terrible to say in the textile area, but when I buy a garment, I don't look and see if it's made in the U.S.A.; I don't care. Anyway, what's made overseas anymore? You have to read, go so far deep to know. But it doesn't matter." For some, this reflects a generational shift. One young woman said: "I'm getting married in May. I registered my china, and my mother went with me and said, 'Do not pick anything out of Noritake or the Japanese china, because it was Japanese.' I'm like, 'Wow, Mom, it doesn't matter.' " Another agreed: "The older generation didn't like Germans when they were young; my grandfather is not too happy about BMW coming in. But really, Germany is a lot like the United States." And one said, "I have to admit, I think foreign made is better."

More remarkable is the feeling of career security LGE people manifest despite facing the same restructuring turmoil as many American companies. This is a tribute both to the company's progessive human resource policies, which offer employability security, and to the economic health of the area. For example, LGE downsized from five hundred people in 1990 to three hundred in 1994 but did it through use of temporary employees "brought on for the purpose of being able to destaff," an official said, and the downsizing in general was less severe in terms of percentages than what other consulting firms did. A professional reported, "A lot of department managers do a lot of things to help people stay here. I see them transfer people not just to the other offices, but to the other engineering firms, and loan them out, just to keep them employed, renting them out for a period of time. We get a feeling of security because we see that happening a lot. That comes down from the top. They want to keep people employed."

As a result, people feel they have employability security. For example: "I feel that with my abilities, even if I didn't retain the job I've got now, I can still do the things that the people who work for me do. . . . So I feel like there's a place here for me, but maybe it's not the job I've got now." Or: "I echo what others say. I don't feel insecure. I think if I was to lose my job, I'm proud enough to believe it would be because of business conditions and not because of the job I'm doing. And therefore I don't worry about job security. I don't lose sleep at night, even when there's layoffs going on." And: "You learn your security is equal to how you can produce. In this business, if you don't produce, your security is very slim."

THE CHALLENGE: EXTENDING PROSPERITY TO THE URBAN CORE

Like many American cities, Spartanburg and Greenville face a variety of problems related to the movement of businesses and people out of the inner city. Peripheral highways such as I-85 are the new business districts, shopping malls have replaced center-city Main Streets, and the core city often is left with a deteriorating physical plant and a Third World–like population.

The international presence in the area has done little to address these issues, but it has put more pressure on the cities to do so while contributing to problems of explosive growth, which makes the locals edgy about their quality of life. A county administrator found "so many eyesores in downtown, you don't want to drive people through there and show that." A community leader informed us that Austrian, Swiss, and German companies—whose expatriates are from European towns with lively, historic centers—have let it be known they are concerned about the deterioration of downtown, more concerned than American companies—but they have not given money to do anything about it.

While business gets better and better in Spartanburg, urban social problems have been getting worse. An annual report on critical indicators for Spartanburg County compares it with twelve upstate counties.[8] In the 1991 report, Spartanburg was better than other counties in hotel/motel rooms, business openings, low unemployment rate, and retail sales per capita. But twenty-six out of thirty-nine factors had deteriorated since 1989, including crime (aggravated assault, motor vehicle theft, rape, breaking and entering); adult education enrollment; divorce rates; youth (high school dropouts, births out of wedlock, juveniles committed, juveniles on probation, births to women under twenty, high school graduates attending college); and motor accident injuries. Fundamental literacy and numeracy are often lacking in the urban population; Spartanburg Steel has to teach reading and writing.

Race relations is a continuing challenge, as it is for local Third Worlds in urban areas throughout the United States. The 1990 census revealed that the population of Spartanburg County is 21 percent black, and 17.3 percent of the county's population lives in households with income under $10,000 a year. "I don't think minorities have participated fully in the economic opportunities," commented Spartanburg County Foundation's Barret. "A lot of that is due to education and other social factors. They are in the low-skilled jobs, and that's where the significant unemployment is." To remedy this, 1994 goals for the Greenville Chamber of Commerce include minority business development, especially attracting high-profile minority businesses to serve as community role models. And plans were proceeding for a German-style apprenticeship program.

LEVERAGING THE SKILLS OF MAKERS

World class production competence rests on work force skills, on the ability to learn and continuously improve, on the involvement of people in analyzing and solving problems. That is why technical training is so important for manufacturing centers and why improvements in education are key to maintaining production preeminence.

The story of Spartanburg and Greenville illustrates both what it takes to attract significant new jobs in manufacturing and also how foreign investment can play a positive role in helping communities become world class. To recruit international companies, civic leaders mounted active campaigns over a long period of time, bent over backward to help new companies, and spoke with a unified voice. They first sought suppliers with large customers in the area, building on natural ties within industry supply chains, and they found midsize companies that dispatched entrepreneurs who would make a long-term commitment to the area. Initially the incentives they offered were human more than financial: customized training, a strong work ethic, and a welcoming community. Because of a commitment to world class quality, companies operating in the area, both foreign and domestic, became manufacturing innovators, applying their skills to new products and markets, which helped the area diversify away from reliance on a single dominant industry. Cosmopolitan companies from outside the area brought new technology and high standards that raised the aspirations of locals, taught them new skills, and brought an international outlook to the community.

The world came to Spartanburg and Greenville to make products largely for North American markets, and now those communities need to strengthen their connections back to the rest of the world. One solution to the problem of those left behind in the urban core is to create more jobs and economic multipliers from the presence of international companies—to help local companies link with global networks, as exporters and supply partners. Spartanburg business leaders in our survey want expanded international air service for passengers and freight, free trade zones around the airport, national distribution centers, information about establishing business partnerships with European firms, and intensified global networking. In this respect, makers have something to learn from traders.

Traders: International Connections Through Miami

To visualize cities specializing in trade, flash back to the famous bar scene in the film *Star Wars*. There a mix of characters from around the galaxy, whose strange appearances are matched by the equally weird languages they speak, gather to make deals.

Trade centers are polyglot. They stand at the confluence of cultures. They are staffed by cosmopolitans who can move between cultures, interpreting one to the other and facilitating the flow of goods and services. The world's great trade centers are crossroads through which people can pass comfortably from one culture to another, often because they contain a host of expatriates as well as immigrants, wealthy investors as well as unassimilated newcomers. They are bridges, New York City to Europe in the nineteenth century, San Francisco to China and Japan somewhat later, or Hong Kong and Singapore spanning the Anglo and ethnic Chinese worlds of today.

The essential resource of trade centers is connections. If Boston flourishes first through world class concepts and Spartanburg through world class manufacturing competence, Miami thrives because of world class connections. Central city of Dade County and anchor for south Florida, Miami has transformed itself from a sleepy, deteriorating Southern city into an international urban center, often compared to Hong Kong in its dynamism. It has been called the northernmost Latin city and the capital of Latin America. As the joke goes: Why do people vacation in Miami? Because it's so close to the United States. Ruth Shack, president of the Dade Community Foundation, recalled, "My husband and I returned from six weeks traveling through Australia and New Zealand. We got off the plane in Miami and felt the heat, saw the density of people, heard many languages. For the first time in six weeks we were in a foreign country, and it was ours."

The modern Miami has been built on modern infrastructure—air-conditioning, jumbo jets, fax machines, and modems—which link the area to the Caribbean, Latin America, and beyond. Many Latin Americans view Miami as a kind of suburb: a place to shop, invest, obtain medical services, make deals, and catch up on events in the region. Latin Americans follow Miami's news media and have turned Miami politicians into celebrities. In addition, Europeans and, increasingly, Asians arrive as tourists and investors. They purchase real estate, start businesses, and contribute to the city's cosmopolitan air.

The Beacon Council, Miami's award-winning economic development agency, trumpets the city as "the Business Capital of the Americas" and hails its location "at the center of a hemispheric market of more than 700 million people." Miami houses 330-plus multinational companies, 29 binational Chambers of Commerce, 49 foreign consulates, 20 foreign trade offices, and the third largest international banking center in the United States. It also has numerous homegrown entrepreneurs. Sixty-one of Florida's top 150 public companies and 43 of its top 150 private companies on *Florida Trend*'s annual rankings are from Dade and adjacent Broward Counties.

The Summit of the Americas, held in Miami in December 1994, brought President Clinton and heads of state from thirty-three Latin American and Caribbean countries to discuss hemispheric cooperation, providing an opportunity for nearly every Miami professional group concerned with trade, from customs brokers to health products exporters, to increase connections. With the spotlight on Miami, the summit's temporary international press center was made a permanent facility at Miami's airport, with a satellite downtown; Florida International University's engineering school planned a hemispheric center for sustainable technology to implement postsummit environmental accords. Other local colleges and universities accelerated advertising of international trade programs such as St. Thomas University's evening certificate program in import/export in Hialeah, Miami's garment district.

Modernization in Latin America helps drive Miami's trade growth through demand for high-technology products—especially those related to infrastructure improvements—as well as for knowledge-intensive services such as health care, legal, accounting, education, and business advice. Charlotte Gallogly, executive vice president of Miami's World Trade Center, estimated that trade surpassed tourism as the number one industry in 1994 to reach an economic impact of over $7 billion. Since the customs district does not track trade in services, the full impact of Miami's international linkages is undoubtedly much higher.

THE MAKING—AND MAKEOVER—OF MIAMI

Miami is so young as a city that the first person on record to be born there just died in 1993. Miami was founded in 1896 by Julia Tuttle, a Cleveland widow, who persuaded financier Henry Flagler to bring his railroad south from Palm Beach and build the Royal Palm Hotel to lure tourists. Tuttle's legacy is both economic and political. Reputedly she foresaw the city's potential as a great future center of South American trade.[1] She also started the practice of turning parcels of near vacant real estate into full-fledged municipalities, which eventually balkanized Dade County into dozens of cities.[2]

Transportation was enhanced when the federal government created a deepwater port for small freighters in 1905. A few years later the Miami Canal was dredged, and the U.S. Army Corps of Engineers created the Intracoastal Waterway. Carl Fisher and John Collins then developed Miami Beach, a sand spit between the Intracoastal and the Atlantic Ocean. Like many Southern cities, it was segregated until after World War II. Miami Beach enjoyed a postwar tourist boom that gave an economic lift to otherwise sleepy and undistinguished Dade County. The population of Dade County nearly doubled between 1940 and 1950.

But during the next decades Miami's tourism industry suffered a precipitous decline while the state of Florida boomed. Between 1950 and 1970 Florida's population grew from the twentieth to the ninth largest in the country. By 1987 the state was the fourth most populous, despite the fact that it is not noted for natural resources, eminent universities, Fortune 500 corporate headquarters, or nationally dominant manufacturing industries. In 1993 the state led the United States in job creation.

Florida's growth was stimulated by developments such as Disney World in Orlando and Cape Canaveral's space program on the coast, which brought high-tech jobs to the center of the state. Miami lost many tourists to Orlando, and jets enabled others to fly to the Caribbean, skipping Miami altogether or simply passing through the airport. While wealthy vacationers headed through Miami to the Caribbean, natives there sought desperately to get to Miami, creating a pool of poor black immigrants joining ghettoized African-Americans. Meanwhile, Fort Lauderdale, historically an insular community in neighboring Broward County, became a youth playground for students on spring break, drawing vacationers away from Miami Beach's deteriorating real estate and aging population.

Miami's rebirth as an international city is not just a comeback, but a complete transformation. Five elements were at work. Some appear unique to Miami, yet in different form they represent factors critical to the development of any city's international trade capabilities:

- strong cultural connections to another region of the world, as a starting point for trade;
- events that flip the focus from a domestic-only economy, stimulating explicit international strategies;
- an atmosphere conducive to foreign comfort that attracts foreign capital;
- development of trade skills and infrastructure through entrepreneurs as well as multinational companies;
- leveraging of trade connections in other major industries.

■ SUCCESS ELEMENT #1: NEW CULTURAL CONNECTIONS FROM THE CUBANS

Miami's single most important economic development agent turned out to be Fidel Castro.

Miami's international success can be traced, first, to a transformation in the city's ethnic composition that facilitated strong connections to Latin America. For the first time in history, a Miami writer has argued, it was an asset, not a liability, for immigrants to retain their cultural and linguistic heritage.[3]

Miami could have been left in the dust in the 1960s had it not been for the proximity of Cuba—a country so close to Florida's southern tip that an early explorers' map briefly showed the two as a single landmass. Castro's Cuban revolution in 1959 began the Latinization of Miami.

Although Florida was originally a Spanish colony, few traces of early Spanish influence can be found in Miami. The city's Latin character derives from recent times and from the New World. Some ties with Latin America existed even before Castro's regime caused Cuban flight to Miami. In 1946 the *Miami Herald*'s news editor began the *Clipper Edition*, a streamlined version of the *Herald* for distribution in twenty-five Latin American countries. The *Herald*'s Miami edition began to specialize in coverage of Latin America. In 1960 John Knight, the newspaper's president and publisher, gambled on Miami by constructing a $30 million building with offices and printing presses; at the time, it was the biggest building in Florida and the biggest newspaper printing plant ever built.[4] The same year he hired Alvah Chapman Jr. as his assistant; Chapman eventually became CEO of parent company Knight-Ridder and perhaps Miami's most important civic leader. Meanwhile the Cuban exodus had begun, a migration that would soon make Miami attractive to people of means throughout Latin America. A Miami writer observed, "Over the next twenty years, Miami would prosper when Latin America prospered. It would also prosper when Latin America faltered, attracting money and people north to the safe haven of Miami's bank vaults and walled condominiums."[5]

Between 1962 and 1968 almost 1.25 million people left Cuba, three-fifths of whom traveled to the United States. The U.S. government attempted to disperse them throughout the country; by 1978 almost half a million settled away from Miami.[6] Many Cuban-Americans who later became leaders of Miami grew up elsewhere. Xavier Suarez, elected mayor in 1985, was heralded during his campaigns as a Cuban refugee. But Suarez, the son of a nuclear engineer, was raised in Washington, D.C., and received an engineering degree from Villanova and two graduate degrees from Harvard. Upon moving to Miami to begin his political career, he had to relearn Spanish.[7] Suarez and leaders like him look like cosmopolitans to the locals of Miami because of their elite American educations, not because of their Latin origins.

Because Americans viewed the Cubans' exodus as a flight from communism, the immigrants were hailed as "freedom fighters," "citizens of an invaded neighboring nation," and "an important ally in the fight for Cuba and Latin America" rather than categorized as "illegal aliens" or a "domestic ethnic minority."[8] As a consequence they received much support from the federal government. Between 1962 and 1976 the government spent $2.1 billion on direct assistance to Cuban refugees, more than the total budget for Alliance for Progress and the largest federal assistance effort in U.S. history.[9] Local agencies and private organizations spent millions more, raising the total to at least $4 billion, according to one estimate.[10]

Miami's population in the early 1960s was less than one million people. By 1970 the Latin population alone, almost all of it Cuban, was 300,000; by 1980 it had climbed to 580,000. The exiles came to Miami in a series of waves, beginning with upper-class and middle-class professionals; each new group possessed a lower educational level and occupational status than the previous one. In Miami this pattern produced a growing market as the population expanded but, more important, provided low-cost, hardworking labor for Miami enterprises. In addition, as Alejandro Portes and Alex Stepick observed in their excellent study of Miami's ethnic communities, Castro's decision to permit wholesale migration meant that entire groups could relocate themselves, and families could remain intact.[11] Castro did not allow young men of military age to leave Cuba but did allow women and older men to do so, a move that strengthened the social fabric of the exile community by excluding those least likely by age and gender to espouse communal responsibility and including those who did.

Self-definition as exiles who intended to return, not immigrants who intended to stay, shaped the economic life of the Cuban community in Miami, which became a bounded community favoring economic transactions among its members.[12]

TIGHT CONNECTIONS: THE CUBANS' MUTUAL-HELP ECONOMY

Cuban employers faced a moral expectation to hire fellow exiles, who would accept low wages from an employer willing to overlook their lack of education or English. Cuban consumers patronized Cuban establishments. According to sociologist Alejandro Portes's periodic surveys, by 1979 63 percent of 430 refugees who had arrived six years earlier reported buying everyday goods from Cuban stores; 32 percent bought their cars and appliances from Cubans. A comparable survey of Mexicans in the United States showed half the coethnic purchases. In 1976, 39 percent of Cubans were employed by Cuban-owned firms or were self-employed; by 1979 the proportion had climbed to 49 percent. The comparable figure for Mexicans was 15 percent. About 21 percent of all Cubans were self-employed and enjoyed generally high earnings.[13] Carlos Arboleya, vice chairman of Barnett Bank and one of Miami's highest-ranking Cuban-American executives, claimed, "Never in the history of the United States has there been such a number of immigrants concentrated in one specific area with an economic, social infrastructure that does not need the regular infrastructure of the place they live."[14]

While Miami Cubans built dense interpersonal connections within their own community, they were also well connected outward. Cuban communities sprang up in Europe, in Paris, London, and throughout Spain; in Venezuela, Puerto Rico, Canada, and Mexico; and in other large U.S. cities. This created a vast network resembling that of the overseas Chinese, an ethnic network with Miami at its center. "One reason Miami today is such an important international center of trade, communications, and finance is that so many Cubans did *not* settle there," an observer commented.[15]

Good connections through social networks transformed refugees into entrepreneurs. Both local collaboration and networks spanning countries could help seed businesses. A bounded community could be the basis for trust, just as it is for the overseas Chinese, which enables community members to invest in each other's business concepts. Cuban bankers, for example, boasted to interviewers that they had "zero losses" on loans in the Cuban community.[16] When capital was difficult to obtain from banks, Cubans lent to each other. Cubans found they could get ahead by helping others.

Take the case of Remedios Diaz-Oliver.[17] She rose quickly from young exile to business leader by building on her Latin ties and seizing business opportunities in Miami's Cuban community. In 1961, at the age of twenty, Diaz-Oliver left Havana with her husband after spending eleven days in a Cuban jail for opposing Castro. After settling in

Miami, she went to work as a bookkeeper for Richford Industries, a container distributor for Owens-Illinois and other large corporations. Within a year Richford had opened its international sales division, and Diaz-Oliver, with her husband, carried a bag of samples to pharmaceutical houses in Honduras and Nicaragua. She returned with $300,000 in orders.

Soon Diaz-Oliver became active in helping Cuban exiles who had business experience, but no capital or contacts, start their own companies. She sold them packaging, helped them with translations and brand development, explained U.S. packaging regulations, and introduced manufacturers and distributors to each other. In 1962 Diaz-Oliver asked her company to extend $30,000 in credit to an exile who had been a successful manufacturer in Havana and offered to cover the debt with her salary. She did the same for many others. As accounts grew, so did her commissions. In 1965 she became vice president of domestic sales and president of Latin American sales.

When Richford sold out to a non-Florida firm, Diaz-Oliver left to found her own company, American International Container, in a construction trailer in West Dade. She had a ready-made group of customers in Miami. Two years later Richford's buyer decided to exit the business, so she bought its inventory. By 1988 her company was a distributor for leading packaging manufacturers, had over $60 million in sales, and planned to expand to other states. Diaz-Oliver took on community leadership roles as Dade County chair for the American Cancer Society and national co-chair of Hispanics for Bush. A few years later she left her company under difficult circumstances, re-emerging as president of All American Containers.

Cuban exiles from the first wave often moved from taking any job they could get to owning the business. For example, apparel manufacturers from New York began moving to the Miami area in the 1960s for a better climate with respect to labor as well as weather, clustering in Hialeah, visiting parents wintering in Miami Beach's Jewish sections, and hiring Cuban women. By the mid-1970s, when Nicaraguans replaced Cubans as garment workers, Cubans owned garment factories, often started in their garages, acting as subcontractors to apparel companies.[18]

Other early companies started by exiles built on competence brought from Cuba. Diego Suarez started Inter-American Transport Equipment (ITE) to provide equipment for the sugar industry in Latin

America and Florida. Growing to become one of world's largest suppliers in that industry, ITE sponsored the first Pan-American seminar on sugar cane diseases. In 1988 NCNB National Bank of Florida named Suarez Hispanic Entrepreneur of the Year.

Cubans began outperforming blacks in business soon after they arrived. By 1977 there were more than eight thousand Cuban-owned firms in Dade County, four times the number owned by blacks, according to figures compiled by sociologists Portes and Stepick. Average gross receipts at those businesses reached almost $84,000, twice that of the typical black. By 1980, though only 5 percent of the total U.S. Hispanic population lived in Miami, the city was the site of about half of all firms or banks owned by Spanish-origin groups or individuals. Federal agencies bolstered these trends by favoring the city's Latin population. In 1968 the U.S. Small Business Administration awarded more than $1,078,950 in loans to Cubans and just $82,600 to blacks. From 1968 to 1980, 46 percent of SBA's Dade County loans went to Cuban and other Spanish-origin businesses; 6 percent went to black companies.[19]

By the mid-1980s Miami's Latin community was generating a yearly income of over $7.5 billion, more than that of many Latin American countries. Spanish-language media included over thirty newspapers and magazines, including two dailies, nine twenty-four-hour Spanish-language radio stations, two full-time television stations, and four Spanish cable channels.[20] Cubans owned over twenty thousand businesses. An estimated 4,500 Cuban-American doctors, 500 lawyers, and 400 high-level bank executives worked in the city.

Gradually, Cuban exiles have become Cuban-Americans. A survey in the 1980s by a Miami radio station found that while 97 percent of Latins were proud of their ethnicity, 80 percent saw themselves as Americanized and enjoyed both Anglo and Latin friends.[21] Michael Lewis, publisher of *Miami Today*, told the story of a Cuban who became an American citizen. Asked by (then) Senator George Smathers how he felt after the citizenship ceremony, the exile replied, "Sir, today I went from being a Cuban who speaks English badly to an American who is very fluent in Spanish."

■ SUCCESS ELEMENT #2: FLIPPING THE FOCUS—DOMESTIC LOSSES, INTERNATIONAL VISIONS

There is often both push and pull in the transformation of cities as well as companies. The Chinese symbol for change reflects this in combining the signs for danger and opportunity. Losing share in one market can allow visionary leaders to step forward who completely shift the focus.

Bypassed by many Americans in the 1960s and 1970s, Miami was later embraced by foreigners. The years around 1980 transformed the city, tarnishing its image in the United States—from winter resort to war zone, an observer said—just as it was discovered abroad.

A series of pivotal events occurred between 1977 and 1981 that presented both dangers and opportunities. From 1977 to 1981 sixty thousand Haitian boat people swarmed upon the city. The Haitians created a new neighborhood, Little Haiti, but unlike the Cubans, they were needy: they came without relatives and without job-finding networks. In 1980 an influx of criminals and "less desirables" arrived in Miami by boat along with the so-called Marielitos, and the black community called Liberty City exploded in riots. Also in 1980, an antibilingualism referendum banned Spanish from official Dade County documents. FBI crime statistics showed Miami as the most crime-ridden city in the United States. Miami was distinguished by the nation's highest murder rate; the federal government estimated that 70 percent of all cocaine smuggled into the United States passed through Miami's ports.[22]

Yet the city's "rise to international prominence [was] as stunning as Miami's simultaneous fall from American grace."[23] In 1977 an international banking statute permitted foreign banks to open in Miami, and after 1980 the city underwent the biggest building boom in its history. Over $3 billion was spent on nineteen major projects in the early 1980s, including more than $250 million to expand the seaport and $1 billion to expand the airport. By 1983 the city was issuing nearly ten thousand building permits per year. Arquitectonica, a firm whose designers included Ivy League–educated Peruvian, Cuban, and Anglo Miami natives, developed what is now known as the "Miami look." In 1981 British tourists spent more money in Miami than tourists from Ohio and Texas; wealthy Latins spent $1.5 billion, more than twice as much as New Yorkers. Miami became the world's biggest cruise ship port. Its airport grew to be the largest in the United States in international air cargo and second largest in international passengers. By 1994 it handled more air freight than all but five other airports in the world.

In 1964 Miami was the site of almost no foreign trade; by 1980 its port was handling $9 billion per year of trade, and in 1981 the city's airport handled $4 billion per year of trade. By the early 1980s more than 130 banks in Greater Miami were engaged in international operations, and more than 250 multinational corporations had opened offices there. South Florida was handling over 40 percent of all U.S. trade with Latin America, and together finance, banking, and international trade accounted for two-thirds of all income and jobs. Miami also had the dubious distinction of being a "military supermarket" for combat supplies; its flourishing arms trade was heralded in a 1985 Greater Miami Chamber of Commerce brochure on emerging industries.

THE HEMISPHERIC VISIONARY

While some Anglos worried about crime and immigration, other leaders saw that Miami's Latin connections could make it a great international center. Most important among them was Maurice Ferre, mayor of Miami from 1973 to 1985. His dream for Miami: to become the first hemispheric city. Ferre came to Miami as a wealthy Puerto Rican married to an equally prominent Venezuelan; he later lost the family fortune, made through a Florida cement company. He is credited with encouraging the building boom of the early 1980s, including the construction of the Miami International Center, the Bayside Marketplace, the Miami Arena, and landmark high-rise office buildings. He promoted a new skyline for the city that he called "Manhattan South."

Ethnic battles and corruption—two themes that echo throughout Miami politics—shaped Ferre's career directly and indirectly. A liberal Democrat, he lost a race for mayor in 1970 but was later appointed to the post following Mayor David Kennedy's suspension from office after indictment for bribery. Kennedy returned to office six months later when his case was thrown out of court, but he did not run again when his term was over. Ferre was elected in 1973. In 1983 he defeated challenger Xavier Suarez by getting 97 percent of the votes of the black community. Ferre's campaign was galvanized by a radio crusade warning of a "Cuban takeover" if Suarez won. His loss to Suarez in

1985 was attributed to Ferre's firing of a black city manager, triggering a recall movement.

Ferre returned to politics in April 1993 with his election as one of thirteen Metro Dade County commissioners. Supported by a stellar group of community leaders, he created Metro-Miami Marketplace Destination 2001, a grand vision of airport and seaport expansion and rail links to Orlando. Destination 2001, a planning project with committees of business and political leaders co-chaired by Ferre and Charles Zwick, assessed Dade County's future needs for transportation, tourism, and industrial development, recommending $10 billion in infrastructure improvements. Barely touching his breakfast bagel when we met, Ferre painted a vision of such possibilities as a large flower market surpassing the Dutch original, which he had just visited, or an airport shopping mall better than the one at London's Heathrow, or high-speed French trains to help tourists go from Orlando to Miami in an hour. The world was his inspiration, Miami his canvas.

William Delgado of the Latin Builders Association summarized the reaction to Ferre: "In the Hispanic community, and I can only speak from the Hispanic side, Ferre has got a lot of friends and a lot of enemies. He's the kind of individual who doesn't sit in between; you're either his friend or his enemy. But one thing we all have to recognize: the vision of Maurice Ferre brought the best years that the city of Miami has had."

■ SUCCESS ELEMENT #3: FROM SOUTHERN COMFORT TO FOREIGN COMFORT—ATTRACTING FOREIGN CAPITAL

Just as Spartanburg became a place in which Germans, and later other internationals, felt comfortable, Miami became a home away from home for Latin Americans and eventually cosmopolitans of many nationalities. "Miami has the infrastructure of North America and the comfort level of South America. You can't beat it," commented Peter Reavely, a Miami International Airport executive and former British pilot.

FOREIGN BUYING

A new, more cosmopolitan city was emerging, and Miami real estate became a magnet for foreign money. In 1979 a full square mile of south

Miami Beach with more than four hundred art deco buildings was designated a national historic district, becoming an artsy hangout known as South Beach with resemblances to the French and Italian Rivieras. In Coconut Grove, Grand Bay Hotel was marketed as European chic and managed by CIGA, an Italian hotel corporation. In 1981 foreigners made the largest number of purchases and spent the most money in Miami ever, for a total of 1,029 purchases at almost $1.4 billion; in 1982 foreign companies purchased 844 properties for $870 million.[24] Law firms began to specialize in representing foreign property buyers.

Foreign real estate investment has waxed and waned with the fortunes of Latin America. German Leiva, head of Miami Free Zone Corporation (MFZC), recalled: "We had a tremendous development here in real estate, and it made a lot of people wealthy. Brickell Avenue was the center for high-rises, very prosperous. A lot of buildings were under construction, people coming from Venezuela, from Brazil, from Colombia, from Peru, Chile, and so on, to acquire apartments and to have offices and to develop new businesses. With the Latin American financial crisis in 1982–83, everything stopped. They were in bankruptcy or they closed places. I can tell you that I had tenants here in the free zone who came with the keys and said, 'Mr. Leiva, I cannot pay rent anymore. Take my keys, take my business.' "

As Miami became an international center in the 1980s, affected by foreign events that threatened to cut off the flow of capital, Miami politicians had to reach out for foreign investment. They found themselves in the middle of foreign affairs. Soon after reelection in 1987, Mayor Xavier Suarez met with Madrid's mayor and banking leaders to promote economic ties. He spoke out about political turmoil in Haiti. He intervened in a Cuban prisoner uprising in Atlanta.[25] His outreach was not limited to Latin issues. He also marched to publicize the plight of Soviet Jews and visited London to court companies thinking of moving to Miami.

Although property sales stalled, Latin Americans continued to shop for other goods in Miami. Daniel Fernandez, now an official of Miami's World Trade Center, recalled the changes wrought in his family's agricultural equipment export business when Latin Americans began to operate directly in Miami: "In the mid-seventies, we started exporting agricultural equipment, and back then, I think there were sixty-nine pages of exporters in the Yellow Pages in Miami. Everybody was in the export business. It was easy, because suddenly there were people here who spoke Spanish and were the obvious bridge to Latin America. When my dad started his business, he spent a hundred thousand dollars just going to Ecuador to make connections, and after a year of that, he got his first order. We had a successful multimillion-dollar business.

"But then, before the Latin American financial crisis in 1982, 1983, our clients started coming over here. Their kids were studying at the University of Miami, they'd buy a condo on Brickell Avenue, they'd come shopping, they'd go to Disney World. And they started seeing that a lot of what we were shipping them, they could buy themselves. And American companies like Ace Hardware and Wal-Mart opened stores in Lima or Quito. So a lot of the export business that was being done out of Miami suddenly became business that was being done directly from the manufacturer or wholesaler to customers in Latin America, skipping the middleman. We had to close our business; frankly, the job we were doing could be done by a freight forwarder.

"Miami changed. Now we have fewer exporters but a more important export industry because more value is added here."

By the 1990s foreign capital was heading back toward the peak. Foreigners invested 54 percent more money in south Florida commercial real estate in 1993 than in 1992, for a total of 277 purchases at $823 million, the highest since 1989. Investors were mostly German, Brazilian, and Canadian—or a mix, such as the firm of Swiss origin based in Rio de Janeiro that purchased the Tarleton Hotel in Miami Beach in the fall of 1993. In 1994 Sotheby's International Realty named Miami one of the "hottest" residential markets in the world because of foreign purchases from Europe, South America, and the Pacific Rim, which constituted 50–60 percent of Miami's luxury real estate market.

The health of Latin American economies continues to be felt in Miami, often by the shopping barometer. Ruth Shack of the Dade Community Foundation, who lives in a small high-rise off Brickell Avenue, reported: "In my building alone we can track what's going on in Latin America by the number of shopping bags. If the Brazilians are here buying like crazy, the economy must be good. If the Venezuelans are not here, they can't get their money out."

INTERNATIONAL BANKING AND FINANCIAL SERVICES

Financial service companies, even small ones, are more internationally oriented in Miami than manufacturers, a pattern that is reversed in other cities, as I found in comparing 412 Greater Miami area companies with those from the other four cities in my survey.

An international finance infrastructure helped bring foreign capital to Miami through international banks. The Edge Act of 1919 allowed U.S. companies to create subsidiaries to accept deposits from non-U.S. citizens and provide loans to finance international trade. Edge Act banks are supervised by the Federal Reserve, but deposits are not federally insured. In 1977 Florida's international banking code built on the Edge Act to allow foreign banking agencies to operate in Florida. A Federal Banking Act in 1978 modernized the organization of international banking in the United States. In 1978 and 1979 about ten foreign banks opened offices in Dade County, mostly from Latin America, but including two from Israel that serviced Miami Beach's Jewish population. In the first years of the 1980s, European and Asian banks joined Latin American ones, including Schroder's (United Kingdom) in 1980, Credit Suisse (Switzerland) and Barclays (United Kingdom) in 1981, and Credit Lyonnais (France) and Bank of Tokyo (Japan) in 1982.

Miami ranks fourth in the United States in concentration of international banks, after New York, California, and Chicago, and has the largest number of Edge Act corporations. As of September 1994 there were ninety-eight financial institutions with international operations in Greater Miami: twenty-eight Edge Act banks, twenty of them domestic-owned and eight foreign-owned full banks; forty-seven state-licensed and one federally licensed foreign bank agencies; and twenty-two representative offices.

International banking in Miami revolves around private banking for individuals who want U.S. dollar accounts as well as trade finance for companies. The Latin American debt crisis halted bank expansion in Miami but also stimulated foreign deposits, which grew from $6.2 billion in 1987 to $9.1 billion in September 1992. In 1991, in response to scandals such as the failure of the Bank of Commerce and Credit International (BCCI), the federal Foreign Bank Supervision Enhancement Act tightened requirements for foreign banks operating in the United States, making entry more difficult and expensive.

The flavor of Miami's international banking derives not just from Latin America. Banks from other countries have been attracted to the city as well. In August 1992 the Fierro family of Spain acquired Westchester Bank, a community bank whose name was soon changed to International Finance Bank, opening new English clubroom–style headquarters in March 1994. The group's companies, also dealing in tobacco, matches, liquor, and oil, span Spain, Guatemala, Costa Rica, Venezuela, Colombia, Ecuador, Argentina, and the United States. Alumni of the Spanish banks now head banks throughout Latin America, from Guatemala to Argentina.[26]

Like Mochtar Riady's Lippo Group, Fierro started as a family group with a dizzying array of multinational connections. Unlike Lippo, it has experienced a roller-coaster ride of zigzagging fortunes. One of many Spanish family groups once protected from foreign competition by Franco's dictatorship, it hit financial problems after Franco's death. The group had to sell off many holdings from the family group—Fosforera, founded in 1882—including Banco de Finanzas, which Fierro sold to Chase Manhattan. The Fierros bought back a South African group's 26 percent stake in Fosforera in 1989. In 1988 they bought Sindibank, a small bank in Barcelona that grew profitably to forty branches; the group added a minority partner, the Italian bank Monte dei Paschi di Siena, in 1990, to which they sold a majority stake in 1994.[27]

The Fierro purchase of Westchester was almost an exception. Regulation slowed down foreign bank expansion in Miami in the 1990s, and then a crisis threatened to halt it altogether. Both Miami's importance in Latin American banking and its vulnerability to foreign affairs were exemplified by the sudden failure of a Venezuelan bank's Miami subsidiary.

The Failure of Banco Latino International

Banco Latino International, an Edge Act bank in Miami, had served 5,700 foreign depositors through 1993, holding $230 million in deposits and $20 million in equity; it was considered solid and healthy. But on January 14, 1994, the Venezuelan government seized BLI's parent, Banco Latino, and by January 18 hundreds of depositors flew from Caracas to Miami, lining up even before the security guards arrived at seven A.M. Barnett, the clearing bank, suspended payments after $45 million was withdrawn. On January 19 BLI suddenly declared bankruptcy, a first for an Edge Act bank in the United States.

The Venezuela side of the story was significant and steamy. Charges of fraud, mismanagement, and insolvency had led to a $500 million run on deposits at the parent bank, Venezuela's second biggest. The bank was suspended from the national check clearing system on January 13 and closed the next day. According to *The New York Times*, after regulators locked Banco Latino, bank officers, operating from offshore, entered the bank's computer electronically with a modem, altering thousands of records. Venezuelan police issued eighty-three arrest warrants but found only six suspects. The rest were presumably abroad; speculation was that many were in Miami. The bank's former chairman, who resigned in December 1993, granted his first interview exclusively to the *Miami Herald*.[28]

Federal Reserve officials met with their Venezuelan counterparts and monitored other banks in Miami. Some uncertainty developed over which country's regulators have full responsibility for foreign Edge Act banks. Regulators in Venezuela hired Swiss Bank in August to evaluate BLI. At least one other troubled Venezuelan bank was under pressure to sell its U.S. offices.

One fallout for Miami banks was that many Latin American depositors moved their money to U.S. banks, including Barnett Bank International. Group senior vice president Robert Duckworth, former president of the Florida International Bankers Association (almost all of whose members are in Miami), commented on other consequences: "The desirability of being in Miami is still there. However, impediments to opening foreign banks in the United States are slowing Miami's growth as a financial center. And since the problems in Venezuela, half the trade isn't going anymore. Venezuelan companies must buy dollars through the central bank, which imposes currency restrictions."

Wilfred Bascom, international banking chief for the Florida Bureau of Banking and Finance, stated flatly, "It has arrested the emergence of Florida as an international banking center. More rigid control has occurred at the wrong time. Now that Latin America is liberalizing its financial markets, the time is ripe for freedom of entry with freely convertible currency flows." Meanwhile some foreign banks have entered Florida as "near banks," that is, foreign corporations that provide financial advice, which means, according to Bascom, funneling money outside of regulated channels, creating an undermarket reducing the transparency of money flows.

The more money put into trade financing, Bascom said, the more trade. And the development of trade capabilities is the essence of Miami's strength.

■ SUCCESS ELEMENT #4: ENTREPRENEURS, MULTINATIONALS, AND THE DEVELOPMENT OF TRADE COMPETENCE

Foreign investment by itself does not build a city's capabilities. To build on its international connections, Miami needs trade competence—people and companies with trade skills and knowledge and an infrastructure to support them. And competence grows as a result of both entrepreneurs and established companies taking advantange of connections to Latin America. Both were necessary to make Miami a preeminent magnet for trade.

Entrepreneurs in the Cuban community such as Remedios Diaz-Oliver and Daniel Fernandez's father jumped into export sales with little value added, initially, except their own cultural capital and connection-making skills. More recent arrivals from other parts of Latin America augment this tradition but add more value.

Maria Elena Ibanez is president of International High-Tech Marketing (IHTM) and a mentor for the U.S. Small Business Association. As a girl Ibanez helped run the family fruit-processing business in Barranquilla, Colombia, where she was born. When she was fifteen, Burroughs moved an office nearby, and Ibanez attended their computer course—and was the only student in town to complete it. She came to Miami in the 1970s to attend Miami-Dade Community College, despite her lack of English. Later she transferred to Florida International University and graduated with a computer science degree, taking a job at FIU as a programmer.

In 1979, with $15,000 of savings, Ibanez founded International Micro Systems to sell computers and software throughout Latin America and the Caribbean. In 1986 her company achieved sales of almost $7 million. In 1987 *Inc.* magazine listed the company fifty-fifth among the fastest-growing firms in the United States. Then Ibanez sold her company to the then Boston-based computer comglomerate Micro America, and in 1991 she launched International High-Tech Marketing out of her home, with a $35,000 investment and a plan to sell to Africa. She spent the first three months negotiating freight rates to ensure she could offer competitive prices to ship to any country. After six months, and two weeks before Hurricane Andrew, the company had billed almost $1 million and moved into a small warehouse in

Kendall. Soon Ibanez expanded her sales to the Middle East and Asia and, with the end of the noncompete agreement with Micro America, to Latin America.

Ibanez found she had to persuade Africans that Miami could be a valuable source and convince manufacturers that Africa could be a profitable market. "They told me that people are not going to need computers in Africa—they use smoke signals," she said. To counteract risks to suppliers, Ibanez asks buyers to prepay. Low sales volume in Africa is offset by lack of competition from major distributors.

Ibanez has helped suppliers such as Leading Edge gain a handsome share in new markets that Compaq and IBM are still waiting to enter. She has found a demand for high-end products; buyers want the most expensive, most recognized brands. Initially Ibanez entered a market by offering seminars on state-of-the-art solutions that can revolutionize local business productivity; large audiences attended these seminars in Kenya and Nigeria. She used the best principles of networking to make friends first, then discuss business; in Kenya she attended parties and danced with government officials. Eventually she discovered that she could use her credibility to do most of IHTM's business by fax. By 1992 her company was active in five African countries and had accounts in Indonesia, Malaysia, and Singapore. It enjoyed revenues of $8 million in 1993, reaching $15 million in 1994 with a growing staff of specialists she screened by IQ tests.

Ibanez is a pragmatist. She packed a veil for her trip to Saudi Arabia in early 1994, and planned to enter Haiti and Rwanda as soon as democracy was restored. She is also fun loving (Rollerblading and dancing) and enterprising, two good traits for cosmopolitan entrepreneurs. Discovering while vacationing in Japan that she could buy the goods she saw there for less in Miami, she has sold Japanese computers purchased in America back into the Japanese market at 20 percent under wholesale prices.[29] After Hurricane Andrew, Ibanez bought cellular phones and operated out of employee homes that still had electricity.

Anywhere one turns in Miami, there are trade entrepreneurs:

- Bernard and Carmen Von Rietsenstein started Advanced Generation Motors to convert Mitsubishis into $70,000 cars called Rhinos for export to the Middle East and South America.
- Fernando Paiz founded Carben, Inc., to export private label products, such as a nondairy coffee creamer, to El Salvador, Argentina,

and Honduras. His company competes with others it previously represented, such as Kraft and Del Monte, which have set up their own distribution facilities in Latin America.[30]

Moving up the competence scale, Miami entrepreneurs began to create businesses to facilitate trade in sophisticated ways. This, in turn, solidified the area's desirability as a trade center.

TRADE INFRASTRUCTURE ENTREPRENEURS

The Miami Free Zone Corporation is more than a warehouse offering customs benefits; the MFZC is a facilitator, consultant, and promoter of trade. German Leiva, MFZC's head, was born in Colombia and attended university in the United States. After returning to Bogotá to work in family businesses, he missed America. About 1976 his father-in-law was contacted by the Greater Miami Chamber of Commerce for investment in a new venture to be the free trade zone for Miami. Miami was then "very provincial," he recalled. Leiva and his family started passively as investors, got more active, and now manage MFZC under the Chamber's license. The three C's of world class concepts, competence, and connections are apparent at MFZC.

In April 1979 MFZC started operations with half a building. The first year's volume of goods handled was $170 million; for the year ending 9/30/94 the volume was $1.4 billion, involving over one hundred countries. One of America's few foreign trade zones with a positive balance of payments and the first with a computer system for inventory control, it received the 1992 U.S. Presidential E award for export excellence. Currently, the Customs Service works with software created by MFZC, applying it for use in other trade zones.

A believer in massaging networks, Leiva works closely with the Florida District Export Council for the U.S. Commerce Department, the Miami World Trade Center, Camacol (the Latin Chamber of Commerce), the Greater Miami Chamber of Commerce, and the Beacon Council to promote Miami around the world and around the United States through a coordinated network that makes business trade missions especially effective. About ten of MFZC's seventy employees are dedicated to bringing new business to the area. He claims that MFZC has created 4,500 jobs and brought one thousand companies to Miami. The MFZC prides itself on a capacity to grow to handle increasing amounts of cargo, twenty-four-hour security, and extensive staff training on customs and trade matters. "You see many other cities that are trying to take away from us the trade," Leiva said. "Palm Beach. Tampa. Jacksonville. New Orleans. Houston. Atlanta. But we have something that they don't have. We have other nationalities. We have the infrastructure."

Miami's population may have possessed the language capabilities for making connections to Latin America, but its trade capabilities had to grow beyond that. Latin American trade requires a high level of competence. Companies must cope with complex challenges, such as small customers requiring more frequent shipments because they lack adequate financing, differences in regulatory requirements among countries, bilingual labels, and growth in local competitors who undercut prices. Sophistication in trade matters was helped along by the presence of large numbers of corporate giants locating trade offices in Greater Miami and hiring the local population.

CORAL GABLES AND THE ATTRACTION OF MULTINATIONAL FIRMS

Miami's educated and prosperous community of Cuban Americans began to attract the attention of companies operating in Latin America. The most aggressive business recruiters were just across the Miami municipal line in Coral Gables. One of Dade County's most attractive residential communities, Coral Gables became home to the headquarters, regional, Latin American, or European offices of almost half of the multinational corporations with offices in south Florida. These companies' jobs were not just white collar, but "gold collar"—jobs in highly paid managerial and professional occupations. Although most offices are small, some (like AT&T) have two hundred or more people carrying out trade management functions.

Coral Gables' founder had deeded sixty-five acres to the University of Miami, wanting Coral Gables to be a city of culture that could be a gateway to the South. "Son of a gun if he wasn't right," declared city development director Cathy Swanson. When Esso Interamerica (then Standard Oil of New Jersey) opened its office in Coral Gables in 1951, the city established an economic development board known as the Committee of 21. Other companies followed over the next three decades, some creating a new facility, others relocating from Latin America or other parts of the United States to Greater Miami: Goodyear, which eventually closed every other satellite office but the one in Coral Gables, handling all other trade from its Akron headquarters; Armstrong, which moved its Latin base from Puerto Rico; or Cooper Industries, which moved Latin American coordination out of various Latin American countries.

By 1982 there were 106 multinational companies operating in Coral Gables alone. By 1987, because of economic cycles in Latin America, the number had fallen to 69. But in 1994 Coral Gables housed 140 multinationals, with a very different flavor. International high technology, from Asia as well as the United States, came to Miami and Dade County. Daewoo, the Korean conglomerate, had opened an office in 1980, as had AT&T in 1983, and when Latin American markets—and Miami's assets—became more attractive in the late 1980s, multinationals multiplied again. Epson came in 1985; Yamaha of Japan in 1988, moving from Panama and gradually expanding its products from music items to motors and motorcycles; Acer in 1989, choosing to put a main Latin American office in Greater Miami instead of representatives in each country. In 1989 AT&T expanded in Coral Gables, changing its focus from domestic to international activities and choosing south Florida over Mexico as its Latin American base.

The 1990s brought a range of consumer products companies and midsize companies. Seagram relocated from Brazil because it could set up an information system more easily from Miami. Disney Consumer Products, the licensing arm of Walt Disney Company, moved from Mexico upon realizing that contacts there tended to be confined to Mexicans; more Latin Americans could be seen in Miami, since they traveled there so often. "We met with more clients in our first three months in Coral Gables than we did in a whole year in Mexico," reported Stephen de Kanter, Disney's head for Latin America.

Latin American companies have also built Miami bases. The Venezuelan conglomerate Corporación Venezolana de Guayana (CVG) relocated to Miami from Plainfield, New Jersey, when it needed to expand and consolidate shipments to Venezuela, a country that imports more goods through Miami Customs District than through any other port, especially industrial machinery, computers and related equipment, vehicles, precision instruments, and aircraft. CVG worldwide procurement office buys about $250 million per year. Miami's port facilities and collection of similar businesses provided the company with a network of suppliers and services to facilitate purchasing, cargo consolidation, and shipping, and the city offered a labor pool experienced in international marketing.

Coral Gables focused on getting multinationals what they need. My research group's interviews with twenty of them show what they like about the area, in addition to its bilingual work force with Spanish accents considered more appropriate for the rest of Latin America than accents in Mexico. They like the amenities for Latin American visitors: nightlife, shopping, resorts, and restaurants; so Coral Gables, Cathy Swanson said, sought a desirable mix of stores and restaurants. They like access to other multinationals; so Coral Gables made contacts and held events to help them network. They were concerned about crime; so Coral Gables provided a two-minute emergency response by police. Moreover, Coral Gables Senior High is one of two high schools in Dade County offering the international baccalaureate and has 550 students trying to earn it.

Multinational companies also use a range of trade services now widely performed in the Miami area: freight forwarders, customs brokers, international consulates that process visas quickly, law firms and accountancies with an international focus, internationally oriented marketing and public relations firms. The larger companies arrange to have many services provided by their corporate headquarters outside Florida. But for smaller and midsize enterprises increasingly in the trade game, such business services are essential.

And just as the set of companies in Dade County is diversifying from the original base of American companies trading in oil and heavy equipment in Latin America to international consumer products and information age companies, the companies themselves are often expanding the number of things they do in Coral Gables and Miami. Eastman Kodak, which moved its Latin American and Caribbean offices from corporate headquarters in Rochester in 1991, now has a staff of 110 in Coral Gables. Products are still warehoused in Atlanta, but the Port of Miami is used for shipping, and the number of Kodak business units represented in Miami is increasing rapidly, which will add still more jobs to the area. Indeed, Miami operations for most companies are unique; for other parts of the world, trade is managed either from corporate headquarters or from countries in Europe or Asia.

Other Greater Miami advantages our interviewees mentioned are infrastructure related, from good telecommunications systems to a great airport to a trade-informed work force.

The Jet Set at MIA

Company leaders in all five cities in my survey view their airport very positively, but Miamians rate theirs the most highly of all as a helpful resource for their business. By 1994 Miami International Airport (MIA) surpassed New York's JFK Airport to become the handler of the largest amount of international cargo in the country, 1.1 million tons. Over 310 air transportation businesses operate in Dade County, employing almost twenty thousand people; total airport-related employment is estimated to be over 120,000, with 33,000 people working at MIA itself. International passengers have grown from 32 percent of Miami's total in 1970 to 43 percent of almost thirty-three million passengers in 1995. There is more air service out of Miami to Latin America than from all the other U.S. airports combined, according to Peter Reavely, assistant director of international air service at MIA. And MIA is self-financed, as it plans for forty million passengers and two million tons of cargo in the year 2000.

Reavely, a former British Royal Air Force pilot with experience in airport development at London's Heathrow Airport, began to work with MIA as a consultant when the construction of a new airport in the Everglades was under consideration in 1970. Fortunately the Everglades plan was scrapped, avoiding a battle with environmentalists, and MIA expanded in its city location, a decision that proved to add another business advantage to Miami. In 1980 Reavely joined MIA to head a major cargo development program, working with airlines in Europe and Latin America to become a connecting hub between those continents. At 20–25 percent of airline revenue but 30–35 percent of profits, cargo is essential to the health of airlines and thus to the health of Miami International Airport and Miami.

As a sign of MIA's growing importance as an international hub, Airbus chose MIA for its international training center in 1986 because Eastern, American, and practically every other airline buying Airbuses served MIA. Airbus brought eighty jobs and the economic benefit of two thousand extra airline crew members passing through MIA each year for training. Although the demise of Eastern Airlines, which had been headquartered at MIA, caused enormous job loss in Miami at the end of the 1980s, American Airlines alone has more than replaced the traffic and now employs 8,200 people as Miami's largest private employer; two other airlines also rank among the top twenty largest non–locally headquartered employers.

Tapping collaborative advantage, new airline alliances have brought more traffic from Latin America into Miami: United Airlines allying with Trans Brasil, ALM Antillean Airlines, Sunaire Express, Lufthansa, British Midland, and Ansett. A group of five privately owned Central American airlines created a new Miami-based corporation in 1994, America Central, to combine sales and marketing, tour development, and reservations systems, for which it will use an El Salvador–based 800 number.

MIA has actively promoted Miami in Europe. Although most European air service to the United States passes through JFK in New York, MIA has scored some big wins. Reavely worked personally to get Air France and Alitalia to Miami. Spain's Iberia consolidated its U.S. operations in Miami and expanded its service. In 1994 Russia's Aeroflot made Miami its primary North American gateway, expanding service there and reducing it to Havana.

Asia is the next target. Reavely envisions long-haul cargo aircraft that will bring freight destined for Latin America from Asia to Miami. He is working on a Miami-Anchorage-Asia route for cargo. Passenger service is another opportunity. "One million people in São Paulo, Brazil, are of Japanese descent," he reported. "They go back and forth to Japan all the time. Now they use Los Angeles; we want them to come through Miami, which they would prefer." Early in 1995, Dade County's aviation department hired an airport development director to work with Chambers of Commerce, the Beacon Council, and the World Trade Center on a collaborative strategy for even more international marketing of MIA.

Information Age Information

Miami's World Trade Center (WTC) was opened in 1987. Its foundation was the International Center of Florida, started in 1971 by a group associated with the Greater Miami Chamber of Commerce. WTC's main service is trade information. Almost a thousand company members can dial into a unique on-line database system, obtaining information on distributors in Brazil, for example, or buyers in Colombia or Miami companies that are trading with China. WTC also has a large trade library with telephone books from every city, directories from all over the world, country marketing plans, and product marketing reports. About sixty programs a year include seminars, longer classes, conferences, and trade shows on themes such as "Textiles of the Americas" or "Air Cargo Americas"—the biggest of its kind in the Western Hemisphere. WTC officials add their own cosmopolitan value. Before Daniel Fernandez, who grew up in Miami, joined the WTC in 1993, he had been trade commissioner for Hong Kong for seven years in Latin America and Cuba.

More and more Miamians, particularly those in small businesses, are involved in international trade, in part because the industry creates a demand for many different services. Efforts to diversify the economy in the 1990s led to a focus on small businesses and international trade on the part of Florida state officials. Over half of a 1993 sample of Miami businesses, most of them small service companies, were involved in international trade in some way,[31] a finding supported by my 1994 survey. Barnett Bank's Charles Umberger reported a jump in trade interest on the part of the bank's smaller company customers: "Domestic Florida companies that have a good niche are saying, 'Last year we exported five times more than the year before, next year we're going to export ten times more, and a year or two from now exports will be 50–60 percent of our business.' "

International skills and awareness are growing throughout the business service sector. Umberger continued: "I follow elections in many more countries than I ever did five years ago. I've been taking Spanish for about nine months. A number of our people serve on task forces throughout the community that are focused on international trade. Our commercial lenders—we now call them relationship managers—are learning trade finance, documentation, how international funds move. These are skills that are going to serve us well for decades to come."

As an example of business interest in trade matters, there are 350 firms in the Brazilian American Chamber of Commerce of Florida and 250 in the French American Chamber of Commerce of Miami–Ft. Lauderdale, which was founded in 1983; it is one of sixteen in the United States. Camacol, the Latin Chamber of Commerce, founded in 1967, is the largest Hispanic organization at almost 1,700 members. Director Jay Rodriguez called it "the strongest Hispanic organization in the area and maybe in the country." For over fifteen years it has been the convenor of an annual hemispheric congress in Miami for

Chambers of Commerce throughout Latin America; Europe and Canada also sent people in the last few years; and Russia joined in 1994. Rodriguez's group also runs seminars in Latin America on how to do business in the United States via Florida. "Today we are the organization best known in Latin America for international trade," he said. He serves as secretary of a Mexico City–based trade association that is only for Spanish-speaking countries. He convinced them to let his Miami group join on the grounds that the United States is the world's sixth largest Spanish-speaking nation.

Once trade competence grows beyond language or cultural similarity, it is possible to diversify connections to include more countries. Lewis of *Miami Today* watched the blossoming of a French business community in Miami after the French consulate opened in the mid-1980s, followed by the Spanish and then the Italians. "An awful lot of the development in Miami Beach is funded by Italian money run by Italian interests," Lewis said. "In Coral Gables, Italians have been buying restaurants and other properties. There have always been British interests, but never that visible. The Italians are very hot." New European residents add glamour; Italian fashion designer Gianni Versace renovated a mansion on Ocean Drive, the stretch of Miami Beach called "America's Riviera."

International connections are extending to fast-growing Asian countries as well. Far East Venture Inc., for example, has offices in Miami, Hong Kong, and Chengdu, China. The firm finds Chinese companies that can manufacture and export goods and services to the United States. U.S. customers include Coca-Cola licensees, for whom the firm finds Chinese companies to produce promotional material; a video rental corporation; and a retail hardware chain. The company also brokers joint ventures.

Some have come from Asia to invest, others to sell. Swire Properties, part of the powerful Hong Kong–based Swire Group mentioned in chapter 4, won the Downtown Development Authority's monthly award for its construction of a new residential tower. Febena Fashion Co. Ltd., also introduced in chapter 4, opened its regional headquarters in Dade County early in 1994, becoming the first of Taiwan's textile industry to invest there (but not the first Taiwanese company).

■ SUCCESS ELEMENT #5: LEVERAGING INTERNATIONAL CONNECTIONS IN OTHER INDUSTRIES

Every city relies on a mix of industries in its economic base to provide jobs to locals, but not all are equally important for the city's core capability. Garment manufacturing, an entry point for immigrant labor, employs seventeen thousand people and represents over 20 percent of Dade County's total manufacturing jobs; the county's apparel industry is the third largest among U.S. counties. But its low skill levels and fragmentation (about seven hundred small companies in Miami) mean that it does not contribute much community leadership or figure prominently in the future of cosmopolitan Miami. There is a growing base of high-tech facilities in Broward County and technology entrepreneurs in fields such as software, but these do not dominate. "Miami is not an industrial city," one Hispanic leader said. Another argued, "We don't want to be Silicon Valley, we want to be Service Valley."

Miami's other two large sectors—leisure and health technologies—better link locals to cosmopolitans.

Leisure

Miami is working to expand its tourist industry. In March 1994 it took bids from top American hotel companies for a convention hotel on Miami Beach and offered a $50–$60 million inducement package. At the time of bidding, there had not been a new hotel on the Beach for twenty-seven years. Commissioners voted a month later to fund a twenty-four-hour tourist information and emergency hot line in Portuguese, Italian, French, and German and twenty-one positions within the police department to aid tourists.[32]

The area is attractive to entertainment companies; a large number of affluent visitors are already involved in the industry. Yamaha, one of the Coral Gables multinationals my research group interviewed, mentioned Miami's video production capabilities as a frequently used resource. Spanish-language cable television originates in Miami; Caribbean Satellite Network (CSN) was formed in Miami in December 1992 by Jamaican entrepreneur Delroy Cowan. The station is beamed from Miami throughout the region. Famous residents Emilio and Gloria Estefan run Estefan Enterprises out of Miami, producing albums for Gloria and other Latin artists; they also own South Beach hotels and restaurants.

Miami has become so important for the state's film, TV, fashion, photography, and music industries that the state relocated operational headquarters for its entertainment commission from Jacksonville to Miami even though Universal and MGM movie studios still operate in Orlando. During one week in January 1994, I counted forty-six permits for filming in Dade County. A year later, the City of Miami Office of Film and Communications issued a record number of permits, over two hundred for the month of January 1995, including about twenty music videos, commercials, or television and film productions. Sylvester Stallone had just moved his home to Miami from Los Angeles, dazzling the community with his largesse on behalf of causes from ballet to United Way and considering locating a major film studio in the area, according to Rosario Kennedy, an honorary co-chair of the burgeoning Miami Film Festival.

Health Technologies

Miami's health services have long been attractive to retirees from the North and foreigners from the South, and biomedicine is considered one of Miami's most important future industries. Over 150 biomedical companies operate in the area, employing an estimated ten thousand people, the fastest growing of all employment sectors; Dade County ranks tenth among U.S. counties in jobs in medical instrument manufacturing and eighth in jobs in biomedical products. If other health care services such as hospitals and medical schools are added to the mix, the total impact jumps to rival trade as one of Miami's largest industries. Boston also features health technologies, and Miami does not have Boston's innovation advantages—but it can offer this industry its international connections.

Miami's climate and strategic location for world trade attracted Coulter Electronics, global leader in blood cell counters, south from Chicago in the 1950s. Coulter employs half of its more than five thousand worldwide employees in Dade County at its technical center and world headquarters; it has operations in twenty-four countries and distribution to more than one hundred others. The other local star is Ivax, the world's largest generic drug manufacturer since its acquisition of Zenith Laboratories; Ivax lured the former director of the National Cancer Institute to Miami as its chief scientific officer.

Dade County houses Florida's only biomedical incubator. The Center for Health Technologies (CHT) opened in 1990 with its first state appropriation, later receiving funds from Coulter, the University of

Miami, and two other sponsors. Beyond its role in nurturing twenty-five start-ups, CHT symbolizes two important aspects of Miami: linkages both to the local black community and to international trade. CHT sits in the midst of Miami's medical centers, is active in the black community of Overtown, and supports black-run ventures such as HealthNet Data Link, started by an osteopath from Grenada. Tessa Martinez Pollack, president of Miami Dade Community College medical center, also heads Minority Medical Technologist Entrepreneurs, a training program affiliated with CHT. At the international end, CHT participates in international trade fairs because its products—new drugs or bone-cutting instruments—have export potential. Many of CHT's baby companies focus internationally; for example, VideoMed provides physician consultations by video link to developing countries, and BioNucleonics supplies radioisotopes from Moscow to Mexico and Guatemala.

CHT is thus one force attempting to bridge a cosmopolitan-local gap in Miami. Despite the city's cosmopolitan flavor, that gap is in danger of widening.

COSMOPOLITANS VERSUS LOCALS, LOCALS VERSUS LOCALS: THE UNDONE TASKS OF AN INTERNATIONAL CITY

Perhaps Miami's youth—a frontier in which the line between opportunity and speculation blurs—accounts for its political immaturity, its difficulty producing leadership to solve community problems. Miami has clear trade capabilities on which to build its future. But like other cities, it offers global opportunities to cosmopolitans while threatening to leave unconnected locals behind. In Miami's case the cosmopolitan-local split has ethnic and racial overtones that add to the problems of overcoming it. Furthermore, while the area's business leadership is increasingly learning to collaborate, its political leadership mirrors Dade County's ethnic and jurisdictional fragmentation. High crime rates and a troubled school system are symptoms.

A HISTORY OF BACKLASH: ANTIBILINGUAL MOVEMENTS

"The first time I came to this city was 1947," an older businessman recounted. "It was a small city and a gringo, gringo, gringo city. This was a city where if you couldn't speak English, you were dead, man. And then here comes this invasion."

To respond to a growing Spanish-speaking population after the first Cuban migration, Dade County enacted a bilingual ordinance in 1973 requiring county documents to be available in both English and Spanish. Studies showed that Hispanic immigrants were learning English faster than many other previous immigrant groups. But fear of lack of assimilation of immigrants that had surfaced during other periods of heavy immigration[33] continued to plague the area. In 1980 Citizens of Dade United placed on the ballot a county ordinance prohibiting spending county funds "for the purpose of utilizing any language other than English or any culture other than that of the United States." It passed overwhelmingly.

Feelings about language were justified—however inappropriately—by fears of crime. The 1981 mayoral race coincided with an upsurge in crime in 1980 after the Mariel boat lift, including the machine-gun murder of a bailbondsman running for mayor. Grace Rockefeller, a white-haired civic leader supporting incumbent Maurice Ferre's chief rival, vacated her house after a tear gas bombing. She told a national reporter: "Anglos in Miami have come to feel like they're living in Russia or Iran. We hide behind double-bolt-locked doors with a gun. Ferre's attitude is, 'Anyone who doesn't want to speak Spanish can move.' " Some called Miami "the Banana Republic on Biscayne Bay."[34]

The antibilingual ordinance led to many dilemmas: Could county libraries buy books in foreign languages? Did tourism promoters have to use English when advertising in foreign newspapers? Could the formal Latin names of animals be included on the plaques in the county zoo? And compromises: 911 emergency network and hurricane warnings remained available in Spanish. But bilingual public safety ads and bus schedules were abandoned. There were repeated attempts to repeal the ordinance through 1984; but at one county commission meeting, defenders carried signs urging that the commissioners be hanged.[35]

To advance their status with the larger Miami community, Cuban exiles organized the Cuban-American National Foundation and Facts about Cuban Exiles and developed plans to run political candidates. Then, in 1988, Citizens of Dade United, in alliance with Florida English, pushed an English Only amendment to the Florida State Constitution. The opposition, English Plus, was formed by Unidos, an alliance of nineteen Cuban-American business leaders and the multicultural awareness subcommittee of the Greater Miami Chamber of Commerce's Hispanic Affairs Committee. English Plus was headed by an Anglo bilingual attorney, Jon Weber, who had come to Miami to specialize in legal and investment counseling for Latin Americans. When "it came to my attention that this movement was afoot to restrict Spanish or foreign languages," he recalled, "that threatened the very reason why I found moving to Florida attractive. I mean, I didn't go there to get a tan. I went there because I saw it as a gateway to Latin America."[36]

Racist, inflammatory language characterized the English Only side of the debate, although Anglo business leaders distanced themselves from pro-nativist groups like Citizens of Dade United. Weber's strategy for the opposition to English Only was to appeal to the self-interest of the majority—for example, the specter of restrictions on companies doing business with the Spanish-speaking world. A Miami banker concurred: "Why should you lose something that is helpful to the area, is helpful to the nation, is helpful to you? In Switzerland or in Germany or in Spain or in France, people are supposed to be cultivated, educated—they speak three to four languages. This is a blessing that we are able to speak two languages so well."[37]

Ultimately Hispanic business leaders in Miami didn't back the protest against the English Only amendment, and 84 percent of Florida voters approved it in the November elections. Part of the lack of interest among Hispanic business leaders in fighting English Only was a conviction that they would not be affected. Carlos Arboleya, vice chairman of Barnett Bank and one of the highest-ranking Cuban-American executives, wrote: "I don't believe in the melting pot. Nobody is going to melt me. Nobody is going to make me speak anything I don't want to speak. I believe in the blending of the cultures, that takes best of all and creates the finished mosaic which is America."[38]

Meanwhile the Spanish-language tide was growing anyway, and business cosmopolitans were acknowledging it. The *Miami Herald*, which was considered the voice of the Anglo establishment, promoted change. In 1985 *El Herald*, the *Herald*'s first stab at a Spanish-language edition, began to change; it had been under the direction of the parent's English-language editor and largely featured translations from the English edition. There were many open confrontations between Cuban-American activists and the *Herald* in 1987, culminating in a full-page ad by the Cuban-American National Foundation in October,

"The *Herald* has failed us."[39] In November 1987 *El Herald* was transformed into *El Nuevo Herald*, a newspaper virtually independent of the English edition, with its own news staff and editorial positions. But the once sleepy *Herald*—which many Miamians of all ethnic groups thought had been out of touch—was waking up. A new leadership team was brought in, including (as executive editor) Janet Chusmir, an advocate of diversity programs. It started holding neighborhood town meetings through 1986 and 1987. "It seemed pretentious, but it worked," a Miami leader told me. One sign of change was a column by the *Herald*'s new publisher, David Lawrence, on March 24, 1991, headlined GET ON THE BALL . . . LEARN A LANGUAGE. The *Herald* continued its community outreach, convening about two hundred Community Conversations between 1993 and 1994; at the same time, *El Nuevo Herald* held "Tertulias"—luncheon roundtables in Spanish.

William Delgado, head of the Latin Builders Association, feels that the English Only law did not make much difference, except perhaps to inflame tempers or encourage Anglo bosses to ban Spanish at work. But Spanish speakers keep on speaking it, and in some parts of Miami it is hard to find English-speaking shop clerks. In a revealing turnabout, one business head responding to my survey wrote this recommendation for Miami: "Don't make English-only-speaking professionals feel alienated." But the other reason Delgado thinks the English Only law didn't much matter is because the next generation is more comfortable in English anyway. "In my house, I speak Spanish," he said, "then I get the answer from my kids in English." Still, in 1994 Dade Community Foundation received its first million-dollar gift from a Cuban exile, a man in business for over thirty years in Miami who built a chain of storefront medical clinics. He speaks no English.

ETHNIC PLURALISM AND FRAGMENTATION

"Miami is a city of unresolved pain," observed Modesto (Mitch) Maidique, president of Florida International University and an influential civic leader, referring to the Holocaust for Jews, slavery for blacks, and exile from communism for Cubans. "When we get together and try to solve problems, there is an underlying feeling of exile, of displacement, of loss of generations. We spend a lot of time tied up in knots of our own heritage as opposed to saying 'There's this great opportunity, let's capture it.' "

Resentments surface repeatedly. Blacks who cannot access international connections blame it on Hispanics. Some argue that they are left out of Latin business opportunities, like this black activist: "Most black people here are hired by white people. You're very seldom hired by Latin people if you are black." A black business leader says, "It's vicious here. A black with a bus company, not a big one but a good one, bid on a contract with an institution, got it, and went to buy extra buses. But the buses he needs, special ones out of New York, were bought up by the Latin company that lost the bid—just so he couldn't get the contract." But a Latin community leader claimed, "When a group of people believe that this has to be mine because I was here first, because I am poorer than you are, it's very difficult to work together."

To the outside world, Miami is a triethnic city: Latino, Anglo, and black. Insiders see numerous distinctions within each group—fragmented communities crumbling into ever smaller pieces. Within the Anglo community is a large, vibrant Jewish community. The Hispanic community includes everything from Mexican Latinos to aristocratic Cubans. Some Cubans divide Hispanics into groups not only by country, but also by skin tone—Euro-Hispanics, Afro-Hispanics, and Indo-Hispanics. The black community is similarly split. Migrants from the North have different expectations from African-Americans long in the South and sometimes find Miami's black community too Latin, too Caribbean. Jamaicans with their English heritage are different from Haitians with their French roots or from Trinidadians or Bahamians. Haitians are insulted when a newspaper serving the area including Little Haiti published a page in Creole, because Haitian-American leaders consider French the language of Haitians of quality.

Because the black community has the greatest economic need, a number of initiatives center around them. Tools for Change, an organization of the Black Economic Development Coalition, serves 650 clients a year, packaging eighty-one loans at over $10 million in value and helping incorporate 160 businesses in a recent year. Director Elaine Black sees numerous international trade opportunities for Miami's black-owned businesses in the Caribbean, where "everyone has a relative in south Florida, and in Latin America, where the population is 15–20 percent black." The Business Assistance Center has a different focus; director Gregory Hobbs sees opportunities for black businesses in minority procurement programs under municipal contracts supporting international development such as airport improvements. A third activity is Partners for Progress, headed by John Copeland, through which Miami Anglo leaders committed to raise an equity pool for black businesses and help recruit talented black professionals nationwide with Miami ties to return to Miami businesses. They also sought to develop a first-class hotel in Miami Beach managed principally by blacks.

There are many groups starting to look out for the pieces. Someone has to look out for the whole. That's the vacuum Dade Community Foundation (DCF) is trying to fill. For the last decade DCF's mission has centered around building a more cohesive community. Organizations applying for funding must show how they intend to cross ethnic barriers or cooperate with neighboring groups. President Ruth Shack is a former county commissioner and unsuccessful Miami mayoral candidate who has refused invitations to run for office again because of Dade's governance problems, concluding she can have more positive impact through DCF.

POLITICAL CLASHES

Miami's political climate sends temperatures rising. Mitch Maidique of Florida International University said, "Miami's still a poor town, an undereducated town, a place where an incredible amount of energy is dissipated in friction."

Shack points to problems built into the very design of local government: "We established professional government that is manager driven as opposed to politics driven. It doesn't serve, it doesn't work. While there were aberrations to the political type, there are even worse aberrations to the professional system. You have bureaucrats who make certain the community just runs, and they stay within budget. It gets the trains there on time sometimes, but it isn't dealing with larger, cosmic issues of a community that wants to be the capital of Central and South America. I see very little leadership. I go to communities like Kansas City, Minneapolis, and I ache with longing when they say things like 'We pulled our community leadership together.' Our asset is that we have multiple power bases and activities, but that makes it hard for us to develop any cohesive image for this community." There is even talk in the affluent neighborhoods of Coconut Grove about seceding from the City of Miami.

The division of Greater Miami into tiny jurisdictions from its beginning was counterbalanced by strong county government, including a county school system, with members elected not by district, but countywide. Recent changes, however, have occurred to make these elected officials respond to particular constituencies. Janet McAliley, former chair of Dade County School Board, told my research group in October 1994: "We've had a movement to go to single-member school board districts instead of countywide elections. I think it would be the kind of disaster that Metropolitan Dade County is now. The county manager resigned on Wednesday. Supposedly part of his reason for resigning was the difficulty of working with thirteen commissioners who each represent a distinct racial and ethnic geographic area, and they all want to deliver for their little community. There is a lack of thinking about the whole and the needs of the whole."

I first met McAliley and Shack when a dozen of Miami's women leaders convened to discuss the community early in 1991. One leader present said that if cities had personalities, "Miami would need to see a psychiatrist." Another described the city as a "frontier town full of carpetbaggers. Everyone is in transit." A third complained about corruption: "The 'old boy' network doesn't work, but it exchanges favors." Then the 1992 election of county commissioners demonstrated the divisiveness of Miami's political scene. After the election, the *Herald* ran a series based on total access to the inner circle of Conchy Bretos's unsuccessful campaign. Her winning opponent apparently played dirty: he produced inflammatory Spanish language ads and allegedly offered payoffs for votes, received donations in paper bags, and called married Cuban-American Bretos a lesbian, a Castro-loving Communist, and an anti-Semite. After she lost, Bretos was further trashed when fired without cause from her job as head of the county Commission on the Status of Women. The governor ordered a grand jury investigation.

Dade County "*still* has a leadership gap at the highest level," Michael Lewis wrote in April 1994, repeating his *Miami Today* headline of three years earlier. He argued that the county's weak mayoral, eight-commissioner system leaves it with no single civic group or powerful individual to provide community direction. Then, "Dade was growing more powerful economically, even in difficult times, and more important on the world scene. But haphazard growth and disjointed efforts in most civic, business, and governmental realms were frittering away our natural advantages." Today, "It is drifting in the right direction but is beset by internal squabbles, no mayor, and 13 commissioners. It would be hard to have less coordination for this community than we have today."

Others similarly call for Dade to put its political house in order and promote high-tech industries instead of "tourism for the wealthy and self-indulgent," as an academic put it. Many of my survey respondents recommended coherent leadership for nontourism aspects of south Florida business activity. Some went further, urging a tricounty alliance among Dade, Broward, and Palm Beach Counties.

Governance problems were reflected in the view of some in the business community that Miami's quality of life and image were deteriorating. Miami is still crime ridden, and crime reaches the best protected; in 1990, for example, thieves held Mayor Xavier Suarez's family at gunpoint. Crime and the bad publicity that accompanies it was a primary concern of the 412 business heads in my survey with Miami collaborators. Business leaders also want a more business-friendly and accountable government, a more qualified nonprofessional work force, and better public school education—although, like other places, they have voted down taxes to support it. While individual businesses reported the highest recent profitability in Miami of any other place in my survey and were optimistic about their own futures, Miami's average annual employment growth rates were among the lowest in the state in 1994 and Fort Lauderdale's rates not much higher.[40] A respondent to my survey worried about how to "stem the white gringo flight from south Florida."

Miami's reputation in these regards is worse than reality. Laura Jack, corporate staffing manager for Coulter, explained: "The area has a bad image nationally, with crime and everything else, so it's sometimes difficult to attract people here from other areas. What's really kind of comical is people live in Broward County and commute into Dade, thinking Broward's a safer place to live. Well, hah, there's nothing magic about crossing the border to Broward; it's just twenty-six miles to the north. Miami has a bad reputation, but an awful lot of people move here. I am a good example. I love it in Miami. I would have to be blasted out of here. There is no way in the world I would leave here."

BUSINESS LEADERSHIP

At the center of the work of making Miami as world class a community as it is a trade center is a nonprofit business-funded economic development agency, the Beacon Council, created in 1986 to help make Miami a leading center for international business, culture, education, health care, and recreation, supported by a large number of member companies. Beacon offers databases and business assistance services, recruits companies to locate in the area, and organizes marketing events, including thirty-seven international trade missions in the first nine months of 1994. It received federal funds to assist in the cleanup after Hurricane Andrew, offering $11 million in bridge loans to over five hundred companies, and earned awards for its efforts.

To increase civic engagement, Beacon Council organizes communitywide working teams. Together with the Greater Miami Chamber of Commerce, Black Team Miami obtained commitments from eighteen of Dade's major employers to procure goods from minority businesses. Latin Team Miami assisted in the development of videos and brochures in Spanish to market Dade internationally.

In 1992 international development became a major focus for the Beacon Council. Since then it has signed strategic alliances with seven economic development organizations representing thirteen countries in Latin America, the Caribbean, east Asia, Europe, and India. Its world marketing head oversees regional directors for Asia, Europe, Latin America, and North America; regional directors visit their respective markets for at least two weeks every ninety days.

Other collaborative efforts help market and improve Miami. About four thousand companies and eight hundred individuals belong to the Greater Miami Chamber of Commerce, the third largest Chamber in the United States and highly regarded. In 1994 the Coral Gables Chamber of Commerce revived its Committee of 21, which had earlier worked to attract multinational corporations. In other examples of cooperation, Dade County hospitals and the University of Miami medical school work together to market Miami's medical service capacity internationally. And there are signs of greater collaboration between Dade and Broward Counties, extending sometimes to Palm Beach County in a rising south Florida regional consciousness.

The standout example of what the community can achieve when it pulls together was the December 1994 Summit of the Americas, for which Miami hosted thirty-four heads of state flawlessly and received worldwide accolades. David Lawrence, the *Herald*'s publisher and a relative newcomer to the area, headed local arrangements and deliberately brought new people to the volunteer committees. Miami, more than most large cities, must rely on newcomers and nontraditional leaders. There have been some exemplary long-term civic leaders, but

Miami has lacked a cadre of locally rooted large company executives that tends to constitute the leadership base for other cities. "We have a lot of talent pass through, they come to visit or do business, and they leave," Ruth Shack said.

Because Miami has so few large companies, each one feels pressure to do a greater share of community service than would be true in other cities, according to Ray Goode, Ryder System's senior vice president of public affairs. Ryder, one of the few Fortune 500 headquarters in the area, has been a heavy giver of money, stresses employee volunteerism, and lends executives to many causes. Anthony Burns and other senior executives have chaired the Chamber of Commerce and United Way and served on the Orange Bowl Committee and as trustees for the University of Miami and FIU. But Ryder does business in fifty states, and Burns has national involvements; he chaired the Urban League board. Knight-Ridder, the *Miami Herald*'s parent and another Fortune 500 company, is more local in its concerns and has produced Miami's foremost leader.

Alvah Chapman Jr. began work at the *Herald* in 1960 and by 1976 had risen to CEO of Knight-Ridder, becoming board chairman in 1982 and then executive committee chairman on retirement in 1989. Throughout his career Chapman was the force behind civic efforts like the revitalization of the once stagnating Greater Miami Chamber of Commerce in the early 1970s, which spawned the plan to rebuild downtown. Chapman's leadership is moral as well as economic. When he moved to Coconut Grove in 1991, he took a different route to work that confronted him daily with the suffering of the homeless. A lay leader at his Methodist church, he got to work developing a plan to help the homeless adopted by Metro Dade Commission and funded by a one-cent food and beverage tax, serving also as chair of statewide commissions and community partnerships on homelessness.

Chapman led a campaign to get $8.5 million from Miami corporate and financial sources to rebuild Liberty City after its riots, formed Miami Citizens Against Crime, helped form President Reagan's drug task force, and was founding chairman of the Community Anti-Drug Coalition of America. He chaired the board of the Business Assistance Center for minority businesses and headed We Will Rebuild, a group organized after Hurricane Andrew. He led a statewide fight to stop casino gambling, an issue since revived in Miami. Not every cause he has supported has prevailed; a proposal to salvage the Florida Philharmonic with an "orchestra tax" on business was defeated by Latin businesspeople.

Chapman has been described as possessing "an unexpected ability to bend to the changing times."[41] It is not clear whether the same is true of another civic group Chapman formed: a set of business leaders called the NonGroup. One Miami leader commented that the NonGroup "used to be five men, and now it is forty-odd men and women, ethnically appropriate but completely inappropriate to moving this community forward. No one asked them to make policy, and nobody listens to them when they do."

As Cuban-Americans come of age as business and political leaders, will they repair Miami's infrastructure for collaboration? University president Mitch Maidique, a former Beacon Council chairman, and Carlos Delacruz, owner of Eagle Brands, Ford, Honda, and Hyundai distributorships, began a dinner group of a dozen Cuban-American leaders, since expanded to about twenty-five members, known as Mesa Redonda (roundtable). Among other activities, Mesa Redonda has an outreach program to the black community: six to ten Latin couples invite black couples for a social evening to get acquainted and break down stereotypes. They are creating social capital.

A Latin leader offered this view of the NonGroup and Mesa Redonda, accompanied by laughter and a few side comments in Spanish: "We have, basically, two groups. They have titles, but we're not sure what they do. They operate in a very secret way. They're very important people, and I believe that they have done a lot for this community. They are secretive, but they get involved in a lot of community activities." A prominent Anglo civic leader echoed their importance but worried about their impact: "They are probably listened to by their own community. How they bring the rest of Miami along is something else."

But others are not so skeptical about the efforts to create community spirit across Miami's divides. Barnett Bank executive Charles Umberger quoted Carlos Arboleya's optimistic observation: "For so many years Miami tried to build the bridges, and now, since the hurricane, people are starting to walk across them."

LESSONS FOR TRADING ON TRADE

Traders rely on connections in and out of their home base. But if they cannot collaborate to move their city forward, its attractiveness as a center for trade will decline. The Miami story illuminates both conditions that create an international city and tensions that can keep it from realizing its full potential.

Many of Miami's success elements are replicable and, indeed, being cultivated by other cities: a cultural base providing linguistic abilities and natural ties to foreign markets, a vision of international prominence, financial opportunities and institutions that attract foreign capital, amenities for international business visitors, sophisticated international companies that teach the local work force, a transportation and trade infrastructure, entrepreneurs and professionals with trade skills, and ways to capitalize on international connections in industries not directly trade related.

But the Miami story also sounds cautionary notes. First, natural strengths must be bolstered by strong business and civic programs. Cities should not take their natural advantages in connection making for granted. South Florida business heads in my survey recognize that the area's trade capabilities must increase to get the most out of its connections. They asked for an even better support system that requires more active, focused, collaborative civic leadership—for example, faster development of a planned international exhibition center, better transportation to link airport and seaport and to distribute goods from south Florida nationally, more trade missions, export tax credits, low-cost export education for small businesses, marketing of the area as a trade link between Mexico and the rest of Latin America.

Second, overspecializing is risky. Strengths easily become weaknesses. Miami's foreign flavor could potentially make it less comfortable for domestic businesses that also contribute to the economy and need to recruit domestic talent. There need to be reasons to locate in the area besides tourist amenities or international air service or trade seminars easy for other cities to duplicate. Specialization in countries is also risky. Miami should avoid overdependence on the health of Latin American economies and forge links to companies in Europe, Asia, and the rest of North America based on more than its link to the South.

That's why trade capitals that thrive on connections also need to increase their stock of the other two C's of concepts and competence. Trade centers must add functions and capabilities in addition to facilitating the flow of goods and services, or locals will gain limited benefits from the cosmopolitans that pass through. A 1993–94 company recruitment campaign brought thirty-five new companies but a projected investment of only $28 million and only one thousand new jobs to Dade County—a modest payoff for a great deal of effort. Companies must see more in Miami than a convenient airport, more in Miami's work force than the ability to speak Spanish.

Trade centers must increase their innovation and manufacturing skills, as Singapore did, attracting activities that add value rather than simply move goods from one point to another. For example, Miami could increase its innovation capabilities, which are already strong in health technologies. It could increase light manufacturing and assembly of high-tech products destined for export; computers and office machines constitute the largest export out of Miami. It could facilitate partnering between transient multinational companies and smaller local ones that could act as local parts suppliers and value-added assemblers and benefit from learning what their larger partner has to teach about meeting world standards. With an even wider regional focus, Miamians could link Florida's manufacturing and high-technology base farther north with its trade base in the south of the state.

Miami is already starting to build social and civic bridges to improve quality of life. Ultimately that is the key. The global economy will bring significant local benefits only if institutions work together to increase their collective strength.

PART FIVE

BECOMING WORLD CLASS: HOW TO CREATE COLLABORATIVE ADVANTAGE

Becoming world class means joining the world class. Success in the global economy derives not just from meeting high standards for competition in world contests, but also from strong relationships—networks that link to global markets and networks that build collective local strength. In the future, companies that flourish will be "best partners" to their customers, suppliers, employees, and allies in joint ventures. Their leaders will know how to create productive partnerships that span companies, sectors, countries, or communities.

Companies need collaborative advantage; cities can help them get it. The task for a community is to be the best place for businesses to operate and for people to work and live—a place where cosmopolitans can replenish their stock of concepts, competence, and connections and where locals can link to global markets.

Cities need their own foreign policy. They must be world-ready, foreign-friendly, globally skilled, and partnership oriented in order to attract resources to enhance local quality of life. They must strengthen their infrastructure for collaboration—the linkages that produce civic engagement and unity of purpose. An action agenda for cities starts with core local strengths as the foundation for a global vision, a vision that embraces the opportunities of a new century and builds bridges to help people reach them.

World Class Businesses: Leadership across Boundaries

Regardless of industry or profession, cosmopolitan business leaders are in the construction game. They should change the title on their business cards to represent their most important responsibility:

Destroyer of Walls. Builder of Bridges.

The year 1989 was a watershed for many geopolitical trends, but its most important event signaled that the global economy was about to reach nearly everywhere: the destruction of the Berlin Wall. Now the job of cosmopolitans is to tear down the invisible walls between countries, companies, cultures, customers and suppliers, and departments and levels within organizations, replacing walls that divide with bridges that link. This is cosmopolitans' most important class interest, source of opportunity, and basis for success.

Cosmopolitans are popularly defined by their international ties. Certainly many of the world class businesses encountered in this book are led by people who cross cultures: Henri Termeer, Dutch head of Boston's Genzyme; Maria Elena Ibanez, a Colombian entrepreneur in Miami selling computers to Africa; Pierre Everaert, the Belgian-born U.S. citizen formerly at the helm of a Dutch company creating a multicountry supermarket alliance; Joanna Lau, Asian-American leader of a defense company spin-off; Kurt Zimmerli and Hans Balmer, German-speaking Swiss immigrants to Spartanburg, taking U.S. citizenship, building American-German joint ventures, and leading Chamber of Commerce activities; or Mochtar Riady, ethnic Chinese founder of a Pacific Rim conglomerate friendly with both the premier of China and the president of the United States. But in all these cases it is their open minds and outreach to partners, not their cross-country affiliations or multicultural backgrounds, that make these leaders cosmopolitan.

Let us not mistake one aspect of some cosmopolitans for the entire world class. Many cosmopolitans are domestically oriented, locally rooted, community spirited, highly patriotic, single-passport holders—like Ben Holmes at Hewlett-Packard or Mitchell Kertzman and his team at Powersoft. But they also cross boundaries, bridging company cultures as they establish networks of business partners and dreaming of new opportunities that may take them to new international frontiers. They are cosmopolitan in outlook because they think beyond established boundaries. They are open to information from outside their current framework. They take pleasure in new experiences and ideas. They are a step ahead of others in envisioning new possibilities that break the mold.

How often I hear cosmopolitan leaders described as broad-minded people who are good listeners. Olof Lundberg, Swedish head of Inmarsat, a global satellite telecommunications consortium headquartered in London and owned by sixty-five companies from sixty-five countries, has to balance many interests very diplomatically and convince a set of diverse rivals to embrace new directions. He can do this, he said, because he is from a small country where he had to learn how to listen to people who did not speak his language or share his assumptions. Cosmopolitans can forge links with many kinds of companies and places because they are able to understand others on their own terms, becoming like insiders in every place as they create strong local ties—in many places.

GLOBALIZATION, CUSTOMER POWER, AND COSMOPOLITAN PERSPECTIVES

The global economy sets in motion forces that shift power to customers and give advantages to cosmopolitans. Ever more rapid mobility of capital, people, and ideas means that ever more products or concepts are introduced simultaneously around the world, closing the gap between countries. The ability to bypass the establishment because of new choices across borders and technologies means that dominant players that once monopolized a particular channel are losing power. Changing technology and global sourcing make it easier to go around dominant players, finding an alternative way to meet a need. For example, the huge installed base of mainframe computers is bypassed by personal computers and workstations; telephone companies' monopoly of public land telephone lines is bypassed by private networks, cellular or satellite communications; television broadcast networks' monopoly on entertainment is bypassed by cable. Large installed bases or control of a particular means of distribution to a particular set of customers no longer guarantees future success.

The first three forces—mobility, simultaneity, and bypass—reinforce pluralism, the rise of multiple centers of expertise and influence. "Superpowers," whether superpower countries or companies, cannot easily dominate a world of mobile resources where establishments can be bypassed by alternative technologies. Nor can companies control all activities from a single headquarters or center. They need to tap the moving sources of information, expertise, or capital wherever they are found, in many parts of the company or the world, through their own internal network or through partners. In the race to improve, wide networks provide an advantage.

Globalization creates choice-led revolutions. Customers have more choices, because they can cross borders to get the goods and services they need. Customers are more informed about choices available elsewhere, because of the power of information technology and world communication systems. Some individual consumers cross borders to shop, but organizational customers are even more likely to treat the whole world as their shopping mall. Institutional customers are consolidating their purchasing power to get the best they can anywhere for the best terms. So, in industry after industry, power is systematically shifting from *producers* who make goods and services to *customers* who use them.

Globalization forces companies to embed a customer perspective in all of their activities. They must stop "thinking like producers" and start "thinking like the customer." This means becoming more cosmopolitan—to open minds as well as borders, to join networks rather than remain closed hierarchies.

Producer logic suggests a focus on products as tangible entities, trying to push products on customers who might not crave them. Customer logic suggests a focus on applications—the use value to customers, the ability to solve a problem for them.

Producer logic suggests an internal focus on assets owned: trying to maximize the use of what the organization already owns, rewarding people for internal asset size, growth, and return, encouraging building of closed internal empires. Customer logic suggests a focus on resources mobilized: pulling together resources from any source, inside or outside the company, owned directly or borrowed for the current venture, domestic or international, to deliver value for customers.

Producer logic suggests a focus on transactions, tracking particular events and tending to view them one by one as isolated events, product by product or account by account. Customer logic suggests a focus on relationships, identifying the totality of any customer's dealings with the company as well as seeing the linkages among customers—for example, that a set of customers live together in a single household or are part of the same network.

Producer logic suggests a focus on uniformity and standardization, to create internal efficiencies, and on masses and aggregates, to determine how well things are going "on the average." Customer logic suggests a focus on differentiation and variety, on serving particular needs, on treating each customer as a "segment of one" more interested in "what's in it for me" than in what is done "on the average" for customers in general. And producer logic suggests a focus on avoiding visible mistakes, errors, or defects in existing activities. Customer logic suggests avoiding "invisible mistakes"—the failure to innovate fast enough.

Learning to "think like the customer" requires organizations that are entrepreneurial, learning oriented, and collaborative—focused on core skills, fast to innovate and incorporate new knowledge, flexible in their use of people, and friendly in reaching out to partners.

To succeed in the customer-driven global economy, businesses of all sizes must be world-ready, even if they choose to stay at home. They must

- meet B-I-W (best-in-world) standards;
- pioneer in the best ideas and technologies;
- invest in work force skills and offer employability security;
- act as partners to suppliers and customers;
- connect to networks providing broad reach and additional resources.

World class companies are rich in the three golden intangible assets, the three C's of concepts, competence, and connections. Those assets are hard to measure, but they are more critical for building the future than tangible assets of capital, plant, and equipment.

In contrast, local isolates or chauvinistic companies without the three C's are likely to face deteriorating businesses with work forces paralyzed by insecurity. Both isolated businesses and insecure workers are tempted to retreat into protectionism and xenophobia, as we saw in chapter 5, but this pulls them farther away from future opportunities by closing their minds to what the world has to offer.

In the global economy, leadership is an outward-looking, not an inward-looking, function. This is why "Best Partner" is such a good label for aspirations to attain world class quality. Quality is a matter not of internal processes only, but of excellence in relationships with suppliers, distributors, venture partners, and end users as well as with employees. And as linkages across boundaries become more important to success, influencing the quality of what occurs within an organization itself, leaders must build, manage, and nurture their organizations' networks of relationships to ensure that they have the best concepts, competence, and connections.

THE POWER OF NETWORKS

Look at the diversity of collaborations encountered in this book. We saw giant Gillette learn about global markets through a joint venture in China, reorganize to treat North America and Europe as one enormous seamless market, build closer ties with major suppliers, and share ideas on-line between Boston and Berlin plants. We saw Roger Milliken of Milliken & Company help create a manufacturing renaissance in South Carolina by establishing closer connections with equipment suppliers; then, Swiss and German companies established in Spartanburg encouraged others to come over, forming joint ventures and sharing space or technologies. We saw Powersoft grow up with hundreds of partners for development, marketing, and training; local collaboration with Lotus to share facilities, technologies, volume discounts, and expertise; a key partnership with Attachmate in Seattle; and an eventual marriage with Sybase. Good connections even helped five-person Bamboo Fencer in Boston share Orvis's bamboo from China.

Pick a field, and find networks of all kinds growing in importance. Marketing partnerships among Latin American airlines in Miami. Cleveland and Seattle law firms joining Lex-Net, an international referral network. A&A/Carey in Boston thriving through its membership in an international limousine network. Miami Beach hotels finding they must be part of a worldwide reservations network. There are product joint ventures such as the one Hewlett-Packard has with Boston Scientific for medical equipment; community service joint ventures that cement industry ties in a local area, such as Wellfleet's collaboration with AT&T to provide telecommunications services to homeless veteran shelters; and business-social enterprise joint ventures to make money while strengthening a community, such as Bank of Boston's partnership with Organization for a New Equality to help low-income people buy foreclosed properties.

Networks form around a common industry, such as the software council in Massachusetts, to augment informal industry connections and help emerging companies in those industries get the best talent and operate to the highest standards. Alternatively, they form around a common culture, such as overseas Chinese in California and Southeast Asia or Cubans in Miami; recall Remedios Diaz-Oliver, founder of American International Container, who supported other Cubans in using Latin connections to open trade opportunities. For overseas Chinese entrepreneurs like Mochtar Riady of Lippo Group, the business concept begins with linkages—a banking network that could provide end-to-end Pacific Rim trade financing. Lippo Group's domestic and international partners provide new venture possibilities, financial resources to pursue them, a stock of new business concepts, external know-how that enhances internal competence, and long-term connections that boost Lippo's reputation while promising to open more doors in the future.

Alliances are an asset in helping small and midsize companies cover the world. Smaller companies can take advantage of industry opportunities if they have a superior concept, as Tech Ridge does in photo ID cameras, thus attracting a well-endowed partner like Polaroid that introduces it to international opportunities. For smaller companies lacking the resources of global giants, international distributors are an educational resource and even a source of financing. Globally savvy suppliers, too, can be resources in learning how to work internationally, helping smaller companies master different banking systems, business systems, or cultures. Newer companies that form or join networks while still young soon come to understand the B-I-W standards necessary for local success.

Connections are especially important in foreign markets. Sometimes local laws require foreign companies to have a domestic partner. More often it is simply sound practice to build strong local alliances in markets where local knowledge and connections are valuable. Companies benefit from the endorsement of others with high reputation; organizations, like people, are often known by the company they keep. Sometimes relationships bring unexpected benefits when new markets open. Netas, Northern Telecom's long-standing joint venture in Turkey, now provides a fortuitous window into the Turkish republics of the former Soviet Union that Northern's competitors lack.

Networks come in many forms. There are *consortia* of similar companies within an industry, pooling resources for a mutual service (sometimes casually, like Greenville's Chamber of Commerce members lending staff to a new company in the area); *joint ventures* that link companies with different assets in pursuit of a single opportunity; and *supplier-customer partnerships* that stretch across the supply chain.[1] Large international companies increasingly operate like networks, building linkages among highly focused units that could be independent businesses. Many networks have an open-ended, multipurpose quality that can make them hard to define. Powersoft's Kertzman called his company part of the Lotus *keiretsu*, using the analogy to Japanese business groups to describe relationships that are still new in the United States. A Foote, Cone & Belding (FCB) executive conveyed frustration as he tried to describe the relationship with Publicis described in chapter 3: "What is an alliance? Did we acquire these guys? No. Did they acquire us? No. Did we merge? Well, no, not exactly. We moved some operations around in Europe, we bought each other's stock, and we sit on boards together. But how do you say what this is?"

Furthermore, the specific purpose that brings companies together is not the whole story. All relationships contain the potential for additional connections. Network ties represent a mutual desire to continue to get together, an agreement to continue to meet. New possibilities can emerge from the fact of having the relationship.

For cosmopolitans, relationships are more than "the deal," and they have to be managed as living systems. The behavioral side of networks, their cultural, organizational, and human dimensions, often pose the greatest challenges, not the business side. Collaboration can be messy and emotional, involving ineffable feelings like "chemistry." Compatibility, trust, and communication determine whether relationships succeed or fail.

SKILLS FOR COLLABORATIVE ADVANTAGE

Productive business collaboration is built in overlapping phases that resemble a marriage process. First there is the romance of courtship, followed by the deal making of getting engaged. Once partners start to work together, setting up "housekeeping," difficulties and differences are discovered, which require adjustments and formal mechanisms for planning or problem solving. The partners come to respect differences and learn from each other. And as their relationship evolves, they accept the possibility of change or termination.

Successful network leaders abide by fifteen principles:

1. *Be open to romance, but court carefully.*

There's an element of romance in the formation of new relationships. Good connections rely on personal chemistry. Company relationships generally begin with a small number of direct interpersonal connections, leader to leader. Deals often turn on personal rapport between leaders. The feelings between them that clinch or negate a relationship transcend business to include personal and social interests that serve as a signal of mutual understanding and a basis for trust. Maria Elena Ibanez opened doors for International High-Tech Marketing in Africa because she first seeks personal relationships.

Relationships are initially romantic in another sense. Their formation rests on hopes and dreams—what might be possible if particular opportunities are pursued. Strategic and financial analysis might provide guidance and confidence that it is right to enter into a relationship with that particular partner. But the rest, the view of what will emerge, is a matter of hope, as in all new ventures. Desire not to miss a rare opportunity is also a motivation for relationships that contain open-ended possibilities rather than clear financial payoffs. For example, telecommunications companies in Europe, Latin America, or Asia that seek foreign suitors as part of government privatization or international growth aspirations often find many bidders for their affections, even when the financial prospects are problematic and the venture strategies confusing, because they represent one of the few chances for outsiders to get inside positions in that country's market. And "distance lends enchantment." Company leaders often do not know each other well enough to be aware of the other company's subtle flaws.

At the beginning of new relationships, selective perceptions reinforce dreams, not dangers. Leaders see in the other what they want to see, believing what they want to believe. In retrospect, when inevitable management problems surface, executives realize that the warning signs were there all along; they just chose to ignore them in the warm glow of beginning the relationship.

Hopes and dreams are necessary for innovation and entrepreneurship. But balancing hope with a clear-eyed assessment of self and other helps ensure that the relationship is right.

2. *Know yourself. Build your strengths.*

The best relationships begin with self-awareness. Voluntary suitors who understand their own strengths and weaknesses well are better than the reluctant, the naive, or those who have no other choice. Companies should avoid grabbing the nearest good-looking prospect after a short courtship in which potential partners shower each other with praise and promises. One of the dangers for Boston-area entrepreneurs seeking partners through the MIT Enterprise Forum or Route 128 Venture Network is that they do not know the needs of their fledgling businesses well enough to join forces with another one. In the rush to get something going, they settle for the wrong things.

Ideally all partners have pursued independent analyses of opportunity and come to similar conclusions. Each is experienced in testing partners; leaders will not be dazzled easily. Each is clear what it wants in a partner, often because of a long prescreening process involving casual "dates" with other possible partners without finding compatibility. Each partner has a long-term vision and sees a new relationship as an asset in realizing that vision. And, most important, each has built its own internal strengths first, so as to have desirable assets to offer.

Networks of the weak do not survive; the best alliances join strength to strength. Powersoft could find so many development partners because of the asset it brought in its PowerBuilder product line. In contrast, the African-American parts supplier described in chapter 6 had little to offer but "minority vendor" status; when its largest customer had a business downtown, the customer cut the weak link to the parts supplier and took the work in-house.

3. *Seek compatibility in values.*

The courtship period tests compatibility on broad historical, philosophical, and strategic dimensions—common past experiences, values, and principles and common hopes for the future. While analysts examine financial viability, leaders assess more intangible aspects of compatibility.

When British retailer BhS decided to form partnerships with a small number of core suppliers, as we saw in chapter 4, David Dworkin (then CEO) met personally with the heads of potential supply partners to explore business philosophies; Cohen & Wilks International, which was prepared to accommodate BhS and shared its perspective on quality and design, became a significant partner. FCB and Publicis thought they had the partner of their dreams when they found each other: they shared Nestlé and other clients, knew they could not grow alone, and had similar creative principles for advertising. Compatible philosophies and values create a comfort zone that sway preferences for partners or for places—the reason so many German and Swiss companies chose Spartanburg and Greenville over places offering better financial incentives to locate there.

In rapidly changing industries, compatibility in values, philosophy, and goals is more important than specific features of an immediate business deal; because business conditions change rapidly, the basis for collaboration must be more enduring than a transitory opportunity.

4. *Treat the "family" respectfully.*

What starts out as personal rapport, philosophical and strategic compatibility, and shared vision must be concretized, institutionalized, and made public. Other stakeholders get involved; new partners have to the meet the family. Rapport between leaders must be supplemented by the approval of other people and organizations: investors, large customers, key suppliers, other venture partners, government regulators, or local officials. Acceptance by their own work forces of Honda as a Japanese company in central Ohio and St. Gobain as the French acquirer of Norton was determined in part by how these companies treated other local institutions, as we saw in chapter 7.

Relationships are jeopardized when a potential partner does not exhibit proper behavior toward those other stakeholders in the extended family. Consider this instance of bad behavior. An American CEO who was introduced by a potential French partner to the French government minister regulating such deals proceeded to lecture the official about the virtues of free market capitalism. Because the minister was a socialist from a culture taking pride in intellect, both the substance and process of the meeting were an insult to the French, causing significant problems that almost jeopardized the partnership. "Ultimately you are going to go in and sort out all the economics for yourself and your shareholders. But if you don't pay attention to the relationships, you will never get to the economics," a senior executive said he learned from this event. "In North America, the economics is a driving force. It is not a driving force with the French people." In many emerging markets that North American companies seek to enter, showing respect and taking time to make sure the surrounding "family" feels good about the alliance are essential. In China, for example, taking time to cultivate personal relationships at many organizational levels smooths business transactions and adds to the fund of good *guanxi* (the Chinese term for connection)—a principle prevailing in nearly every country outside of the Anglo-Saxon world.

5. *Put the lawyers in their place.*

Since leader-to-leader relationships are important, network formation cannot be turned over to third-party professionals, such as lawyers, investment bankers, or staff analysts. A unit of Brown & Root discovered this after a bad experience with a French company in an alliance that fell apart in less than three years. After a few perfunctory meetings between the chief executives, legal and financial staffs handled details under the guidance of external law firms. Later dissection of what went wrong pointed to the fact that these professionals were more interested in financial terms and contract niceties than in what it would take to operate the joint venture and whether the two companies approached management the same way. Learning from experience, Brown &

Root's subsidiary next formed a productive alliance with a Dutch company, but this time the chief executives and their key managers spent a great deal of time together discussing principles; the lawyers' and analysts' roles were minimized.

6. *Vow to work together till business conditions do us part.*

The best agreements have four components:

- A *specific joint activity, a first-step venture or project.* The specific project makes the relationship real in practice, helps the partners learn to work together, and provides a basis for measures of performance. It makes it possible to get started; the longer a courtship drags on without consummation, the more conditions can change and jeopardize the relationship.

- A *commitment to grow the relationship through side bets.* Companies must put something into the network besides support for the first project: loans of equipment, equity swaps, exchange of personnel, exchange of information, performing extra functions in the case of supplier-customer networks, and so forth. This reflects a willingness to connect the fates of the companies by investing more generally in each other. The side bets ensure longer-term investment in each other.

- *Clear signs of continuing independence.* New partners have to balance their aspirations for cooperation with signals of reassurance for other relationships that they will not disappear. The FCB-Publicis alliance appointed an American as chairman of the European joint venture so that FCB's European staff and clients would not think that FCB was simply ceding its European operations to its French partner. Powersoft has to reassure its customers and development partners that despite the merger with Sybase, Powersoft products and standards will be maintained. Tech Ridge shows Kodak that it is still available for partnerships despite the close tie with Polaroid but also does Polaroid managers the courtesy of informing them.

- A *way to exit gracefully if things don't work out.*

7. *But don't count on the contract.*

Formal agreements cannot anticipate everything, and they are often interpreted differently depending on which network partner is asked.

Indeed, the very meaning of an agreement—whether it is seen as general guidance or the letter of the law—varies with country customs.

Early conflicts in TGNT, Northern Telecom's Chinese joint venture with Tong Guang Electronics, were over contract interpretation. The Chinese managers were perplexed by the dearth of equipment and documents arriving at start-up. Northern Telecom (Nortel) managers knew the venture was not ready for more equipment until the first weeks of the venture's third year, as stipulated specifically in the contract; they thought their Chinese counterparts understood that. But there was a similar misunderstanding on the Nortel side. In 1989 TGNT used most of its regulated sales quota, so the Nortel managing director asked the government for more permits. He was told the venture would not get them until they fulfilled an export requirement of five thousand lines and transferred more Nortel technology. Nortel representatives had thought those numbers in the contract were guidelines, not absolutes.

Agreements in principle, based on the warm glow of compatibility in philosophies, turn out to mask very different expectations for what the other is prepared to commit. The regional partner of a multinational company thought that as soon as the deal was struck it would get control of all the business of both companies in its region. But the larger partner never intended to transfer a significant business to a minority partner, nor to allow complete management control; in fact, it was seeking a second partner for other products.

Interpreting and acting on agreements is made more complicated by differences among units within each company in a network. For some departments the network might be critical; for others it is a nuisance. Some immediately get along with their network counterparts because they share a technical language and professional orientation—often true around information systems. Conflict tends to revolve around financial and commercial issues more than technical matters. In one newly formed alliance, technical and market information was exchanged freely. Sharing technology and consolidating R&D went smoothly, despite fears of turf battles and technical pride. Much more difficult were questions of transfer pricing, licensing, distribution agreements, management fees, and compensation levels for each company's staff deployed to a joint team, because each company had a different pay and bonus arrangement.

8. *Keep communicating, face-to-face.*

Matters are more easily sorted out when network partners keep talking long after their initial deal making and dedicate people to watch over the relationship—which is why Powersoft, Lotus, and other software companies, even small ones, now have entire departments dedicated to their alliances. Relationship managers should be close to the top, able to commit their company to changes in a flexible manner. For nearly two years after their alliance was under way, FCB and Publicis deployed a transition team in Europe to sort out operations, rationalize offices, make key personnel decisions, and handle policy conflicts.

Because so many matters remain to be defined, and communication is essential, the location of key managers makes a difference in effectiveness. Disney Consumer Products moved its Latin American headquarters from Mexico, inside the region, to Miami, outside it, because President Stephen de Kanter learned that Disney's licensing partners from every other country came to Miami much more frequently than to Mexico City. The Publicis-FCB transition team, based initially in London as neutral territory between FCB's U.S. base and Publicis's base in France, ran into resistance from local European offices and had difficulty scheduling formal meetings or getting to know managers informally. Support increased when the team moved to Paris, where it could forge bonds with key people at Publicis headquarters.

To many managers, geography is destiny. They take it for granted that they should have power on their own turf, so if a network or joint venture is located in one partner's territory, that partner will expect to dominate. Power will shift to the place with the most frequent face-to-face contact. Because the venture linking COMCO of Switzerland and Martech of Alaska for environmental cleanup was housed in COMCO's Swiss headquarters, the American venture manager lent by Martech could simply go up the elevator to see his European bosses. Soon the middle-of-the-night calls from his American boss nine time zones away, who rarely traveled to Europe, seemed like unhelpful intrusions.

Locals always resist direction from those they never see. This is why cosmopolitans must be willing to travel; Gillette's CEO Alfred Zeien spends a high proportion of his time meeting with country managers in their own offices. Smaller company leaders must go personally to the places where they have significant relationships, as Tech Ridge's Stephen Comeau did in watching Tech Ridge cameras being used on Polaroid contracts in Mexico and the Dominican Republic. In addition to providing an on-the-scene opportunity to sell more business for Tech Ridge, Comeau's presence helped him learn about customer use and local infrastructure, which made clear the need for innovation in battery-powered cameras.

9. *Spread involvement. Create more ties for more people.*

Networks begin with a few direct connections among top leaders. As projects unfold, they are translated to the next tiers in each organization, implicating more people. Powersoft's alliance manager makes an agreement with a development partner, but then programmers must carry it out. City Year gets company sponsorships from senior executives, but other employees must decide whether to join Serv-a-Thons.

This creates dilemmas and, sometimes, problems. The next tiers might not experience the same attraction and rapport that the chief executives did. For example, during their alliance's early years, top executives at Publicis and FCB maintained close contact, the French traveling often to Chicago and the Americans to Paris. The two CEOs spent a great deal of time together informally as well as in formal meetings, strolling the hills of San Francisco, for example, talking about strategies. However, lower levels were not in touch and, in some cases, were reluctant to work with their overseas counterparts; they had to be pushed by senior management.

Other things can go wrong as networks get under way. Implementers in local operations might be less visionary and cosmopolitan than top management, less experienced in working with others who are geographically distant or different from them in industry, company culture, professional field, or ethnicity. They might not understand the strategic context in which the relationship makes sense, seeing only operational ways in which it does not. There might be only a small number of dedicated staff for the network. Others who have only partial involvement are measured on their own responsibilities, not on relationship success, so they neglect network duties.

"Locals" might oppose the relationship and have the power to undermine it. This is especially true in organizations with strong local subsidiaries, independent business units, or professional groups whose incentives are not totally aligned with the interests of the organization as a whole. For example, a group of hospitals in a Southern city formed a network with a medical laboratory company to create a single new clinical testing lab serving all the hospitals. The hospitals invested substantial capital in the network and, it was assumed, would send enough testing business to make it profitable quickly. But although the hospital chiefs made a commitment, physicians and staff in several hospitals did not want to see their labs closed, and they fought back. They invoked quality reasons for not sending tests to the new external lab, cut their own prices, and refused to send their staff to work with the venture. The new venture began to lose money badly; soon the network collapsed.

Getting people in every key function in the organization committed to the network, involved in its activities, and rewarded for its success ensures that its promise can be realized. Multiple ties at multiple levels ensure communication, coordination, and control. Kohler involves Spartanburg workers in direct relationships with suppliers and sends them on observational tours of Europe. Within Gillette, Sally in Boston and Rudy in Berlin exchange data on-line weekly to improve production of SensorExcel razors. Foreign expatriates cannot build international networks alone; everyone in the company has to work on them, from wherever they are.

One cosmopolitan observed that getting more of his own people directly involved in an alliance is a better guarantee of control than voting rights: "In reality, the way you have management control is by staffing the organization with strong people from your company at the working level as well as at the key decision level. Because if the proposals that come up for approval or rejection are written by your people, then the boss from the other company either blesses them or rejects them. And if they are well done, he is going to accept them." There is a similar lesson for local community partnerships; CEOs must be personally committed, but many more associates must be involved.

For these reasons, FCB and Publicis expanded their initial Alliance Operating Committee to include more people, then started holding worldwide conferences for executives and country managers, and next involved creative directors and worldwide account managers. Telecommunications equipment producer Dynatech uses a corporate "university" to build a common culture and commitment to joint action for its many entrepreneurial business units, so they can gain power from the whole network as they deal with customers that demand more resources and services than a single small unit could provide on its own.

Broad synergies on paper do not translate into synergies in practice without social capital: many people who know each other personally and are willing to put in the effort to get the most from the network. Many strong interpersonal relationships help resolve small conflicts before they escalate.

10. Build bridges—formal structures.

Active collaboration takes place when companies develop mechanisms—structures, processes, and skills—for bridging organizational and interpersonal differences and getting value from the relationship.

Leader-to-leader bridges involve continuing contact among top leaders to discuss broad goals or changes in each company. It is important that leaders not form the alliance and then abandon it largely to others, confining contact to infrequent meetings of a venture board or service on each other's boards of directors. The more contact, the more warnings of changes, the more chances to work things out, the more information about possible new relationship benefits, the more chance for the companies to evolve in complementary rather than contradictory ways.

To have these broader conversations, chief executives of the three companies in the European Retail Alliance introduced in chapter 3 devote a day a month to their meetings, rotating among countries. The Wertheim Schroder relationship began with infrequent board meetings but soon saw the need for more contact. FCB and Publicis built their Alliance Operating Committee after seeing that it was not enough for the chief executives to sit on each other's boards. Claude-Alain Tardy's personal involvement on bank boards and in civic activities in Worcester after St. Gobain acquired Norton created goodwill with community institutions whose support Norton needs. Cleveland Tomorrow, an exemplary civic partnership for economic development, has the active involvement of fifty-six CEOs.

Leaders must put in their own time to ensure that network ties work to their advantage, whether at home or away. Smaller companies' leaders must be willing to travel, meeting with customers, distributors, and partners at their home base. They cannot rely on distant representatives to make decisions for them because reps do not know the business as well. Direct communication must be maintained, to share vision and strategy.

Joint project teams bring together middle managers or professionals from each company to develop plans for specific projects or joint activities, to identify organizational or system changes that will better link the network, or to transfer knowledge from one company or unit to others.

The European Retail Alliance developed projects in insurance, information technology, and transportation that involved staff from member companies; leadership for the project came from the company with the most experience or the best practices in that area. A telecommunications alliance deployed four working groups of a dozen professionals for close to a year to define specific details of cooperation in domains where potential synergies existed. Small supplier Cohen & Wilks and large retailer BhS developed joint team efforts to improve computer linkups based on a ledger system designed by CWI. And civic collaborations become real only through the specific tasks tackled by active representatives from each partner organization.

Designated integrators are another form of bridge, like the department dedicated to management of alliances at Powersoft. Worldwide account directors (WWADs) at FCB and Publicis mobilize resources of both companies on behalf of specific major global clients. WWADs roam the world as a bridge among countries, clients, and advertising agencies, acting as cross-fertilizers of ideas and a connection among diverse places. Their task is complicated by another relationship dynamic—the fact that each client relationship is itself very different; some clients are highly centralized for global marketing efforts, others give each company or region autonomy to develop their own. Integrators must be flexible, operating as diplomats, not controllers.

Joint ventures are also often new ventures, running into the same problems as any start-up—but with the additional complication of many parents. Networks that are significant for the business need dedicated resources and managers with power.

11. Respect differences.

Networks are most helpful when they involve differences—when partners give each other something they do not already have, whether geographic reach to another place, special expertise, new business concepts, or the clout of larger size from combining forces. But differences in business specialty or geographic location desired by partners are accompanied by more inconvenient differences in behavioral style, operating methods, or cultural assumptions. This is especially true when more than one country is involved, but cultural differences can be found even across neighboring towns or industry lines.

Stereotypes about cultural differences among ethnic groups, countries, or cities roll off managers' tongues easily. Behavior that fits common characterizations of an ethnic pattern is used to confirm a generalization, and soon that generalization is used to explain everything that goes wrong, even when other examples contradict the stereotype, as I argued in chapter 5.[2] It can be easier to invoke a stereotype to explain things than to look deeply into the situation. An exporter of specialty goods moved his business from New York to Miami and joined a freight-forwarding network associated with an airline; he attributed inferior service he found in Miami to "those laid-back Latin workers" rather than to the poorly run U.S. airline that later proved to be at fault.

Certainly cosmopolitans need to know about differences in customs among areas and people—that showing the bottom of the foot is an insult to Muslims, for example. But when such differences are constantly mentioned as a handicap of the other that is the cause of all problems, then a helpful hint has become a straitjacket. Stereotyping polarizes people, setting up us-them dynamics that undermine the desire to collaborate. Just when people should be getting closer, their generalizations about each other push them farther apart. A vicious cycle is set in motion. Mistrust makes success harder to attain. Lack of success sets up a search for blame. It is easier to blame the outsiders and condemn their differences. This increases mistrust.

Cultural differences are inevitable; the closer the collaboration, the more noticeable the differences. But whether people choose to invest the time in understanding them and working through them is a matter of how much they feel valued and respected for what they bring to the relationship. Trust begins with an assumption of equality—that all parties bring something valuable and deserve to be heard. Norton employees were motivated to respect French ways, not only because St. Gobain rescued Norton from a hostile bidder and promised training opportunities, but also because St. Gobain demonstrated its commitment to Norton's Worcester home base by extending community service. In contrast, a few Marysville residents were less willing to tolerate Japanese culture because they felt some Honda managers were condescending or neglected the needs of their town.

Respect and reciprocity are essential. A Chinese manager commented about the resentment engendered by companies assuming that their superior Western technology gave them the right to make all decisions: "The focus here is on face, reputation. Even if people are very poor, you need to give them face. Americans feel that because they gave us jobs, we can't argue. But the Chinese people don't need their jobs. We can replace them with another foreign company; we can import from another place."

Respect is a two-way street. German, Swiss, and other foreign companies chose to locate in Greenville and Spartanburg, and international companies put Latin American headquarters in Miami because of a "foreign comfort" zone: that people will be surrounded by others who respect their differences. But foreign companies were welcomed in South Carolina because the first wave wanted to be close to valued American customers, learn from Americans, and be Americans. Showing respect engenders respect.

If problems exaggerate differences, success submerges them. The ultimate trust builder is delivering on promises. Early successes prove that a partner has something to contribute. It makes others more willing to listen. Suddenly, annoying differences dissolve into amusing foibles or easily fixed misunderstandings.

12. Teach partners. Learn from partners.

Often the purpose of networks is innovation, to speed concepts from one place or company to another quickly, as in the dense networks of development partners surrounding software companies like Powersoft. FCB and Publicis considered the formation of their alliance an occasion to rethink the nature of an advertising agency. Tech Ridge used its partnership with Polaroid in Mexico and the Dominican Republic to learn about international markets, bringing back ideas for product innovations that shifted its focus.

Cosmopolitans cross both external and internal walls. They create "learning organizations" that disseminate knowledge widely. Powersoft has rapid communication loops between its customer service organization and its product design teams so it can act fast to incorporate customer problems and needs into the next product release. Education-oriented companies such as Hewlett-Packard, Lau Technologies, or Kohler are not only rich in training programs, they also build more cross-functional teamwork that spreads ideas across the organization and minimizes resistance to learning. Companies that derive greater value from their outside networks also have greater communication across functions and share more information inside the organization. There was a strong statistical correlation in my five-city survey of 2,655 companies between closer relationships with suppliers, customers, or venture partners, and greater internal teamwork.

Companies often fail to get advantage from their relationships because of the internal barriers they erect between levels and functions. They confine the possible learning from partners to the small set of people involved directly in the relationship. Or "not invented here" attitudes mean that staff remote from the relationship reject out of hand ideas or technology created elsewhere. A large American company's highest-quality award went to a joint venture in Turkey, yet people from facilities in North America and Western Europe did not want to believe that managers from a less developed country had anything to teach them.

People from across the network must become teachers as well as learners. Timberland sponsors City Year and provides the City Year board chair, teaching business management principles; City Year teaches team building to its large benefactor. A Mitsui trainee from the giant Japanese trading company was deployed to tiny Cohen & Wilks to learn about British markets from CWI.

13. *Be prepared to change.*

Cosmopolitans become skilled at crossing boundaries and linking many places because they are willing to be influenced by the people and companies in their network. To make linkages possible requires operating compatibilities, which in turn means learning others' language or inventing a new one, changing to their system or creating a joint one. Productive external relationships require internal change.

Companies must strike a balance between holding on to their own way and letting go of it entirely. The need to work together on a partner's terms as well as on one's own terms means a partial loss of control, a ceding of some independence. Cosmopolitans must avoid imposing their home culture on their partners while preserving the strengths that make them desirable partners. They must be ready to change or reverse role. Rieter Machine Works opened an American sales office in Spartanburg over thirty years ago, gradually expanding into manufacturing dominated by "Swiss ways" and technology from Switzerland; now the American plant beats European facilities in productivity and innovation, and technology flows from South Carolina to Switzerland.

14. Help everyone win.

Mutuality is the hallmark of business collaboration. Network members need to make the linkage beneficial not just for themselves, but for the others. There are power differences in networks that join larger and smaller organizations (big retailer BhS has more control than small supplier Cohen & Wilks, Cohen & Wilks has more control than its Asian factory partners), but unless larger companies help the smaller ones remain profitable, they lose their dedicated supply base or eager innovator.

Balancing benefits is hard to do in the short term. It is not subject to strict economic rationality, because relationships can be complex, with network members playing a variety of roles with respect to each other. Tech Ridge is a supplier of cameras to Polaroid, a customer for Polaroid's film and camera backs, and a source of new concepts in technology and manufacturing. Many of Powersoft's development partners are also customers, distributors, and competitors; Powersoft is active in the Massachusetts Software Council, where it helps potential rivals. The dozen largest partners in Inmarsat, whose mobile telecommunications satellites were used by CNN for live broadcasts during the Gulf War, are simultaneously investors, regulators (setting international standards), suppliers (of technology), customers (for Inmarsat systems and satellite slots), and competitors (seeking to enter the same consumer markets as telecommunications is deregulated). People involved in complex relationships must distinguish between what they must keep separate and secret, because of rivalry, and what they can offer freely to their partners, to support victory for all.

Relationships are simpler to manage when they are narrow in scope, with few points of contact between the organizations and few overlapping operations, but that weakens commitment and brings fewer long-term benefits. When partners extend areas of collaboration, it becomes more difficult to put a monetary value on every contribution from each member, allocate costs and benefits, or determine compensation for extra services.

The best relationships operate by an implicit "relationship value maximization" logic that is hard to quantify. By providing an opportunity for Tech Ridge to sell cameras well suited to a contract, Polaroid gives up a chance to push its own cameras but sells more film and gets first crack at Tech Ridge's innovations.

15. Get closer, change course, or exit gracefully.

Leveraging connections has to be balanced against all the other things the company is doing. Organizations can handle only so many significant relationships before their demands begin to conflict and perceived benefits diminish in the face of investment requirements—not only capital, but management time and attention, partner-specific learning, and staff for joint project teams. Sometimes one connection swamps others in business importance; A&A Limousine would be just a struggling local chauffeur service without its Carey International link.

As living systems, relationships evolve in their possibilities. Sometimes an alliance serves to try out a few ways of working together before doing more or to live together before getting married, as Powersoft did with Sybase. Some Japanese acquirers of American companies ensured smooth transitions by beginning with a joint venture, to build the relationship slowly and help local managers feel comfortable.

A suitable partner for one purpose might not be adequate for others. Relationship managers or venture participants might be needed for more urgent tasks. Shifts in business conditions and strategy changes mean that a particular relationship no longer fits as well. Lotus and Powersoft might have to differentiate among their many partners as technology changes, reducing commitments to older relationships while seeking new ones.

When it is necessary to change partners, they should be informed fully and treated with integrity. If they are not, future relationships will be jeopardized. In Asian countries, for example, business and government leaders have long memories.

Networks should not be entered into lightly. Promiscuous alliances usually result in failed promises and broken hearts. Only those relationships with full commitment endure long enough to create value for their partners.

The best business relationships, like the best marriages, are true partnerships that meet eight criteria; call them the "eight I's that make We":

• *Individual excellence.* Partners are strong in their own right. They have things to contribute to the relationship. Their motivations for entering into it are positive (to pursue future opportunities) rather than negative (to mask weaknesses).

• *Importance.* The relationship fits major strategic objectives of the partners, so they care about making it work. Partners have long-term goals for which the relationship plays a key role.

• *Interdependence.* Partners need each other. They have complementary assets and skills. Neither could perform alone what is possible if all work together.

• *Investment.* Partners invest in each other (lending equipment, equity swaps, personnel exchanges, cross-training of staffs, mutual board service), which demonstrates a stake in the relationship. They show their long-term commitment by devoting resources to the relationship.

• *Information.* Communication is reasonably open. Partners share information required to make the relationship work. They disclose objectives and goals, provide technical data, and inform each other about conflicts, trouble spots, or changing situations.

• *Institutionalization.* The relationship is given a formal status; clear responsibilities and decision processes govern it. It extends beyond the particular people who formed it and cannot be dissolved whimsically.

• *Integration.* Partners develop linkages and shared ways of operating so they can work together smoothly. They build bridges between many people at many organizational levels. Partners become both teachers and learners.

• *Integrity.* Partners behave toward each other in honorable ways that justify and enhance mutual trust. Partners do not abuse the information they gain, nor do they try to undermine each other. If they must terminate the relationship, they do so honestly and fairly.

Consider these the *Scout's Handbook* principles for cosmopolitans, the rules for joining the world class.

THINKING ACROSS BOUNDARIES

Picture this scene: It was a meeting of the minds at a crossroads of world trade. In a Singapore ballroom, the British head of Castrol, maker of high-quality motor oil, was about to reveal to managers from thirty-seven countries the characteristics necessary for success in their global company. The audience squirmed in anticipation of the usual list of sensible but bland clichés about biases for action and putting people first. Then he spoke. "Brains," he said. "You need brains." And he sat down.

How unexpected. How refreshing. How appropriate.

Mental agility is essential in the global economy. Ideas and events are reshaping social and economic institutions. In every area, received wisdom about categories, distinctions, and groupings is being challenged. Trying to conduct business while the system itself is being reshaped puts a premium on brains—to imagine possibilities outside of conventional categories, to envision actions that cross traditional boundaries, to anticipate repercussions and take advantage of interdependencies, to make new connections or invent new combinations. Those who lack the mental flexibility to think across boundaries will find it harder and harder to hold their own, let alone prosper.

Boundaries are sometimes a mental imposition, a decision to divide the world a certain way. They become real when social patterns come to enforce the imaginary walls and when once deliberate choices become mindless habits. But history teaches us not to assume their permanence. For every barrier there seems to be a patient entrepreneur who eventually finds a way around it—and then tries to erect a new one to defend his or her position.

A familiar brain teaser is often used to illustrate the need to think across boundaries. Arrange nine dots in three rows and three columns. Now try to connect all the dots with four lines. If you stay within the boundaries defined by the dots, as most people think they must, the task cannot be done. A solution is found only by going outside the apparent boundaries. Now try using just three lines to connect the dots. Impossible, you say? Not if you challenge another apparent constraint. Enlarge the dots enough, and the puzzle is solved.

Generating new ideas is boundary challenging. Innovations grow out of unexpected, surprising, and even irreverent mental connections. To develop them requires collaborations and adjustments by many parts of organizations and the networks surrounding them. Entrepreneurial opportunities do not respect territories; they do not present themselves in the boxes established on organization charts. The more rigid the walls between functions or between companies, the less likely that people will venture out of their boxes to try something new.

Cosmopolitan leaders must destroy those walls, even at the cost of resistance by locals. Cosmopolitans, who value choices and want the world to operate as a qualitocracy in which everyone has access to the world's best, can be feared or mistrusted by locals who want those walls to protect their own territory. But locals sometimes fail to realize that the same walls that keep outsiders out also hold insiders in, confining them to a shrinking set of opportunities.

The ultimate walls that cosmopolitans must destroy are walls in the mind: insular thinking that limits aspirations, resents outsiders for their differences, and shrinks away from collaboration. Then cosmopolitans can build the bridges that connect islands of resources to the rest of the world.

World Class Regions: Strengthening the Infrastructure for Collaboration

I started this book by invoking a magical island of beaches and nature preserves five miles off the coast of Massachusetts and raising the question of how we are connected to the world. Now we have traveled to many places and left islands of all kinds far behind. We have examined the networks and partnerships of world class companies, toured international cities in which businesses thrive, and seen how those who are isolated risk retreat into self-defeating nativism. Success, it is clear, is not insular but collaborative.

Communities must open their connections to the world. Success for locals in the global economy will derive from their ability to become more cosmopolitan, to forge linkages to the rest of the world. And local communities must exert leadership to develop these links, with or without the help of national governments. In the global economy of the future, national opportunities will be led by world class metropolitan centers within nations. National social problems will be solved the same place they are manifested—at the grass-roots level. National governments will be standard setters, supporters of local development, suppliers of resources, and facilitators or guardians of economic and political activity across borders, but countries will be only as strong as the localities they contain.

World class businesses need the three C's of concepts, competence, and connections. World class places can help grow these global assets by offering innovation capabilities, production capabilities, and trade capabilities—that is, investing in entrepreneurship and innovation, quality skills and learning, networking and collaboration. America's strength in the world stems not from military might, but from marketing savvy, not from the power of size, but from the power of innovation.[1] Cities and surrounding regions must work together to foster world-ready businesses, workplaces with employability security, communication and learning within and across industries, civic engagement, more inclusive community leadership, and regional bodies that look across jurisdictions to create larger benefits for the whole.

The global economy makes it clear that the success of businesses derives heavily from their linkages. They draw strength from relationship-based social capital as well as from financial capital. Therefore cities need to be the places where linkages can be forged and facilitated. Cities will thrive as international centers to the extent that the businesses and people in them can learn more and develop better by being there, in communication with each other, than somewhere else.

The clearest danger to the viability of communities is not globalization, but a retreat into isolationism and protectionism. In the global economy, those institutions that are fragmented and those people or organizations that are unconnected and isolated are at a disadvantage. They are targets of nativists who capitalize on discontent by blaming outsiders, scapegoating foreigners, and urging that barriers be erected to stem the global tide. But if communities retreat into nativism, they are unlikely to find solutions to the very problems that led to their discontent in the first place. And just as ironically, the best way for communities to preserve their uniqueness and control is to be globally excellent.

Those that set the standards can call the shots.

Cities can be sources of each of the three C's. They can be places where new concepts are developed, where innovators exchange expertise with others in their industry, come into contact with new ways of thinking about businesses, technologies, products, or services, and find support for translating their concepts into commercially viable businesses. They can be places where production competence is enhanced because B-I-W quality standards are promulgated and reinforced and the work force is trained and applauded for operational excellence. They can be places where connections are made and international networks form, where businesses find resources and partners to take them to other markets.

CITIES AS GLOBAL SKILL CENTERS

To help businesses and people thrive at home in the global economy, cities must become centers of globally relevant skills, offering ways their occupants can link to the world.

World class cities gain that status from a "core capability"—a central orientation that is flexible and can be renewed, updated, and generalized over a variety of industries. World class cities are centers of deepening, widening skill that links them to the global economy.

This represents a new way of thinking for cities whose agenda is still dominated by traditional downtown banks, utilities, and real estate interests, because their view of economic development centers around bricks and mortar, not global skills. Much of the economic development debate in Boston in 1994, for example, centered around what kind of convention center and sports stadium to build, and where. But it is not sports teams or events for out-of-towners that distinguish Boston from Memphis or Kansas City; Boston would lose more of its long-term viability if world class technology companies or research laboratories decided to move to Atlanta than if large conventions went there.

The emphasis on a core global capability also represents an enlargement of Michael Porter's important theory that places derive strength from the industries that cluster there, the set of suppliers, customers, and rivals that make a place a center for the industry and stimulate innovation[2]—like autos around Detroit, insurance around Hartford, films around Los Angeles, leather goods around Milan, computers around Boston and the San Francisco Bay, tires and other polymers around Cleveland and Akron, or aircraft around Seattle. Industry clusters are apparent and powerful, especially at early stages of business development. But clusters are concrete manifestations of more generic skills that cut across particular industries and outlast them. As companies develop, they extend their ties beyond localities, dispersing functions to many places, spreading a cluster over a widening territory, or multiplying the number of industry centers, making them interchangeable or making it important for businesses to have a foothold in all of them. New entrants, such as foreign investors, create satellite centers, as Michelin did in moving tires to South Carolina.

Creativity and innovation in companies are facilitated by cross-fertilization, by flexible organizations encouraging people to think across boundaries and combine ideas across fields.[3] In *The Economy of Cities*, Jane Jacobs argued that cities grow faster and are able to renew themselves periodically because their diversity of institutions stimulates a similar cross-fertilization or clash of ideas; and recent economic studies confirm that adoption of new technology is more likely when companies are located in places with diverse economies rather than near those specialized in their particular industry.[4]

Cities need to be places that help people in an industry gain strength not just by talking to each other, but by talking to those who think differently, challenge assumptions, and bring ideas and resources from outside the industry or locality. Detroit's downhill slide starting in the mid-1970s developed because the industry cluster there was so strong, it became insular; there was little external stimulus to innovation. With major rivals and suppliers clustered in the area, there was no need to look beyond the Detroit region, auto executives apparently thought, to stay abreast of new developments in the industry. The Japanese auto companies proved them wrong. By the end of the next decade Detroit–Tokyo flights were packed, some of the most important centers of innovation were at NUMMI in Northern California, Saturn in Tennessee, and Honda in Ohio, and American automakers were embedded in dense webs of global alliances drawing on many centers of expertise.

Furthermore, too much reliance on particular industries can lead to a company town writ large, one that is highly vulnerable to industry cycles and capital flight once companies no longer need their founding location. Tying a city's success to a small number of large industries means that Seattle would have busted long ago when the forest products boom ended and never risen from the ashes of periodic Boeing layoffs. Or that Boston would still be in the doldrums from defense industry cutbacks and computer hardware industry crashes.

Core global capabilities, in contrast, are more general and permit more diversity. They create new industries as old ones die—like software and telecommunications replacing computer hardware around

Boston because of a fertile environment for new concepts and the means to start businesses based on them. An area's core skills can be generalized over a variety of industries, bringing related diversity in many companies, as happened with manufacturing skills in Spartanburg and Greenville; textile manufacturing attracted equipment suppliers that used machine-making skills to diversify the area's industrial base beyond textiles. An unexpected combination of diverse industries can create new ones: aerospace engineers + Hollywood = Los Angeles' multimedia companies. Core global skills take a long time to embed in community institutions—like Atlanta's twenty-five-year climb to technology prominence—and are long lasting, occasionally even for centuries—like northern Italy's core competence in artistic design, making Florence a capital of the Renaissance and Milan a fashion capital today. And a region's core skills give additional power to what would otherwise seem like unrelated industries. For example, Miami's health technology firms take advantage of trade connections with Latin America, while Boston's larger set of health technology firms take advantage of computer software and other technological innovation in the area.

Sometimes an area can contain an industry cluster that is largely unrelated to a generic global skill and therefore likely to wane as an economic strength in the future. Miami is home to a significant garment manufacturing cluster that is the city's largest employer in manufacturing, but Miami's strength as an international city—and its future —lies elsewhere. Unless Miami's core trading skills give its apparel industry special features, apparel will wane in importance.

Core capabilities emerge and grow because cities have two critical features: magnets and glue.

MAGNETS: THE FOUNDATION OF WORLD CLASS CITIES

Supporting institutions, sometimes unrelated to particular industries, help to transform an area's core skills into an economic asset by attracting and retaining the resources businesses need to succeed at using the area's core skills. *Magnets* are the key institutions that attract potential members of the world class to a particular place. Social *glue* includes the quality of industry interaction and quality of life that hold them there.

Magnets draw their power of attraction from foundation organizations, often decades old. Out of these foundations grow an area's characteristic skill as well as the suppliers and services to support major industries. Often this evolution has occurred slowly, without a clear strategy. Foundation organizations may themselves change shape or pass from the scene, but they have started a process in motion. Each foundation organization attracts people and organizations from outside its borders that reinforce the skill implied by the foundation. Public and private investment builds the core skill. Even when the whole area prospers, the benefits of this investment can flow disproprortionately to some parts of the community, attracting more people and organizations relevant to the core skill.

For Boston, whose global linkages stem from success as a thinker, exporting concept-based products and services, the magnets are institutions of higher education, research laboratories, and academic medical centers. The people they attract are students, faculty, and knowledge-oriented professionals. The most significant public investment has been federal defense and research spending; the most important political decisions affecting the area between 1940 and 1980 were federal decisions to pursue new technologies for World War II and the cold war. The most significant private investment has been venture capital; together with an array of technology transfer programs, state financing opportunities, and informal networks, this has translated new concepts into commercial enterprises. The primary beneficiaries of the core skill in thinking tend to be successful entrepreneurs and the professional work force.

For Spartanburg and Greenville, models of makers, the foundation organizations in the 1950s were textile factories, and the first flow of external resources were European equipment manufacturers persuaded to locate near their American customers. The most significant public investment was in customized worker training. The critical political decision at the state and local level was to pursue outside investment actively, including foreign companies. The most significant private investment has been foreign capital, accompanied by foreign expertise. As the area gained increased manufacturing competence, American subsidiaries of foreign companies became models for their foreign parents, outperforming them. Skilled production workers and suppliers to manufacturing are the primary beneficiaries.

For Miami, an example of a trader, foundation organizations perhaps reach back to the post–World War II resort hotels that provided the area's first flow of external resources in the form of tourists; some decided to settle in that warm climate, like Jewish garment manufacturers from New York, who formed an ethnic colony in Miami Beach. That Miami faded, only to be revived by a significant political decision to admit refugees from Castro's Cuba and a significant public investment in aid to the exiles to build an economic base. A bilingual, Spanish-speaking population, facilitated by another political decision, the foreign banking act, attracted the most significant private investment: Latin American and then European money. Public investment in the physical infrastructure for trade, the airport and seaport, supported the growing trade skill of the area in those business services that make the city the place to go to communicate or make deals across cultures. Benefits tend to accrue to "gold collar" workers (highly paid executives and professionals) who can make international connections.

Each of these cities can seem unique or exotic, a product of historical accidents and the independent actions of business entrepreneurs rather than of conscious strategies. Yet at some point luck was converted into strategy. Civic leaders recognized potential skills and made decisions that supported them. And other places strong in these generic skills have similar combinations of foundation organizations and investments that make them magnets for the resources that support the skills: the San Francisco Bay Area or Austin, Texas, as centers of technological thinking, building on great universities and federal funding; Greater Cleveland or northern Indiana as centers of manufacturing competence, building on foreign as well as domestic investment in world class quality; New York City or Los Angeles as global trade centers, benefiting from a combination of cross-border population flows, transportation links, and strength in finance, communication, and other business services.[5]

Core capabilities can also bring core rigidities—an overreliance on known technologies and an inability to change.[6] Becoming so strong at industries based on one core skill that others are neglected creates tensions in the community between the cosmopolitans who benefit from the core skill—or can pick up and move elsewhere—and the locals who are left behind. It creates weaknesses and vulnerabilities. For example, thinkers can fall prey to arrogance, orthodoxy, and elitism; because knowledge industries are so central, they can emphasize knowledge work to the exclusion of other fields, like manufacturing, that employ a wider range of people than simply the techno-cosmopolitan elite. Makers can stress reliable performance over innovation, training the work force for production efficiency but neglecting to support organizations and people whose thinking creates new concepts. Traders can become conduits for the exchange of goods and services without adding value through concepts or production competence originating in the trade center. Miami's success at creating "foreign comfort" might reduce domestic comfort; some Dade County companies complain that the foreign flavor of the city makes it hard to attract talent from other parts of the United States.

Even where one core skill is central, it is not enough by itself to guarantee global success. Thinkers need makers to serve as local test centers for new concepts and as customers in regular contact whose problems and needs give rise to new concepts. Thinkers and makers need traders to make connections with international markets, for direct export income, outside investment of new capital and expertise in the area, and the quality stimulus of being forced to be world-ready, meeting B-I-W standards. Traders need makers and thinkers, or they become simply deal makers and freight handlers who add no extra value and can easily be bypassed as trade connections grow elsewhere.

Whereas cities might have grown through special strength in one skill area, they can slip in the global economy if they do not emphasize the others. The renewal of Cleveland's success as a maker was supported by investments in thinking and trading. The Cleveland Advanced Manufacturing Program was created in 1984 to bring new technological concepts that would restore manufacturing competence. Its affiliates include a range of local universities engaged in basic research and community colleges offering customized job training, including experience in a "teaching factory" that helps workers learn new technologies.

With Cleveland's competence augmented by concepts, connections came next. Recognizing that one in three manufacturing jobs in the Midwest is related directly to exports (compared with one in four nationally), Cleveland leaders such as Eaton Corporation CEO William Butler decided in 1991 to increase the area's trade connections, forming the Greater Cleveland International Trade Alliance as a collaboration of the city, county, port authority, and the Greater Cleveland Growth Association, the city's largest business membership association. The alliance opened a World Trade Center in 1993. In support of this international strategy, former Ohio governor Richard Celeste said, "You can always buy something in English; you can't always sell something in English." Now Ohio governor and former Cleveland mayor George Voinovich touts such trade facilitators as an export tax credit, a cooperative relationship between the state and Japan's External Trade Organization to help Ohio exporters enter the Japanese market, and an Ohio on-line export directory that includes product catalogs in multimedia form.

To succeed in the global economy, places must nurture the core capability that gives them international distinction, but they must also invest in other skills to support their core strength. They must seek interactions among strategies: for example, offering both education for professionals who will pioneer in new technologies and new concepts and training for production workers in world class operations that can use those technologies; or seeking international connections both to export local products and to attract foreign investment.

In every case, new possibilities are brought to a city by a flow of new people, often outsiders with different ideas and international connections. It could be politically unfashionable today to note the importance of immigrants to the vitality of cities. But consider the role that students, exiles, foreign-born professionals, and foreign companies have played in bringing new capital, ideas, or standards to places we have visited in this book, including smaller places such as Marysville, Ohio. This influx of fresh know-how then combined with classic American strengths to produce even higher performance; both Japanese-owned Honda in Marysville and Swiss-owned Rieter in Spartanburg eventually outperformed units in their parents' countries, and Americans became the teachers.

For those locals who feel threatened by global change, it seems clear that the best "protection" is to embrace global possibilities, strengthening rather than cutting their linkages to the world. By fostering high standards and encouraging local companies to meet them, communities can both produce locally for local needs but also have strengths to offer global businesses.

Currently prosperous places must do this along with those in economic distress. Take Seattle, selected as America's number one city for business by *Fortune* in a 1992 article featuring its strong economy and such world class Seattle-based companies as Boeing, Microsoft, and Nintendo of America. Seattle's Trade Development Alliance was the inspiration for Cleveland's program and that of other cities, and it builds the area's international connections in numerous ways: from intercity visits that have taken hundreds of local leaders to Europe and Japan to an international press center for visiting foreign journalists. Even schoolchildren are influenced to think globally—for example, through the Seattle *Post Intelligencer*'s issue on "Pacific power" in its color magazine for kids. The Seattle-Tacoma airport, a leader in the sea-air cargo link, partners with Miami for Latin American–bound cargo.

This active strategy to build trading skills for a city better known for its making and thinking skills is necessary because of a tendency for local residents to turn inward. The beautiful natural environment surrounding Seattle is sometimes called "Ecotopia," a term echoing the closed-system feel of a Utopia content to be self-contained. Seattle struggles with the proper balance between protecting its environment and saving jobs by changing what business leaders on my survey called an unwieldy regulatory apparatus and slow permitting process that could cause companies to leave the area. It aspires to be an international city, but its economic development strategy focuses largely on indigenous entrepreneurs rather than attracting international investment to the city, and its airport faces stiff competition for important Asia-to–North America connections from Portland, Oregon, and Vancouver, British Columbia.

Looking inward will not help locals join the world class; they must also reach outward. To do this effectively, with a coherent strategy, requires a second ingredient of world class cities: social glue.

GLUE: THE INFRASTRUCTURE FOR COLLABORATION

Cities must not only attract resources, they must hold them and grow them. What keeps brainpower, labor, or investors in an area is quality of life and quality of community—the ways that businesses gain strength from association with others in the area, that talented people gain well-being from staying there.

Therefore communities must offer more than their connective physical infrastructure of roads, bridges, buses, subways, airports, seaports, electric power lines, and telecommunications networks. They must also have a social infrastructure that helps forge linkages relevant to global success: networks among small and large companies in related industries, between suppliers and customers, between ethnic groups and neighborhoods, or among institutions in a community that contribute to quality of life. I call this the infrastructure for collaboration.

The infrastructure for collaboration consists of the pathways by which people and organizations come together to exchange ideas, solve problems, or form partnerships. It helps people move across the barriers of localism, parochialism, or provincialism that divide them. It is the means by which people and organizations can come together across sectors to recognize, value, and leverage their area's assets for mutual gain. It might take concrete form as civic leadership groups, public-private partnerships, industry councils, or other institution-spanning bodies. It is broader but less formal and more fluid than government and, in some cases, much more important in getting things done. Roger Milliken in Spartanburg or Alvah Chapman Jr. in Miami have outlasted local and regional officials and held multiple leadership roles.

Civic life consists of a range of institutions beyond government and a range of issues beyond politics. Politics involves battles over distribution: who gets which slices of the pie. A community's social infrastructure, in contrast, offers the prospect for expanding the pie. Yet, as we have also seen in Boston and Miami, this social infrastructure, and the social capital or human relationships that support it, are too often neglected, allowing the area to remain fragmented and balkanized.

Crises sometimes galvanize leaders to improve the infrastructure for collaboration. Cleveland's social infrastructure, for example, had too many potholes by the 1970s—dying industries, lost jobs, racial tensions, deteriorating education, incompetent politicians, and a river declared a fire hazard. So business leaders went to work to lead a remarkable turnaround through collaboration across sectors. Cleveland Tomorrow, formed in December 1981 as a result of a study undertaken in 1979, brought together the heads of thirty-six major businesses to create strategic plans that revived community spirit while bringing new industry, new jobs, and new tourist attractions, such as the Rock and Roll Hall of Fame and a new sports stadium. With fifty-six CEOs now on board, Cleveland Tomorrow continues to encourage other civic partnerships. Leadership Cleveland's eight hundred multiracial graduates form a network infusing nearly every major organization in the area, the Council of Small Enterprises gets small and midsize companies involved, the Business Volunteerism Council links companies to community service, and the New Cleveland Campaign sells the community.

Opportunities as well as crises can bring leadership to the social infrastructure. For Atlanta, the 1996 Olympics is a community connections builder and a vehicle for encouraging long-term improvements in the city. Well in advance of the Olympics, Atlanta used its prospect to increase community volunteerism and address urban problems; opportunities to work on Olympic events, for example, are restricted to those residents who have a long volunteer résumé in other aspects of community service. The Atlanta Committee for the Olympic Games is handling the Olympics itself (the construction of venues, for example); but Atlanta's commissioner for planning and development is working to convert Olympic construction into a permanent legacy. To coordinate neighborhood and city development outside Olympic fences, the mayor formed CODA (Corporation for Olympic Development Authority) in January 1993. The jobs accompanying Olympic preparations are expected to provide training, upgrading work force skills. Whatever they bring to Atlanta's physical plant, the Olympics are an energizing force strengthening the city's social infrastructure by providing common direction and a timetable for action.

Sometimes both crises and opportunities teach a community how to work together. For Miami, Hurricane Andrew in 1992 was the crisis that started to repair ethnic tensions as people rallied for the rebuilding effort; the Summit of the Americas in 1994 was the opportunity that increased civic engagement, identified new leaders, built new organizations such as an international press center, and gave the community the sweet taste of shared success.

The need is urgent in many places. America's cities and surrounding regions must strengthen their infrastructure for collaboration in order to solve pressing urban problems of crime, education, housing, and welfare that trap local isolates in a cycle of disadvantage. Deteriorating quality of community life not only hurts locals directly, but also encourages cosmopolitans to take their concepts, competence, and connections—and their jobs—elsewhere. Cities and their regions must strengthen their community problem-solving and skills-building capacity in order to compete in the global market for investment.

THE WORLD COMPETITION TO JOIN THE WORLD CLASS

There is already a world market among places to attract and hold business investment. Communities everywhere must develop their direct economic connections to the world. To compete, cities need economic development strategies that include, in effect, their own foreign policies.

Look at the brochures of cities all over the world, and you will see that they are showing off their international offices and factories the way they once boasted about their local museums and churches. The slick brochure for the city of Lodz, Poland, for example, features foreign companies located there: Boston's own Gillette as well as Shell, PepsiCo, Sara Lee, ABB, Coca-Cola, and VF Corporation, parent of Wrangler jeans.

Cities like Newcastle, England, are international role models for collaborations that revitalize declining regions and ready them for twenty-first-century competition. Newcastle is a quintessential maker, an international manufacturing center with strong linkages to North America and Europe. In 1993 the Newcastle area in the northeast of Britain was named by the World Economic Forum's magazine as the number one new plant location in the world, based on data collected by the international consultancy Price Waterhouse and Plant Location International, a Brussels-based firm.

One of the oldest relics of the last century's Industrial Revolution, the Newcastle region now creates jobs faster than all but two other parts of the United Kingdom; houses over 380 foreign companies, including 130 from the United States and 50 from Japan that use the area to reach British and European markets; and exports 45 percent of its output, a higher percentage than any other U.K. region. Between 1986 and the fall of 1994, foreign companies alone spent almost £4 billion ($6–$7 billion) on 370 projects that created or safeguarded fifty thousand jobs. In 1994 Samsung established an electronics complex in Teesside involving at least five manufacturing plants and a training center for an investment of over $1 billion, the largest in Europe by a Korean company. Instead of bringing coals to Newcastle, companies are bringing capital.

Northern Development Company (NDC), the development catalyst in Newcastle's area, is one of the largest regional development organizations in the world. Its head office is in Newcastle, with branch offices in Teesside and Cumbria to ensure linkages across city jurisdictions. NDC also has foreign offices in Brussels, Bergen, Chicago, San Francisco, Tokyo, Hong Kong, Osaka, Seoul, and Taipei. International companies loan employees to these offices, as Bridgestone Tire did to NDC's Tokyo office.

NDC reaches over ten thousand companies regionwide with programs to boost their competence and connections. A Quality North campaign launched in 1990 spreads B-I-W quality principles; the area's world class companies like Japan's Komatsu have taught their techniques.[7] Quality North has involved over three thousand organizations in three stages: first, emphasizing quality tools and service; second, forming networks to exchange ideas across companies and partnering between customers and suppliers; finally, engaging three hundred executives as ambassadors to attract new companies to the region while NDC's Fit for Europe export campaign helps companies find international markets.

The quality theme seemed a natural for the region in 1989, when all three winners of the 1989 British Quality Awards—ICI, British Shell, and 3M—had northern-area operations and Greater Newcastle already had a reputation as a preferred European site for Japanese industry. David Williams, architect of the program, recalled: "What struck me was the opportunity this provided to position the region as a quality leader in international terms, to 'badge' it distinctively with a quality branding, and to underline the clear competitive advantage to be enjoyed by a business locating here among such illustrious company." But because Williams and his colleagues found that many local companies had a long way to go to reach world quality standards, Quality North began with broad and deep education for the region.

Northern's quality education programs are extensive and practical: a quarterly public forum; road shows to carry the message and techniques to organizations throughout the region; kits of materials; a quality hot line to answer questions or make referrals; a Service with a Smile award for front-line workers such as receptionists, shop assistants, and taxi drivers; and Open to View, behind-the-scenes visits to quality companies, which attracted twenty thousand visitors eager to learn from other companies' quality practices. A challenge to manufacturers to improve work force skills was supported by over one thousand companies. Many companies receive awards for their achievements, reinforcing the quality message, and often the region's awards go to foreign companies, which makes them feel welcome and encourages them to transfer still more know-how to Newcastle. Northern also holds a competition in schools that spreads awareness to kids, deploying schoolchildren to search the area for examples of quality.

While Quality North focuses on competence, other programs actively market the region and enhance connections. NDC offers exhibition services for small and medium-size enterprises at trade shows abroad. A regional procurement office provides opportunities for smaller local suppliers to be matched with larger companies' supply needs; and events such as Great North Meets the Buyer promote almost four thousand local suppliers to purchasing agents. In October 1993 a live videoconference from Teesside to Europe helped manufacturers and suppliers discuss mutual business opportunities, and 450 of the area's small and midsize companies attended three thousand prebooked appointments to see 31 buying organizations. Since 1986 NDC has conducted over eighty-two trade missions involving over 1,200 companies to open trade connections in countries as diverse as Japan, Egypt, Poland, India, and Malaysia. A symphony tour in Germany helped local officials meet influential investment decision makers from the automotive sector. A telemarketing campaign by the U.S. desk reached over 300 American semiconductor companies.

The Newcastle region is unusually active, and its activities are paying off handsomely in new investment and job creation for an area that has faced dying industries and high unemployment. But Newcastle is only one of many places mounting collaboration-based campaigns to strengthen linkages to the global economy. Cheltenham, England, uses Spartanburg and Greenville, South Carolina, as role models for improving its success as a maker. Sydney, Australia, seeks prominence as a thinker. Sydney and its region in New South Wales have developed numerous strategies to strengthen its already core knowledge-based industries such as financial and business services, information technologies and telecommunications, environmental industries, and advanced manufacturing technologies. There are echoes of Boston and Massachusetts in New South Wales's Science and Technology Council, Technology Development Board, Information Industries Advisory Council, and Cooperative Research Centres linking universities and industry.

Other efforts to join the world class borrow from Boston's Route

128 and California's Silicon Valley while adding programs that aim to compete with successful U.S. high-tech regions. It is no accident that Scottish Enterprise, the development arm for Scotland, is trying to duplicate American high-tech success. Its Scottish chief executive since 1991, Crawford Beveridge, previously worked in management positions for Hewlett-Packard in California, Oregon, and Switzerland; Digital Equipment in Switzerland; Analog Devices in Boston; and Sun Microsystems in California. In this case, a cosmopolitan has returned to his roots, bringing global experience to boost his home locality.

By 1992 Scottish Enterprise had an ambitious vision involving an environment for innovation, inward investment ("Locate in Scotland"), enhanced export capability of Scottish businesses, and development of industry linkages. Its programs for world readiness feature many forms of collaboration: big companies allowing smaller ones access to training facilities and skills; employer-school partnerships; a "Eurogateway" program involving Scotland's linkages to France and Germany; a Euromatch database to help local companies find partners throughout Europe; and a Euro Information Centre in Glasgow.

The region seeks strength as a thinker breaking new technology ground, a maker with good manufacturing jobs, and a trader exploiting close connections to the European continent. Its foreign investment program targets firms that will carry out research and development in the region. A new medical complex in Edinburgh intends to compete in international health care services and is already trying to lure physicians from Boston's teaching hospitals. Duplicating Greater Boston's entrepreneurial success is an uphill battle because the small-business sector is comparatively weak in the United Kingdom compared to the United States and even weaker in Scotland. But Scottish Enterprise has developed partnerships with banks and a venture fund for start-up capital; training for potential entrepreneurs, including a special program for women; and an advice-plus-networking program modeled on the MIT Enterprise Forum. The city of Glasgow's New Business Ventures Program trains Scottish venture teams and then helps them form partnerships with smaller and midsize American companies with promising products but no European distribution.

Throughout Europe, cities not only are making their own foreign policy and foreign connections, they are forming groups to help them do it. Eurocities, formed in 1986, is an association of fifty-eight European regional centers—among them Barcelona, Spain; Cologne, Germany; and Lyon, France—that play an international role. Its goal is to facilitate its member cities' international linkages and to gain "political recognition of the position and role of cities in Europe" at European Union deliberations in Brussels. The voice of cities is being heard. As part of his European jobs platform, Jacques Delors called for the formation of local and regional partnerships to help develop small and medium-size firms in new industries.

As cities and regions develop explicit strategies and foreign policies, competition among places to be world centers of thinking, making, and trading promises to be increasingly fierce. Cities can no longer afford complacency. They must actively create their own futures. They must do so as leaders of regions that acknowledge their shared fate. Cities and suburbs, edge cities and downtowns, prosper—or fail to prosper—together.

Whatever their core skills, localities face five challenges:

- To nurture their core capabilities and create inspiring visions of quality and excellence, uniting business and government across jurisdictions to remove obstacles to excellence and build on the strengths of the area.
- To increase business-to-business collaboration, helping small and midsize enterprises join industry forums, find partners, tap international markets, transfer best practices, and become connected to wider networks.
- To develop a world-ready, foreign-friendly environment that attracts new outside investment, increases exports, and uses international connections to help locals become globally skilled.
- To spread employability security and build the work force of the future—one that is learning oriented, performs to high standards, and finds opportunities even in the face of continuing corporate change.
- To use new models for civic engagement and leadership development, in which community service is an integral part of a business career and social capital is developed by teams of diverse people working together on community projects.

CAMPAIGNING FOR LEADERSHIP AND EXCELLENCE: AN ACTION AGENDA

Cities would benefit from a single bold stroke to take action on many of these fronts simultaneously—an overarching campaign to set and achieve high goals that could be endorsed by business and government, management and the work force, private enterprise and the social sector. This would be led by the central city but unite the region, including both traditional downtown leaders and those from emerging companies in the edge cities and beyond. Such a bold stroke would involve many people from many parts of the community, joined through a common purpose and using common tools, who see the direct benefits to their own careers and their own enterprises from improving linkages to the global economy. This initiative would directly improve business and community performance.

Cosmopolitans and locals can be united around a vision of excellence. This vision should build on the area's historical advantages to increase its stock of world class concepts, competence, or connections —its skills as thinker, maker, or trader. It should rest on a set of linked premises, which show how cosmopolitans and locals can succeed together:

- that the best social program is good jobs;
- that the best jobs are those that provide linkages and capabilities for the global economy;
- that the best source of those jobs and capabilities is a world-ready business;
- that the way to attract and keep world class companies is to build a strong community, one that adds value to the company's business through its core global skills, welcomes newcomers, and offers a high quality of life;
- that a desirable community is one that can work together to address its problems and build a healthy business climate that creates good jobs . . . which is the best social program.

A campaign for leadership and excellence—spearheaded by an existing civic organization, a coalition of organizations, or a new public-private partnership—would invite locals to join the world class. It would promote world-readiness for local companies and employability security for the local work force. It would serve as an umbrella for initiating, publicizing, and extending areawide actions. Imagine possibilities such as those that follow, which build on this book's success stories.

ACTIONS FOR QUALITY AND EXCELLENCE:
BECOMING THE BEST-IN-WORLD

• *Develop regular areawide civic forums for communication and mutual understanding between business and government.* Use these forums to develop visionary goals, as well as action plans to remove obstacles to a healthy business climate and community life. Form regional councils linking public officials and business leaders across the area to create a shared agenda, working together in their own jurisdictions to implement it.

• *Identify the area's core skills and the investments required to increase the area's stock of world class concepts, competence, and connections.* Create a vision of excellence that will show how those key global assets will increase in the future.

• *Define B-I-W performance standards for every aspect of the community that supports its core skills*—from airports to schools, from recreational opportunities for foreign business travelers to incubators for new technology companies. Compare the area's performance against the world's best places in both private industry and the public sector. Benchmark against comparable places to illuminate strengths and weaknesses; create action plans to enhance the strengths and eliminate the weaknesses.

• *Celebrate excellence.* Create achievement awards, and use the criteria for receiving them to help educate organizations about best practices. Publicize role models. Produce tools for performance improvement that can be disseminated widely across sectors, creating a common vocabulary for the community as well as spreading high standards.

• *Promote a customer focus in government, business, education, and service industries.* Use it as an attraction for tourists, conventions, business travelers, and new outside investors.

• *Extend education in quality problem-solving skills to the schools.* Offer this to the adult community as well, in evening programs at the schools. This would prepare students for jobs of the future, provide a common educational experience for both parents and children, and improve the at-home dialogue critical to school performance.

• *Launch or reinforce "best partner" quality campaigns to educate companies throughout the area about world standards (such as Baldrige quality criteria, ISO 9000, value-added through customer-supplier partnerships) and criteria for success in global markets, complete with awards and recognition.* Create international road shows to market area companies exemplifying "best partner."

ACTIONS TO ENHANCE BUSINESS-TO-BUSINESS NETWORKING AND PARTNERING

• *Develop mechanisms to facilitate small-business collaboration.* Possibilities include purchasing, marketing, importing, exporting, ideas, exchange of personnel at slack times, sharing of facilities. Use directories, computer networks (bulletin boards), resource kits, local trade shows, seminars, and forums.

• *Create one-stop business service centers dispersed throughout the region that combine information from both the public and private sectors.* Provide information on government resources and support services, assistance for meeting regulatory requirements, and information from industry associations, civic groups, free trade zones, World Trade Centers, and other resources. These centers can act as places for small businesses to initiate a search for collaborators.

• *Develop databases of local suppliers and their skills.* Introduce new companies from outside the region to local companies that could support them. Ensure that local companies get information about potential procurements from large customers.

• *Hold regular minitrade shows at technology parks and research labs to connect developers of new concepts with potential entrepreneurs and suppliers who will commercialize them.*

• *Create welcoming kits for newly incorporated businesses that give them trial memberships in civic associations and offer them the chance to announce their existence to the membership.* Create networks to help smaller businesses make contacts that are inclusive of newcomers.

Partnering requires active initiative; businesses cannot wait for it to happen spontaneously. Small businesses must take the initiative to find partners and sell their skills. While it is not the role of government to form business collaborations, government resources could help jump-start collaborations in industries where this is difficult—or for populations where this is difficult.

• *Help minority companies join networks as equal players.* Small minority businesses emanating from the inner city need a link that connects them to other places. Create financing pools or government-backed loan guarantees for small businesses that invest in the inner city. Identify investment opportunities in the inner cities that can attract nonminority businesses as partners for inner-city firms. Dollars tend to be available for the inner city for philanthropy but not for business activities; for this reason many of the strongest leaders in the black community of some cities head social sector enterprises rather than businesses. Encourage these leaders to form job-creating businesses.

• *Ensure that mentoring programs for minority businesses make them "world-ready" from the start.* Include connections with companies that operate internationally as well as domestically; educate them about world class standards; and identify strengths that would make them appropriate local partners for new companies coming to the area.

ACTIONS TO BECOME WORLD-READY, FOREIGN-FRIENDLY, AND GLOBALLY LINKED

• *Identify the criteria used to select new locations that are important to international companies in industries related to the city's core skills.* Use those criteria to identify improvements the community must make —not only to attract outside investment, but also to encourage current companies to expand activities in the area rather than taking them elsewhere.

• *Actively market the area to potential international investors, but look beyond multinational giants.* Find midsize outside companies that are already links in a supply chain into the area and could relocate to serve large customers who would otherwise purchase outside the area—an "import substitution" strategy. Seek investors who will make long-term commitments to the area, bring innovation and new knowledge, and become involved in civic affairs—in the way that European middle-market companies contributed to Spartanburg. Find companies that are performing one function in the area, such as sales, and encourage them to perform others.

- *Follow the trade routes.* Identify the key trade connections of major companies in the area and develop strategies for transportation, telecommunications, and language skills that build on existing ties. For example, if Germany and Korea receive the highest number of exported products from the area, then work on bringing German and Korean airlines to the airport, expanding routes for cargo and passengers.

- *Examine the points of entry to the city to see how they look to outsiders.* This was what the Atlanta Chamber of Commerce did in asking about the experiences of international visitors to Atlanta. Develop amenities geared to international business travelers and not just to tourists—activities that make them feel comfortable and welcome or places where they can find items from their home, culturally appropriate entertainment, and resources to facilitate their visit, such as those that Seattle's international press center offers. Tourists bring onetime dollars, but business travelers bring continual investment.

- *Build ties in other countries with civic associations and economic development bodies as the basis for exchange of information about joint venture, plant location, and export market possibilities.* Send local executives as temporary ambassadors to other countries or take advantage of their business trips and help them sell the region.

- *Create databases of products developed by local companies that are candidates for export markets.* Bring them to trade fairs in other countries. Exchange information with economic development agencies in other countries to help link producers to international distributors or joint venture partners.

- *Multiply the payoff from trade missions.* Offer slots to groups of companies; ask those who participate to teach others and share connections; ask large companies to sponsor a small-business executive who could not otherwise afford to go.

• *Offer trade finance help to smaller companies before they enter foreign markets.* Tiny grants to seed the business are often more helpful for international trade than large loans after the company already has the business.

• *Identify international companies with extensive international knowledge and connections.* Determine how to tap their expertise and relationships for synergies with other area companies—for example, a manufacturing executive bringing knowledge of the German apprenticeship system; a bank with long-standing Latin American connections opening doors in that region for other local companies.

• *Bring newcomers and expatriates into local business councils to add an outside perspective or international presence.* Make them feel welcome. Determine how to use foreign companies as teachers for community institutions and in public school classrooms—a role Honda played in Marysville.

• *Set up mentoring relationships linking large international companies in the area with small companies seeking international opportunities.* Encourage the local press to report about the international activities of area companies.

• *Develop registers, directories, and information clearinghouses to help connect emerging companies with potential international partners.* Collect and provide data on companies capable of and interested in serving globally oriented, world class customers.

• *Publicize local educational resources for learning about international opportunities, companies, and business practices.* The resource pool is extensive: universities, foreign students, language institutes, World Trade Centers, foreign Chambers of Commerce, translators, expatriates, and retired executives are all possibilities. Use foreign students in the area as a source of knowledge about their countries; they are eager to get work experience, and they often come from prominent families with excellent connections. Invite foreign dignitaries or speakers to visit the schools, meeting with schoolchildren.

ACTIONS TO CREATE EMPLOYABILITY SECURITY AND SPREAD WORKPLACE EDUCATION

• *Support "learning alliances" to offer training, compare best practices, share success stories, and provide internships across companies.* Nashville's Peer Learning project, for example, is a management development consortium of local companies, organized into groups of a dozen companies—with only one company in each group—which share educational programs and exchange best practice ideas, supported by a local university.

• *Develop human resource and job banks linking networks of related companies.* Help companies to see their network of suppliers, customers, and venture partners as a resource for skills development, personnel exchanges, internships, or job placements. Encourage companies to invite speakers together, create training programs together, and help their people's skills become known to one another.

• *Offer customized job training for new companies bringing large investment to the area.* Use this training to increase the skills of the potential pool of workers, before they are chosen, to upgrade more people than the number to be hired immediately.

• *Bring ideas to and from the workplace.* Offer "open visit" days in which managers and workers can visit excellent companies in the area and ask questions about their activities and approaches. Create mobile education units (like Bookmobiles) to bring portable seminars or materials from local colleges to work sites.

• *Enhance support (financing, role models) for internal corporate entrepreneurship—new ventures, buyouts, and spin-off businesses* around promising ideas that the established company cannot use. These are important sources of innovation in technology, and they smooth employment fluctuations. Such programs also have a cascade effect inside the established company: they encourage entrepreneurial behavior, which can come back into the core business in the form of innovation that helps the company compete, saving jobs.

• *Expand entrepreneurship skills at both ends of the life cycle.* Beginning in early grades, give children opportunities to practice running small businesses, using programs such as Junior Achievement or An Income of Her Own, which helps teenage girls start businesses. Create "Senior Achievement" programs to help older workers get education and encouragement to start new businesses after hours, while still employed, as a transition to retirement or an alternative to large-company employment.

• *Develop school-to-work apprenticeship programs that offer students the chance to gain job skills.* Extend apprenticeship programs to displaced workers from declining industries—such as the Massachusetts Software Council's internship program to help people move from hardware to software jobs.

ACTIONS FOR CIVIC ENGAGEMENT AND LEADERSHIP DEVELOPMENT

• *Mount tours of other cities for current and future community leaders, to stretch their horizons and give them a shared view of what is possible.* Use cosmopolitans with experience in other places as critics, idea sources, or sounding boards.

• *Mount a civic leadership development program in which the next generation of leaders forms project teams to tackle community problems.* Younger and rising leaders can be sponsored by companies from downtown, urban neighborhoods, the suburbs, and the exurbs, where emerging companies reside, inclusive by race, gender, and foreign experience, and fellowships can be offered to not-for-profit and government organizations. This would address critical issues while enlarging the connections across ethnic groups and organizations, building social capital and future networks.

• *Link community service to employee development and training, and help volunteers get credit or credentials as part of their career development.* Companies that send managers on Outward Bound expeditions for team building might send them to "Inward Bound" community service programs that are equally physically challenging and team oriented, the way Timberland uses its City Year involvement. Time for volunteering is limited, but time for training is increasing. Smaller companies that do not have their own staff development programs could be included, and emerging new technology companies that see little value in traditional cultural or civic organizations would see value in leadership development for their staff.

• *Use the agenda of newer, technology-based industries as the basis for new forms of civic contribution.* Offer schools and not-for-profit institutions as sites for demonstrating the value of new technologies. Take advantage of the professional resources and products emerging companies offer to make the community a laboratory for testing and using the latest technologies—which also helps spread technology know-how, includes locals, and reinforces the city's status as a world class center.

• *Create short-term private sector–public sector job exchanges to foster greater understanding and develop multifaceted leaders.* Teacher apprenticeships in industry would be one example; another, businesspeople on loan to the public sector. Develop databases of available people and opportunities.

• *Help not-for-profit organizations understand the implications of strategic philanthropy and become better business partners by teaming with others to multiply their impact.* Find ways to measure the quantity and quality of community service, so that not-for-profits can value the time they receive (not just the dollars) and those engaged in community service can reach a high performance standard and get "résumé credit" for their activities.

Actions like these are important elements of a community's strategy for joining the world class—its domestic economic development plan and its foreign policy. Such actions should not be isolated initiatives; they should be linked to a vision for excellence based on the city's distinctive global capabilities.

BUILDING BRIDGES TO EACH OTHER AND THE WORLD

All change needs a champion. But I am convinced that every community already has potential champions for the global economy waiting in the wings—enlightened public officials, business leaders, community activists. They need to be brought together to agree to apply for membership in the world class and helped to imagine all the possibilities for becoming world class.

Like the physical infrastructure, a community's infrastructure for collaboration is a network that makes possible timely and productive action because of the power and connections it provides. An infrastructure for collaboration is not a set of centralized initiatives that forces everyone to do the same thing; it is an overaching framework, an agreement about priorities that stimulates many diverse initiatives but then links them so that they result in significant impact. As long as there is a guiding vision and an infrastructure for collaboration to ensure cooperation and coordination, then change proceeds best when a thousand flowers can bloom, when multiple experiments and grass roots programs translate the vision into local action. From diversity comes innovation; from unity comes the capacity for effective action.[8]

Globalization of the economy encourages businesses to extend their ties beyond local areas, changing the meaning of community and the agenda for regions. Communities need to break down the walls that separate organizations, institutions, sectors, jurisdictions, neighborhoods, or people. They must concentrate instead on helping to link them. Only if communities are strong in terms of the united efforts of their residents and able to enhance their connections to the world can they attract and hold job-creating businesses whose ties reach many places.

Instead of walls that divide, regions and their people should build bridges that connect. Then the fault line between cosmopolitans and locals will be healed, and globalization will be embraced as an opportunity for locals to thrive.

ACKNOWLEDGMENTS

Only when I looked at the burgeoning list on my computer screen of all the people who have contributed in some way to this book did the full scope and magnitude of the projects behind it become clear to me. I want to thank many people at many institutions throughout America and the world who made the task of organizing and managing numerous teams and team efforts a pleasure and a learning opportunity. I hope all of them will be proud of what is conveyed here. Of course, they bear none of the responsibility for it; that is solely mine.

Principal funding came from the Harvard Business School Division of Research under Warren McFarlan, who was generous and supportive, as well as community service funds from Dean John McArthur, also generous and supportive. Ann Walter and her competent group at the Division of Research helped me both travel around the world and make a contribution to my home community. Professionals from the school's external relations, executive education, and word-processing departments helped make the Boston civic leaders/business leaders forum a great success. Throughout everything, Willa Reiser was there for me, doing whatever needed to be done, as she has for the past half dozen years with grace and cheer; thanks, Willa. I am fortunate to have such a loyal staff and access to such great talent and resources.

For the global side of the research and analysis in this book, I also received invaluable help. My cases on international networks, alliances, joint ventures, and consortia were developed with an excellent group of research associates: at varying times, Kalman Applbaum, Lisa Gabriel, Paul Myers, Gina Quinn, and Pamela Yatsko. I exchanged ideas about this field with faculty colleagues in a new executive program on international alliances: Benjamin Gomes-Casseres, Joseph Bower, Dorothy Leonard-Barton, and Philip Rosenzweig. Doors were opened, contacts facilitated, and/or visits to Harvard classes made by Maurice Lévy and Gerald Pedraglio in Paris; Olof Lundberg, George Symeonidis, and Gene Jilg in London; Mochtar Riady, James Riady, Roy Tirtadji, Markus Parmadi, Charles de Queljoe, José Hanna, and Kenneth Wynn in Jakarta; Stephen Riady, John Lee, and Roger Lacey in Hong Kong; David Dworkin, Liz Broughan, Sandee Springer, Bryan Spink, and Derek Doyle in Britain; Pierre Everaert, Sir Alistair Grant, and Antoine Guichard in Europe; Paul Fruitt at Gillette in Boston; and many others, too numerous to name, on several continents, who employed my service as a consultant and adviser—and from whom I learned much. I hope that the lessons in this book are useful for all of you.

On the local front, the Boston project was the first of my five-area national initiatives and the role model for the others. Madelyn Yucht performed many tasks for the Boston project with charm and diplomacy, working on the survey instrument, profiling a dozen companies, conducting focus groups, and helping organize the collaborations in other cities. Pamela Yatsko did her usual professional research and writing, pitching in even while en route to a new position at the *Far Eastern Economic Review* in Shanghai. Jane Katz, James Sailer, Allison Hughes, and Robert Lightfoot also conducted interviews and focus groups and worked on the civic forum, as did Michael Gorman; Jane put in extra time that was very valuable to me before starting her new career at the Federal Reserve Bank of Boston. William Simpson did a superb job of quantitative analysis of survey results nationwide, as he had done earlier for the *Harvard Business Review* global survey in 1991. Doctoral students Richard Corn and Todd Pittinsky collaborated with me skillfully on analysis of foreign acquisitions of U.S. companies and workplace changes.

A number of talented Harvard Business School faculty helped make the 1994 Boston civic leaders/business leaders forum a success: Michael Porter, to whom I owe special thanks and am pleased to work with on other civic initiatives; and Michael Beer, Gregory Dees, Janice Hammond, Dorothy Leonard-Barton, George Lodge, Gary Loveman, and Debora Spar. Herminia Ibarra, Linda Hill, Jeffrey Bradach, John Kotter, Nitin Nohria, and Richard Myers also contributed ideas at critical points. In addition, my thinking about community service was stimulated by participation in the school's new social enterprise initiative led by James Austin, Gregory Dees, Kash Rangan, and Robert Burakoff.

Kudos also to my collaborators in the main cities in this project, who devoted their own time, energy, and resources to our comparative survey and civic dialogues. Working with them on our joint venture taught me a great deal and gave me the privilege of contributing directly to their efforts to meet the local challenges of the global economy.

• *Boston.* Thanks to Paul O'Brien, William Coughlin, Flash Wiley, and members of the executive committee, Greater Boston Chamber of Commerce, especially Sherry Penney, and to John Gould, André Mayer, and Brian Gilmore, Associated Industries of Massachusetts, for collaboration on the survey and dissemination of its results.

• *Miami.* Thanks to Mitch Maidique, Harold Wyman, Mary Ann von Glinow, Florida International University, and John Anderson and John Cordrey, the Beacon Council, and other faculty and doctoral students from Florida International and Florida Atlantic Universities for collaboration on the survey and civic forum for south Florida, including Ana Azvedo, Linda Clarke, Deborah Cohen, Meredith Downes, Shawnta Friday, Peggy Golden, Peter Goumas, Richard Hodgetts, Bill Jerome, Sherry Moss, Mark Rosenberg, Susan Ross, Anisya Thomas, Lori Zalka, and John Zdanowicz. FIU and the Beacon Council also assisted with arrangements for Madelyn Yucht, Barry Stein, and Nancy Fuerst Hexter from my own research group, enabling them to help me conduct the Miami interviews reported in this book. Mary Ann von Glinow deserves special appreciation for being south Florida project leader while serving as president of the Academy of Management.

• *Cleveland.* Thanks to Scott Cowen, Michael Fogarty, and Paul Gottlieb, Case Western Reserve University Weatherhead School and Center for Regional Economic Issues, Joseph Roman, Cleveland Tomorrow, and Carol Hoover and Peggy Gallagher, Greater Cleveland Growth Association, for contributions to the Cleveland portion of the survey and the symposium on international trade. Rena Blumberg, community all-star, facilitated the collaboration. Other Ohio information, especially about Honda and Marysville, was gathered competently for me by Myra Moss, Ohio State University economic development expert.

• *Spartanburg.* Thanks to Roger Milliken, Milliken & Company, for local arrangements and hospitality, Laura Corbin, Paul Foerster and Ben Haskew, Spartanburg Area Chamber of Commerce, for help with the survey, and Weston Milliken for joining Pamela Yatsko and Barry Stein from my research group to conduct interviews.

• *Greenville.* Thanks to Richard Blouse, Sandra Roth Dreibelbis, and Tamara Cope, Greenville County Chamber of Commerce, for local arrangements and help with the survey.

• *Seattle.* Thanks to Michael Luis and Susanna Malarkey, Greater Seattle Chamber of Commerce, William Stafford, Trade Development Alliance of Seattle, and Kenneth Knight and Jim Goebelbecker, Seattle Pacific University, for help with the survey, interviews in Seattle-area companies by Michael Krohn, Mary Mader, and Sunny Kim, and the opportunity to work with the Greater Seattle Chamber of Commerce's annual leadership conference.

Additional research assistance was provided by Goodmeasure Inc., the consulting firm that Barry Stein and I co-founded in 1977 and that he leads. Wendy D'Ambrose, vice president, conducted interviews and checked facts with her usual skill at building great relationships; Paul Loranger, Tiffan Rosenfeld, and Marta Grace were helpful in many ways; and Barry flew to South Carolina and south Florida to join my Harvard staff in interviews there.

I digressed partway through my research to produce an updated 1993 afterword for my earlier book, *Men and Women of the Corporation* ("A View from the 1990s: How the Global Economy Is Reshaping Workplaces and Careers"), which contributed to some of my thinking for this book. So did my 1994 *Harvard Business Review* article, "Collaborative Advantage: The Art of Alliances," which Daniel Niven and Judy Uhl did me the honor of using to plan a Harvard Business School Publishing Corporation joint venture.

Conversations with Connie Borde of Paris and Martha's Vineyard and William Reinfeld of Taiwan and Martha's Vineyard—that little island is indeed connected to the world—helped me clarify ideas at critical stages in writing the book. Julia Wells, Eleanor Lake, Pamela Yatsko, and David Lehrer helped me with crafting the first drafts of some of the longer chapters, and David Lehrer also volunteered his time for research assistance. Thomas Teal, a talented writer and *HBR* editor with first-person experience of cosmopolitans and locals, provided three valuable days as an editorial consultant at the final stages. Bennett Harrison, Herminia Ibarra, Marisa Lago, and Alejandro Portes provided helpful comments.

Frederic Hills, Simon & Schuster senior editor, has contributed his professionalism and insight since the publication of *The Change Masters* and *When Giants Learn to Dance*; he believed in this book when the project was still just a few incoherent thoughts. And Fred and Burton Beals gave so much time and help, expediting the editing stage.

Thank you, all of you, for being world class.

And thanks beyond words to my support system at home, which is what makes it possible for any of us to take on the world: Barry Stein, Matthew Moss Kanter Stein, Browser ("animal companion"), and Ed. Barry, you contribute so much intellectual substance as well as so many other things. Matt, I couldn't have done it without those inspirational signs you made for me with your graphics program: "Just Do It," "Avoid the gumption trap," and the aphorism I coined in *The Change Masters*, "Everything looks like a failure in the middle."

I managed to make it over those difficult slumps in the middle because of the help and support from so many collaborators and friends. If this book is a success, it will be a tribute to collaborative advantage—the numerous contributions of colleagues, partners in other cities, friends, and loving family. The measure of success will be that it stimulates further collaboration within communities everywhere, helping the businesses and people in them succeed in the global economy and the new century.

Cambridge, Massachusetts
April 1, 1995

APPENDIX

RESEARCH AS CIVIC ACTION: A NOTE ON SOURCES, METHODS, AND COLLABORATIONS

Research on the new business alliances was the starting point for work on globalization. It was extensive but straightforward: several hundred interviews and compilation of industry statistics by my research group at the Harvard Business School to develop cases on international partnerships and joint ventures. In 1993, when I began to look at how those new global relationships changed the nature of local transactions, I embarked on a more complex effort. Guided by what I had learned about joint ventures, I created a national action project on local challenges in the global economy.

I looked for areas that reflected various approaches to globalization; I was not trying to single out particular places as the best in their class. I wanted to include cities that represented an important U.S. region with distinctive strengths in the global economy, were manageable in terms of size and logistics, offered willing partners, and would be credible as examples of global change. New York and Chicago were too large to cover given the project's resources. I wanted to include Los Angeles despite its size because it is an important trade center with connections both to Asia and Latin America, and I had begun discussions with potential partners. Then the earthquake struck in January 1994, which made it impossible to pursue a Los Angeles initiative, although I conducted interviews in Greater Los Angeles with affiliates of Asian banks and worked as a consultant to aerospace companies in the area.

I found excellent collaborators in five American metropolitan areas that met my criteria: Boston/eastern Massachusetts, Cleveland/northeast Ohio, Greenville-Spartanburg/South Carolina's "upstate," Miami/south Florida, and the Seattle/Puget Sound region. To look further into the role of foreign companies in smaller places, I added a subventure in two areas just outside the core regions: Marysville, Ohio, home of Honda USA, and Worcester, Massachusetts, west of Boston. I also continued to work as a consultant to large international companies in telecommunications, autos, and aerospace and to economic development initiatives in Europe and Great Britain, which provided useful global perspectives.

The approach in the five main cities was to carry out a kind of high-level community organizing, in which research would be the catalyst for business education and civic engagement.

With the help of my Harvard group, I formed or tapped into a local coalition in each city that would carry out portions of the project in collaboration with us. Large civic organizations would provide access to their members and would help link the project to ongoing civic actions. Local university business school researchers would help customize the research instruments to the region, assist with gathering data, and contribute to the analysis. Together, the university and civic organizations would host a forum for senior business executives, public officials, and community leaders to engage in dialogue about the formal research findings and set priorities for additional action.

This collaborative model was used fully in Boston, Miami, Seattle, and Cleveland, and partially in Greenville-Spartanburg, to carry out six steps.

1. *Large-sample survey.* To create a broad profile of each area's businesses and their ties to the global economy, an extensive questionnaire was developed. Modified slightly by local teams, it was largely comparable from place to place, including specific information on

- basic facts about the company: industry, form of ownership, location of headquarters, five-year revenues, profits, employment, and source of competitive strength
- views about fourteen aspects of business and government relationships and government policies, including trade policies, local procurement, and the use of public funds to help business
- ratings of the degree to which twenty-six to thirty local resources help or hinder business effectiveness (resources such as airports, public schools, unions, state legislators, the press)
- frequency of community service of thirteen types (such as donations, loaned executives, summer jobs for youth)
- frequency of local business collaboration of fourteen types (joint research, for example, or joint skills training for workers)
- changes in thirty-four organizational strategies and practices in the past three years and expectations for the next three years (expanding operations in the area, changing compensation systems, making acquisitions within or outside the United States, installing/reinforcing quality improvement programs, and so on)

- geographic scope: the proportion of business factors such as customers, suppliers, people, capital, ideas, competitors, and allies found locally, regionally, nationally, or internationally
- open-ended comments about the three most important things that should be done to improve the prospects for job creation and business growth in the area

The questionnaire was mailed to business heads and other senior executives, accompanied by letters intended to help raise consciousness about the new challenges of the global economy. In several cities follow-up phone calls were made. By August 1994 we had received 2,655 completed questionnaires:

- 521 from the Boston area (out of 1,950 mailed to members of Greater Boston Chamber of Commerce and nonoverlapping eastern Massachusetts members of Associated Industries of Massachusetts)
- 653 from the Cleveland area (out of 4,220 mailed to manufacturers, large employers, and international trade lists of Greater Cleveland Growth Association and a private list vendor's code sort for service companies)
- 378 from the Greenville and Spartanburg area (out of 2,500 mailed to members of Greenville County Chamber of Commerce and 1,800 mailed to members of Spartanburg Area Chamber of Commerce)
- 412 from the Miami area, plus an additional 60–70 received too late to analyze (out of 4,250 mailed to members of the Beacon Council, Miami MetroDade Chamber of Commerce, Broward and Palm Beach County economic development council lists, and Camacol, the Latin Chamber of Commerce)
- 691 from the Seattle area (out of 5,350 mailed to members of the Chambers of Greater Seattle/King County, Everett/Snohomish County, and Tacoma/Pierce County)

The returns were reasonably representative of each membership group as a whole, except in Cleveland, where manufacturing companies were oversampled because that was the population of greatest interest to the local collaborators at Case Western Reserve University's Center for Regional Economic Issues.

2. *Company interviews*. Extensive interviews with over 150 executives were conducted in nearly 100 companies, primarily by my Harvard group but also by Seattle and south Florida teams, using a standard protocol. Many of the interviews were tape-recorded. Those interviewed varied with company size; in larger companies multiple interviews were conducted with the chief executive or chief strategist and heads of purchasing, human resource, public/government/community affairs. Interviews plus company documents were used to create company profiles covering their strategic challenges, experience with global markets, alliances, human resource policies, and purchasing patterns. In Miami the in-depth interviews and company profiles were supplemented by

briefer telephone interviews with officers of twenty multinational companies in the area.

3. *Employee focus groups.* To include the voices of people outside the executive suite, my Harvard team conducted over forty tape-recorded group discussions of two to three hours each with five to seven people per group in three of the cities. Most groups included a cross-sectional mix of middle managers/professionals or direct production/service workers in the same company; several groups mixed professionals across companies in Miami, Marysville, Ohio, and a town outside Boston. The structured protocol for these discussions covered

- participants' current position and brief history with employer
- strengths and weaknesses of the company in the marketplace
- strengths and weaknesses of the company as a place to work, changes in participants' jobs, and their expectations for their careers over the next three to five years
- strengths and weaknesses of the community as a place to live, desire to leave, amount/kind of own community service, and attitudes toward corporate involvement in community service
- large consumer purchases and awareness of their domestic/foreign content, perceptions of the best products made in the United States and five other countries
- experience with and attitudes toward outside or foreign ownership of local companies, attitudes toward free trade and protection of local jobs
- views of the area's public officials and priorities for community improvement

4. *Broad community interviews/information.* Company and employee perspectives were supplemented by interviews in person or by telephone with a wide range of public officials and civic leaders about events or issues that emerged from our interviews. I also reviewed economic reports, community documents, and local press.

5. *Business leaders/civic leaders forum.* The research was meant to stimulate dialogue and action. Before a report was issued, several hundred business and civic leaders, including elected officials and questionnaire respondents who provided their names, were invited to participate in a discussion of the findings. The goal was to encourage leaders to agree on a perspective, a common vocabulary, a set of priorities, and commitment to action. The discussion content and priorities identified at the forums became an important part of the final report.

In Boston the forum was held at Harvard Business School; in Cleveland, under the auspices of the Weatherhead School at Case Western Reserve University; in Miami, at Florida International University; in Seattle, as part of the Greater Seattle Chamber of Commerce's annual leadership conference in

1994 and 1995; and in Spartanburg and Greenville with the sponsorship of the two Chambers of Commerce.

6. *Follow-up actions.* Follow-up appropriate to each city went beyond dissemination of the final report. Actions included educational briefings for public officials such as mayors, state legislators, and their staffs; presentations to local and regional civic associations; and discussions with the editorial boards of major local newspapers about how the findings might contribute to their agenda. In my home area, I joined Michael Porter on Governor Weld's Council on Economic Growth and Technology, co-chairing the task force on international trade, and worked with Associated Industries of Massachusetts on a follow-up leadership forum in addition to other actions. In other places my collaborators took the lead in ensuring that the issues we illuminated stay on the civic agenda and contribute to productive change. Dialogue and action projects are ongoing.

The complete process was a method not only for learning about the infrastructure for business and civic collaboration, but also for helping to strengthen it.

NOTES TO CHAPTERS

Chapter 1. The Rise of the World Class

1. John Newhouse, "Earth Summit," *The New Yorker*, June 1, 1992, p. 78.

2. Simone de Beauvoir, *The Second Sex*, trans. by H. M. Parshley, New York: Vintage Books, 1989, originally published in 1952.

3. Neil Peirce, with Curtis W. Johnson and John Stuart Hall, *Citistates: How Urban America Can Prosper in a Competitive World*, Washington, D.C.: Seven Locks Press, 1993.

4. William R. Barnes and Larry C. Ledebur, *Local Economies: The U.S. Common Market of Local Economic Regions*, Washington, D.C.: National League of Cities, 1994.

5. Joel Garreau, *The Nine Nations of North America*, Boston: Houghton Mifflin, 1981.

6. Paul Krugman, *Geography and Trade*, Cambridge, Mass.: MIT Press, 1991.

7. Benjamin Barber, "Jihad versus McWorld," *The Atlantic*, March 1992.

8. Claire Sterling, *Crime without Frontiers*, New York: Little Brown, 1994.

9. James Fallows, *More Like Us*, Boston: Houghton Mifflin, 1989.

10. Figures on investment and employment are from Arthur Andersen & Company, *Foreign Direct Investment in the United States: Analysis and Outlook* and *International Business*, 1993.

11. Robert Putnam, "Bowling Alone," *Journal of Democracy*, vol. 6, January

1995, and Putnam, *Making Democracy Work*, Princeton, N.J.: Princeton University Press, 1993.

12. Eminent thinkers from a number of other fields have been attracted to this challenge. My Harvard colleague Michael Porter has extended his framework from *The Competitive Advantage of Nations* (New York: Free Press, 1990) to a variety of regions and states; economist Paul Krugman has helped revive the field of economic geography (*Geography and Trade*, above); and marketing expert Philip Kotler has applied his knowledge about the marketing of products to the marketing of places (*Marketing Places*, New York: Free Press, 1993). Even before he wrote about reinventing government, David Osborne saw localities as appropriate units for testing new ideas (*Laboratories of Democracy*, Boston: HBS Press, 1988).

13. Peter Drucker makes clear the growing importance of the social sector in the future in *Post-Capitalist Society*, New York: HarperCollins, 1993, and helps guide its reinvention in *Managing the Non-Profit Organization*, New York: HarperCollins, 1990.

Chapter 2. Winning in Global Markets

In addition to direct interviews and the works cited, statistics in this chapter have been compiled from industry associations such as the Food Marketing Institute and cable television trade associations, company records, automotive industry tracking services such as *Ward's*, and United Nations and U.S. government publications that regularly report industry statistics, such as *Statistical Abstracts of the United States.*

1. William B. Johnston, "Global Work Force 2000: The New World Labor Market," *Harvard Business Review*, vol. 69, March–April 1991, pp. 115–27.

2. Joel Kurtzman, *The Death of Money*, New York: Simon & Schuster, 1993.

3. Josh Hyatt, "DEC pays $45,000 in wages, fines," *Boston Globe*, January 11, 1994.

4. Johnston, "Global Work Force 2000."

5. *Chronicle of Higher Education Almanac* for 1993.

6. John Maxwell Hamilton, "Keeping up with Information: On Line in the Philippines and London," in Rosabeth Moss Kanter, Barry A. Stein, and Todd D. Jick, *The Challenge of Organizational Change*, New York: Free Press, 1992, pp. 108–24.

7. Kenichi Ohmae, "Managing in a Borderless World," *Harvard Business Review*, vol. 67, May–June 1989.

8. The Food Marketing Institute referred us to several research services in the United States and Britain that confirmed this impression and offered to go shopping in a few dozen countries for a hefty fee in order to prove it.

9. Hamilton, "Keeping up with Information."

10. *Ibid*.

11. Emiko Terazono, "Hong Kong Stamps on Japan's Postal Pride," *Financial Times*, November 2, 1994, p. 7.

12. William Taylor, "The Logic of Global Business: An Interview with ABB's

Barnevik," *Harvard Business Review*, vol. 69, March–April 1991, pp. 90–105, and in Kanter, Stein, and Jick, *The Challenge of Organizational Change*.

13. "The Global Suit," *Harvard Business Review*, vol. 69, March–April 1991.

14. Hamilton, "Keeping up with Information."

15. The three C's, and the practices behind them, reflect the underlying vision of business excellence conveyed by the criteria for the U.S. Baldrige National Quality Award. The Baldrige has added considerably to the conventional definition of quality as process assurance, which is only one aspect of operational competence; the award now emphasizes work-force skills and human resource development along with organizational processes. Innovation in customer-driven product and service concepts is stressed in the strategic planning section. Customer and supplier collaboration are highlighted. See *The Malcolm Baldrige National Quality Award 1995 Criteria*, Gaithersburg, Maryland: National Institute of Standards and Technology, 1995.

Chapter 3. The New Business Cosmopolitans

1. Christopher A. Bartlett and Sumantra Ghoshal, *Managing across Borders: The Transnational Solution*, Boston: HBS Press, 1989.

2. Richard Barnet and John Cavanaugh, *Global Dreams*, New York: Simon & Schuster, 1994.

3. Taylor, "The Logic of Global Business," p. 105.

4. John Naisbitt, *Global Paradox*, New York: William Morrow, 1994.

5. Ohmae, "Managing in a Borderless World."

6. Rosabeth Moss Kanter, Kalman D. Applbaum, and Pamela A. Yatsko, *FCB and Publicis (A): Forming the Alliance* (case #9-393-099), *FCB and Publicis (B): Managing Client and Country Diversity* (case #9-393-100), and *FCB and Publicis (C): The German-Led Network* (case #9-394-079), Boston: Harvard Business School Publishing, 1993 and 1994. Industry data cited in this portion of the chapter come from industry publications, *Advertising Age*, FCB research, or directly from the companies (magazine circulation figures, for example). Late in 1994 FCB changed its corporate holding company name to True North, but the advertising agencies retained the FCB name.

7. *Statistical Abstracts of the United States*, 1994–1995 edition.

8. Kanter, with the assistance of Barbara Feinberg, Lisa Gabriel, and Barry Stein, *The European Retail Alliance* (case #9-392-096), Boston: Harvard Business School Publishing, 1992.

9. See Joel Kotkin, *Tribes: How Race, Religion and Identity Determine Success in the New Global Economy*, New York: Random House, 1993.

10. Kanter, *Lippo Group (A): Mochtar Riady's Vision, 1960–1990* (case #2-393-110), *Lippo Group (B) Synergizing (1990–1992)* (case #2-393-111), *Lippo Group (Supplement 1): History in Hong Kong* (case #2-393-108), *Lippo Group (Supplement 2): The California Connection* (case #2-393-109), Boston: Harvard Business School Publishing, 1993.

Chapter 4. "Best Partner": Transforming Supply Chains to Global Webs

1. One of my Cleveland collaborators, Paul Gottlieb, focused his analysis of the Cleveland survey data on a comparison of manufacturing firms with a more international scope. Gottlieb, "Local Infrastructure in Support of Global Trade," Working Paper, Center for Regional Economic Issues, Weatherhead School of Management, Case Western Reserve University, December 1994.

2. Ernst & Young, *Biotech '94*, San Francisco: Ernst & Young, 1994. On the global thrust of emerging technology enterprises, see also Hama Bahrami, "The Emerging Flexible Organization: Perspectives from Silicon Valley," *California Management Review*, vol. 34, Summer 1992, pp. 33–52.

3. *Computerworld*, August 8, 1994.

4. Kanter and Applbaum, *Cohen & Wilks International Ltd.* (case #2-394-029), Kanter and Lisa K. Gabriel, *BhS plc (A): Opening Boundaries* (case #9-392-082) and *BhS plc (B): Global Sourcing* (case #9-392-083), Boston: Harvard Business School Publishing, 1992 and 1993. For industry background see also James Lardner, "The Sweater Trade, from Hong Kong to New York," in Kanter, Stein, and Jick, *The Challenge of Organizational Change*.

5. Joel Bleeke and David Erst, *Collaborate to Compete*, New York: Wiley, 1993; Rosabeth Moss Kanter, *When Giants Learn to Dance*, New York: Simon & Schuster, 1989; Kanter, "Collaborative Advantage: The Art of Alliances," *Harvard Business Review*, vol. 72, July–August 1994.

6. Benjamin Gomes-Casseres, "Group versus Group: How Alliance Networks Compete," *Harvard Business Review*, vol. 72, July–August 1994.

7. Jeffrey E. McGee and Michael J. Dowling, "Using R&D Cooperative Arrangements to Leverage Managerial Experience," *Journal of Business Venturing*, vol. 9, January 1994, pp. 33–48; and Andrea Larson, "Partner Networks: Leveraging External Ties to Improve Entrepreneurial Performance," *Journal of Business Venturing*, vol. 6, 1991, pp. 173–88.

8. This strategy revolves around "import substitution," an important item on local economic development agendas. See Myra L. Moss and David Kraybill, "Industrial Linkage Analysis as a Tool for Targeted Economic Development," paper presented at the International Community Development Society conference, Lincoln, Nebraska, July 25, 1994, working paper, Ohio State University Industrial Extension Service.

9. Hortense Leon, "Many Hotels Turn to Franchises to Help Stay in Business," *Miami Today*, March 17, 1994.

10. Tone A. Ostgaard and Sue Birley, "Personal Networks and Firm Competitive Strategy," *Journal of Business Venturing*, vol. 9, July 1994, pp. 281–305.

11. Andrea Lipparini and Maurizio Sobrero, "The Glue and the Pieces: Entrepreneurship and Innovation in Small-Firm Networks," *Journal of Business Venturing*, vol. 9, March 1994, pp. 125–38.

Chapter 5. Wallets and Ballot Boxes

1. Kanter, "Transcending Business Boundaries: 12,000 World Managers View Change," *Harvard Business Review*, vol. 69, May–June 1991.
2. Bernard A. Weisberger, " 'The Chinese Must Go,' " *American Heritage*, February–March 1993, pp. 24–25.
3. Liah Greenfield, *Nationalism*, Cambridge, Mass.: Harvard University Press, 1992, pp. 438, 439.
4. Donna G. Goehle, "The Buy American Act: Is It Irrelevant in a World of Multinational Corporations?" *Columbia Journal of World Business*, Winter 1989, pp. 10–15.
5. Michael G. Harvey, " 'Buy American': Economic Concept or Political Slogan?" *Business Horizons*, vol. 36, May/June 1993, pp. 40–46.
6. Japan Society, "The Dilemma of Japanese Investment," *Directors & Boards*, Spring 1990, pp. 52–53.
7. Candace Howes, *Japanese Auto Transplants and the U.S. Automobile Industry*, Washington, D.C.: Economic Policy Institute, 1993. See also Robert Perrucci, *Japanese Auto Transplants in the Heartland*, Hawthorne, N.Y.: Aldine de Guyter, 1994.
8. Goehle, "The Buy American Act."
9. James Bennet, "Want a U.S. Car? Read the Label," *New York Times*, September 18, 1994.
10. Pamela Varley, *Language and the Melting Pot: Florida's 1988 "Official English" Referendum* (case #C-16-90-990.0), Cambridge, Mass.: John F. Kennedy School of Government, Harvard University, 1990, pp. 9, 11.
11. William Echikson, "Adieu l'airbag: France Fights Franglais Anew," *Boston Globe*, April 12, 1994.
12. My research group's telephone interviews were supplemented by John Teopaco and Stephen A. Greyser, *Crafted with Pride in U.S.A. Council*, (case #9-587-110) and *"It Matters to Me"* (case #9-591-067), Boston: Harvard Business School Publishing, 1987; and Kay Brinker, "Made in the USA—Does It Still Matter?" *Discount Merchandiser*, March 1992, pp. 52–72.
13. From my research group's phone interviews and review of Wal-Mart literature; see also Steve Jacober, "Wal-Mart: A Boon to U.S. Vendors," *Discount Merchandiser*, November 1989, pp. 41–46.
14. Raymond Serafin, "Car Industry Embraces 'Buy American' Theme," *Advertising Age*, January 27, 1992.
15. See Janeen E. Olsen, Kent L. Granzin, and Abhijit Biswas, "Influencing Consumers' Selection of Domestic Versus Imported Products," *Journal of the Academy of Marketing Science*, vol. 21, Fall 1993, pp. 307–21.
16. Christy Fisher, "Will marketers rally 'round the flag?" *Advertising Age*, vol. 63, June 1, 1992, p. 12. See also Yankelovich Clancy Shulman, "Drawing a Bead on Car Buyers for the Nineties," *Brandweek*, September 14, 1992, pp. 19–20; Carol Ukens, "Red, White, and Blue over 'Buy American' Pitch," *Drug Topics*, vol. 136, March 23, 1992, pp. 14–15; and Stanley J. Modic, "Imports Still Stir Emotions," *Purchasing World*, January 1990, pp. 25–26.
17. Greenfield, *Nationalism*, pp. 15–16.

18. Kanter, *Men and Women of the Corporation*, New York: Basic Books, 1977, 1993, chapter 8, dramatized on videotape as *A Tale of "O": On Being Different*, Cambridge, Mass.: Goodmeasure Inc., 1994.

19. R. Hastie and P. A. Kumar, "Person Memory: Personality Traits as Organizing Principles in Memory for Behavior," *Journal of Personality and Social Psychology*, vol. 37, 1979, pp. 25–38; Henri Tajfel, "Social Psychology of Intergroup Relations," *Annual Review of Psychology*, Stanford: Annual Reviews, 1982; J. Howard and M. Rothbart, "Social Categorization and Memory for In-Group and Out-Group Behavior," *Journal of Personality and Social Psychology*, vol. 38, pp. 301–10. I am grateful to Richard I. Corn for his helpful literature review.

20. Social psychologists call this the "fundamental attribution error." See Thomas F. Pettigrew, "The Ultimate Attribution Error," *Personality and Social Psychology Bulletin*, vol. 5, 1979, pp. 461–76, and E. E. Jones and Robert E. Nisbet, "The Actor and the Observer: Divergent Perceptions of the Causes of Behavior," in E. E. Jones, *et al.*, *Attribution: Perceiving the Causes of Behavior*, Morristown, N.J.: General Learning Press, pp. 79–94.

21. Rosabeth Moss Kanter and Richard I. Corn, "Do Cultural Differences Make a Business Difference? Contextual Factors Affecting Cross-Cultural Relationship Success," *Journal of Management Development*, vol. 13, Winter 1994, pp. 5–23.

22. *Ibid.* Also David K. Perry, "News Reading, Knowledge About, and Attitudes Toward Foreign Countries," *Journalism Quarterly*, vol. 67, Summer 1990, pp. 353–58.

23. Greenfield, *Nationalism*, p. 482.

24. Robert Reich, *The Work of Nations: Preparing Ourselves for 21st Century Capitalism*, New York: Knopf, 1991.

Chapter 6. Workplaces, Careers, and Employability Security

1. Tetsui Jimbo, "Cutbacks Shake Japan's Social Contract," *Toronto Globe and Mail*, March 30, 1993, pp. B1–2.

2. Fred C. Shapiro, "Letter from Hong Kong," *The New Yorker*, June 29, 1992, pp. 74–82.

3. Kanter, *The Change Masters: Innovation and Entrepreneurship in the American Corporation*, New York: Simon & Schuster, 1983.

4. *Boston Globe*, July 3, 1994.

5. See Kanter, *When Giants Learn to Dance*; also Kanter, Stein, and Jick, *The Challenge of Organizational Change*.

6. I first defined employability security in *When Giants Learn to Dance*; recently the new shape of corporate careers has received considerable attention. See Michael Arthur, "The Boundaryless Career," *Journal of Organizational Behavior*, vol. 15, July 1994; Jeffrey Pfeffer, *Competitive Advantage through People*, Boston: HBS Press, 1994; and Thomas A. Kochan and Paul Osterman, *The Mutual Gains Enterprise*, Boston: HBS Press, 1994.

7. Arthur L. Stinchcombe and Carol A. Heimer, "Interorganizational Rela-

tions and Careers in Computer Software Firms," *Research in the Sociology of Work*, vol. 4, Greenwich, Conn.: JAI Press, 1988, pp. 179–204.

8. Alejandro Portes and Alex Stepick, *City on the Edge: The Transformation of Miami*, Berkeley, Calif.: University of California Press, 1993, pp. 14, 11.

9. *Miami Herald*, January 17, 1994.

10. Michael Porter, "The Competitive Advantage of the Inner City," working paper, Harvard Business School, May 1994.

11. Bennett Harrison, *Emerging CDC Trends: Networking to Enhance Job Creation and Training Initiatives*, Boston: Economic Development Assistance Consortium, and New York: Ford Foundation, 1993.

12. Ricardo Semler, "Why My Former Employees Still Work for Me," *Harvard Business Review*, vol. 72, January–February 1994, pp. 64–74.

Chapter 7. Business Leadership in the Community

1. *The New York Times*, September 18, 1994.

2. David A. Heenan, *The New Corporate Frontier: The Big Move to Small Town USA*, New York: McGraw-Hill, 1991.

3. Joel Garreau, *Edge City: Life on the New Frontier*, New York: Anchor Books, 1991.

4. Juliet Schor, *The Overworked American*, New York: Basic Books, 1991.

5. Craig Smith, "The New Corporate Philanthropy," *Harvard Business Review*, vol. 72, May–June 1994, pp. 105–16.

6. Joel Makover and Business for Social Responsibility, *Beyond the Bottom Line*, New York: Simon & Schuster, 1994.

7. John Logan and Harvey Molotch, *Urban Fortunes: The Political Economy of Place*, Berkeley, Calif.: University of California Press, 1987.

8. Allison K. Hughes, *Corporate Impact on the Community: A Study of Charitable Contribution Patterns for Corporations with Local, Non-Local Domestic and Foreign Headquarters in Three U.S. Cities*, unpublished honors thesis, Department of Economics, Harvard University, 1994.

9. Marilyn Adams, "Big Banks' Battle for Florida," *Miami Herald*, February 21, 1994.

10. Larry Birger, "Texaco Staying in the Gables," *Miami Herald*, January 17, 1994.

11. Robert N. Storn and Howard Aldrich, "The Effect of Absentee Firm Control on Local Community Welfare: A Survey," in John J. Siegfried (ed.), *The Economics of Firm Size, Market, Structure, and Social Performance*, Washington, D.C.: USGPO, 1980, pp. 162–81.

12. *Mergers and Acquisitions Almanac*, 1992. For an earlier overview, see Norman J. Glickman and Douglas P. Woodward, *The New Competitors: How Foreign Investors are Changing the U.S. Economy*, New York: Basic Books, 1989.

13. Kanter and Corn, "Do Cultural Differences Make a Business Difference?" *Journal of Management Development*.

14. Andrew E. G. Jonas, "Corporate Takeover and the Politics of Community: The Case of Norton Company in Worcester," *Economic Geography*, vol. 68, 1992, pp. 348–72.

15. Portes and Stepick, *City on the Edge*, p. 13.
16. *Ibid.*, p. 200.
17. Gerald F. Russell, "The Cases for and against Wal-Mart," *Boston Globe*, September 24, 1994, p. 29.
18. Charles Whited, "Alvah Chapman, Business and Community Leader," *Miami Herald*, September 29, 1989, p. 1C.
19. Makover and Business for Social Responsibility, *Beyond the Bottom Line*.

Chapter 8. Thinkers: The Brains of Boston

In addition to interviews, the five-city survey, company reports, and the works cited below, statistics have been compiled from city, state, regional, and national statistical reports, including those issued by the Bank of Boston, Associated Industries of Massachusetts, New England Council, and Federal Reserve Bank of Boston; reports prepared for Challenge to Leadership in 1993; CorpTech's *Technology Resource Guide: Massachusetts* for 1993 and 1994; and *Choosing to Compete*, the economic vision issued by the Commonwealth of Massachusetts Office of Economic Affairs in 1991.

1. Robert L. Turner, "State of Decline: Is Massachusetts Sliding into Mediocrity?" *Boston Globe Magazine*, October 9, 1994.
2. Citizens League Research Institute, *Rating the Region: Closing the Gap*, Cleveland: Citizens League, 1994.
3. Alexander Ganz and L. François Konga, "Boston in the World Economy," in R. V. Knight and G. Gappert, *Cities in a Global Society*, Newbury Park, Calif.: Sage, 1989, pp. 132–40.
4. Craig L. Moore and Edward Moscovitch, *The New Economic Reality: Massachusetts Prospects for Long-Term Growth*, Amherst, Mass.: University of Massachusetts School of Management, 1994, for the Massachusetts Taxpayers Foundation.
5. Garreau, *Edge City*.
6. AnnaLee Saxenian, *Regional Advantage: Culture and Competition in Silicon Valley and Route 128*, Cambridge, Mass.: Harvard University Press, 1994.
7. Paul Herbig and James E. Golden, "How to Keep that Innovative Spirit Alive: An Examination of Evolving Innovative Hot Spots," *Technological Forecasting and Social Change*, 1992.
8. Stephen Sass, "What Is So Special about Manufacturing?," *Regional Review*, Federal Reserve Bank of Boston, Spring 1994, pp. 19–24.
9. Ganz and Konga, "Boston in the World Economy."
10. Everett Rogers and Judith Larsen, *Silicon Valley Fever*, New York: Basic Books, 1984.
11. Nitin Nohria, "Information and Search in the Creation of New Business Ventures: The Case of the 128 Venture Group," in Robert Eccles and Nitin Nohria, *Networks and Organizations*, Boston: HBS Press, 1992.
12. Roger Miller and Marcel Cote, "Growing the Next Silicon Valley," *Harvard Business Review*, vol. 63, July–August 1985; Nohria, *ibid*.
13. See the discussion of Powersoft in chapter 2. On agglomeration effects

in technology ventures, see Herbig and Golden, "How to Keep that Innovative Spirit Alive."

14. Nohria, "Information and Search . . ."

15. Massachusetts Software Council, *The Complete Guide to the Massachusetts Software Industry, 1994–1995*, Boston: Massachusetts Software Council, 1994.

16. See coverage in the *Boston Globe* and *The Wall Street Journal*, December 16, 1994.

17. *Massachusetts High Tech*, February 21, 1994.

18. Bank of Boston was influenced by the South Shore Bank of Chicago; see Ronald Gzryzinski, "The New Old-Fashioned Banking," *Harvard Business Review*, vol. 69, May–June 1991.

19. Turner, "State of Decline."

20. Massachusetts Software Council, *The Complete Guide*.

21. *Boston Globe*, July 7, 1994.

22. Citizens League Research Institute, *Rating the Region*.

23. Garreau, *Edge City*.

24. William S. Ellis, "Boston—Breaking New Ground," *National Geographic*, vol. 186, July 1994, pp. 2–34.

25. Elizabeth L. Useem, *Low Tech Education in a High Tech World: Corporations and Classrooms in the New Information Society*, New York: Free Press, 1986, pp. 1–2; Turner, "State of Decline," cites data on state spending for education.

26. Robert M. Krim and Laura Rossin Van Zandt, "Kids, Cops, and Consultants," *Journal for Quality and Participation*, January–February 1994, pp. 6–12.

Chapter 9. Makers: Foreign Manufacturing in South Carolina

In addition to interviews, the five-area survey, company reports, and the works cited below, statistics have been compiled from Greenville County Chamber of Commerce and Spartanburg Area Chamber of Commerce reports, U.S. Commerce Department data, and Spartanburg County planning documents, including *Spartanburg County Demographic and Economic Projections*, 1993, and Jeanie Gilmer, *Market Profile of Greenville 1993–1994*, for the Greenville Chamber of Commerce.

1. Greenville Chamber of Commerce, *International Business Guide 1994*, Greenville, S.C.: Multimedia Publishing, 1993. "International" means international affiliations and includes independent U.S. subsidiaries with licenses from foreign parent companies that formerly wholly owned and controlled them, but it does not include U.S. companies begun by foreign nationals.

2. For concept of industry clusters see Porter, *Competitive Advantage of Nations*, and for a review of industry agglomeration and localization theory in economics, see Krugman, *Geography and Trade*.

3. James R. Hines, "Altered States: Taxes and the Location of Foreign Direct Investment in America," Faculty Working Paper R#93-17, John F. Kennedy School of Government, Harvard University, 1993. For example, with

respect to British and Japanese companies, for every 1 percent rate of taxation, those who cannot claim credits appear to reduce their investment shares, relative to those claiming credits, by about 7–9 percent.

4. Scott Gould and Mark Olencki, *Spartanburg: Portrait of the Good Life*, Memphis, Tenn.: Towery Publishing, 1993, p. 129.

5. According to the Greenville Chamber of Commerce's *International Business Guide*, the 215 upstate firms with foreign affiliations in 1993 had 38,776 employees. Germany was first in representation with 65 companies that employed 9,411 people; 29 Japanese companies employed 5,954 people; and 16 French companies employed 8,075, most of them at Michelin. There were also 43 British companies, 22 Swiss companies, and companies from Australia, Austria, Belgium, Canada, Denmark, Egypt, Finland, Italy, Korea, the Netherlands, Singapore, Spain, Sweden, and Taiwan—a diversified group that included thirteen joint ventures combining foreign parents from more than one country. Foreign investors brought new manufacturing jobs to the upstate, as shown by these figures:

ACTIVITY BY BUSINESSES WITH INTERNATIONAL AFFILIATIONS

Percentage of companies that are	
Start-ups	68%
Relocations	12%
Acquisitions	23%
Percentage of companies engaging in	
Manufacturing	67%
Sales	42%
Service	42%
Distribution	23%
Research & Development	12%

6. Heenan, *The New Corporate Frontier.*

7. Gould and Olencki, *Spartanburg.*

8. Spartanburg County Foundation, *Critical Indicators* and *Critical Indicators II*, Spartanburg, S.C.: Spartanburg County Foundation, 1989, 1991.

Chapter 10. Traders: International Connections Through Miami

In addition to interviews, the five-area survey, company reports, and the works cited below, statistics have been compiled from Beacon Council publications, including *Annual Report* for 1992–93 and 1993–94, *Miami Business Profile* for 1993–94 and 1994–95, *The Smart Business Choice*, 1993, and others; *Inside Miami*, 1993; and county and state statistical reports.

1. Arva Moore Parks, *The Magic City: Miami*, Tulsa: Continental Heritage Press, 1981, pp. 63, 151.

2. T. D. Allman, *Miami: City of the Future*, New York: Atlantic Monthly Press, 1987, p. 224.

3. *Ibid.*, p. 374.

4. Scott M. Lewis, "Knight-Ridder, Inc.," *International Directory of Company Histories*, 1988, pp. 628–30.
5. Allman, *Miami*, p. 299.
6. Portes and Stepick, *City on the Edge*, p. 104.
7. Allman, *Miami*.
8. Portes and Stepick, *City on the Edge*, p. 29.
9. Thomas D. Boswell and James R. Curtis, *The Cuban-American Experience: Culture, Images, and Perspectives*, Totowa, N.J.: Rowman & Allanheld, 1983, p. 3.
10. Allman, *Miami*, p. 307; Jan Lutyes et al., *Economic Impact of Refugees in Dade County*, Miami: Florida International University, 1982, p. 2.
11. Portes and Stepick, *City on the Edge*.
12. *Ibid.*, p. 135.
13. *Ibid.*, pp. 145–46.
14. Varley, *Language and the Melting Pot*.
15. Allman, *Miami*, pp. 315–16.
16. Portes and Stepick, *City on the Edge*, p. 136. See also Alejandro Portes, "The Social Origins of the Cuban Enclave Economy," *Sociological Perspectives*, vol. 30, October 1987, pp. 340–72. For a review of ethnic business issues, see Ivan Light, "Immigrant and Ethnic Enterprise in North America," *Ethnic and Racial Studies*, vol. 7, April 1984, pp. 195–216.
17. Dory Owens, "Her Faith in Hispanics Paid Off Big," *Miami Herald*, October 10, 1988, p. 9BM. The story that follows is based on this article with updates from informants and correspondence with Diaz-Oliver.
18. Portes and Stepick, pp. 127–28.
19. *Ibid.*, pp. 45–46.
20. Varley, *Language and the Melting Pot*, p. 3; the figures are from Carlos Arboleya, Barnett Bank.
21. Allman, *Miami*, p. 338.
22. *Ibid.*, p. 31.
23. *Ibid.*, p. 34.
24. *Miami Daily Business Review*, January 14, 1994.
25. *Miami Herald*, January 11, 1988.
26. *Miami Today*, March 17, 1994.
27. *El País*, November 27, 1987, and July 28, 1989; *Financial Times*, August 2, 1985, December 19, 1990, and March 25, 1993.
28. James Brooke, "Failure of High-Flying Banks Shakes Venezuelan Economy," *The New York Times*, May 16, 1994. For the rest of the Banco Latino International story, see Jane Bussey, "Insider's View of a Crisis: Ex-Chief Defends Job at Banco Latino," *Miami Herald*, April 8, 1994; coverage in *Miami Herald* on January 19, 20, 21, 22, 26, 1994, February 19, 1994, March 10, 1994, April 6, 1994, September 13, 1994; *Los Angeles Times*, February 14, 1994; *Miami Daily Business Review*, January 20, 1994, April 1, 1994; *Financial Times*, January 17, 1994; *The Wall Street Journal*, November 16, 1994.
29. This comment appeared in *Miami Herald*, August 8, 1994; the rest of her story is from my interviews.

30. See *Miami Today*, March 17, 1994.

31. BDO Seidman, *The Business Pulse of Greater Miami 1993*, Miami: Greater Miami Chamber of Commerce, 1993.

32. *Miami Today*, April 21, 1994.

33. James Crawford, *Bilingual Education*, Crane Publishing, 1989, p. 60.

34. Art Harris, "In Miami, Puerto Rican Mayor Faces Politically Macho Cubans," *The Washington Post*, October 25, 1981, p. A11.

35. Varley, *Language and the Melting Pot*, p. 8.

36. *Ibid.*, p. 13.

37. *Ibid.*, p. 7.

38. *Ibid.*, p.1.

39. Portes and Stepick, *City on the Edge*, pp. 173–75.

40. University of Florida Economic and Business Research, cited in *Newcomer's Guide to Florida Business*, St. Petersburg, Fla.: Florida Trend Magazines, 1994.

41. Alison Turner, "Who's Who: 100 People Who Make Things Happen in South Florida," *South Florida Business Journal*, April 29, 1994.

Chapter 11. World Class Businesses: Leadership across Boundaries

1. Portions of this chapter are based on my article "Collaborative Advantage: The Art of Alliances," *Harvard Business Review*, 1994. For analysis of success factors in business alliances and partnerships, see Michael Yoshino and U. Srinivasa Rangan, *Strategic Alliances*, Boston: HBS Press, 1995; Bleeke and Ernst, *Collaborate to Compete*; Benjamin Gomes-Casseres, *The Alliance Revolution: The New Shape of Business Rivalry*, Cambridge, Mass.: Harvard University Press, forthcoming.

2. Kanter and Corn, "Do Cultural Differences Make a Business Difference?"

Chapter 12. World Class Regions: Strengthening the Infrastructure for Collaboration

1. Kanter, *The Change Masters*.

2. Porter, *The Competitive Advantage of Nations*. This work builds on economic theories of comparative advantage and well-documented studies of industry localization. For a useful review stressing the "standard Marshallian trinity" of labor market pooling, a supply of intermediate goods, and knowledge spill-overs as the basis for industry agglomeration or clustering, see Krugman, *Geography and Trade*.

3. Kanter, *The Change Masters*, and "When a Thousand Flowers Bloom: Structural, Social, and Collective Conditions for Innovation in Organizations," *Research in Organizational Behavior*, vol. 10, Greenwich, Conn.: JAI Press, 1988.

4. Jane Jacobs, *The Economy of Cities*, New York: Random House, 1967; Bennett Harrison, Maryellen Kelley, and Jon Gant, "Specialization versus Diversity in Local Economies," *Cityscape*, vol. 1, 1995, forthcoming.

5. For the role of producer services in the economies of the world's financial

capitals, see Saskia Sassen, *The Global City: New York, London, Tokyo*, Princeton, N.J.: Princeton University Press, 1991.

6. Dorothy Leonard-Barton, "Core Capabilities and Core Rigidities: A Paradox in Managing New Product Development." *Strategic Management Journal*, vol. 13, Summer 1992.

7. For an insider's account of quality lessons from Komatsu and others in the region, see Clive Morton, *Becoming World Class*, London: Macmillan, 1994.

8. Kanter, *Change Masters* and "A Thousand Flowers," and Kanter, Stein, and Jick, *Challenge of Organizational Change*, chapter 14, "Where to Begin." Decentralization and centralization must be balanced in the change process. Decentralization produces more ideas, experiments, and alternatives to choose from and learn from; centralization produces faster implementation or adoption of innovation. When leaders have weak mandates, an effective approach is to build coalitions of diverse groups around a shared vision, which each implements in its own way.

INDEX

A&A/Carey Limousine, 111, 138, 332, 349
Actinvest Technologies, 231
ADIA personnel services, 97
advertising, 74–83
  global integrators in, 80–83
  mergers in, 77
African-Americans, 165–69, 286, 291, 315–17
African market, 300–301, 334
Ahold, 84
Airbus, 39, 306
airline industry, 39–40, 46, 110, 306–307
AirTouch, 110
Alcatel, 79
All American Containers, 290
Alliance for Economic Development, 237
Alton, Jim, 103, 105–6
American Airlines, 43, 306–7
American Automobile Label Act (1992), 125
American Celanese, 139
American Cyanamid, 79
American International Container, 290, 332
American Research and Development (ARD), 210
Ameritech, 110
AMR, 43
Analog Devices, 209, 223
Anheuser-Busch, 76
apparel industry, 290, 310, 357, 359
Arboleya, Carlos, 101, 103, 108–9, 289, 314, 322
Argentina, 231, 301
Argyll, 84, 85
Armonk, 47
Arquitectonica, 292
Arthur D. Little, 209, 238
Asea Brown Boveri (ABB), 47–48, 71, 72
Asian-American Bank, 165
Asia Pacific Economic Cooperation (APEC), 142

Associated Industries of Massachusetts, 236, 237
Associated Marketing Services, 85
AT&T, 26, 31, 47, 49, 58, 110, 148, 193, 217, 218, 234, 304, 332
Atlanta, Ga., 357, 364, 374
Attachmate, 58, 163, 332
Austin, Tex., 205–6
Australia, 82, 209, 367
Austrian companies, 29, 246, 254, 281
automobile industry, 20, 27, 46–47, 125, 186–89, 356
  see also BMW

Baldrige, Malcolm, National Quality Award, 49, 52 (*n*), 249, 268, 392
Balmer, Hans, 34, 257, 260, 263, 276, 278, 328
Bamboo Fencer, 34, 332
Banco Latino International (BLI), 24, 42, 298–99
banking industry, 24, 148
  African-Americans and, 166–68
  in Miami, Fla., 296–99
  see also financial industry
Bank of Boston, 180, 192, 196, 209, 210, 216, 226–27, 231, 234, 237, 332
Bank of Commerce and Credit International (BCCI), 297
Barings plc, 42
Barker, Peter, 57
Barnes, Jhane, 48
Barnett Bank, 179, 190, 308, 322
Barnevik, Percy, 48, 72
Barrett, James, 243, 276–77
Bascom, Wilfred, 299
BBDO, 77
Beacon Council, 109, 174, 284, 302, 307, 319–20, 322
Beauvoir, Simone de, 19–20
Belanger, Michael, 213
Bell Atlantic, 110
Bellingham, Wash., 41
BellSouth, 110
Beveridge, Crawford, 368
BhS, 100, 104–8, 336, 344, 348
bilingual debate, 312–15
Bi-Lo, 259
biotechnology industry, 42, 93, 219–220, 224, 229
Biotechnology Industry Organization, 221
Black, Elaine, 316
Black Economic Development Coalition, 316
Bleustein-Blanchet, Marcel, 78, 79–80
BMW, 125, 245, 265–66, 267, 269, 280
  relationship to Spartanburg, 270–273
BMZ, 77, 80
Boeing, 39, 147, 356, 361
Boone, Charles, 247, 250, 274
Boots, 63
Bose, Amar, 209
Bose Corporation, 209
Bosnia, 19, 47
Boston, Mass., 32, 111, 113–15, 128, 135, 136, 139, 141–42, 143, 150, 151, 154, 163, 165, 178, 179, 180–181, 182, 183, 192–93, 196, 201–241, 260, 267, 332, 335, 342, 355, 356–57, 358, 363, 367–68
  arrogance in, 232–33
  as comeback city, 203–7
  commercialization in, 209–12
  health care industry in, 218–22
  industry "schmoozing" in, 212–23
  international connections neglected in, 229–32
  magnets for brainpower in, 207–8
  manufacturing lost in, 228–29
  political fragmentation in, 233–36
  quality of life in, 223–27, 238–39, 240
  repairing infrastructure in, 236–40
  software industry in, 213–16
  supplies to, 95–96
  telecommunications industry in, 216–18
  as thinking center, 30–31
Boston College, 235
Boston Computer Society, 213
Boston Globe, 224, 236, 237
Boston Management Consortium, 238
Boston Private Industry Council, 230–31, 236
Boston Scientific, 219, 332

Boston Symphony, 231
Bradbury, Katherine, 206
Braun, 61–62, 66, 70
Brazil, 69, 170, 231, 304
  education in, 42
Brazilian companies, 296, 308
Bretos, Conchy, 318
British Airport Authority, 40
British Petroleum (BP), 20, 99, 184
British Steel, 67
Broward County, Fla., 284
  see also Fort Lauderdale, Fla.
Brown, Michael, 195
Brown, Norman, 76, 77, 79
Brown & Root, 99, 337–38
Brown Boveri, 72
BTR, 20, 185
Buckley & Mann, 223
Bull, 139, 154
Burns, Anthony, 321
Business Assistance Center, 316, 321
Business for Social Responsibility, 176, 226
Butler, William, 194, 360
Buy American Act (1988), 125
Buy American efforts, 125, 126–27, 134, 135, 137, 140, 279
bypass, 45–46, 329

Calyx & Corolla, 46
Camacol, 302, 308
Campbell, Caroll, 270
Campbell Soup, 76
Canada, 142, 209, 309
  education in, 42
  Québecois separatists in, 125–26
Canadian companies, 296
C&C Information Resources, 169
CARE packages, 226
Caribbean, 109, 284
Carolina Panthers, 248
car services, 111
Carter, Jimmy, 86
Casino, 84, 85
Castro, Fidel, 286–87
Castrol, 315
catalog industry, 45
Cazalot, Clarence, 183
CBS Records, 125
CDs, 44
Celeste, Richard, 361
Center for Health Technologies (CHT), 311–12
Center for Quality Management, 222
Central America, 108, 109
Certainteed, 186
Challenge to Leadership, 236
Chapman, Alvah, Jr., 178, 192, 287, 321–22, 363
Charles, Prince of Wales, 176
Chase Manhattan Bank, 95, 209, 298
Chavez, Linda, 126
chemical industry, 258
Chile, 231
China, 34, 67, 86, 108, 219, 309, 332, 337, 339, 345–46
  education in, 42
  Gillette in, 62–63, 331
  human rights in, 19, 47
  job security in, 146
China Resources, 87
Chinese, overseas, 26, 85, 332
Chinese-Americans, 165
Chipcom, 217–18
Chusmir, Janet, 315
Citibank, 86
Citizens of Dade County United to Protect English, 126, 313
CityACCESS, 226
City Year, 194–97, 226, 341, 347, 377
Cleveland, Ohio, 20, 31, 178, 184, 194, 267, 332, 343, 359, 360–61, 362, 363–64
Cleveland Tomorrow, 183–84
Clinton, Bill, 47, 86, 264, 284
CNN, 43, 74–75, 138, 348
Coca-Cola, 76, 309
Cohen & Wilks International (CWI), 34, 100–109, 336, 344, 347, 348
  BhS and, 104–8
  Mitsui and, 101–4
Colgate-Palmolive, 76, 78
  advertising strategy of, 82
collaborative advantage, 325–53
  action agenda for, 369–78
  globalization and customer power in, 329–31
  skills for, 334–50
  strengthening infrastructure for, 353–79
  see also networking

colleges and universities, 19, 42–43, 80
  in Boston, Mass., 207, 230, 235
  in Florida, 285
  research funding at, 206
  in South Carolina, 261–62, 266
Collins, John, 285
Colombia, 82, 251–52
Columbia Pictures, 125
Comcast, 110
COMCO, 29, 340
Comeau, Leonard, 113
Comeau, Stephen, 113, 114, 341
Commerce Department, U.S., 86, 124, 210, 302
Commonwealth of Independent States (CIS), 87
communitarian values, 26
community development corporations (CDCs), 169
community interests, 172–73
  in Boston, Mass., 225–26
  in Miami, Fla., 290
  in South Carolina, 273–80
  see also social responsibility
community resources, 32
competence, 23, 30, 32, 37, 51–52, 59, 136, 147, 157, 165, 168, 169, 170, 197, 200, 241, 242, 302, 324, 331, 354
  CWI and, 106–7
  Powersoft's use of, 55–56
Compton, 77
Compton, Karl Taylor, 210
computer industry, 48, 52–58, 96, 204, 205, 300, 329, 356–57
computer services, on-line, 43, 307
computer skills, 154–55
concepts, 23, 30, 32, 37, 51, 59, 136, 147, 157, 165, 168, 169, 170, 197, 200, 302, 324, 331, 354
  CWI and, 106
  Powersoft's use of, 53–55
connections, 23, 30, 32, 38, 52, 59, 136, 147, 157, 165, 168, 169, 170, 197, 200, 241, 302, 331, 354
  CWI and, 107
  Powersoft's use of, 56–58
Conoco, 99
Conran, Sir Terence, 104
Consensus project, 267–68
consumption, as preeminent, 48–52, 329–31
Coopers & Lybrand, 150
Cope, Tamara, 269
Copeland, John, 316–17
Coptech, 215
Coral Gables, Fla., 303–9
Corporación Venezolana de Guayana (CVG), 304–5
cosmopolitans, 60–61
  locals vs., 22–25, 312–22
Coulter Electronics, 311, 319
Council on Economic Growth and Technology, 213, 221, 236–37
Cowan, Delroy, 310
Cox Communications, 110
Crafted with Pride (CWP) in USA Council, 127
Creative Artists Agency, 110
Creative Staffing, 151
Crich, Bill, 225
Cuban-Americans, 165, 189–90, 286–291, 292, 303, 313, 314, 315, 322, 332, 359
Cullinet, 53
Customs Service, U.S., 302

Dade Community Foundation, 284, 296, 317
Dade County, Fla., 109
  see also Miami, Fla.
Dadeland Shopping Center, 41
Dallas, Tex., 174
Dareshori, Nader, 224
Day-Timer, 152
Dayton Hudson, 108
defense industry, 158–59, 205, 207
De Graan, Edward, 66–67
de Kanter, Stephen, 304, 340
Delacruz, Carlos, 322
Delgado, William, 294, 315
Dell Computer, 45
Delors, Jacques, 369
Deming, W. Edwards, 250
de Toledo, Fabrizio Alvarez, 231–32
Detroit, Mich., 46, 356
Diaz-Oliver, Remedios, 289–90, 300, 332
Digital Equipment, 42, 53, 148, 196, 204, 209, 210, 368
Dillard's, 108

Massachusetts Biotech Council, 221
Massachusetts Business Roundtable, 236
Massachusetts High Technology Park, 212
Massachusetts Institute of Technology (MIT), 67, 201, 206, 209–10, 213, 215, 220, 222, 223, 235
Massachusetts Office of Business Development, 237
Massachusetts Science and Technology Foundation, 211
Massachusetts Software Council, 53, 214, 216, 225, 348, 377
Massachusetts Technology Development Corporation (MTDC), 211
Massachusetts Telecommunications Council, 217
MassJobs, 215
Mass Tech Corps, 215
Mayrose, Bill, 258
Mazda, 48
MCI, 26, 217
media, 74, 78, 232, 291
Menino, Thomas, 239
Menzel, 256
Menzel, Gerd, 256
Merlin Metalworks, 91, 137, 141, 154, 177
Mesa Redonda, 322
Metro-Miami Marketplace Destination 2001, 294
Metromont Materials, 248
Mexican-Americans, 289, 316
Mexico, 34, 69, 82, 114, 115, 129, 133, 223, 304, 323, 340, 341, 346
MGM, 46, 311
Miami, Fla., 32, 34, 41, 46, 110–11, 123, 151, 165, 168, 169, 178, 179, 180, 182–83, 189–90, 192, 267, 283–324, 332, 340, 345, 346, 357, 358–59, 360, 362, 363, 364
  attracting foreign capital to, 294–299
  bilingual issue in, 312–15
  business leadership in, 319–22
  community involvement in, 189–190
  Cuban-Americans in, *see* Cuban-Americans
  developing trade competence in, 300–309
  ethnic tensions in, 315–17
  foreign real estate investment in, 294–96
  health technologies in, 311–12
  history of, 285–86
  international refocusing of, 292–94
  leisure in, 310–11
  leveraging international connections in, 310–12
  as trading center, 31
Miami, University of, 303, 311–12
Miami Free Zone, 190
Miami Free Zone Corporation (MFZC), 295, 302–3
Miami Herald, 179, 287, 299, 314, 318, 320, 321
Miami International Airport (MIA), 306–7
Michelin, 141, 180, 244, 259, 265, 268, 269, 271, 356
Micro America, 300, 301
MicroMentor, 214–15
Microsoft, 148, 182, 361
Middle East market, 301
Milliken, Roger, 97, 127, 135, 178, 242, 249, 250–52, 254, 268, 270, 276, 331–32, 363
Milliken & Co., 97, 127, 135, 178, 242, 249–51, 256, 262, 270, 273, 275, 332
minorities, 281, 315–17, 373
  inner-city, 165–69
Mita South Carolina, 262–63, 269
Mitsubishi, 86
Mitsui & Co., 101–4, 105, 347
mobility, 42–43, 145–46, 329
Monsanto, 127
Montgomery, Walter, Sr., 250
Motorola, 171
Mountain Bell, 43
Müller, Klaus-Jürgen, 80
Murdoch, Rupert, 75

Nashville, Tenn., 173, 376
National Bank of Georgia, 86
National League of Cities, 22

nativists, nativism, 123–34, 143
discussion among, 128–32
history of, 124, 140
internationalism's triumph over, 139–42
psychological processes of, 132–34
NEC, 49, 222, 230
Needham Harper, 77
Neiman-Marcus, 104, 174
Nestlé, 20, 71, 76, 77–78, 80, 81, 164, 188, 336
advertising strategy of, 82–83
Netherlands, 84, 259, 338
networking, 85–89, 331–34, 372–73
employability security and, 163–164
inner-city minorities and, 165–169
in software, 213–16
supply chains and, 109–12
see also collaborative advantage
Newcastle, England, 27, 365–67
New England Council, 237
New England Shelter for Homeless Veterans, 193
newspaper industry, 43, 148, 224, 287, 291, 314–15
see also media
New York City, 359
New Yorker, 19
New York Times, 224
Nicaragua, 290
Nicaraguan-Americans, 290
Nigeria, 301
Nohria, Nitin, 213
Noltemy, Stephen, 195
NonGroup, 322
Nordstrom, 108
North American Free Trade Agreement (NAFTA), 25, 129, 130, 135, 137, 138, 143, 279
North Carolina, 205
Northern Development Company (NDC), 365–67
Northern Telecom, 333, 339
Norton Company, 20, 164, 173, 185–186, 337, 343, 345
Nuevo Herald, El, 314–15
Nynex, 110, 163–64, 234, 239
Nypro, 67, 95
O'Brien, Paul, 232, 239–40
Ocean Spray, 51, 154
suppliers to, 98–99
Office Depot, 31–32
Ohmae, Kenichi, 73
Olsen, Kenneth, 210
Olson, Morrie, 92
Olson's Food Stores, 92
Olympic games, 364
Omnibus Trade and Competitiveness Act (1988), 125
Omnicon, 77
O'Neill, Thomas P. "Tip," 24
128 Venture Group, 213
Open Software Foundation, 214
Oral-B, 62, 66, 70
Organization for a New Equality, 227, 332
Organization for Economic Cooperation and Development (OECD), 231
organized crime, 24
Osburn, Arthur, 127
Owades, Ruth, 46

Pacific Bell, 43
Pacific Telesis, 110
Packard, David, 219
Palmer and Dodge, 220, 221
Panama, 34
Parker Pen, 61
Partners for Progress, 316–17
Peer Learning Network, 173, 376
Peigh, Terry, 83
PepsiCo, 76
Perot, Ross, 25, 143
pharmaceutical industry, 48–49
Philip Morris, 76
Philipp Holzmann AG, 279
Philippines, 42, 82
education in, 42
Philips, 76
photo industry, 113–15, 333
PictureTel, 217
Pittsburgh Airport, 40
Plotkin, Joyce, 214–15, 216
Poe, Sherri, 176
Poland, 365
Polaroid, 34, 113–15, 209, 333, 338, 341, 346, 348

politics, 120–21
  in Boston, Mass., 233–36
  foreign investment and, 187
  of language, 125–26
  as local, 24–25, 73
  in Miami, Fla., 293, 317–19
Pollack, Tessa Martinez, 312
Pompidou, Georges, 126
Porter, Michael, 237, 355
Portes, Alejandro, 190, 288, 289, 291
Powersoft, 52–58, 93, 108, 110, 136, 138, 173, 177, 180, 211, 216, 328, 332, 333, 336, 338, 340, 341, 344, 346, 348, 349
  employability security at, 159–163
Pradere, Claude, 82, 83
Preston, John, 209
primary education, *see* education, primary and secondary
Prince of Wales Business Leaders Forum, 176
Prince's Trust Volunteers, 197
Procter & Gamble, 76
Project Pro-Tech, 231
protectionism, 125
Protestant Ethic and the Spirit of Capitalism, The (Weber), 26
Prym-Dritz, 248
Publicis, 74, 77–83, 87, 333, 336, 338, 341, 342, 343, 344, 346

Quaker Fabrics, 223
Quality Institute of Enterprise Development, Inc., 261–62
Quality in the Workplace program, 268
Québec, 125–26

Rabins, Richard, 214
Ramada Resort Deauville, 110–11
Raytheon, 209
Reader's Digest, 74
Reagan, Ronald, 321
Reavely, Peter, 294, 306
Reebok, 176, 193, 196
Reebok Foundation, 239
regions, competition among, 365–369
  rise of, 22
Reich, Robert, 142
Relational Courseware of Boston, 215
religious institutions, 260
Renault, 73, 76, 79, 80
Research Triangle, 205–6
Reznicek, Bernard, 237
Riady, James, 86
Riady, Mochtar, 85–86, 87, 165, 298, 328, 332
Richardson, Jerry, 248
Richford Industries, 290
Rieter Machine Works, 254–55, 260, 278, 347
Riley, Richard, 264
Rio de Janeiro summit (1992), 18
RJR Nabisco, 76
Roberts, Edward, 209
Rockefeller, Grace, 313
Rodriguez, Jay, 308–9
Ronald McDonald House, 192
Roosevelt, Theodore, 140
Rose Foundation, 176
Rossellini, Isabella, 79
R. R. Donnelley, 267
Russia, 307, 309
Ryder System, 190
Ryka, 176

Saatchi & Saatchi, 77
Safeway, 63, 84, 85
St. Gobain, 21, 164, 185–86, 337, 343, 345
Salto, Salomon, 83
Sansbury, Olin, 243, 251
Sara Lee, 76, 268
Saudi Arabia, 147
Saxenian, AnnaLee, 205
Saxonia-Francke of America, 257
Saztec, 43
SBC Communications, 110
Schettino, Susan, 219
Schmid, Ueli, 254, 260, 278
S. C. Johnson, 78, 79
Scotland, 27, 99, 368
Scottish Enterprises, 27, 368
Scott Paper, 85
Screw Machine House, 113
Sculley, John, 215

Seattle, Wash., 22, 26, 31, 58, 111, 142, 147, 163, 182, 184, 232, 267, 332, 355, 361–62
secondary education, *see* education, primary and secondary
Second Sex, The (Beauvoir), 19–20
Semco, 170–71
Semler, Ricardo, 170–71, 173
SEW-Eurodrive, 257, 272, 273
Shack, Ruth, 284, 296, 317, 318, 321
Sheraton, 111
shoe industry, 176, 229
Sidell, Chet, 108
simultaneity, 43–44, 329
Singapore, 26, 42, 301
Sisson, Coleman, 55
skill requirements, 154–56
  see also employability security
Skychannel, 75
Smathers, George, 291
Smoot-Hawley Tariff Act (1930), 124
Snowden, Gail, 226–27
social responsibility, 174–97, 226–27, 278, 281, 321–22, 362–63, 377–378
  City Year model of, 194–97, 226, 314, 347, 377
  foreign business leaders and, 184–190
  headquarter dispersion and, 178–184
  strategic philanthropy in, 190–94
software industry, 26–27, 32, 42, 45, 111, 173, 193, 213–16, 225, 230, 300, 340, 356
  see also Powersoft
Sohio, 20, 184
Sony, 125
South Africa, 193
South Carolina, 180, 184, 185, 242–282, 332, 346, 356
  active outreach in, 248–52
  BMW attracted to, 270–73
  community impact of foreign presence in, 273–80
  foreign companies welcomed to, 259
  inner cities of, 280–81
  raising quality through collaboration in, 266–70
  Southern work ethic in, 259–60
  training and education in, 260–66
  work ethic in, 252–60
  see also Greenville, S.C.; Spartanburg, S.C.
South Carolina, University of, at Spartanburg, 243, 262
South Carolina Economic Development Board, 262
South Carolina State Board for Technical and Comprehensive Education, 261
Southeast Bank, 190
Southern Bell, 190
Southwest Airlines, 72
Southwest Missouri University, 127
Soviet Union, 87, 333
  education in, 42
space research, 206
Spain, 79, 309
Spanish companies, 297–98, 307
Spartanburg, S.C., 27, 31, 34, 99, 125, 127, 135, 137, 139, 155, 170, 173, 178, 242–82, 332, 336, 342, 346, 347, 357, 358, 363, 367, 374
  active outreach in, 248–52
  BMW attracted to, 270–73
  community impact of foreign presence in, 273–80
  economic overview of, 243–48, 281
  foreign companies welcomed by, 259
  foreign surge in, 252–57
  Greenville's joint development with, 269–70
  inner city of, 280–81
  raising quality through collaboration in, 266–70
  Southern work ethic in, 259–60
  training and education in, 260–66
  Tukey's role in European investment in, 251–52
  work ethic in, 252–60
Spartanburg Chamber of Commerce, 173, 245, 249, 251, 257, 258, 262, 267, 268
Spartanburg County Foundation, 243, 250, 267, 276–77, 281
Spink, Bryan, 100, 101, 104, 107
sports teams, 248